Praise for *Racehoss: Big Emma's Boy*

———

"As remarkable as Wright's [*Black Boy*]."

—Richard Stern,
Chicago Tribune

"Startling as a cell-door clanking shut . . . Sample has made it, and *Racehoss* is his proof."

—Peter C. Wyckoff,
The Houston Post

"Of the most remarkable stories I've come across, perhaps the most remarkable is the story of Albert Race Sample, known as Racehoss. This book is more than a searing indictment of the Southern prison system. It is an outcast's eloquent testament to life."

—Studs Terkel,
Pulitzer Prize–winning author

"Scores of listeners have written and called to tell me how they sat, spellbound, hearing Sample relive his spiritual experience. Many said they wept right along with him. Others were moved to reflect on their own lives because of his inspirational words."

—Diane Rehm,
The Washington Post

"The book reads like good naturalistic fiction: strong narrative and dialogue, and many incidents of raw, shocking and absolutely convincing authenticity. . . . [The] book is also warmly funny. The prisoners are brought to life through Sample's accurate ear for how people talk, and it's clear that humor is one of the means for surviving in hell."

—Don Graham,
The Dallas Morning News

"[Sample is] an affecting storyteller."

—Brian Moss,
New York Daily News

"Extraordinary . . . The prison stories are raw, horrible and occasionally funny. Again, the absence of bitterness is remarkable. Sample doesn't tell you about it—he puts you there."

—Molly Ivins,
Dallas Times Herald

"The book does read like a novel. . . . It offers glimpses into characters any master of fiction would have been proud to have created . . . the speech, spiced with folksy sayings and simile, is a joy to read."

—Mike Cox,
Austin American-Statesman

"[At] the end I knew I had read a classic. If you accept *Racehoss* in the right spirit, it will blow your mind."

—Maury Maverick,
San Antonio Express-News

"Albert Sample's book offers a powerful chronicle of the Texas penal system, life in Depression era East Texas and of how, despite seemingly insurmountable odds, one man rose above the scum that life can dish out and still came out a winner."

—Mike Elswick,
Longview Morning Journal

Racehoss

Big Emma's Boy

—

Albert Race Sample

SCRIBNER

New York London Toronto Sydney New Delhi

Scribner

An Imprint of Simon & Schuster, Inc.

1230 Avenue of the Americas

New York, NY 10020

First Scribner hardcover edition May 2018

SCRIBNER and design are registered trademarks of The Gale Group, Inc., used under license by Simon & Schuster, Inc., the publisher of this work.

For information about special discounts for bulk purchases, please contact Simon & Schuster Special Sales at 1-866-506-1949 or business@simonandschuster.com.

The Simon & Schuster Speakers Bureau can bring authors to your live event. For more information or to book an event contact the Simon & Schuster Speakers Bureau at 1-866-248-3049 or visit our website at www.simonspeakers.com.

Interior design by Kyle Kabel

Manufactured in the United States of America

1 3 5 7 9 10 8 6 4 2

ISBN 978-1-5011-8397-3
ISBN 978-1-5011-8399-7 (ebook)

Dedicated in memory of my mother, Emma.
And to Carol, my wife and best buddy.
For without her love, help, and inspiration, this book
would not have happened. But I thank her most of all
for walking back in time with me and holding on to my
hand so Raw Hide and Bloody Bones wouldn't get me.
And to Amber, my daughter and helper.
And to all the children of the world who suffer.

Contents

Contents

Foreword

Tolstoy got it wrong. Unhappy families are also all alike. Albert Sample came from one of them. In this extraordinary memoir, he writes hauntingly and elegantly about a life a middle-class white guy like me can scarcely imagine. The son of a poor black prostitute and a relatively wealthy white john, he witnessed as a young kid a shooting, a stabbing, and a near lynching (of his own mother, no less). In school one day, he stabbed a teacher with a pocket knife. On another day, he beat a classmate with a broom handle. He had to duck whiskey bottles thrown at his head by his drunk, enraged mom and watched helplessly as she was abused. By the time Sample was six years old, he was on his own. At the age of twelve, he started hopping freight trains and riding across the country. At twenty-two, he went to prison for the first time.

But while a reader like me might be unable to fathom the granular details of Sample's life, most everyone in prison has lived it for himself. In a quarter century of representing inmates, I've heard more verses of the same song than I can remember: abusive or absent parents; drug or alcohol dependency; physical, sexual, or psychological abuse, or a combination thereof; poverty so extreme it belongs in an undeveloped country, not America. I've learned that what separates the people I've represented from the kids I grew up with is the horizon line of their vision. Middle-class kids plan for the future: college, a career, a partner, kids. Impoverished kids plan for tomorrow, or the next meal.

Other than his flair for telling it, there is nothing all that special about Albert Sample's circumstance. One in three black men go to prison. Anyone who knows anything about the biographies of inmates could have told you it was a near certainty that Sample would be one of them. And like so many inmates, if Sample felt even the least bit sorry for himself, he doesn't reveal it. His description of prison life, written in matter-of-fact and unsentimental prose, should be required reading for anyone who still harbors the illusion that our criminal justice system has advanced much beyond medieval times. Consensual homosexual sex, because that is the only sex available, is not uncommon, but neither is violent rape; vicious fights between inmates, some involving weapons and others only fists, is constant; so too is sadistic abuse from racist guards. The racism Sample recounts is exactly what one would expect in rural Texas in the 1950s: so pervasive it is normal. When Sample describes being handcuffed and hung by the cuffs from a steel rod by one of the sadistic guards, the description is so vivid I felt my own wrists sear in pain.

Except for the nation of Seychelles (which also imprisons pirates), the United States incarcerates more people per capita than any country in the world. We have nearly seven hundred people in prison for every one hundred thousand in population. (Including juveniles in the statistic would add nearly fifty thousand to the number already held in custody.) By contrast, France incarcerates 103 per one hundred thousand and Germany imprisons seventy-eight.

Michelle Alexander wrote a recent book about the relationship between racial discrimination and the American criminal justice system. To oversimplify only slightly, in *The New Jim Crow* Alexander argues the caste system of race in the United States has not disappeared; it has simply moved. Instead of cotton fields or sugar plantations, we now use prisons. Texas, where Albert Sample served his time, is Exhibit 1 for Alexander's thesis. For every hundred thousand white people in the state, 768 are in prison; the figure for blacks is 2,855.

As a prisoner in a unit on the Texas Gulf Coast, Sample was one of four hundred inmates who maintained sixteen thousand acres of cultivated cotton. That's twenty-five square miles of crop planted and picked without a machine. But backbreaking work doesn't prepare an inmate for life after prison, and because we devote so much more money and ingenuity to incapacitation than we do to rehabilitation or job training, it is not surprising that within five years of being released, nearly 80 percent of black inmates return to prison. Sample fell in the fat part of the bell curve. Two years after being paroled, he was back, and he'd return yet one more time.

But what is harder to predict than whether someone will go to prison, maybe impossible to predict, is how any given inmate will respond. Extraordinary people are not people who face extraordinary moments; they are people who respond to mundane moments in an extraordinary way.

It began for Sample with a trivial offense: signing a guard's name to some forms that had to be mailed. As punishment, Sample was sent to a torture chamber that would make the likes of Saddam Hussein or Idi Amin envious. The four-foot-by-eight-foot cell had a solid-steel door, a concrete slab for a bed, and a hole in the floor for a toilet. There was no window and no light. The ventilation came from the slit of space between the bottom of the door and the top of the floor. Once a day Sample received a cup of water and a single biscuit. He got a full meal once a week. Standing straight, he could reach his arms to the side and touch both walls, or above him to the ceiling.

On his first day there, he felt what he calls a Presence. At the end of his stay, four weeks later, he had gained five pounds. Sample's explanation for what happened to him in that hole, and his explanation for the one-hundred-eighty-degree turnaround in his life that started in solitary confinement, is mystical; Sample attributes his fortune to forces that are religious in nature. But I think that interpretation is far too modest. Sample's essential goodness and decency burned their way to the surface of his actions long before he spent twenty-eight days with no company besides his thoughts. When he became the first ex-con in Texas to serve as a probation officer and thereby help other cons turn their own lives around, his character was the same as it was the day he was sentenced more than three decades before. The proof is this entire book. Until he finally earns his release from prison, virtually every detail of Sample's life is some combination of brutal, sad, sadistic, or unjust. Yet there is not a single page of *Racehoss*, maybe not even a single sentence, that is depressing, oppressive, or remotely self-pitying. Sample has taken raw material comprising one tragic scene after another and created something beautiful and full of hope. I know there are pages where I gasped or winced. But the pages where I laughed or nodded outnumbered them by a ratio of at least twenty to one.

It's not a spoiler for me to call attention to the book's subtitle: *Big Emma's Boy*. Emma is Sample's mom. He's hardly the only prisoner who forgives a mother for deeds that might in fact be unforgiveable, but he is one of the few who is able to see his mother's weaknesses as the reverse side of her strengths and to understand he was shaped by both. We learn from both good people and bad. The former we try to emulate, the latter we don't.

This is a story not just about Albert Sample, but about the culture and the families into which our Albert Samples are born and the humanity and dignity that cannot be beaten from them no matter how relentlessly an oppressive society tries.

There is one thing I have not said anything about, and I am not going to. It's about Sample's prison nickname: Racehoss. I wish you the pleasure of discovering for yourself how he earned that moniker. I promise it will make you smile.

—David R. Dow
January 8, 2018
Houston, Texas

Emma

___

Prelude

Standing in front of the mirror, Lillie Barnes hastily fumbled with the pearl-tipped hairpin as she pushed it through the bun in the back. While fitting on the flower-laden straw hat, hurrying not to be late for the eleven o'clock church service, she hollered into the kitchen, "Bama, y'all hurry up now or we gon be late!"

"Yes mam, we hurryin, Mama."

"Be sho an wipe that baby's face an tie her shoes up."

"Yes mam."

Taking a last glance and smoothing down her Sunday gingham dress, she thought about how nice it would be if Son Buddy were here to go to church with them. He was seventeen, the oldest of her four children, and already out on his own. Smiling, she thought, *But even ef he wuz heah, me an him would be goin roun an roun. That boy got slow as cream risin when it come time to go to church.* Rushing the children, she called into the kitchen again, "Bama, y'all bout ready?"

"Yes mam, Mama. We ready."

"Well, come on now, les go."

Her husband, Charlie, was already seated on the wagon and waiting for them. Lillie cautioned as she turned the skeleton key in the lock, "One uv y'all betta ketch holt uv that baby's hand so she don't fall goin down them steps." Sally B grabbed it—she was eight. Bama was twelve, and the "baby," Emma, was four.

His patience worn thin, Charlie said, "Lillie, y'all hurry up ef'n

3

you want me to drive y'all down there." He had other plans. As soon as he dropped them off, he was heading straight for the gambling shack. Grumbling still, he went on, "Damn, Lillie, it takes y'all longer to git ready than anybody I ever seen. I been settin out heah nelly a hour."

"Oh bosh," she said, "you ain't been settin out heah no hour. Quit yo fussin. You'll have plenty time to gamble," settling herself on the hard oak seat.

Looking over his shoulder, Charlie said, "Y'all hurry up an git in." Sally B couldn't lift Emma up onto the wagon bed alone; Bama had to help her. "Y'all on?" he asked.

"Yessir, we on."

"Y'all set down back there an behave," he ordered.

Lillie added, "Bama, you an Sally B bet not let that baby fall out."

Charlie snapped the reins and started the mules in motion. "Come up heah, Jake, Ol Blackie!" he called, whacking them on the rump as they struck up a trot.

Bouncing on the springless seat and holding her hat down on her head, Lillie said, "Charlie, don't git to gamblin an forgit to come back an git us."

Irritated, he said drily, "Don't worry, Lillie. I won't forgit y'all."

It was miserably hot, and each time the wagon ran over a bump in the dusty road, Lillie complained. "Slow down a little bit, Charlie. You ain't gotta be in such a great big hurry to git rid uv us. I'm gon make a cushion for this hard thang or start brangin me a pillow to set on." She was nine months pregnant and expecting their fifth child any day now.

"Oh shet yo mouth, Lillie. I ain't goin all that fas."

Aggravated, he coaxed the mules to speed up. They had less than a mile to go after crossing the branch. The mules were trotting at a rapid pace when the front wheel on Charlie's side bounced over a big rut and suddenly rolled off. Everyone was thrust sideways when the wagon jerked and tilted to the left. Frightened, little Emma started crying. Charlie had his hands full getting the spooked mules to slow down. Lillie grabbed on to the seat tightly with both hands. When she let go of her hat, the wind whisked it away and it was crushed beneath the wheels.

Pulling back on the reins with all his strength, Charlie hollered, "*Whoa! Whoa, Blackie! Whoa, Jake! Whoa! Whoa!*" The mules slowed and finally stopped.

"Y'all awright?" Lillie quickly asked Bama. "Is the baby hurt?"

"Yes mam, we awright. No mam, Emma ain't hurt. She jes scared."

"You awright, Sally B?"

"Yes'm, I'm awright, Mama," she sniveled.

It took some slow doing for Lillie to climb down the jacked-up side of the wagon. Nervously rubbing her overswollen belly, she told the girls to unload as she walked around to Charlie's side. While he stood looking down at the wheelless axle, she nagged, "I tole you to slow down, but you so bullheaded an won't lissen to nobody. At least you could'a hep'd me git down fr—"

"Lillie, jes shet up an leave me alone so I kin fix the damn wagon! Sally B, go back down there'n git that wheel an roll it up heah."

"Yessir." Sally B about-faced and took off down the road.

"Take Emma witcha so she kin git my hat," Lillie yelled. She added to herself sorrowfully, "I know it's all messed up."

"Yes'm. C'mon, Emma."

While they waited for Sally B's return, Lillie asked, "Do you thank you kin git it back on?"

"Yeah, I bleeve so," Charlie said while rummaging through the junk he stored underneath the seat. "*Gotdammit!*" he bellowed. "I thought I had another pin but I ain't. Well, ef I kin jes git the wheel back on the axle, I'll use a nail. Maybe it'll stay on long nuff to git y'all to church."

Emma had found the hat and ran back eagerly. "Mama, it's all broke," she said, handing it over to Lillie.

"Yeah, baby, I know." Lillie put on the crumpled hat, smiled at her daughter, and made a funny face. Emma laughed.

Sally B rolled the wheel up to the wagon and leaned it against the side. Charlie bent down and lifted the bed up. The beads of sweat popped out on his forehead as he strained to keep it hoisted. Realizing he needed help, he said, "Bama, git over heah an ketch holt."

Obediently, Bama rushed to his side and began lifting. She grunted and strained shoulder to shoulder with her father. When the heavy oak bed was up a little higher, he yelled, "Sally B, roll that wheel roun heah 'n git ready to shove it on." Sally B quickly rolled the wheel in front of the axle and stood waiting, but they couldn't raise it high enough before Charlie's arms gave out. "Les ease it down, Bama," he said, winded. After wiping away the sweat with his bandanna and catching a breath, he bent back down. "Okay, les try it, Bama," he said, prodding, "but this time lift hard as you kin."

"Yessir." Bama drew a deep breath and bent over.

Before they could start lifting, Lillie, with motherly instincts, stepped up and nudged Bama away. She took her place, saying, "Charlie, you know this thang's too heavy for that gal to be tryin to pick up."

Shoving Lillie away from the wagon, Charlie shouted, "I didn't tell you to do it! I tole her to do it! Bama, git back over heah!"

"Naw. Charlie, I dun tole you thas too—"

Charlie stood up, hollering, "Thas whut's the gotdam matter now! You pamper these rotten chillun all the time an won't let 'em do nothin. You the reason they ain't worth a shit."

Angered, Lillie blurted out, "Charlie Barnes, sometimes you make me so mad I could jes wring yo neck off! Lemme—"

"You jes git yo ass outta my way! C'mon, Bama!"

Unhesitating, Bama tried to heed his order, but Lillie would not relinquish her. She got a lifting hold on the bed. Without looking back, she snapped, "Ef you tired uv foolin roun, les git this thang up. We late enuff as it is."

In deathly silence Charlie reached into the wagon and grabbed the extra singletree. Gripping one end in both hands like a club, he raised it high above his head and powerfully crashed it across Lillie's lower back. As she lay writhing and gasping on the roadside, he stared at her a moment, then dropped the singletree and fled into the woods.

Bama took off running for the church to get help. Horror-stricken, Sally B and little Emma clung to each other and looked on while their sister was born and their mother drew her last breath.

As soon as she got word of her daughter's death, Louduskie came down by train. Her husband had been dead for years, but she brought along the rest of her family for the funeral. Lillie, at thirty-six, was the oldest of her nine children. The other four daughters and four sons, whose ages ranged from fourteen to thirty-two, still lived at home with her. In addition, the clan had four grandchildren belonging to two of her unmarried daughters, and one daughter-in-law.

After the funeral was held and the man came and got his wagon and mules, for which Charlie still owed him, there was no more business to transact. Lillie and Charlie had been renting the house, and the meager insurance policy on her was just enough to cover the funeral and burial. With no reason to remain any longer, the tribe would be leaving in the morning.

Louduskie dug deeper into the large purse, corralling and smoothing out the crumpled dollar bills as she laid them on the ticket counter. Good thing she thought to get some more money from the coffee can before she left; she was buying three extra tickets for the trip back to Big Sandy, Texas. The infant, whom Bama named Elzado, could ride free. Grammaw Duck, as she was known to her grandchildren, held on to the round-trip tickets she'd bought in Big Sandy for the family and handed Bama their three tickets for safekeeping.

Apart from the others, sitting on one of the waiting benches to give her feet a much needed rest, Grandma Duck watched her grandchildren playing on the station platform. Noticing they were getting too close to the tracks, she yelled, "Y'all git back away frum the edge uv that platform!"

Her mind drifted: *We barely makin it off them three acres as it is. Four mo moufs to feed sho gon be hard on me an wit that low-down Charlie in jail, he won't be no hep atall. Only reason I'm takin his chillun in's cuz nobody else would. His mama an papa both dead an his four brothers an sister didn't even show up at the funeral. They ain't nothin but a low-down, stankin bunch uv thievin, gamblin heathens whut ain't hit a lick'a work since they be grown. An Son Buddy can't keep 'em. He jes a porter livin in the back room uv a hotel where he works at in Gilmer. He never did git 'long wit that ol devil an got away quick as he could. First time Lillie Mae come draggin him up to my house, I tole her then. She wuzn't nothin but a baby, not even eighteen. Everbody in town knowed bout his drankin, fightin, gamblin, an carryin on. Bless my po chile's heart, she wouldn't lissen. Hard as I tried, Lawd, she jes wouldn't lissen. I know you do's thangs for a reason. She in yo hands now, Lawd. Rest her soul.*

Louduskie's shoulders sagged and her tears flowed freely. While dabbing them away, she heard the train whistle in the distance. She stood and yelled, "Git back frum that edge! Rat now!" The ducklings scampered over and started shouting and pointing at the huge rumbling mass of steel.

Bama quickly covered the baby's face with a blanket to protect her from the swirling dust storm the engine kicked up as it went by. Emma's dress blew over her face as she gleefully jumped up and down, excited about her first ride on a "choo-choo." When Grandma Duck heard the porter's "All aboard!" she gathered "her" flock together at the coach's boarding steps and stood to one side, making sure everybody got on. Then she boarded.

Afterward Bama stepped on, carrying Elzado in one arm and lugging a cardboard suitcase. Sally B helped Emma up the steps and they trailed behind Bama as she looked for seats. She found two with the backs already flipped the right way so they could sit facing each other. Taking a window seat, Bama told Sally B to sit next to her, giving the active Emma a whole seat to herself.

The train slowly pulled out and then picked up speed. The telephone poles went zooming up through the window. Emma was taking it all in and merrily swinging her feet back and forth when she asked, "Sally B, how come Mama didn't go on the choo-choo wit us?"

"Cuz she can't, Emma. Mama dead."

"How come she dead, Sally B?"

"Cuz the preacher say it wuz time for God to come 'n take her away to heaven."

"Is God gon let her come back?"

"Naw, she ain't never comin back."

"Well, God ain't nice an I don't lak Him no mo if He ain't gon let Mama come back frum heb'n."

Rocking Elzado in a motherly way, Bama gently scolded, "Sally B, y'all hush up. Emma, you look out the window at the moo-cows," quickly turning her face toward the window to keep them from knowing.

When Emma saw some she pointed out the window, exclaiming, "Look, Bama! Look! There go some moo-cows!"

"I saw 'em, Emma."

"How come you cryin then?"

"Watchin moo-cows through a train window always make me cry."

"Oh," Emma answered and looked back out the window, a blank stare on her face.

1

When the Barnes girls walked into the house, Grandma Duck told them to wait in the hall. She went in one of the rooms, put away her hat and purse, and returned. At fifty-six, she was a robust giant of a woman, standing nearly six feet tall and weighing over two hundred pounds. Ill-tempered and worn out from the funeral and trip, she didn't mince words.

"Y'all kin come to the table to eat afta we git through. Bama, far as I'm concerned, them chillun b'long to you an you gon hafta keep that baby quiet. I hear enuff cryin in this house. You gon hafta see afta 'em. I dun raised all the young'uns I'm gon. Sally B kin hep you wit y'all's washin an ironin. She kin tend to them other two while you hep in the kitchen wit the cookin."

With hands on her hips, Grandma Duck towered ominously over the girls as she continued, "I'm tellin y'all rat now, I ain't gon put up wit one bit uv y'all's foolishness. An y'all bet not be sassin out none'a these grown folk roun heah neither. Ef you do, I'll burn y'all's hind ends up. Do y'all hear me?"

"Yes'm, Grammaw Duck," they replied in unison.

Beckoning for them to follow, she said, "Y'all c'mon in heah an put y'all's thangs up under one'a these beds."

Bama's arm was cramping from holding Elzado for so long and she asked, "Grammaw Duck, where kin I lay the baby down?"

Pointing to the open door, Louduskie said, "Take her in yonder an lay her on one'a them beds. Make sho you put sump'n else under her so she won't pee all over everthang."

"Yes mam."

Grandma Duck's final order came as she fixed her eyes on Emma. "An, Bama, you keep this lil ol Charlie-lookin devil outta my sight! I hope that low-down heathen rots in jail for whut he dun to my Lillie!"

The paintless wood-framed house, weathered gray with age, had an arched tin roof and no porches. The ground around it was feet-packed hard and bald. All the grass had been trampled away. The water well was in the backyard. The old house had four medium-size bedrooms. Two were on either side of the hall. For the married son and his wife, the brothers rounded up enough scrap lumber to build a shack with a separate entrance onto one of the back bedrooms. All the bedrooms, except Grandma Duck's, were overcrowded with beds and single metal cots, with only narrow trails for passageways. Elzado slept in the bed with Bama and two aunties. Sally B and Emma slept in the kitchen on two single canvas fold-up cots shared by four other children.

Little by little the Barnes girls were subjugated to being the family Cinderellas. When the inside work was caught up, it was on to the washing board and tubs. Then the garden had to be hoed and the hogs slopped.

With free time on her hands, Grandma Duck taught Emma to tie her shoelaces and button the back of her dress. For a teacher's aid she used a thin board that she had driven a nail through at one end. Every morning when the children were getting dressed, Grandma Duck called Emma up to her and pecked her hands with the nail board while she desperately tried to button her four back buttons. The pecking ended when they were all buttoned. She got the same lesson while tying her shoelaces.

When Grandma Duck let her go, with bloody hands Emma ran crying to her surrogate mother. Bama took her to the well to wash the blood away and dried her hands gently with the tail of her dress. Standing behind the well, Bama held her sister close, stroking her hair and consoling, "Sshhh, hush up now. Don't cry. It's gon be awright," while crying herself. "You know whut, Emma?"

Her lips still quivering, Emma said, "Naw, whut?"

"One'a these days when I git growed up, I'm gon have a great big ol house to live in wit room enuff for everbody. When I do, I'm comin back afta y'all."

"I wanna go wit you, Bama."

"If you hush cryin, I'll come back an gitcha real quick."

"Awright," Emma agreed, wiping her nose with her arm.

"You be a big girl now an go on an play."

"They won't play wit me, Bama."

"How come?"

"They call me Charlie-lookin devil an won't play wit me."

"Well, play by yosef." Looking toward the back door, Bama said, "I gotta go befo Grammaw miss me."

There was hardly elbow room on the cot with the three of them sleeping in it. Emma scooted as close to the edge as she could, trying to get out of the puddle of piss that hadn't seeped through yet. Reaching back, she tugged some of the raggedy, wet quilt they shared over her cold back. In an effort to squirm farther away from the wetness, Emma slung her arm and leg over the side and lay sleeping, exposed to the chilling night air.

When it felt like somebody was turning her over, she opened her eyes to see who was tucking in the flimsy quilt. It was her mother! In the second it took to wipe the sleep from her eyes to get a better look, Lillie had disappeared.

Emma untucked the quilt, jumped off the cot, and tiptoed over to Sally B's cot. Shaking her vigorously, she said, "Sally B! Sally B! Sally B, wake up! Wake up, Sally B! Mama come back! Wake up, Sally B! You tole me—"

"Emma," one of Sally B's cot mates interrupted, "if you don't go back to bed, Grammaw gonna give you a whuppin!"

The many trips Sally B made to and from the well drawing up and toting wash water had taken their toll. She was dead asleep.

Emma crawled back onto her cot. She got a "whuppin" the next morning from Grandma Duck anyway when her bunk rats ran and told, "Emma peed the bed."

A few days after Bama, now eighteen, took some jars of Grandma Duck's watermelon rind preserves to the county fair, she ran off with a soldier and got married. Her leaving didn't even put a dent in the overpopulated household. Grandma Duck's two oldest daughters stayed neck and neck producing another baby apiece, and the two youngest had come up with three between them. Seemed like every time they had a revival, her daughters got full of the "spirit" and had another one on the way. After Bama absconded, Grandma Duck tightened the screws of vengeance down on Emma six more notches. She got a "whuppin" almost daily from her, and the "grown folk" were unleashed to fill in the gaps.

Grandma Duck walked into the kitchen; Emma knocked over her glass and buttermilk spilled all over the oilcloth covering on the table. "Git up frum that table an clean up that mess you made, you triflin heifer!" Hovering over Emma and watching her wipe the tablecloth with a dishrag, the mean-spirited old woman yelled, "You ol Charlie-lookin devil, you! Don'tcha lemme ketch you settin at my table no mo till I tell you. Frum now on, you eat out on them back steps." Shaking her finger in Emma's face, she demanded, "You hear me?"

"Yes'm, Grammaw, I hear you." Emma bristled and flashed a defiant look.

Enraged, Grandma Duck grabbed the iron skillet from the stove and drew it back. "Don'tcha be standin there rollin them eyes at me! You betta gitcha ol Charlie-lookin sef outta heah befo I bust yo brains out!" she shouted.

On an errand to the store Emma was hailed down by one of Grandma Duck's church-member neighbors, "Emma."

"Yes mam?"

"Stop by heah, chile," the woman said, beckoning her to the

porch. "Heah, take this quarter an brang me a small box uv KC bakin powder when you come back. An you stand there an wait cuz you got some change comin. Now git!"

When Emma delivered the baking powder, the woman handed her a dime and thanked her for doing the errand. On the way home, mad and frustrated, Emma kicked the road. "I sho wisht she hadda give it to me on my way *to* the store." She quickly crawled under the house and hid her dime on one of the rafters, then went in. With an overabundance of anxious errand runners on standby, it took a while for her turn to rotate around again. Until it did, she checked on her dime two or three times a day.

Next time she was in the store, the owner asked, "Whut else you need today, Emma?"

"An Grammaw wants a dime's worth uv Rough on Rats."

"Gotta rat problem, have ya?" the store owner said, walking around to the other counter.

"Yessir, Mr. Riley. They be gittin priddy bad."

After scooping the yellow, mealy-looking rat poison from the barrel and putting it in the small paper sack, he weighed it. Looking at the scales, he said, "Well, that looks like a whole dime's worth. This'll surrre git 'em. You tell Duck I said be careful with that stuff." Folding down the sack, he warned, "And don't git any on your hands, you hear?"

"Yessir, Mr. Riley. I ain't."

When Emma hit the straightaway for home, she ran to keep from being too late. Closer to the house she started walking again. Before she'd left for the store, supper was on the stove and everybody was sitting out in the yard waiting for it to cool. She was glad to see they were still there.

As soon as she walked onto the yard, Grandma Duck asked, "Didja git everthang I tole you?"

Not slowing down, Emma said, "Yes'm, I got it."

"Take it on in there an set it down an come on back outta the house."

"Yes'm."

The oblong pan of cream corn cooling on the stove top was still plenty hot as Emma dumped in the whole sackful of rat poison. Hearing somebody coming, she had no time to get a spoon, and she burned her fingers while stirring the corn frantically.

Out on the yard, she casually played her way up to Sally B and Elzado. Without raising suspicion, she had to tell them before Grandma Duck called suppertime. "Sally B, les you an me an Elzado go over by the well 'n play." When they got to the well, she motioned for them to squat down behind it so Grandma Duck couldn't see them.

"Whut is it, Emma?" Sally B asked.

"I got sump'n to tell y'all."

Glad to be in on the secret, Elzado wanted to know, "Whut is it?"

"Y'all bet not eat none'a that corn we scraped."

"Why, Emma?"

"Never mind why, I'm tellin y'all, don't eat none."

"But why, Emma?"

"Cuz it'll kill y'all, thas why."

"Whut'd you do to it?"

"Never mind, Sally B. Jes don't eat none uv it. An y'all bet not tell nobody neither."

The threesome sat down on the back steps, waiting for the others to finish eating. All the while, Emma glanced through the screen door and couldn't sit still. Puzzling it over in her mind, *Frum the way that man wuz tellin me bout how much poison Rough on Rats is, they oughta be keelin over dead in they plates any minute now.*

Every time she quit watching, Sally B or Elzado asked anxiously, "Whut they doin, Emma?"

"Nothin yet."

When Grandma Duck's army finished, she called, "Sally B, Elzado, y'all come on to the table 'n eat."

They were too scared to eat anything and sang back, "We ain't hongry, Grammaw."

"Suit y'all's sef. But don't be ramblin roun in this kitchen afta while lookin for nothin to eat."

"No mam, Grammaw, we won't."

Emma fixed her pan, minus the corn, and sat between her sisters on the back steps and ate. Disappointed, she wished she had her dime back. In a few minutes Grandma Duck called them, "Sally B, y'all git in heah 'n clean up this kitchen."

"Yes mam, Grammaw, we comin."

After supper, as usual, the rag buckets were lit to smoke the mosquitoes away. Grandma Duck and her swarm sat outside in the cool of the evening. With the kitchen cleaned, Sally B, Emma, and Elzado joined them. Over the noisy playing of the smaller children, Emma heard Grandma Duck cry out, "God, I'm so sick," as she held her stomach.

Then another, "Me too."

And another, "Mama, my belly crampin me to death." One by one, they began sweating, moaning like sick cows, and vomiting all over the yard.

Nudging Sally B, Emma said, "C'mon, les play lak we sick too."

They lay down and started rolling around on the ground holding their bellies, groaning and giggling. Elzado wasn't putting on a very good act mimicking the others and drew Grandma Duck's attention. With stern eyes, she looked at Elzado for a minute and knew she was "jes puttin on." Then she looked at Emma, then at Sally B. Then back at Emma again. Pointing her finger at Emma, she declared, "Ain't nobody dun this but that ol nasty, stankin Charlie-lookin devil! That heifer dun sump'n to our suppa."

"No mam, I didn't, Grammaw," Emma defended quickly.

After Grandma Duck puked again, she hollered, "Sally B, run down yonder an tell Doc Hines I say come rat away. An don't you tarry!"

As Sally B turned to go, Grandma Duck said, "Take Elzado witcha."

"Kin I go wit 'em, Grammaw?" Emma asked eagerly.

"Naw, you set yo tail down over yonder where I kin see you!"

By the time Sally B and Elzado got back, that Rough on Rats had Grandma Duck and her gang's bellies swole up like balloons. When Doc Hines got through pumping them out, he had enough shit to fill up a wagon. In a few days Grandma Duck recuperated, and Emma took her "whuppin" with a smile. Even though things didn't go as planned, it was a whole dime's worth.

Sally B was always so quiet and shy. It sure surprised everybody when she got saved at the revival. She kept it a secret as long as she could, but the "spirit" was in her and kept getting bigger and bigger until she got shamefaced and ran off with the jackleg preacher who filled her with it.

Sitting with her sister on the back steps, Elzado urged, "Emma, les run off. Bama an Sally B been gone so long. They ain't never comin back afta us," she said forlornly.

"I know they ain't."

"Well, les run off then! I'm tired uv doin all the work an me an you gittin all the whuppins, specially you. Grammaw hates you! Look at my back, Emma," she said, pulling down the neck of her tattered dress to bare the rows of freshly inflicted coat-hanger welts.

Looking at Elzado's shoulders, Emma said, "I know, mine looks the same way, but you too little to ru—"

"Naw I ain't too little! I'm big is you is, an I do as much work as you do."

"I know that, but you still jes 'leven. Hush, I hear somebody comin."

Emma, at fifteen, had blossomed. Though her five-foot-five frame was slim, it bore the signs of womanhood, and her long dancer legs were striking. She kept her wavy, reddish, dark brown hair in a braid that hung midway down her back, exposing an interestingly beautiful face. The tiny moles dotting her cheeks were unignorable and accentuated her dark, intense eyes and pouted lips.

Unlike her sisters, Emma took her caramel-colored complexion and wavy hair from Charlie's light brown Cajun-Negro side of the family. Bama, Sally B, and Elzado, with their kinky black hair and dark mahogany skin, resembled Lillie and the rest of Grandma Duck's offspring.

Grandma Duck was crowding seventy. She wasn't as agile as she used to be, but she was just as hateful. Because she'd gotten too short-winded, she delegated "Big Auntie," her oldest daughter, full authority to do all of her "personal whuppin" while she oversaw to make sure it met her satisfaction.

Big Auntie was still sitting at the kitchen table while Emma and Elzado cleaned off the dirty supper dishes. She was just as ornery as Grandma Duck, and Emma decided now was as good a time as any. She had been wanting a chance to talk to Big Auntie away from all the others. As she raked the leftovers into a bucket for the hogs, she said, "Big Auntie?"

"Whut!"

"I wisht you'd make them ol boys a' yourn stop meddlin me."

"They be meddlin me too," Elzado chimed in.

"Shet up, Elzado, an git yo tail outta this kitchen!" Elzado glanced over at Emma. "I said git on outta heah!" After Elzado left, Big Auntie asked with indignation, "Meddlin you how?"

"They puttin they hands up under my dress, pinchin my titties an stuff."

Big Auntie pushed her chair back abruptly and stood up. "You jes shet yo lyin mouf! They ain't dun no such a thang! You low-down cow, none'a my boys wouldn't even look at you!"

"They did, Big Auntie!"

"I tole you to shet yo mouf! I been seein you sassy wigglin yo high-yella tail up an down that hall lak you got sump'n special!"

"Naw I ain't, Big Auntie!"

"You ol Charlie-lookin devil!" she shouted angrily, coming around the table to get at Emma. "Don't you 'spute my word!"

They clashed, and the noise of their battling soon brought

Grandma Duck. Emma was fighting Big Auntie like a tiger cat and had her down on the floor. Grandma Duck rushed in, hitting at her until Emma grabbed the butcher knife off the table.

Holding them at bay with the long-bladed knife poised in a striking position, she threatened, "If y'all come up on me, I'm gon stick y'all's hearts out. I ain't gon take no mo whuppins!" as she eased her way out the back door.

2

A motherless children have a hard time.
Motherless children have a hard time, Mother's dead.
They'll not have anywhere to go,
Wanderin around from door to door.
Have a hard time.

—Blind Willie Johnson,
"Motherless Children"

Emma didn't stop running until she got to the railroad trestle. She stayed under it all night long, and as soon as the dark lifted at dawn she got on the railroad tracks and hoofed it the twenty miles to Gilmer. Son Buddy was not hard to find. He was still living in the back room of the same hotel. He'd been working and living there for so long he was practically a landmark.

He could offer her no refuge. His quarters were too small for two people; besides, the manager of the hotel wouldn't allow it. However, he did know that the owners of the dry goods store were looking for some live-in help and offered to take her there.

"Thas awright, Son Buddy, you needn't do that. Jes tell me how to git there. I'll find it," she told him and left.

Emma walked up to the white lady behind the counter. "Mam?"

"Yes, can I help you?"

"Yes mam, I wuz by the hotel a while ago an the porter over yonder say the folks who own this store wuz lookin for somebody to work. Is you the one?"

"Yes, I am. Well, that is, me and my husband," the lady said, smiling. "We need somebody who can live in. It's just me and Jim and our three-year-old boy. We've been dropping him off at a woman's house, but we'd rather somebody be at home with him while we're gone. We spend most of our time here in the store," she explained, adding, "and usually when we get home, I'm dead on my feet and need some help with him at night."

"I kin do it, Miz . . ."

"Swift. My name's Mrs. Swift and that's my husband, Jim, over there," she said, pointing to the white man behind another counter.

"Miz Swif, I kin do it."

"What's your name?"

"Emma."

"Emma, do you know anything about taking care of smaller children?"

"Oh, yes mam, I growed up in a house full uv 'em."

"Where you from, Emma?"

"Big Sandy," she replied, dropping her head.

"What brings you to Gilmer?"

After taking a deep breath, she said, "I run away frum home, Miz Swif."

"Why on earth did you do that?"

"Cuz they whupped me all the time for nothin." With tears streaming down her face, Emma showed Mrs. Swift her scarred back.

"Lans sake! Why would they do a mean thing like that?" she exclaimed.

"Well, Miz Swif, afta my daddy kilt my mama, me an my other three sisters had to live wit Grammaw. She already had other chillun uv her own an didn't want us to begin wit. An afta the two biggest growed up an left, Grammaw got meaner an meaner to me an my baby sister. We didn't have nobody to go to or take up for us or nothin an got whuppins all the time."

Sympathetically, Mrs. Swift said, "Emma, child, you just stand right here and I'll be right back," and she fetched her husband.

"Jim, this is Emma. She's gonna be living with us and taking care of Bobby Joe."

After hearing his wife's version of Emma's plight, Mr. Swift looked the young beauty over and smiled. "That's fine, Irene, but first we've got to find her some clothes. I'll take her home and let her git herself cleaned up." Looking at Emma, he said, "I bet you'd like that, wouldn't you?"

"Yessir."

"Come with me then."

With Emma cooking, the Swifts started taking turns coming home every day to look in on Bobby Joe and eat a hot lunch. Today it was Jim's turn and he was seated at the kitchen table. Emma had her back to him, putting some things away in the pantry. He eyed her shapely legs and hourglass figure. "Emma."

"Yessir?"

"You're honestly about the prettiest colored gal I ever saw."

"Thank you, Mr. Swif."

"Why don't you call me Jim . . . when Irene ain't here."

Soon after, Jim started giving her money and getting more than just a hot meal when he came home while his wife tended the store. And, in addition, Emma could go to the dry goods store and Jim let her pick out anything she wanted. She quickly learned that a white man was willing to pay for "it."

Whenever she went to town in her off time, Emma expanded her profitable "trade" beyond Mr. Swift. When she stopped by to visit Son Buddy, the conversation drifted to her pretty clothes. "Emma, I thought you wuz workin for them people for jes room an board. Ever time I see you, you got on sump'n new. Where you comin up wit all them priddy new hats an shoes an dresses?"

"It ain't none'a yo bizness where I got 'em frum. I sho as hell didn't git 'em frum you!"

"You didn't answer me. Where you git the money for that stuff?"

"Mr. Jim give it to me."

"Whutcha do to git it?"

"None'a yo damn bizness!"

"Emma, you bet not be no whorish gal, messin roun wit that white man an takin money frum 'em!"

"Who you to talk? You been livin a few measly miles away frum us all this time an never come seen bout us, not one time! An you ain't never raised a finger to help us! So don'tcha be tellin me shit!"

Smack! The hard slap across the face sent her reeling. As soon as she cleared her head she lit into him, forcing him over backward. Realizing he had a ferocious wildcat on his hands, he used his fists a couple of times to get her off.

Emma's dress was torn, and by the time she got to the Swifts' house, her bloody lip had swollen to twice its size and the bruised skin under one of her eyes was bluish black. Still fuming, she hurried straight through the house to her back room. Jim looked up from his newspaper in time to see her going past and got a glimpse of the torn dress. He went to her door and knocked. "Emma, can I come in?"

"Yessir," she sniffled.

When he entered and saw her bloodied face, he asked angrily, "What on earth happened to you? Who did this?"

"Nobody, Mr. Jim."

Not masking his concern very well, he called, "Irene, come in here and look at what somebody did to Emma." Irene got a wet towel and was wiping Emma's face when he said, "I tried to git her to tell me who did it, but she won't."

"Well, Jim, maybe she doesn't feel like talking about it right now. Why don't you go on out and let her lie down for a while."

Her shiner had turned good and black by the time Jim came home for lunch the next day. Refusing to let it drop, he said, "Emma."

"Yessir."

"Tell me who did it."

"It wuz my brother." And she told him why.

The next week Son Buddy was found dead in his little room at the hotel with a bullet hole through his chest. After a "thorough" investigation, the authorities were unable to come up with a suspect for the murder. Emma was questioned and said she knew nothing.

As she dressed for the funeral Emma had only one thing on her mind; she raised the corner of her mattress and got her savings, to which Jim Swift and a few others had so generously contributed. On her way out, she stopped by the kitchen doorway. "Mr. Swif, Miz Swif, I'm gone."

Emma took a seat in the back of the little church and wouldn't sit close to them. Grandma Duck and her bunch had the three front benches on both sides of the aisle filled with family. The old matriarch was watching her masses like a chicken does a hawk. It was clear she didn't want them to even look around at her. Finally, Elzado got the chance to glance back long enough for Emma to catch her eye and gesture to go outside. She quickly passed the word down the bench to Grandma Duck, "Elzado gotta pee."

Looking back down the bench at her, Grandma Duck whispered loudly, "G'on! But you hurry up an git yo tail back in heah an don't be talkin to that ol Charlie-lookin devil!"

Soon after Elzado left the church and Emma caught Grandma Duck not looking, she left. She met Elzado on the outside and they stole away. Emma had their getaway prearranged. She handed the driver the thirty dollars for their fifty-mile trip, and they settled into the backseat of the car. Elzado asked excitedly, "Where we goin, Emma?"

"We goin to Longview. They havin a oil boom up there an men is comin frum everwhere bringin lotsa money wit 'em. Don't worry. I got some saved up to rent us a house till we kin git started."

"I don't care if we ain't got a pot to piss in. I'm jes so glad to git away!"

"I know, El. I wuzn't gon leave you behind again."

They were dropped off in downtown Longview. Neither had ever seen so many people in their entire lives. Tin Lizzie horns honking, wagon mules rearing, and all the folks scurrying about had their hearts racing with excitement. Nestled in the piney woods of Deep

East Texas near the Louisiana border, the town was flourishing. After they found a place to stay, it was time to sit down and go over the game plan. Elzado was ready and willing as she listened to Emma's teachings.

"The first time you may have to grit yo teeth. Lak I did wit Mr. Jim. But afta that, you git use to it an it don't hurt or nothin. White men wanna git through quick as they kin an go cuz they don't want nobody knowin it. You kin put on a little baby whine an they'll give you jes about anythang you ask for. They always in a hurry, so the only thang you gon git frum 'em is money. An thas all we want! Soon as he do his bizness, suck yo belly in an git up an pee that stuff out. We gon git us two uv them long pocketknifes, an we don't never wanna be on our backs at the same time. Understand?"

Elzado answered with a laconic "yeah."

"While I'm doin it, you stand guard an be ready to use that knife. When you do it, don't be scared. I'll be guardin for you. We gon be awright, but we gotta stick together an not git separated frum each other. You understand?"

"I understand, Emma, an don't worry. I ain't scared. Not half as scared as I wuz to eat that corn you put poison in that time." They hugged and laughed in remembrance of the occasion. After so much talking, sleep came tinted with solidarity. Although Elzado was big for her age, she wasn't quite fourteen when they hooked up as a team and took to the oil fields.

Emma's bravery shone like pearls in the moonlight as she and Elzado walked toward the oil field derrick lights. The autumn night air stunk with the pungent odors of burning oil and gas. The closer they got, the brighter the glare of the lights and the harder it was to see. Emma could barely make out the figure of a man walking to meet them. "Here come somebody," she told Elzado. "Member whut I tole you." They stopped. The white man kept coming.

"Whut in the Sam Hill are you two gals doin out heah this time uv night?"

Emma stepped closer to him. "Lookin."

"For whut?"

In a sexy tone, "Whutever's out here," she replied.

He got the picture, smiled broadly, and walked them to the toolshed. The roughnecks welcomed them with open arms and billfolds. Very seldom did anybody give them a hard time. When they did, it usually was the foreman rushing somebody back to work so he could take his turn in the toolshed.

Emma always made a lot more money than Elzado and caught tricks three to her one. Elzado was gangly with a boyish figure and wore her kinky black hair in plaits. The ugly harelip that Grandma Duck had left her with, after hitting her in the face with a skillet for "bristlin back," made her no match for Emma's drop-dead good looks. Whenever Emma got on her about "fixin" herself up, Elzado would say in a funk, "I ain't gon play lak I'm priddy when I know I ain't," and wouldn't touch the rouge and lipstick Emma offered. "Anyhow, afta he git on toppa me to do his bizness, he don't give a damn whut I look lak."

Their notoriety spread quickly. The other whores in town even noted how much "guts an gall" it took to be out in the fields tricking, "jes the two uv 'em." Danger or no danger, the team kept hiring the taxi driver to haul them from one site to another and wait. Taking it directly to the front lines, they were shortstopping the traffic before it got to town. They bought plenty of baubles and beads and pretty clothes, and eventually filtered into the "streets" mainstream.

Soon thereafter, Baby Norris joined their team. Semifoxy but with an air of cheapness about her, she was five or six years older than Emma, didn't have a steady man, was tired of waiting on the tricks to come to town, and had the guts. By now Emma was well known and heralded as everybody's favorite. Because Emma and Baby Norris were about the same build and complexion, Baby Norris was passed off as the third sister. To enhance her chances at a greater share of the tricks, she and Emma dressed alike to confuse the "bulls," who picked her thinking she was Emma. But Emma had enough tricks to keep them both busy.

Even though the toolshed business was very lucrative, it was getting old and the trio started having the workers come to the little two-room shotgun house instead. With a few tips from Baby Norris, Emma got in touch with the right people and expanded her enterprise to include bootlegging. As soon as the other whores found out about the crowds that came to her house for a "good time," they started coming in droves.

Emma hung a long piece of cloth over the open doorway separating the one small room from the smaller kitchen. She bought a cot and placed it just inside the kitchen beyond the "curtain." Then she laid down the law to the visiting whores. "Don't ketch no tricks in my house an take 'em off somewhere else. You found 'em here, leave 'em here. When you wanna trick an I ain't usin it, you kin pay me to use the cot in the kitchen. An don't be rollin no drunks. It give my house a bad name." Even though Elzado had moved out and was on her own, living with a white man in the Northcutt Heights, she was still tricking and spent much of her time at Emma's.

Emma's "good time" house was fast becoming the most popular place in town. The bootlegging business was thriving, and, with the other whores hanging around, the shotgun house was always crowded with oil field workers, both blacks and whites. This soon brought the gamblers. "Where there's hoes an boozin, there's sho to be gamblin," Baby Norris explained. With the lure of easy money, some of the "real" gamblers started drifting in. That's how Emma met Allen.

He was a tall, good-looking black devil, so black his friends called him Blue. He was streetwise and smooth as butter, a touch of arrogance mixed with caution. His worldly manner ofttimes belied his mere twenty-three years, and he stood apart from the herd. His expensive tailored clothes fit snugly, accentuating his slim, muscular frame. He was a gambler by profession and always won big at Emma's.

She had smoked him over on several occasions when he was down on his knees shooting dice. Aside from his outright handsomeness, she was magnetized by his gambling skills and always stopped what she was doing to marvel at the way he took them to the cleaners. When he propositioned her about paying her to let him "manage all the gamblin," she jumped at the chance to enter into the contract.

He started coming early and staying late. For the first time Emma was infatuated and didn't view him as just another trick. She dropped her guard and fell head over heels for the impressive young hustler. He soon took up permanent residence and they worked as a team. She tricked on the cot and took care of the bootlegging while he cleaned up with the dice. All the money that came in the house stayed there, one way or another. They became the talk of the streets. The top whore in town hooked up with the beautiful black stallion. All the whores envied her for nabbing the number one hustler; the men envied him for having won over the cream of the crop.

Emma realized that Allen was making more than she was and much quicker. However, many times after he'd won all the money in the game at her house, he left and went somewhere else to gamble, only to lose. When he got broke at the other places, he sent his hat by a runner for identification and she sent money back to him. He wouldn't quit until he used up all of her money too.

Being in the hole was tampering with the bootlegging business. With both of them broke, she had to accelerate her tricking to come up with the money to pay for the loads of whiskey. It was becoming increasingly apparent to Emma that Allen was blowing it faster than she could make it. They began to argue about it more and more. "Hell," she told him, "I don't need nobody to help me fuck it off! I kin do that by myself."

It was late morning when he finally made it home. Clothes rumpled and his eyes bloodshot, he'd been up all night gambling. She noticed it right off; it had looked so good on him. "Where's yo hat?" she asked as he headed into the kitchen.

Stalling for time, he hated to face her. "Whut'd you say, Emma?" he asked in between swallows from the dipper.

"You heard me. I *said* where's yo hat?" She had paid sixty-five dollars for that Borsalino.

"I hocked it last night."

"To who?"

"Aw, I let Pinch hold it for twenny dollars. I'll git it back this evenin." Walking toward the bed, he yawned and said, "Baby, yo man is beat."

She'd been up and down all night herself, waiting on customers who dropped by for bootleg whiskey and getting up to send him money. Irritable and in no mood to cut him any slack, she countered, "You don't look all that tired to me." Wheeling out of the bed, she said, "I'm gon git the crap blanket an you gon teach me how to gamble an shoot dice, right now. I'm sick uv this shit!" She spread the Army blanket on the floor and got down on her knees at its edge. "C'mon, you got some dice in yo pocket. Gitcha no-gamblin ass down here," she taunted.

He whined and hemhawed around for a while but, in hopes of soothing ruffled feelings, agreed reluctantly. "First off," he said, picking up the blanket, "you don't want it spread all the way out lak this. It's too thin." He folded it into a four-by-four square and lay it back on the floor. He took the dice out of his pocket and got down on his knees beside her. "The softer the surface, the easier it is to control the dice when you roll 'em, lak this," he told her, demonstrating. "You don't want 'em bouncin roun lak this," he explained, as he precariously threw them out on the blanket. "You wanna hold 'em wit yo fingers lak this, an jes rollll 'em easy lak this. Jes sorta push 'em 'cross the blanket so they stay together an tumble side by side. You hafta learn how to control the way they roll wit yo fingers. You wanna keep 'em rollin side by side an not let whutever you got locked in the middle come up."

Taking the dice, one in each hand, he showed her what he meant. "Look, I got a three an a two in the middle," he said, joining the two together. "I'm gon roll 'em so they stays where I put 'em." He "rolllled" them time and time again, and the three and two never showed up. "Another thang, they's forty-two dots on a pair uv dice, three sevens on each one." Rotating them in his hand, he told her,

"See, all the dots equal seven. You got five-deuce seven, four-trey seven, an six-ace seven. So—"

"So," she interrupted, "if you know alla that an kin do it so good, how come you git broke all the time?"

"Cuz, Emma, you know well as I do, most uv the whitefolks an nigguhs that hang aroun over heah don't know shit bout gamblin. They be jes havin fun an don't hardly know one dice frum another. I kin git away wit cold-blood murder in a game wit them."

"How come you can't do it when you gamblin in them other games?"

"Cuz they won't letcha set 'em an roll 'em lak that. All them nigguhs know how to gamble, an all uv us know how to roll. So they serve 'em to you. Ever time you shoot 'em out there the houseman or whoever's runnin the game picks 'em up, shakes 'em, an puts 'em back in yo hand. You ain't got a chance to set 'em an you be goin on luck. Specially when we shootin on a pool table, cuz them dice be tumblin ever which way."

"Well, if they won't letcha do whut you showin me, whut the hell do you keep goin over there for an luckin off all our money?"

He looked at her for a moment. "I guess for the same reason you keep on trickin. C'mon, les git back to whut I wuz tellin you. The best way to learn bout the bets is to watch the game. You bet the straight-make on six an eight, an you bet the bar on four, five, nine, an ten. When you throw seven . . ."

Emma went to Shivers Drugstore and bought several pairs of dice. All during the day when she wasn't busy she devoted her time to playing with the pair she carried in her hand, squeezing them, matching them, fitting them, and learning to hold them the "right way." When the crap game at the house started, she got down on her knees and watched. When the game ended, she practiced on the blanket by herself. She had emulated the roll down pat and could "rollll" them across the blanket so close together they looked like they'd been stuck with glue.

Emma added the third dimension to her repertoire. No longer was she a mere observer; she had served her apprenticeship. Now when she got down on her knees at the blanket's edge, she got down there to gamble and "run" the game. Allen's managing steadily diminished and she took over. She loved it, and gambling became her life's blood. Dedicating herself to the perfection of her talents, she became a whiz with the craps and was "lucky as a shithouse rat" in the eyes of the other gamblers.

Along the way she developed into a pretty fair card shark. She dealt Maude, Georgia skin, kotch, poker, blackjack, and was a damn good cooncan player. Allen had been a good tutor, and as soon as she learned the ABCs of gambling, he taught her how to cheat. He explained, "The first law in gamblin is know how to cheat an know when you bein cheated." She knew how to "pike" under each card off the bottom or from the middle of the deck without anyone ever noticing. It was hard for them to imagine such a good-looking woman cheating. She also developed a gift of gab for distraction purposes when she was performing her quicker-than-the-eye-could-see card antics.

Though she became very adept at cards, her passion was shooting craps. She learned to use every trick in the book to throw her opponent off balance and make him break his rhythm. Anything to distract. She'd put on her sexiest dress and a pair of her best black gunmetal hose. She flashed a little dab of thigh and leaned forward enough to let him have a quickie at the breast. When she got the attention she was after, she made her move with the dice, "the hull-gully," setting them as she quickly scooped them up to make her "Hudson" shot. She released them with a side motion, killing the die she had cupped in her little finger and careening the other one out with topspin English. Coming out, that die she cupped in her little finger always stopped on five, eliminating the possibility of throwing "craps"—a two, three, or twelve.

Most of the time she was the only woman in the game, but she cursed just as loud, squabbled just as much, hit, got hit, and hit back. She stood her ground and was just as cold, hard, callous, cunning, and tough as need be, with a natural sense of humor to get by with it. They'd fight one minute and be back gambling and drinking the next. Involving herself in the whole game environment, when the players were ballyhooing and passing the bottle, she took her turn and got just as mean and ornery as the rest of them. When that firewater hit the pit of her stomach and her shot came, she started "talking" to the dice.

First roll, coming out, "Oh! Don't forget to take the dough! *Eleven!* Bless joy, there it tis!" Snapping her fingers as loudly as she could with each roll, Emma begged for each point incessantly while the dice propelled down the blanket. Coming out again, with her Hudson shot, first roll, "Oh! Don't leave me here! Take me witcha when you go!" Got nine for a point, "I bet I bar it."

"You got a bet, Emma, you don't bar. Shoot 'em." She rubbed the dice back and forth on the blanket, talking to them. "C'mon, Emma, quit fuckin aroun an shoot the damn dice!" the fader said, admonishing her.

"How come you in such a great big hurry for me to make nine on yo ass?" she quipped, still rubbing the dice slowly and deliberately to antagonize.

"C'mon, bitch! Shoot the fuckin dice!" he said gruffly, irritated by her delaying tactics.

"Whut'd you say, muthafucka?"

"Shoot the dice."

"No, whut'd you call me?"

"Bitch. You ain't no better'n my sister an they calls her a bitch."

Emma dove over on him and whupped his ass good. He was out cold. Blue and another crapshooter dragged him to the other side of the room and propped him up in the corner.

Going for nine with another fader, she cried, "Oh, Lady! Please be good. Quinine! is a bitter dose! Oh, Alek! Iron, you cold black shine! Oh, Baby! We ain't but *nine miles* frum home! *Nine!* times outta ten!" Still no nine. She stopped and looked around at the players. "Bet somebody some mo I bar nine."

"Thas a bet, Emma. Brang 'em on."

"I'm fixin to make nine on y'all's asses. Watch me make it wit six-trey," she said and sent the dice on their mission. "*Ever!* now an then you meet a stranger. *Stop!* an invite him in." Nine.

Got eight for a point. She "cocked the trigger" (set the combination) and fired. "Oh, Ada! Black gal. Let! yo hair hang down! Oh, Ada! Ross wuz a pacin good hoss!" Sweat rolling down her face. "Oh, Baby! don't leave me here. Come back an git me. Oh! if you please! Ada! frum Decatur, the county seat uv Wise. *Eight!* babies too soon!"

Taking another big swig from the bottle, gets ten for a point. "Oh! Tennessee Toddy! All asshole an no body! Oh, *Big Ben!* Bend double. *Oh, Ben!* Bend down an lift it up. *Oh!* Tom Pane, thas Black Annie's ol man!"

Five. "Oh, Fantail Fanny! Fanny Fites! Ugliest woman in the Northcutt Heights! Oh, Phoenix! Arizona. *Oh!* lemme off! *At!* yo next stop. . . ."

Emma and Allen were making "damn good money." When the crap games ended they had most, if not all, of the money. A band of regulars, blacks and whites alike, made coming to their place to drink and gamble a daily ritual. The workers, gamblers, and whores kept money in circulation at the house all the time. With it rolling in, Allen got Pinch to come over and run the house for two or three days so he and Emma could get away.

He loved to show her off at other gambling places, and they'd take special train excursions to Shreveport regularly. At some of the games the gamblers bet five hundred dollars on a shot, shooting on a pool table! Allen took her there to let her see all the excitement of a big bettors' game. But Emma couldn't content herself to stand at the table and watch.

During one of their trips she could take it no longer and tossed fifty bucks on the table. All the players shied away from such a small amount. "Say," she said righteously, "don't stand there an look crazy.

Somebody fade me. They's plenny mo where that come frum. I kin make mo money in fifteen minutes than y'all seen all day!" Looking at Allen, she asked, "Ain't that right, baby?"

"Thas right, baby."

"I got somethin that'll sell when cotton an corn won't." She had them laughing with her. All she wanted was just *one* shot!

Finally one of the players decided, "Hell, I'll fade a priddy woman lak you *anytime*. I got you faded fifty. Shoot 'em."

Emma had never shot craps on a pool table before, but she knew the dice would be bouncing. Just like Allen had said, it was pure D luck. After she rubbed the dice gently on the green felt until she was ready, her first roll was a natural. "Shoot the hundred," she snapped.

"Shoot 'em."

Eleven, a winner. "Shoot the two."

"Damn!" the fader said and tossed up two hundred more. "Shoot 'em again. I gotcha one mo time." Eight, and she made it. "Somebody else kin fade her. She's too heavy for me."

Emma pulled down and shot two hundred again and caught *four!* Gamblers generally hate four and hope to never catch it. It was her favorite point! She bet her other two hundred that she'd bar it. She took two or three more shots and got all the money Allen had in his pockets, and bet that. Still not satisfied after a few more rolls, Emma wanted to bet some more. She *knew* she was going to make that four. They had no more money to bet. She paused a moment to rub the dice on the felt, then looked around at Allen. "Lemme have yo coat."

"Whut for?"

"Never mind, jes pull it off an give it here."

He began to take it off, but very slowly. She had paid the tailor Louie Rickey five hundred dollars to make Allen's imported camel-hair overcoat. When he handed it to her, she laid it on the table and gave a brief on it. One of the players opened it up, saw the Louie Rickey label, and asked, "How much you wanna bet ginst it?"

"Three hundred."

"Hell, naw. I'll go two an no mo."

"Put it up."

More than a thousand dollars was riding on four. She threw the dice out on the table and the ace stopped immediately. The other spun off down the table and was still spinning as she hollered, "Oh! Little Britches! C'mon!" It settled on three. She won big that night and became famous for making "Little Britches."

Shortly after they returned to Longview, the nightly game at the "good time" house had ended and everybody was gone. Allen had something on his mind. "Emma?"

"Yeah, Blue?"

"I wantcha to stop trickin wit them white men."

"Why?"

"Cuz I thank me an you oughta git married. How long we been livin together? Three . . . four years?"

"Yeah, been bout that long an thas the way we need to keep it. That way, you don't own me an I don't own you. Anyhow, I thought you wanted me to do it." Fighting her case and defending her livelihood, she said, "I been trickin since I wuz fifteen an I ain't never had to ask nobody for shit." Playing up to him, she went on, "You oughta be happy. Havin a good hoe is lak havin money in the bank."

"I wantcha to stop or you kin find you another man! I don't wanna see no mo white men comin in an outta heah 'less they wanna gamble."

"How come you jes now gittin mad bout it? Thas whut I wuz doin when you met me."

"I don't give a fuck whutcha *wuz* doin! I'm tellin you I don't wantcha doin it no mo! Fuck that shit!"

"Say, we don't have to git married for me to stop trickin wit them white men. Jes cuz you want me to, I'll quit."

"I ain't for no bullshit, Emma. I mean bizness. I wantcha to stop doin it."

"Awright, awright, I'll stop. I won't do it no mo." Allen searched her eyes for the truth as she vowed, "I won't, Blue. I swear I won't. I promise."

Because the Great Depression was on the horizon, things were "gittin tighter'n the little E string on a cheap guitar." Both of them hustling barely maintained their style of living and paid for the whiskey. Bootlegging had fallen off considerably after the oil fields trade slacked off. In order to keep on buying Allen a new Borsalino whenever she felt like it, Emma started back to "seein" one of her old standbys, Mr. Albert the cotton broker. Unbeknownst to Allen, she met him somewhere two or three times a week.

As she was lying beside Allen early one morning, the "spirit" moved within her. She had to do something quick, rolled off her side of the bed, ran to the door, and barely got it open before she started vomiting.

Half awake, Allen asked, "Whut's the matter, Emma?"

"Damn! I'm sick at my stomach! Git me a wet rag so I kin wipe my face. I'll be awright in a few minutes."

"Whut the hell you eat? I been tellin you bout eatin all that damn garlic an peppers an onions an shit." Handing her the damp cloth, he said, "It's a wonder you don't blow up."

She vomited again. Regaining her composure, she got back in the bed. "I ain't been that sick since I wuz a kid an ate all them half-green huckleberries. G'on back to sleep. I'm awright now. Must'a been somethin I ate."

Later that day she sneaked off to see Doc Falvey. After hearing about the vomiting, he examined her and broke the news. "Emma, you're pregnant." Speechless, she just stared blankly. She'd missed the count! She ought to tell Allen; no, she ought'n. She decided to just sit on it awhile.

Finally the time had come. "Say, Blue, I been thankin bout whut you asked me. You still wanna do it?"

"Do whut?"

"Git married."

"Do you?"

"Yeah."

"Les do it tomorrow!"

"Okay. I love you, Blue."

"I love you too, baby," he told her, and he held her tight.

That night after making love, Allen quickly fell asleep as Emma lay staring at the ceiling, stirring the deception over in her mind. Like shooting dice without getting to set them, the best she could do was go on luck.

The next day they got the marriage license from the county clerk and headed for the justice of the peace. Allen handed the license to the old redneck judge, who told him, "Awright, ketch holt uv her hand, boy. Do you, Allen Sample, take this woman fer yore lawful wedded wife?"

"I do."

"Do you, Emma Barnes, take this man fer yore lawful wedded husband?"

"I do."

"You got a rang, boy?"

"Nawsuh."

"By the powers vested in me by the state uv Texas, I now pronounce y'all man an wife. That'll be three dollars, boy."

After a couple of months Emma began to show, and Allen commented, "Hey, baby, you suuure gittin full roun the middle!"

"I got ever reason to be," she toyed. "I'm pregnant."

"Since when?"

"Since you know when! Wudn't you there?"

"Well, I'll be damned! I'll jes be damned!" he shouted with joy.

They moved into another shotgun house with wider rooms. It was located right behind the old condemned calaboose. One day the regulars still showed up, as usual, but today they were asked to go outside and be quiet. Doc Falvey was inside. Waiting anxiously, Allen mingled in the yard, drinking whiskey with the others to keep warm.

After Doc Falvey cleaned the baby, he laid it in Emma's arms and left to make the announcement. Then she got her first look at what the stork just "brung." "Aw shit," she uttered in dismay, "white as the drifts uv snow."

Doc Falvey walked out onto the small porch. "It's a boy."

Allen beamed while the others patted him on the back. He rushed inside, stepped to the bed, took one look, and knew it "wudn't his'n." He wheeled around and walked out on her that snowy Friday afternoon at 3:20 in 1930, slamming the door so hard it almost jarred the little house off its blocks. She had dealt him a blow right between his balls. Pride dangling, he kept his eyes glued to the ground and didn't speak as he brushed past the gathering.

Bewildered, they watched him taking long strides down the snow-covered railroad tracks, then stared at one another until somebody declared, "Damn! Blue look lak he jes seen a ghost."

The regulars filed into the house and stood around the bed gawking at the infant swaddled in a blanket and cradled in Emma's arms. A little white hand reached out from the blanket toward her. Their eyes widened. They shook their heads and grunted, "Ummh, ummh, ummh," until one of them piped up, "That sho ain't none'a Blue's baby."

"Y'all git the hell on outta here!" Emma shouted. "This ain't no gotdam circus!" And she nudged the little hand away from her.

> I wuz born in a lion's den
> and suckled by a bear . . .
> I growed two sets uv jaw teefs
> and a double coat uv hair.

Big Emma and Me

———

3

1934

Emma was busy tricking seven days a week. Our house was only a couple hundred feet from the railroad tracks and a hundred yards from the Texas and Pacific station. Every time a train came through, our little house almost rattled off its hinges. It was a real convenience for the engineers, firemen, and brakemen who left their trains for a quickie. When she had "company," I sat on the steps and waited.

There wasn't much for me to do during the weekdays, except get up late at night and sell an occasional half-pint. The weekends were totally different and sleep was out of the question. Emma rose early on Saturday mornings and got me out of my cot in the kitchen to help her with the preparations for the long weekend stand.

She fixed our Saturday morning special: two cans of sardines piled high with hot peppers, a big white onion, cheese, and crackers. "Gitcha a fork an come on." I loved eating out of her plate; the food tasted better.

As soon as we finished, I helped get the scrub waters ready for the wooden floors that already looked bleached from too many scrubbings. My job was to watch the water from the outside hydrant so it wouldn't overflow the buckets, while Emma carried the full ones into the house. When we had enough water, she began her ritual of "preparin'" it by pissing in the buckets after adding a half can of Eagle lye. This was for "good luck," she said. I watched out the front door and we'd pretend we weren't home if a woman came to the house before a man. The first person in the house after the piss and lye scrubbing had to be a man, because "if a woman comes in first, it puts a jinx on the house."

The next step was getting the gambling area set up. An old, green Army blanket was spread in the middle of the floor. When unfurled, the thinly worn wool "crap" blanket was clearly marked u.s. in the center. No matter how it was folded the cigarette holes always showed, causing a special house rule to be made: "Cocked dice in the hole don't go." It tasted the sweat from many palms, saw many a dollar change hands, and made both enemies and friends. That old blanket had as much character as anybody in the house, and was richly deserving of the attention it received from Emma. She tried her best to protect it, but serving combat duty on the front lines was hazardous.

Emma thoroughly briefed me on my jobs before the crowd arrived. I sat on the case of bootlegged whiskey bottled in half-pints until somebody wanted one. I collected the money and gave each customer a dipperful of water with which to wash it down, if it was bought by the shot. Between sales, I kept a sharp lookout for the police and a keen eye on the dice when they rolled off the blanket so nobody could switch in some crooked ones. When Emma was shooting, I watched the cigar box she kept her loose change in so nobody would "clip" her. "You my houseman. You gotta help look out for Emma," she instructed me.

After a short wait the gamblers and whores arrived, and Saturday got kicked off with a bang. Ready for the game to start, Emma pulled off her high heels and knelt at the blanket's edge. "Two bits I shoot." A quarter hit the blanket. She rolled the dice and cursed when they stopped on craps. "Four bits this time," and she rolled craps again. "Damn! I must'a throwed a brick in the church house!" She'd lose a lot at first, then get "lucky" and nail them.

The twenty-five or thirty (black and white) gamblers down on their knees were crammed elbow to elbow around the crap blanket.

At least a dozen more hovered behind the shooters, placing bets over their shoulders. The small shotgun house, with one room and kitchen, was bursting at the seams, reeking of booze and cigarettes. Sometimes the gambling, tricking, drinking, squabbling, and occasional fighting went right on into the next day without ever stopping. Many times, Allen came over to gamble. I knew by the way Emma treated him that he was somebody special.

When there was a lull in the whiskey selling, I watched the dice as they were propelled across the blanket. I knew somebody had rolled craps when Emma hollered, "Toot-toot for Dixie!" glad it was her shot next. I tried not to act like I was paying any attention. I knew she didn't want me pulling for her because it made her have "bad luck." Without fail, whenever she missed a point she had bet on pretty heavily, she glowered straight at me and ordered, "Boy, carry yo jinky peckerwood-lookin ass in that kitchen an git outta my sight!"

I stayed awhile but eased my way back into the crap room to take a peep out the curtains for the police. I lingered in the room too long. After she missed another point, Emma's eyes found me. "Don't y'all shoot till I git back," she said as she got up. "I need to take care uv some bizness in the kitchen for a minute." Goose bumps popped out all over me in dreaded expectation.

When she reached a certain quota in her drinking, her bitterness surged, and I was the target for her explosive temper. None of the gamblers dared to interfere, especially after that time Lakey spoke up, "Emma, you ought not ta whup 'em lak that." She flew into a rage and stabbed him in the shoulder with an ice pick and threw him out of the house for "meddlin."

Beyond the doorway curtain I stood waiting. She walked into the kitchen with the coat hanger and slowly began stretching it out. "Take yo clothes off."

"I won't do it no mo. Pleeze, Mama, don't—"

"I tole you not to call me that! Call me Emma! Now git that shit off. Right now!"

When she finished dealing with me, she returned to the crap game and started shooting again. Soon realizing she needed me, she called me back to the crap room: "Git my bottle."

The gambling went on into the night. The house was dark, except for the kerosene lamp on the kitchen floor and the one placed near the crap blanket. Terrell Latham had been "swinging" the craps all evening, and Emma cursed him with every breath. He hung around every crap game in town and never had more than two dollars to lose. After he was broke, or claimed to be, every time his turn came he sold it to a gambler on the other side of the blanket who already shot. If somebody wanted to give him two or four bits for his turn, well and good, but the players to his right, including Emma, were kept waiting.

When he'd swing the craps, it caused confusion, and she lit in on him. "Terrell, you ain't lost but two chickenshit dollars an I'll be a muthafucka if you gon swing the fuckin dice ever time they git to you. They's some mo nigguhs who wanna shoot an can't for you holdin up the gotdam game!"

Unfortunately for Terrell, he got a little too drunk. After a long evening of swinging the dice and getting cursed out, he flopped down in one of the cane-bottom chairs and passed out. Everybody and his brother went through his pockets, and this time he really was broke.

The game was finally about to end, with Emma winning most of the money. There were only a couple of players left, trying to wrap up the "scrappings" (scraps). Emma had quit shooting and I noticed her staring at Terrell with a mischievous look on her face.

She got up and walked into the kitchen, discovering that our two kittens had shit all over the floor. She rolled several turds onto a piece of paper with the stove poker and brought them back into the crap room. Using a small stick, she smeared the "dookie" all over Terrell's face, especially heavily around his nose and mustache.

I started laughing, but she cautioned me not to be too loud and wake him up before she finished. The few gamblers left in the game had stopped shooting and were watching her too, snickering and trying to keep from laughing out loud. She had figured out an acceptable way to get back at Terrell for being such a nuisance.

With the final touches completed, she opened a bottle on the house and passed it around while everybody waited. After a few minutes, Terrell's nose began to twitch. With closed eyes, he started wiping his nose and mustache, rubbing his chin, and scratching his head. Each time he went through those motions, he spread the shit more and more. Now it was even in his hair. The stink in the room was almost unbearable.

At last Terrell opened his eyes, and, after a few moments of collecting himself, he finally said in a half-drunken stupor, "Gotdam, Emma! You needs ta git ridda dem fuckin cats! Looka heah, dem liddle cocksuckers dun shit all over me!"

I laughed so hard I cried, and forgot all about the zinging of the coat hanger.

If some player in the game happened to catch her fancy, Emma wasn't slow about giving him the "glad eye." I knew the moment it happened. She mellowed her intense gambling expression into a sexy, sleepy-eyed bedroom look and flashed it to him like a lightning bug, "stick around." When she mixed business and pleasure, she'd have two games going at the same time, never missing a shot in either.

It didn't matter who she kept for her late-night lover or how eager she was to go to bed with him, he had to wait his turn. After the others were gone, she told him, "I gotta take care uv my o' man first." She was never too tired and it was never too late. After they'd pulled a long tour of duty, she picked up the old crap blanket, shook it out, and painstakingly folded it up and laid it to rest underneath her pillow. With her "o' man" bedded down, it was on to the next item on the agenda.

To get me to go to sleep "quick," I got the "Raw Hide and Bloody Bones" bedtime story. Rushing me beyond the curtain to my cot, she'd say, "You betta git you some salt an take it to bed witcha so Raw Hide an Bloody Bones won't gitcha! He loves to git little boys who don't go to sleep quick lak they mamas tell 'em to.

"Bloody Bones is *biggg! Big* as a bear. An got big o' bloody chunks uv meat hangin all off uv him! An some loooong sharp claws an big red eyes wit blood drippin all down 'em! An slobberin blood all out his mouth cuz he jes ate up a little boy. He creeeeps up on you at night an if he ketch you not sleepin, the first thang he do is claw yo eyeballs out an eat 'em! Then he'll smear you wit his big o' bloody hands, an you'll turn into a big scab an die!

"Only way you kin keep him off you is to throw some salt on 'em an he'll turn yellow an melt away lak a snail do. But if you don't wanna meet him face-to-face, you betta go to sleep quick! An that way, he won't come afta you. But jes in case, you best take that salt box to bed witcha."

"Yes mam, I got the box an I'm gon eat some too! Emma, kin I keep the lamp on turnt down low?"

"Naw, jes go to sleep quick befo he comes." She blew out the lamp and left.

I covered my head, hiding from Bloody Bones. The squeaking bedsprings quickly lullabied me to sleep until somebody knocked on the door and wanted a half-pint. I handled all the late, late traffic from my cot office. Usually, I woke up on the first knock and moved quickly through Emma's room to answer the door before the knocking disturbed them. Digging into the flour barrel in the kitchen for the half-pints, I waited on the customers, collected the money and dropped it in the fruit jar, lay back down, and re-hid from Bloody Bones under the covers.

Tuesday, things were slow; we closed up shop and went to bed early for a change. I was asleep on my cot when Emma came in and woke me up. "Sshhh, be quiet an lissen. The police is outside. You start cryin the minute they come through the door. If you cry, they won't take Emma to jail."

When I heard the heavy knocking on the front door, I got my cry ready. The white man's voice was gruff: "Open up this goddamn door! It's the law!"

Very quickly she opened the door and stepped back to the center of the room, gathering me close to her. Feigning fear, I started whimpering. I knew all three of them by name. They had been here before. All three were notorious for their "head cuttin." "Yessir, whut y'all want?" Emma asked politely.

"You know damn well whut we want, gal!" Mr. Thrasher shot back angrily. "You got some bootleg whiskey in heah an we gonna find it or beat the hell outta you!"

"Naw sir, they ain't none'a that stuff in here," she denied fervently.

"Yore a goddamn liar!" Mr. Bell shouted back.

They began tearing the place apart. After looking under the bed, in boxes, in her trunk, and everywhere they could think of, Mr. Thrasher was really getting irritated and took a swing at Emma. I let out my biggest, best cry. For the moment it worked. They wanted her to stop my loud screaming.

During the pause in the action Emma got a chance to collect herself and go into her command performance. "I'm jes a po ol workin gal tryin to make a livin an raise this half-white baby. I don't steal or do none'a them bad thangs them other nigguhs roun here do, an I *never* give the laws no trouble."

Mr. Killingsworth bent down to me. "Is there any whiskey in this house, boy?"

"No sir!"

Not missing a trick, Emma said, "An jes look at him, y'all. He's one'a yo own. Tell 'em how old you is, baby."

"I wuz born right behind the ol jailhouse in nineteen thurty on a Friday at three twenny the seventh day uv Febewary. It wuz sleetin an snowin. Gregg County Presink Number One. Hoot Garner is the sheriff. I'm four years old."

It took many a lick with the coat hanger to get it in me, but after I had it down pat she could shake me at four in the morning and I'd rattle it off in my sleep.

She had them until Mr. Thrasher noticed the loose planks in the center of the floor where we were standing. "You and that boy move over," he ordered. They lifted the planks, and there it was, two cases of half-pints! I looked at her and she looked at me.

This was one of the few times whiskey was in our house and I didn't know it. When I said "no sir," I thought we were sold out. The deliveryman had brought it without my knowing.

With a look of "aha, we got you now" on his face, Mr. Bell yelled, "We're takin yore ass to jail!"

"Whut am I gon do bout my boy?"

"Leave him wit a neighbor. I don't give a damn whutcha do wit him, yore ass is goin to jail," Mr. Bell reaffirmed.

"Please, sirs, Whitefolks, whutever y'all do, don't make me leave my baby wit none'a these nigguhs roun here," she begged. "Look at him, y'all. If you wuz a nigguh, would you wanna keep him? He's one'a y'all, Whitefolks. He got some'a y'all's blood in him."

There I stood like Mary's little lamb with my light-colored skin and blue eyes staring up at the three of them so innocently, thinking, *I sho don't want no blood uv no policemans in me.*

"All right, git him dressed. He's goin too," Mr. Bell conceded.

Emma took me behind the doorway curtain into the kitchen. As she helped me get into my cowboy outfit and boots, she whispered, "They ain't gon keep *us* in jail long."

While the other two loaded the whiskey into their car trunk, Mr. Thrasher told me he would let me blow the siren on the way. I was tickled pink to be going to jail with Emma. She sat in the back and I sat on Mr. Thrasher's lap up front, blowing the siren all the way to the courthouse.

After booking her in, they were ready to take us upstairs to the jail cells on the fifth floor. I felt the sweat in the palm of her hand as she clutched mine tightly. She was constantly telling me to be a big boy and not to be afraid. I told her I wasn't scared, but that didn't seem to help much. She was getting more nervous by the minute.

On the walk to the elevator leading up to the cells, she told me not to be afraid and not to cry. I kept saying I wasn't and I wouldn't. Inside the elevator, she said it again. When we got off, she said, "Don't cry, baby, an don't be scared. Emma's right here."

When we got to the cells, they had to decide where to put me.

It took a while, but they finally chose a cell across the hall from her. One of them went to the kitchen part of the jail and returned with a wooden apple crate. He told me if I stood on it, Emma and I could see each other. After locking our two cell doors, they left.

I heard the elevator going down. Standing on the box, I could see Emma looking through her barred window at me. "You scared, baby?" she asked.

"No mam, Emma."

I heard the panic when she yelled, "Well, I'm gotdam sho scared an I'm gon cry!" She screamed and hollered so loud the jailer and two deputies came back up quickly. Emma was in hysterics.

They descended again to call the sheriff at his home to find out what to do. By this time I was yelling and sobbing uncontrollably—at Emma's instructions. "Don't let me do all the fuckin cryin an hollerin by myself!" After a few minutes the cellblock was in an uproar and they were unlocking our cells.

"Git the hell outta there," one of the deputies said as he unlocked our doors.

On the elevator ride down, Emma asked for her whiskey back and cab fare home. We got the cab fare.

Once outside, she said, "See there, baby, that wuzn't shit, wuz it? I knowed all the time we wuz gon make it. I bet you thought I wuz scared, didn't you? Shit, I wuzn't scared one damn minute. I didn't want you to be scared, thas all."

We left the courthouse walking, headed for a joint down on the streets. She bought some fried chicken and got herself a bottle. After a while the whiskey began to talk, and she began telling the other patrons how the sheriff demanded her release "soon as he found out" she'd been arrested.

Bright and early the next morning Emma removed the metal washtub hanging from a long nail on the kitchen wall and sat it on the table. "C'mon outside wit me an watch the hydrant while I tote some water." She made two trips, three bucketfuls into the tub and one placed on the stove top to boil. As soon as the water was hot, she poured it into the tub. After testing it with her hand, she told me, "Take yo clothes off."

"How come I gotta take a baff, Emma?"

"Cuz you need one, thas why. Anyhow, we goin uptown an see yo daddy." Drying me off, she said, "When you git bigger an see yo daddy someplace, if he don't say nothin to you, you don't say nothin to him. Walk on by lak you don't know him, you hear?" I nodded. "An don't *never* tell nobody he's yo daddy. Thas our secret till the day we die. Now hurry up an git yo clothes on."

I put on my overalls as fast as I could but needed her help. She was sitting on the side of her bed. "Will ya fix my 'spenders for me? They too tight," I said while backing up to her.

Loosening the clamps to slide them down, she commented, "You growin." After cramming my shirttail into my overall britches, she faced me around, licked her fingers, and tried to smooth down my unruly mass of blond curls. "We got you ready. Now it's my turn."

As we walked the downtown sidewalk hand in hand, the white folks stared at us shamelessly, probably trying to figure out if I looked like anybody they knew. She stopped on the corner across the street from the Hilton Hotel and knelt down beside me. "You g'on 'cross the street now. Watch the cars. Emma'll wait over here for you."

Even with times tough as they were, being a cotton broker, my daddy was always good for at least a twenty. I sat at the hotel drugstore soda fountain like I was a white boy while she paced the sidewalk across the street.

I had met him before. Emma told me, "Here's yo daddy, boy." They had a big laugh when she said, "G'on over to him. Shit, you look jes lak 'em." Then, "Don't he?" Mr. Albert smiled at her, winked at me, and patted his knee for me to come sit on it.

After I finished drinking my milk shake and getting the twenty-dollar bill stuffed in my pocket, he led me to the hotel door and walked me to the corner. While waiting for the traffic, he said, "Bye, son, watch out for the cars," and gave me a nudge. I raced across the street to hand her the money.

Emma was cleaning the kitchen when Baby Norris stopped by late Monday afternoon. She hadn't been by for a spell. Once they finished their "Whut on earth you been up to" and "When's the last time you seen so an so," Baby Norris asked, "Puss, where's that priddy lil man uv mine? I guess you know he gon be my man jes soon as he git a lil bigger. You might as well tell all them other hoes I dun staked my claim on 'em, cuz he sho gon be a heartbreaker one'a these days. I'm gon be the first one to break 'em in. Maybe then I'll have me a man that treats me better'n that sonuvabitch I got."

"Shit," Emma said, "he's jes four an still got the smell uv milk on his breath. By the time he gits old enuff for you, Baby, hell, you'll be on crutches."

Laughing, Baby Norris replied, "Thas why I wanna git a head start so's I kin git as much uv it as I kin. I'm so gotdam tired uv screwin all them old limber-dicked, 'lapidated bastards I jes don't know whut to do. Take that shitty ol man uv mine. Hell, ever once in a while I laks him to take care uv bizness wit me, you know. But I wind up squeezin his dick so long I gits outta the notion. An when he kin git ready, it always bends in the middle an I end up stuffin an crammin it in. Yeah, I'm up to here"—she motioned underneath her nose—"wit them old farts. All that shit bout I'd ruther be a old man's darlin than a young man's fool don't mean shit in my life. I don't want nothin old but money. An I want that to be crisp!"

"Baby Norris, gal, you still crazy. Hell, I thought Jake wuz really layin it to you the way you fuss over him when I see y'all together."

"Yeah, thas the truth, Puss, but I do's that to keep some uv them licks offa my ass. Do you know that nigguh damn near beat me to death a couple weeks ago? Lak'd to knock my teef out when he hit me in my mouf."

"Whut'd he do that for, Baby?"

"Aw, shit. He caught me dead to rights. I held out six dollars so I could git me a pair uv them Mary Jane slippers me an you looked at uptown. He fount the money I stashed an my ass is still so'. But I kin tell you rat here an now that in bed he ain't shit. The muthafucka jes got me scared uv 'em an he knows it. Say, I been over here damn near a hour. I'm sho thirsty. Ain'tcha got nothin to drank?"

"Yeah, Baby, raise up the corner uv that mattress. It's a bottle under there."

"I fount it. Brang two glasses witcha when you come in here."

"I'll brang you one, but you know I don't drank mine outta no glass. Leave my part in the bottle," Emma said, handing her a glass.

"You gon drank some now?"

"Hell yeah, I'm nearly through," she said, walking back in the kitchen. "I wuz tryin to git this shit cleaned up befo I set down. Gal, jes keep on talkin. I kin hear you. I'll be there in a minute."

"Where's that priddy man uv yourn at? That boy sho got lotsa sense an jes as mannerable as he kin be. I ain't never said nothin to him that he don't say 'yes mam' an 'no mam' back."

"He oughta be out in the back somewhere. Why don'tcha call him? It's time for him to be comin in anyhow."

"Come here, you lil priddy thang. Where you been hidin?"

"I ain't hidin, Miz Baby Norris. I jes been settin on the back steps."

"Come here an give me some sugar an hug my neck. An you betta quit callin me *Miz* Baby Norris. Jes leave off that *Miz* shit. Makes me sound too damn old." Pinching my cheeks, she asked, "Don'tcha know I'm waitin on you to grow up an be my sugar daddy?"

She held out her arms and gapped her legs open for me to walk between them. Reluctantly, I did. She grabbed me like an octopus, hugged and kissed me, and even stuck her tongue in my mouth. The way she was smacking and carrying on sounded like I was being eaten up.

Finally Emma said in a joking tone, "You betta leave that baby alone."

Baby Norris untentacled and pushed me back a little. "You might be actin shy now, but jes wait a few mo years. Yo mama'll hafta git a shotgun to keep them black heifers away. An I'm gon be one uv 'em! Puss, he almost too priddy to be a boy."

They sat on the bed drinking and bullshitting and drinking some more until, "Gotdam, Puss, this fuckin whiskey do's shit to my brain. I damn near forgot whut I wuz gon tell you. I ain't never seen so many Mes'kins in my life."

"Where at?"

"Cotton Street. When I wuz on my way to the sto [store] this mornin, I seen one'a them work trains sidetracked over there. It wuz three cars an I seen all them Mes'kins standin round on the outside. I went over an ast one'a the white men whut it wuz there for. He say they'd be there for a few days takin up an layin some mo tracks. I left in a hurry to tell my man Jake. Do you know I couldn't git that no-good bastard to go over there wit me. Even knowin he wuz gon take whut I made. He tole me I didn't have no bizness down there fuckin wit them Mes'kins. Shit, tough as times is now, a dollar's a dollar. Damn who it useta b'long to."

"Thangs been slow roun here an I need some money to git my whiskey stocked back up. Baby Norris, les me an you go down there an make that money, lak we useta."

"Fuck that shit!" Baby Norris exclaimed loudly. "If sump'n happen an that fool fount out I had went down there afta he tole me not to, that sonuvabitch'll kill me. Hey, is that the only bottle you got?"

"Yeah," Emma replied, which I knew was a lie. She was ready for Baby Norris to leave and that was one sure way of making it happen.

"Well, it's gittin late, Puss. Guess I best be gittin on befo that damn ol man uv mine thanks I'm off givin sump'n away. I be seein you, gal."

Night had fallen and with it came the late autumn chill. Emma got off the bed, put on her coat and tam, and grabbed one of her sweaters. "Put this on and come walk wit me. Baby Norris is gittin to be a squeamish bitch, too scared to make money. I don't give a damn if a hundred Mes'kins is in that railroad gang. If they wanna buy somethin, we got somethin to sell. Ain't we, Big Shot?"

"Yes mam, Mama."

"I tole you to stop callin me that!"

"Yes mam, Emma."

She knelt to my size and handed me her switchblade. "Put this knife in yo pocket an keep it open. We goin down there an make that money."

"Yes'm," I said and put it in my pocket.

We walked out of the house hand in hand, heading for the tracks. I was frightened at first, but after she told me how important my part was, I was glad she chose me. With every step, she told me over and over what I was to do.

We walked side by side in the darkness, her sweater down to my knees. The only sound when she stopped talking was our feet crunching the gravel as we neared the tracks. My short steps were no match for her long, determined strides. We followed the tracks until we reached Cotton Street.

We crossed and stopped about a hundred feet from the long Carson fence running beside the tracks and ending at Cotton Street. It separated the railroad right-of-way from the three warehouses on the other side. Straight ahead were the train cars. "I'm goin down there," she said, pointing at them. "I want you to stand right here"—she placed me on the warehouse side of the fence. "Turn aroun an keep yo face turnt to the street. Don't look back. When I come back I'm gon git close to you as I kin. If I call you, don't try to fight 'em. Jes put the knife in my hand. I'll git us outta here."

She began walking toward the train cars but stopped. She turned and asked, "Know why I'm doin this?"

I looked over my shoulder at her, pondering the question. Before I could answer, "For you," she said and hurried down the tracks.

I turned my face back to the street. Always the good little soldier, I did exactly as she instructed. My heart was trying to pound its way out of my chest. I gripped the knife so tight my hand was sweating on its cold steel handle. Her feet crunching the gravel grew fainter and fainter with every step. Then the sound stopped. For an instant I looked around.

I saw her climbing up into the rear of the work train. In a few seconds I heard loud shouts. I didn't know what they were saying, but I could tell they were shouting acceptance. Still, I gripped the handle tighter and tighter.

After a few minutes I heard footsteps on the gravel and glanced back long enough to see her and a man walking toward me. She was slightly ahead of him. He must have seen me standing in the shadows because he said something. I don't know if she understood him, but I heard her say, "It's awright. Thas jes my boy."

I kept my eyes glued to the dark street; I never looked back. I couldn't hear what she told him, but soon after he left, there came another and another and another and another and another. I didn't want to hear, but I heard. I wished my ears were deaf to all the sounds on earth, except her voice should she call out. My chest was on fire and my neck ached from trying to choke back the swelling tears. I couldn't stem the flood and they soaked my face. I didn't know how long or how many. I only knew the very weak voice calling, "Baby, come help me."

I ran to where she lay. The back of her head was resting on one of the rails and her ankles were lying across the other. "Emma, you awright?" I asked anxiously.

Barely a whisper, "Yeah," she said, struggling to get up. I reached down and began pulling her by the arms. "Come closer, baby. There you go," she said, holding on to my shoulders and pulling herself up. "We gon make it, ain't we?"

Her legs trembled and her hands shook as she leaned on my shoulders. One of her shoes was off. I stooped over to pick it up and saw the blood coming down the insides of her legs. "Emma, you got a hankie?"

"Yeah, they's one in my coat pocket." I got it and began wiping at the blood. "Don't throw it away when you git through. I need it," she told me. I handed her the handkerchief and she put it inside her panties.

Kneeling down, she pulled me close and hugged me tight. "You Emma's buddy, ain'tcha?"

"Yes mam. Yes mam," I repeated, reaffirming our buddyship.

"Now, buddy, les me an you go party!"

The "party" didn't last but a hot minute. The next day I came in the house and there sat Arthur Johnson with Emma on his lap. He was a bald-headed railroad porter who wore his navy blue uniform even when he was off duty, sporting a big set of "important" keys from his belt.

"Mr. Johnson's yo new daddy an he's gon live wit us. He laks little boys. So you be nice to Mr. Johnson an behave yoself. You hear?"

"Yes'm."

I couldn't stand him. I had already noticed how he looked at me the other times he came to the house. And those weren't looks of love. Even though he was a top church deacon, he was a cock hound from way back. He had tricked on my cot many times, and not just with Emma.

The house schedule changed overnight. Whenever he got a layover, she was up every morning at the crack of dawn to fix his breakfast. I had to serve his coffee. When I lay back down on my cot, he sat at the table staring at me.

One night on the other side of the curtain I heard him telling her about his high standing in the church and saying, "It jes don't look right when the three uv us be's out together. I don't lak tellin people he's my stepboy." She said she would leave me at the house from now on when they went out.

When she left to take care of her tricking-on-the-side business (namely Mr. Albert) and left me with Mr. Johnson, he told her some big lie when she got back. He said I wouldn't behave and "didn't do a thang I tole him." She'd beat the dog shit out of me in the kitchen. After the beatings I passed through the room on my way outside and he poked fun and made ugly faces at me.

He was a sly old bastard. One day while we sat at the table eating, right out of the clear blue sky he asked, "Emma, how on earth kin I set heah an enjoy my meal wit that boy rollin his eyes at me?"

She slapped me across the mouth and my chair went over backward. I was dizzy and tasted the blood seeping on my gums. "Git yo muthafuckin half-white ass up off that flo an take yo gotdam plate out on the back steps to eat! You the gotdam reason why I can't keep no man! You run ever one I ever had away wit yo peckerwood-lookin ass. You gon treat Mr. Johnson right! You hear me?"

"Yes'm."

From the back steps I heard her say, "He's gon mind you, or I'll wear all the hide off his ass."

He'd been gone a week when he got his next layover. He ate supper and left. Emma left a few minutes later. She was gone about thirty minutes and returned. When he came back, all hell broke loose.

"Where you been, *Mister* muthafucka? I know where you been, you gotdam, sorry, low-down, bald-headed, shit-eatin bastard! Here I am treatin you right, sleepin witcha, feedin yo muthafuckin ass, an I ketch you comin outta Red Sarah's back door!"

He mumbled something, and she yelled back, "You jes a muthafuckin liar! Whut the gotdam hell wuz you sneakin out the back for if you wudn't tryin to hide? You can't keep shit hid cuz it stanks! An I'm gon see that bitch too! She knows I don't let no hoe fuck wit my man."

The more she cussed the angrier she got, and she started throwing his clothes out the front door. He wasn't saying a word. While she was getting his things in the kitchen, she grabbed the butcher knife lying on the table and broke through the doorway curtain like a mad bull.

When she rushed at him with the knife, his eyes got big as silver dollars. He was trying to get out as fast as he could, but just as he wheeled to run, she whacked him across the cheeks of his ass with the knife. I could hardly wait for Old Arthur Johnson to come running by me outside. When she had started cursing, I piled some rocks by the front steps, hoping for a shot. I managed to zero one in, right on the back of his shiny-black bald head. His "important" keys rattled noisily as he ran down the road.

4

Two things our house was never without, dice and men. Old Arthur Johnson was gone, but I knew it wouldn't be long before another took his place. Whenever there was a lull in the action and all was quiet on the southern front, Emma pulled out her old crap blanket. We got down on our knees and she taught me.

"See these burn holes? I always keep 'em spread out to my right. Them holes is my measurin stick an I use ever one uv 'em when I'm shootin for a point. It's a secret, so don't tell nobody."

"I won't, Emma."

Taking the dice in her hand, she said, "See, when I'm shootin for four, I roll 'em even wit this first one. An when I'm shootin for five an six, I roll 'em up to these two. Eight's a long-range point, so I roll 'em all the way up to this last hole." After the strategy lesson, she explained how to "gitcha man," what combinations to use.

Emma bought a pair of peewee dice for me to practice with, saying, "When you learn how to roll them little suckers, you'll have a real good touch when you start shootin big craps lak we use." She taught me how to grip and roll them so that what I set in the middle would stay there. Besides shooting marbles, shooting craps became my favorite game. Now when I watched the shooters, I knew exactly what was going on. And when the blanket cleared, I practiced.

*   *   *

The gamblers, boozers, and whores had been flocking to the house all day. I almost wore a hole in the floor to the flour barrel in the kitchen, retrieving half-pints. Baby Norris paid me four times and Aunt Elzado three times for using my cot. If they were using it and I had to get something from the kitchen, Emma told me, "Don't look. Jes go on through." Terrell, the nuisance, got the "gimmes" (begging), and Emma stopped the game long enough to throw him out. She wouldn't let him back in and he finally staggered away.

It was unusual to have such a large crowd on hand in the middle of the week, but the crosstie loaders had come to town. Their crews were transferred from Beaumont and would be loading railroad ties in Longview for the next few days. Emma had been shooting craps for hours. She took a few seconds to look around the blanket at the onlookers who were already broke. "Say." He raised his eyes. "Whut's yo name, baby?"

"George."

"Well, George, you look lak a honest man," she said, dropping her eyelids like half-pulled shades. "Kin I git you to run the game an git my cuts for me so I kin go pee?" Squirming and holding herself, she declared, "I'm bout to bust!"

"Sho I will. Ain't nothin a good-lookin woman lak you can't axe me."

She flashed him a smile acknowledging the flattery, got up and stretched right in front of him, then headed for the outhouse in the backyard. I watched him while she was gone. He didn't miss putting a single one of her "cuts" (a nickel from every bet for the "wear and tear" on the house, blanket, dice, lamp, and for running the game) in the cigar box. When she returned to the game, George had cut off more than six dollars.

She kept all the small change and pitched him the green across the blanket. "Here, George, take some uv this money to play wit. Maybe it'll make you lucky," she said teasingly.

He scooped up the dollar bills. "I sho thank you, Miz Emma. I could use some luck."

Looking into his eyes, she reached over and patted his hand. "I thank yo luck jes changed," she said, sprinkling the words with plenty of sugar. Finding me in the room, she said, "Baby, hand Emma her bottle."

"Yes'm."

She took a big swig with nothing for a chaser and gave it back to me. "Hand it to George."

"No, I thank you jes the same, Miz Emma, but I ain't much uv a dranker."

When he refused, she exclaimed, "Well, I'll jes be damned! He don't wanna drank wit me. Hand it back here."

"Don't take me wrong, Miz Emma. It ain't that I don't wanna drank wit you," he said, smiling, "but that whiskey sho do tell off on a man when he got a three-hunnert-pound green tie on his shoulder goin up a gangplank to one uv them boxcars."

"Suit yoself." She saluted him with the bottle and took another slug.

It didn't take him long to lose the few bucks she had tossed, and he was back to onlooking. By nightfall the crowd had moved on. There were only three players left in the game, and they were just about broke too. This had been another one of those games where Emma had wiped them out with her Hudson shot. But she wasn't about to quit until the last dollar was in her hand and she heard them sing her favorite song, "Well, Emma, you got me! I'm broke!"

Looking up from the blanket at George again, she said, "Say, sweet thang, I bet them crossties do git priddy heavy. Ain't you tired uv totin 'em, baby?"

She was pouring on the syrup, and George was no fool. "I sho as hell is, Miz Emma."

"Well, kin you cook?"

"As a matter uv fact, Miz Emma, I'm a real good cook."

"Whut kin you cook?"

"Anythang you kin eat."

"Well, maybe you the man I been lookin for. I need a man roun here that kin cook an don't drank." It was her turn to shoot the dice.

All the while she was shooting she was talking to him in between her dice verses. "If you tired uv totin 'em, maybe you'd lak to hang aroun here wit me a while an sort uv help me run thangs. An do the cookin. I'll give you part uv whutever we take in. How's that sound?"

"Sounds jes fine wit me, Miz Emma. When does you want me to start?"

"Soon as you quit callin me *Miz* Emma."

"Awright, Emma, thas a deal."

"Say, George, I'm gon be through here in a few minutes. Me an my boy ain't had a bite all day. I ain't had time to stop an fix us nothin. Look aroun in the kitchen an see if you kin rustle up somethin."

He wasn't in the kitchen very long. "Emma, I looked everwhere. I didn't see nothin in there to cook."

Slightly embarrassed, she told him, "Well, don't worry bout it. Here," she said, tossing him a ten from the bills she kept stuffed between the fingers of her left hand, "the store's aroun the corner. Why don'tcha go git us somethin?"

The game was over. Emma was folding up the crap blanket and I was sweeping the cigarette butts out the front door when he returned. He cooked smothered cabbage, fried pork chops, made a big pan of corn bread, and fixed a peach cobbler. It was the best meal I'd ever eaten. George stayed. Nine months later, my half sister was born.

Long before Emma was due, the cafe part of the business had really picked up. George cooked big pots of chili, stew, chittlins, pinto beans and ham hocks, and all kinds of greens. He even built a barbecue pit out back. Emma helped prepare the meals and I waited tables. Every day at lunchtime the house was packed with railroad workers, filling station attendants, porters, and others there to get a good, cheap meal.

We were living high on the hog, and the integrated cafe went almost unnoticed until a white man brought two white ladies over to eat. Late that night we had a visit from the Ku Klux Klan. They banged on the front door while one of them shouted, "Hey! Y'all nigguhs inside! Open up this goddamn door an come on outta thar!"

George opened the door and stepped outside. I peeped out the window and saw five men with white hoods over their heads. "This is a warnin, nigguh! Next time y'all git a bunch uv white women over heah minglin wit them black bucks, we gonna come back an tar an feather you an yore whore!"

After they left, George told Emma, "We ain't servin no mo white-folks." And he meant it! The very next day when the white customers showed up for lunch, they were turned away, cutting the business in half.

Mama Joe lived in a shotgun house half a block down the road. Even though she was in her sixties, she was feisty. Emma and Elzado had met her long ago when they first came to Longview. She was boot-legging back then and was still plying her trade. She even turned a trick now and again. "Jes for good luck," she'd say.

It was hard to fathom someone turning a trick with Mama Joe. She was about four feet tall and missed being a midget by a toenail. Her bosom was so exaggerated she looked like a bantam chicken, and her head seemed to sit right down on her shoulders, making the hump on her back more visible. To conceal it, she wore middy-collared dresses.

When she came over to our house, she never said more than a few words to me. "How you, Whitefolks? Boy, you sho is growin," or "Emma, Whitefolks's hair ain't gittin a bit darker!" If no gambling was going on, she and Emma talked for hours about years gone by. Mama Joe didn't shoot dice, but she loved to play two bits a game pitty-pat.

She usually walked over about once or twice a week, but since she'd found out Emma was pregnant, she was over every day talking to them about the baby. "Lissen, Emma, George may not know it, but way back yonder, you 'member I tole you afta Whitefolks wuz born, if you ever had another baby, I wanted it. An you promised me if you had another un, you'd let me keep it. Didn't you tell me that?"

"Yeah, Mama Joe, I tole you that, but that wuz a long time ago. I can't jes let you have the baby. George got somethin to say bout it. Ain'tcha, baby?"

George was a slow talker, and Mama Joe seized another opportunity before he answered. "Emma, you an George both know neither one uv y'all ain't got no time to mess wit no baby. Since y'all dun started sellin meals, y'all keeps a house full uv peoples all the time. When y'all gon have time to take care uv it? Emma, y'all both know I wouldn't let it want for nothin. I'd be good to it an take care uv it, jes lak it wuz mine. Y'all wouldn't hafta worry bout nothin. An y'all kin see it ever day." Reeking with self-pity, she went on, "On account'a my condition, I ain't never been able to have chillun uv my own. I didn't even have no sisters an brothers. Please, Emma!" If she came over three times a day, she begged and pleaded with them three times a day.

When Emma and George weren't cooking, they were gambling. He was more of a cardplayer than a crapshooter. Not all that good at either. Soon as they were caught up in the kitchen, she had her crap game going and he had another blanket spread out playing cards. I didn't hear much noise on the other side of the curtain now. When they went to bed they were both dog tired. The good thing for me was she was being distracted and wasn't as quick to get the coat hanger after my ass.

Emma helped with the cooking as long as she could until the summer's heat started getting to her and she fainted on the kitchen floor. As her time grew nearer, she became less and less help. George had his hands full. They realized that even with both of them going full blast, it was almost more than they could handle. With a new baby in the house, she would be spending a lot of time taking care of it. They couldn't afford that; George would be left shorthanded.

"Baby," Emma told me, "run down to Mama Joe's an tell her I said to come over here." She came right away. "Mama Joe, me an George talked it over an want you to keep the baby for us when it comes. The way thangs is goin, I need to git back on my feet quick as I kin. An for a while anyway, I don't see myself havin the time to take care uv it. Lissen, Mama Joe, you best git one thang straight now. It's only gon be while it's little. Soon as it gits big enuff where it don't need so much time, I'm gittin my baby back. You understand?"

Mama Joe was stunned speechless and only nodded her head. "So when the time comes, I don't want no shit outta you either. You hear whut I said, Mama Joe? I'm gittin my baby back!"

Thrilled to get the baby under any terms, Mama Joe whooped and shouted for joy, jumping in jubilation. "If it's a boy, y'all kin name him George or whutever; but if it's a girl," she said longingly, "I'm namin her Patsy Sue an callin her Pat for short. I'm goin home rat now an start makin her some clothes. I already know it's gon be a lil pissy-tail gal!" She got to the door, stopped, and looked back. "Emma, I betcha a half a pint it's a gal."

"You got a bet, Mama Joe."

When the labor pains started, George ran across the road to Miss Bertha's and told her excitedly, "I thank Emma's bout to domino. Kin she use yo place to deliver in an will you midwife for her?"

Ancient looking, as if she just stepped off the slave ship from Africa, Miss Bertha was a tall, jet-black, wiry wisp of a woman who didn't weigh ninety pounds soaking wet but was strong as an ox from a lifetime of backbreaking work. Toiling sunup to sundown, she and her brood of children and grandchildren scratched out a meager existence by doing laundry for the white folks.

The walls of her run-down shotgun house were lined with fruit jars full of home-brewed medicinal concoctions. She was a godsend and the next best thing to a real doctor for the colored folks living in our impoverished part of town known as the Junction. She never took any money for her services, telling them, "I git my crown in glory."

She readily agreed to help and told her gang to go sit out in the yard. George got somebody to run the Saturday night crap game already in progress. He and I kept vigil outside Miss Bertha's house. We got along fairly well. He didn't have much to do with me, nor I with him. We more or less avoided each other whenever possible.

August 15, 1936, and the mosquitoes were driving me crazy singing around my ears before Miss Bertha came to the door and said with a toothless grin, "She got heah at zackly one minute befo midnight. Everthang's awright, Mr. George. Didn't have a bit uv trouble, an

Miz Emma jes fine. You gots a brutaful baby gal. I dun got her all cleant up so y'all kin go on in now an see 'em. But try not to 'sturb Miz Emma. She's a might tired." Feeling around in her large apron pocket, she found the Garrett snuff can and promptly filled her bottom lip.

Once inside the dim lamplit room, I stepped closer to the bed for a better look. Pat was lying in Emma's arms, all wrapped up except for a small part of her face. She was making funny little smacking noises. I told Emma, "She sounds jes lak a little baby puppy." George shot me a dirty look.

A few days after Pat was born, she was handed over to Mama Joe. With very little downtime, Emma was back on the job. She and George were pleased with their decision. Just like Mama Joe told them earlier, she had the baby clothes ready and waiting. Between bottles, she brought Pat to the house to breast-feed and had her dressed up like a doll. At George's request, "I don't want that half-white boy uv yo's foolin wit my baby," I wasn't allowed to have anything to do with her.

Despite losing the white patrons, the cafe business continued to grow; their good cooking saw to that. Most of the time customers had to stand outside and wait for a place to sit, especially at noon. They needed a "bigger place," and George began pushing in that direction. "Emma, why don't we put mo time in the cafe? We kin make a lot uv money if we git a bigger place. You won't need to be gamblin an bootleggin. You kin give that part up an we kin spend mo time wit the baby. Hell, one uv these days I'd lak to go to church for a change. But livin the kind uv life we livin, I jes wouldn't feel right."

With ruffled feathers, Emma told him, "George, anytime you git tired uv the kind uv life we livin, jes let the doorknob hitcha where the Good Lord splitcha."

George persisted more vocally, especially after the brief visits with Pat when she got about four months old. The argument was on as soon as Mama Joe left with the baby in her arms. "Look, Emma! I work jes as hard as you do an jes as long. I hate to be soundin lak a broke record, but whut I'm tryin ta git you to understand is, we don't hafta be killin oursefs. If you'd quit gamblin so much an stop all that other shit you do, we both could git some rest an be wit that baby mo. Thas yo job anyhow."

"My job! George, is you a fool? You must be forgittin who hired who! If you recall, I'm the one that took you in! I ain't got no job! You the one works here!"

"Awright, Emma, awright. But how come you so scared to give it up? Is this all you wanna do the rest uv yo life? We ain't got no privacy! There's nigguhs an whitefolks runnin in an outta heah all through the night! An that boy uv yo's sleeps right on the other side uv the curtain! You may wanna live lak this, but I be damned if I do!"

"I ain't scared uv nothin! Jes cuz runnin a cafe is yo callin, that don't make it mine. If I tole you once, I tole you fifty fuckin times. I got a good place where I am an I ain't gon move!"

"But dammit to hell, Emma, it ain't big enuff."

"It's big enuff for me."

"Oh, so thas the way it is!"

Tempers were rising. "Thas *exactly* the way it is!"

They were in the kitchen and both were working with butcher knives. Glaring at her, George hollered, "I know whut's the matter wit you. You needs a good ass-whuppin! If I git hold uv yo ass, I'm gon tear this lil house up wit it!"

Facing him and gripping the knife handle more firmly, she hollered, "George, anytime you feel froggish, jes hop! An if you do, somebody gon hafta burn me loose frum yo black ass!" She was fighting mad. "An furthermo, nigguh, I don't need you! I wuz makin my livin long befo I met you. I don't need no sonuvabitch on earth tellin me whut to do an how to live my life! An, nigguh, you bet not lay down an *even dream* you whupped my ass! The last time a nigguh tried that, they found 'em dead wit a bullet in his bosom. *Any* time you feel lak you wanna whup my ass, don'tcha let nothin stop you. An another thang, ain't no gotdam chains on yo legs an yo feet ain't welded to that flo! You wanna leave, leave! One monkey don't stop no show!"

"I jes might do that!"

"Well, do it! George, baby, you ain't no *special* nigguh, you jes *another* nigguh! You know whut, George? You way too slow for me! You ain't got sense enuff to steal, you can't gamble, you ain't good-lookin enuff to be no pimp, an you dun let a few white men dressed up lak Halloween ghosts scare you. You right, the best thang for you to do is to go back to totin them big-ass trees on yo shoulders an quit wastin my fuckin time!"

"If it wudn't for that baby, I'd leave yo ass right now!"

"Aw, don't hand me that baby bullshit! Ain't no baby never stopped no man frum leavin a woman yet!" she said and looked at me.

The next morning I woke up when I heard the front door easing shut. I quickly jumped out of my cot and got dressed for school, tiptoeing around in the kitchen trying not to disturb them. The crap game had lasted until the wee hours. Emma had been drinking pretty heavy and I knew she would be sleeping late. I got my book satchel from the nail on the wall and tiptoed out the back door, flipping the latch behind me.

After we got our wraps put away in the cloakroom, we took our seats in the classroom and simmered down. "Good morning, boys and girls," Mrs. Womack greeted.

"Good mornin, Miz Womack!" we sang back in unison.

"Miz Womack?"

"Yes, Murl Dee?"

"Miz Womack, kin I be excused?"

"Not right now, Murl Dee. I think you can hold it a little while longer," Mrs. Womack said with a warm smile, "don't you?"

"Yes'm, Miz Womack."

"All right, boys and girls! Let's get out our pencils and tablets. We're going to work on our writing some more today." Without ever missing a beat, she said, "What's the matter, Calvin? Why don't you have your tablet out?"

Slumped down in his desk with his head lowered, Calvin was semiaudible. "Mama couldn't buy me none."

"That's all right. You just sit up straight in your seat, and we'll get you something to write on." She borrowed a sheet of tablet paper from one of the other kids. "There you are," she said, placing it on his desk. "What's the matter now?"

"I ain't got no pencil." She went back to her desk and got him one.

With writing behind us, it was on to the alphabet cards, where we usually got stuck until recess. Out on the yard, Mrs. Womack kept a close watch over us and had us play together and keep out of the way of the older kids. Seemed like just when the playing got good, the bell rang for us to go inside. Back in the classroom, Mrs. Womack had us going through the daily ritual of singing the alphabet. "Aaaa B! Ceeee D! E F G . . . H I J K Ellaminna P!"

I'd never noticed before how hefty Emma had gotten after Pat was born until I looked up and saw her standing in the doorway. I knew something was wrong; I saw it in her eyes. Acknowledging her presence, Mrs. Womack stopped the singing.

"Yes, Miss Emma, may I help you? Come right on in."

"I wanna talk to my boy a minute," Emma said, scanning the classroom for me.

Mrs. Womack pointed me out. "His desk is right over there, Miss Emma."

"Thank you, Miz Womack," she said, turning up my aisle.

"Hi, Emma."

"Where's yo book satchel?"

"In the cloakroom."

"Go git it!" I ran and got it and hurried back to my seat. "Hand it here!" she demanded, snatching it from me. She looked all through it, turning it inside out. "Where's my gotdam money?"

"Whut money, Emma?"

She hit me with her balled-up fist and knocked me out of my desk, into the aisle. My nose was oozing blood. The kids in the immediate area scampered out of the way as she flung the empty desks to the side to get to me. All the while, Mrs. Womack was shouting, "No! Miss Emma, no! Please, no!"

I was still woozy when she jerked me up by my collar. "Tell me whut you did wit my money befo I kill you!" She hit me again.

"Whut money, Emma?" I cried out.

"Whut money! The money I put in yo book satchel last night! Whut'd you do wit it?"

"I didn't do nothin wit it, Emma. I didn't even know it wuz in there. I don't steal frum you, Emma!"

"Git yo shit! Miz Womack, I'm takin him home."

She hit and kicked me all the way home, saying, "Last night when we got through gamblin an everbody left, instead uv puttin it under my mattress I hid it in yo book satchel. Wuzn't nobody in the house but you, me, an George! I wuz aimin to take it out befo you went to school, but I wuzn't up in time. When I woke up an seen yo satchel gone, I knowed you had my money. An you gon tell me whut you dun wit it, or I'm gon stomp it outta you!" Opening the door to the house and shoving me inside, she hollered, "Git in there!"

"Emma, I didn't know you put yo money in my satchel. I swear I didn't, Emma. I wuz 'sleep when y'all quit gamblin."

She paused and thought a moment.

"I swear I didn't do it! Didja ast George? Didja look everwhere for it?"

"Naw, I didn't look nowhere. I know where I put it! In yo book satchel!"

"Les look, Emma. You might'a put it somewhere else an forgot it!" I started looking in all her familiar hiding places: under the mattress, in her shoe boxes under the bed, in my jacket pockets, and finally to George's footlocker in the kitchen. "Emma!"

"Whut! You find my money in there?"

"Somebody took George's locker. It's gone!"

She began searching through the chest of drawers, frantically throwing clothes everywhere. Before long, "All his clothes is gone!" Standing in the center of the room amidst the strewn clothes, she exclaimed, "That sonuvabitch got me!"

It was back to the two of us again, and it seemed like the roof was caving in. I took the ass whuppin and George took all the money, including the hundred bucks he saw her hide in my satchel. That money was to get us out of arrears with the whiskey man and pay for the two cases on order, which he wouldn't let her have on credit until she paid up.

But, looking on the bright side, there were no worries about Pat. Mama Joe was taking care of her as if she were a little princess. When she heard George had left, she came over to the house and "thanked God" he didn't try to take her away. Regardless of how well Pat was doing with Mama Joe, it didn't change the fact that we were flat broke, out of whiskey to sell, and the rent was past due.

Emma didn't mourn George's vanishing act beyond a long night's drunk. It was time to get into her sexiest rig and head uptown. She put on a hip-hugging red satin dress, black heels with faux diamond buckles, and a pair of black gunmetal hose. She patted and primped with her hair, which was short and parted on the side with large, tapered curls covering each ear. The thirty-or-so pounds she had gained carrying Pat went to the right places in her hourglass figure, emphasizing her already shapely curves. Her long, pretty "white girl" legs with thick calves and her big "nigguh ass" were eye stoppers.

As she was leaving, she told me, "You stay here. I be back afta while."

Emma was like a lure on a fishing line. She caught fish in town, then brought them back to our house to fry. When she returned about an hour later, she pulled off her tam and pitched it on the bed, took off her heels, and busily got ready. "I got some company comin. He'll be here in a few minutes. Watch out the window an lemme know when he gits here." She went behind the doorway curtain into the kitchen to change into her loungewear.

In a little while a car pulled up in front of the house and stopped. "He's here, Emma," I shouted.

"When he knocks, let 'em in. Tell 'em I'll be out in a minute."

"Yes'm," I said and opened the door on the first knock.

"Hi, little fellow. Is Emma here?"

"Yessir, come on in. She be out in a minute."

Emma called, "Jes have a seat on the bed. I'll be right out."

"That's all right, Emma. Take your time. Is this your boy?" he asked, eyeing me.

"Suuuure is. Me an that boy been down the road together, ain't we, baby?" She didn't expect me to answer but knew it sounded good to the white fish.

"I didn't know you had any children."

Stepping from behind the doorway curtain, she said, "There's a whole lotsa thangs you don't know bout me . . . yet," and put them eyes on him. "Baby, you go set out front an if anybody comes by lookin for me, tell 'em I ain't home."

"Yes mam."

In the months that followed, our house became his second home, keeping me practically anchored to the steps. After that first time, he only came at night, explaining to Emma, "It's hard to git away from the hardware store durin the day." The night visits soon became a problem when his timing was off. Answering the front door to wait on my late-night whiskey customers, sometimes I'd find him. Emma already had company; I had to get rid of him, quick!

Whispering to him with the door barely opened, I'd lie, "No sir, she ain't here. She gone. You gotta go now! Ain't nobody here but me."

Trying to peep inside, he'd ask, "Any idea what time she'll be back?"

"No sir. I gotta close the door now. Emma tole me not to open it for *nobody*."

"Well, tell her I came by, will you?"

"Yessir, I'll tell 'er," I'd say and close the door in his face.

On my way past her bed back to the kitchen, Emma would ask, "Whut'd they want?"

"They didn't want nothin, Emma," I'd lie again.

*   *   *

Emma knew why Elzado had stopped coming to the house; she didn't like George. Elzado was a fast talker who didn't bite her tongue about anything. "I can't stand him. Emma, he's jes fulla shit. I be damned if I know whut you seed in him." They cracked up when she quipped, "Must be the cookin." Both of them had spirited senses of humor and neither took offense when they teased each other, especially about their men.

Now that George had gone, she came regularly again. "Emma, you oughta be glad that black bastard left. If it'd been me, I'da run his ass off long befo now. You know whut that tree-totin SOB dun?"

"Whut *else* the nigguh do?"

"Axed me to trick wit 'em! I didn't never say nothin to you bout it cuz I know how crazy you is, so I jes stopped comin over. He wudn't no earthly good! Baby, pass Aunt El that bottle frum yo mama."

"Yes'm, Aunt Elzado."

"I sho wish you'd stop callin me that an call me El lak yo mama do. Who in the hell ever heard uv a name lak Elzado? Emma, I ain't never gon forgive you an Sally B for lettin Bama name me that."

"Don't blame it on me. I didn't have shit to do wit it."

"Grammaw Duck useta make me so damn mad when she'd holler El*zado*. Sound lak a Mes'kin tellin you to git the hell away frum 'em. So, baby, jes call me Aunt El. Okay?"

"Yes'm, Aunt El."

"Say, girl, lemme tell you! I stood out on my gotdam porch this mornin flaggin cars till my fuckin arm nelly fell off. They kept passin right on by. Shit, ain't hardly nobody trickin no mo! Emma, lemme hold sump'n if you kin spare it."

Whatever money we had in the house, Emma produced it and let her take what she needed, expecting no payback. Elzado didn't care much for gambling and generally stuck to the basics. She was fairly well content to have some white man "take care" of her and to turn an occasional trick.

A couple of weeks later, Elzado was at the house again, spitting out words faster than a Red Ryder BB gun. "Emma, I got me a rich white man now, gal! An he don't want me to hit a lick at a snake! All he wants me to do is jes be nice to him every now an then. Emma, gal, he ain't no trouble at all! He's old, gal. I mean old! Hell, he's over sixty!"

With a laugh, Emma asked, "If he's old is you make it sound, whut kin he do?"

"Nothin!" They laughed harder. "He can't do a fuckin thang! He jes laks to play wit it."

"I wish that wuz true wit the one I got. That bastard comes roun two an three times a week, makin sho he gits his money's worth. I can't complain, though. That sonuvabitch sho pulled me outta a hole when George run off. I got caught up on my rent, an he pays for my whiskey jes regular as the man brangs it. That sho takes a load offa my shoulders," Emma said, and she could ill afford to lose such a cushion.

"I know it do, gal! Shit! My ol man's the same way. I don't hafta worry bout no rent, no groceries, no nothin. An thas the kinda man I been wantin. Befo I forgit," Elzado said, running her hand inside her bra, "here." She handed Emma a twenty.

The next time the hardware man paid Emma a visit, he told her humorously, "I'm gonna have to come up with somethin different. I just about wore the Legion Hall out. My wife's called there a couple of times and I wasn't there."

"Tell her you out takin care uv bizness," Emma joked back.

"I can't. I done used that up too."

"Well, looks lak you might be in trouble," she jazzed.

Elzado had a lot of free time on her hands and was back visiting again. I sat out on the front steps listening to them shoot the shit while sharing a half-pint. I heard her telling Emma she found out Sally B and Bama were living in Dallas, 124 miles away. Soon as the news was exchanged, they overwhelmingly agreed, "Who gives a shit!"

When the car stopped in front of the house, I instinctively hollered inside, "Emma! Here come the police!"

Emma told Elzado, "Fuck it, we ain't doin nothin wrong," and slid the half-pint under her mattress. "They early. My whiskey man ain't come yet."

The two deputies got out. When they came near the house, I moved off the steps out of their way. They went inside.

"Whut's yore name, gal?"

"Elzado Barnes," she snapped.

"Git up off yore ass when I'm talkin to you!" the deputy fired back, angered by her curt tone. "Emma, git dressed proper 'less you wanna go lak that." She was still in her housecoat. "We're takin both uv y'all to jail."

"Whut for?" Emma asked as she went behind the doorway curtain to change. "Whut we dun? Y'all kin see ain't nobody here but me an my sister an my boy. Whutcha takin us in for?"

"Never mind, Emma. Jes hurry up in there. All we know is the sheriff wants to talk to y'all." After she got dressed, they put her and Elzado in the police car. I watched until it turned the corner, and then I ran all the way to the courthouse.

I had to stand on a fruit box to see her through the cell-door window. "Whut happen to you?" I asked, grimacing at her battered face.

"I'm awright. El wouldn't hush till she got both our asses whupped."

"She gon be awright? Where she at?"

"They got her in that cell 'cross the hall. She's beat up priddy bad."

"When they gon letcha come home?"

"I don't know," she answered disgustedly. "This ain't for gamblin an bootleggin, an they won't let us pay no fine to git out."

She told me the hardware man's wife had been tailing him and went to the sheriff crying, "Emma, the colored gal over by the railroad tracks, is ruinin my marriage." She said they already had a warrant out for Elzado for "swindlin." Her sugar daddy's children got suspicious when they detected all the withdrawals he was making at the bank and had been watching him closely.

"Go on back to the house an stay there."

I left but didn't go home. I hung around outside the courthouse and found an empty bench on the square with a view of the entrance.

I sat there all day listening to the birds and watching the squirrels run around on the lawn and in the giant oak trees. Later that evening I saw several men wearing white hoods over their heads going in the courthouse. Within minutes they brought Emma and Elzado out the front door and pushed them down the steps. I hid underneath the tall hedges and heard one of the hooded men say, "We're lynchin you whores tonight!"

Emma begged, "Please don't take our lives. At least give us a runnin chance!"

After a brief huddle the men laughingly agreed. "It'd be more fun than runnin rabbits."

One of the KKK members started pushing a few white citizens who had gathered at the steps back away. Another held tightly on to Emma's and Elzado's arms while the rest got in their cars. With engines and headlights on, one of them yelled from a car, "Turn 'em loose!"

Emma and Elzado started running across the courthouse lawn and passed twenty feet from where I was hiding. I ducked down lower because I didn't want Emma to see me. I figured she would have pulled out of that race to give me a whuppin for disobeying a direct order. When they got out on the street, some of the spectators began running behind them and got in the way. The "Klu Kluckers" had to slow their cars down, and blew their horns trying to get through the crowd. This helped.

The sisters turned off the main street, cutting through different alleys. I ran with the crowd and saw them heading for the railroad tracks. Their high heels were hampering their running and the cars were catching up. They started running down the tracks. The drivers stopped and turned around. "C'mon, boys!" one shouted. "We kin head the bitches off at the overpass!"

Lucky or not, a train was coming and slowed down a little to collect any messages from the Y pole. Emma and Elzado hopped it. I raced down the tracks to where I had last seen them. The train was gone; Emma was gone. The revelation buckled my knees. "Em . . .

ma!" I wailed, then withered like the stem of a dying flower. Lightning had just struck the center of my heart.

I wandered aimlessly for a while and went home, quickly latched both doors, and lit the lamps. I got the salt box and lay awake all night to throw some on Bloody Bones if he showed up, and listened for a knock and the sound of Emma's voice.

I did what she told me and stayed at the house until Mr. Booth rented it to somebody else. In lieu of the back rent Emma owed, some men came in a truck and hauled everything away, except the clothes I bundled in her crap blanket and took with me.

I went to Mama Joe's and asked, "Kin I stay wit you?"

Holding Pat in her arms, she shook her head and said, "Naw, Whitefolks, ain't got no room."

I never thought Emma would be gone so long. Six years old and left to fend for myself, I hung around the gambling shacks and slept in cafes, under pool tables, in boxcars, under bridges or rail-road trestles. Stealing food and living down on the streets, I moved among the hustlers like a shadow. Emma left me in a town of faces but no places. Nobody would take me in. Survival was the name of the game. It was save-thine-ass time, not school time. So dodging the truant officer was a full-time job.

5

I was sitting on the bench in front of the Star Cafe when an old gentleman I knew as Wino came walking around the corner. He sat down beside me and struck up a conversation. By now, everybody in town knew about Emma's and Elzado's "messin wit white men an gittin rid outta town on a rail."

"Has yo mama come back yet, Albert?" he asked in a friendly voice.

"Nawsir, but she be back . . . prob'ly by tomorrow."

"Yeah, well . . . where you stayin since she been gone?"

"At diffunt places."

"Lak where?"

"Lak all kinds uv places."

"Who you been stayin with?"

"Nobody. I don't need to stay wit nobody. I kin take care uv myself."

"I see. Oh, I don't doubt yo word for a minute that you kin take care uv yoself. You a real big little man. Do you go to school?"

"Oh yessir," I blurted. "I go ever day," I claimed, fearing he might squeal on me.

"Whut grade you in?"

"The first. You know whut, Wino? You sho ast lotsa fuckin questions."

"Aw, I-I'm sorry, boy. You right. I didn't mean to pry in yo bizness. I jes thought you might need a little help or somethin."

"Naw, I don't need no help. Emma be back . . . prob'ly she be back in the mornin."

"Well, she prob'ly will. But jes in case she don't make it in an you need a place to stay, you kin come keep me company an stay in the room with me. That is, if you don't mind lissenin to an old man's ramblins all the time. We could be . . . pals. I git priddy lonesome sometimes without nobody to talk to. I bet you do too. Don'tcha?"

"Sometimes. But I got me a buddy."

"You do?"

"Yep, name's Floyd. He's my pal." Floyd and I ducked the truant officer together and stole milk bottles to sell for our picture show money. We would sit up in there all day, sucking on our one-cent jawbone breakers, watching the same movie over and over until they closed that night.

"Ain't that one uv Miz Bertha's boys?"

"Yep, she's his grammaw."

"I take it y'all are real good buddies?"

"Yessir! An we don't fight each other neither. I'm waitin on 'em right now. We goin out to the circus grounds an work for us some free passes so we kin git in to see it." Looking down the road, I saw him coming. "Here he comes now. I gotta be goin, Wino."

"Okay. You 'member whut I tole you. If you change yo mind, I live roun there in the roomin house," he told me, pointing, "in the last room on the right, next to the back door." I gave him a noncommittal smile as I looked back over my shoulder running to meet Floyd.

When I got closer to him, Floyd said, "I had ta tote some wash water for Grammaw befo I lef."

"Yeah," I said, "I wuz wonderin whut you wuz doin so long."

Both of us were wearing our Tuf-Nut overalls, but the seat of mine was weighed down ten pounds and almost dragging the ground. I had all my valuables and weapons in my back pockets. I carried at least a half dozen big washers for throwing at older boys, rocks for my slingshot, and for close-range fighting I had a railroad spike. Longview was a hard town to grow up in. Along with my fighting paraphernalia, I carried my peewee dice, marbles, spinnerless spinning top, and, of course, my protective salt wrapped in a piece of newspaper.

On our way to the circus grounds, I said, "Look, Floyd, when we git out there, lemme do the talkin."

"Whutcha thank they have us be doin?" he asked.

"Prob'ly helpin put up the tents or sump'n. I don't know. But whutever it is, me an you kin do it. An we kin sell us some milk bottles an git us some peanuts an stuff."

"Yeah, I'm gon buy me some uv dat cotton candy."

"Me, too!" We were drooling with anticipation. "Now, 'member," I said as we approached the grounds, "lemme do the talkin. Okay?"

"Go 'head! I ain't sayin nothin."

Circus hands were working all over the place, stretching out the tents and pounding the long anchor stakes into the ground with their huge mallets. I finally saw somebody who didn't look extremely busy. "Les go ast that man over there."

"You go axe 'em. You tole me not to say nothin, 'member?"

"I will," I said and walked over to him. "Pardon me, sir."

"Yeah, what is it?"

"Me an my buddy," I said, looking back at Floyd, "wanna work for some free passes to the circus."

"Well, I'm not the man you wanna talk to. See that trailer cabin over there? Go knock on the door and talk to that man."

"Thank you."

I beckoned for Floyd to follow. I knocked and the man opened the door. The trailer was up on blocks, and when he first looked out, we were so short he looked right over us. "Yeah, what can I do for you guys?" he asked, looking down at us.

"Mister, me an my buddy here wanna work for some free passes. An we'll work real hard. Won't we, Floyd?"

"Sho will." He was nine and a head taller than me.

We were so scrawny looking, he thought about it a few seconds before deciding. "Yeah, come to think of it, I can use two more *big* guys like you two." He opened the cabin door wider. "See that guy over there with his sleeves rolled up and all the tattoos?"

We nodded.

"Go over there and tell him I said to put you guys to work. When you finish, come back by here and I'll give you your passes."

"See there, Floyd," I said smugly, "whut I tell you."

We walked up to the tattooed man. "Pardon me, mister."

"Yeah?"

"The man in that trailer said tell you to put us to work so we kin git some free passes to the circus."

He stopped what he was doing. "Okay, follow me." We did until, "Here," he said, handing us two buckets apiece. We followed him again. He stopped at the nozzle of the huge fire hose that lay trickling on the ground. "Okay, I'm goin over there to the fireplug and turn the water up a little," he said. After adjusting the nozzle, he told us, "Watch this nozzle and let me know when it's comin out fast enough to fill up your buckets."

Using the big wrench atop the fireplug, he slowly opened the valve. Floyd and I started waving our hands and shouting, "Okay! Okay!"

He returned. "All right, fill up your buckets and come on. We got some elephant waterin to do."

Water sloshed all over our legs as we hurried to keep up with him. "Do dem elefins bite?" Floyd asked in worriment.

"Nawww, boy," he replied, "elephants don't bite people. Unless, of course, they make it mad. You know what *really* makes elephants mad?"

"Nawsuh," we responded.

"When they don't get enough water."

"Well, I sho don't wanna make 'em mad."

"Me neither."

We could see the elephants standing under a smaller tent with the sides rolled up about four feet off the ground. It had a large walk-through entrance like a barn and was about thirty feet from the bucket-filling spot. When we walked in under the tent, our mouths flew open and our eyes were filled with the biggest "elefins" in the whole world.

Each with one of its back legs chained and anchored down by a stake, about a dozen were rowed up on one side of the tent, leaving only a narrow passageway in front of them. The huge monsters swayed back and forth contentedly, picking up bits of hay from the ground and slinging it up on their backs.

Still holding on to our bucket handles, Floyd and I stood frozen in our tracks. My voice trembled with fear. "Mister, is you sho they won't bite?"

"Nawww, they won't. Here, let me show you," the man said, taking one of Floyd's buckets. He walked up to the first one in line and sat the bucket down in front of it. *Slurp!* He began to pat and pet it. "This is Julie," he told us. *Pat, pat, pat.* "She's a good old girl. Ain'tcha, Julie, baby? Hand me another bucket," he ordered.

I stepped forward to hand him one of mine. He got the empty and gave it back to Floyd. As I reached the bucket out to him, he said, "You sit it down for her." He went on, coaxing, "C'mon, sit it down there where she can get it. She won't hurt you."

I walked closer, sat the bucket down, and jumped back quickly. *Slurp!* "I did mine, Floyd! You do yo's!" I urged as my heart pulsated with fear and excitement.

"See? That's all there is to it. Think you guys can handle it?"

"Yessuh," we chimed with uncertainty.

Left on our own, we started filling the buckets and packing the water back to the tent. We still jumped way back after we sat our four buckets down in front of Julie. She emptied a whole bucket with each slurp and reached her long trunk for another. Even after ten trips each, Julie's thirst was unquenched. Every time Floyd or I tried to walk past her to water one of the other elephants, she stuck out her trunk and blocked our path.

After about thirty minutes of steady toting water to only one elephant, trying not to "make it mad," those five-gallon buckets got heavier and heavier. The railroad spike I had in my back pocket became a real nuisance, kicking me in the ass with every step I took. Back at the spigot waiting for our buckets to fill, I exclaimed, "Whew! Floyd, I'm plumb tuckered out!"

"Me, too! Shucks, dem bucket hannels dun rubbed a so' on my hands."

"Mines, too! The way we goin we ain't *never* gon git all them fuckin elefins watered."

"Sho ain't. Shoots, this heah circus be dun come an gone befo we git through."

"I tell you whut I'm gon do," I declared. "I'm gon take that big o' funky elefin one mo drank an thas all! She kin git mad an scratch her ass till she git glad for all I care!" We delivered those four buckets to Julie and returned to the spigot. "This time les wait till we ketch her lookin off an then run by her," I plotted.

When we tried, Julie saw us and politely stuck out her trunk. Neither of us was brave enough to stoop and run under her roadblock, so we retreated straightaway. We sat our buckets, as directed, down in front of her. She took her usual four slurps and they were empty once more. Then she playfully sprayed water on the other elephants.

"Look, Floyd," I said excitedly, "I got a idea."

"Whut?"

"I know how we kin fill 'er up! An all the rest uv 'em, too!"

"How?"

"Next time we ketch them men not lookin, les drag that fire hose over here."

"Why?"

"You'll see."

Making certain the coast was clear, we started dragging the hose over to the tent. It reached with plenty to spare. "Okay, Floyd, while I keep a lookout you wrap some hay roun that nozzle so she won't see it an ram it in her mouth. Then I'm gon run turn the water up so—"

"Is you crazy! Shit! I ain't stickin my arm up in no elefin's mouf! You do it an lemme go turn the water up."

"Naw, Floyd, I can't reach her mouth. You the tallest," I pointed out.

"That ain't nothin. I kin pick you up."

"We ain't got that much time. C'mon, wrap some uv that hay roun it an stick it in there befo somebody come."

Floyd grumbled as he concealed the long brass nozzle. "You stick it in the next un's mouf." With the camouflage completed, he cautiously approached Julie, reaching the nozzle up toward her mouth.

"I'm gon run out to the fireplug an be ready. When you git it in, wave yo hand." Standing at the fireplug, gripping the big wrench, I waited for Floyd to give me the high sign. It took him several frightened attempts before he got Julie to take the hay-covered nozzle. When she did, he waved his hand affirmatively.

I yanked on the wrench so hard I went completely around the plug and had the valve wide open. With the sudden blast of maximum water pressure, the fire hose pitched and jerked as it wiggled on the ground like a huge snake. The water sounded like it was rushing through in big lumps, instantly swelling the hose taut.

I ran back. Floyd was jumping up and down ecstatically. When the full force of water fired through the hose, it shot the nozzle deeper into Julie's mouth. She had a strange look on her face while an elephant-size tear trickled from one eye. In futile efforts, she coiled and uncoiled her trunk around the hose.

All the while, Floyd and I danced a jig, whooping victoriously. Julie's belly rumbled and shook like an earthquake from the pounding force of gushing water. It got bigger and bigger. She cut loose with a waterfall of piss three hands wide. We were laughing wildly and forgot all about the workers skittering about.

Then someone saw us. "Hey! Just what in the hell do you boys think you're doin!" When he realized what we had done, he shouted, "Hey! Look at what those crazy-assed boys are doin!" They started running toward us. "You goddamn boys get out of there! Get away from those elephants!"

"There they go! Catch 'em!" another hollered.

The chase was on. I took the railroad spike out of my back pocket to lighten my load. When Floyd and I reached the road, we left a jet stream of dust behind and didn't slow down until we got to the intersection. He veered one way, heading home; I took off for the railroad tracks.

Fearing the circus folks might call the police on us, I needed a hideout and an alibi. I was almost out of breath as I tiptoed down the rooming house hallway. Wino's door was slightly ajar and I slowly pushed it open. The shabby little room was dusky, except for the daylight I let in. The curtainless, shadeless window was completely covered over with yellowed newspaper pages. Empty wine bottles lined the walls, and the room reeked of piss, puke, and the stench of stale wine. Wino was lying crossways on the bed, snoring loudly. Careful not to wake him, I eased inside and closed the door. I slept on the floor on some quilts and blankets in the corner of his little dollar-fifty-a-week room.

Wino was a sweet old man who became a dear friend to me. He was a retired railroad brakeman with snowy white hair, a weathered Uncle Remus–looking black man. It was obvious that once he had been handsome, but the booze had gotten the best of him. He cut grass on Nugget Hill for the rich white families, who paid him two or three dollars and gave him their leftovers. He didn't eat any of it until he came home and we'd share. To warm the food, he used a charcoal-filled metal bucket with a little grill on the top. We ate together right out of the pan. Lots of times with one fork because we couldn't find the other one.

He got drunk every night off cheap fifty-five-cents-a-quart sherry. Sitting around listening to his stories of trips to faraway places and different people he met made me forget Emma was gone, sometimes. Like the old folks say, "The shade uv a toothpick beats the broilin hot sun." Wino's room was that toothpick for me, casting its cool shadow over some of my gloomiest nights. When he was drunk he had a unique habit of whistling right in the middle of his sentences. I lay on my pallet while he sat on the side of his bed rambling on and on, and making long whistling noises.

"Well, I'm Alonzo Johnson. I've traveled all over the [whistle] country an I've been in everyplace in Canada [whistle] an everywhere. I've been frum the golden gates [whistle] uv California to the rocky shores uv [whistle] Maine. I've been to the Empire [whistle] State Buildin an the Statue [whistle] uv Liberty. Seen all kinds uv things. An one thing I learnt [whistle], people's the same everywhere. When you got money [whistle], you got friends for miles around, but when you git [whistle] down an out, ain't no need to look for 'em, cuz [whistle] ain't none uv 'em aroun . . . sususususususus."

At first, listening to him was mind-boggling; but after staying with him for four years, I could time his whistles to perfection.

I was just like a coyote. I'd get out at night, steal, hustle, and do whatever I could to help keep the household going. In the early dawn hours, I followed the delivery trucks. As fast as they'd put food out in front of the stores, I took all I could carry and ran for the den. I had to get a bunch; we didn't have an icebox. We ate up everything we had at one time. My hair was long, I was skinny as a rail but tough as a boot, and my eyes were sunk deep in my head. The closest thing I ever got to a bath was swimming in the T & P pond. I didn't bathe, I guess, because Lonzo didn't.

When Emma came back, I thought I was dreaming or had died and gone to heaven. Lying on those raggedy quilts on Lonzo's floor, half-asleep, I heard talking.

"Wake up! It's Emma. I'm back."

I opened my eyes, and there stood Emma and a Mexican. She was much bigger now, close to two hundred pounds, but I never saw anything so beautiful in my life. She was all decked out in a glittering, sequin-covered black dress, fur, and had pretty rings on her fingers. "Miz Bertha tole me you'd prob'ly be over here. Put yo shit on an les go."

She gave Lonzo fifty dollars for "lookin out" for me. Dividing fifty-five cents into fifty dollars was a lot of sherry! We left in a car with a big shiny bird on the front of the hood. Within her first fifteen words, she asked, "Whut do you thank bout this guy? Name's Sabbado. Ain't he good lookin?"

"Yes mam, Emma," I answered indifferently. "Here, I kept it for you while you wuz gone," I said, handing her the crap blanket, which she promptly tossed on the floorboard.

"Whut ees you name?" Salvador asked.

"Let Sabbado hear you tell when you wuz born." I didn't respond. "He'll talk afta he sees whut I brung 'em," she told Salvador.

He drove down to the Nickels Hotel, the aristocratic hangout of the "big-time" hustlers. They'd already been by the room and had clothes lying all over the bed. "I bought these for you," Emma told me. "Go take a bath an try 'em on."

I came out of the bathroom wearing a towel and tried on my new clothes. Nothing fit; everything was too small. Putting my same old rags back on, I said, "You don't even know whut I look lak."

She angrily threw the clothes in the corner. "Well, fuck it! We'll gitcha some mo shit!" she hollered. Later that night as I lay on the crap blanket on the floor, I heard her say, "Not now, Sabbado."

In looks she might have been different, but in principle she hadn't changed one bit. She had met Salvador in Mexico and convinced him to sell his bar and come back to Longview with her. Having used up most of his money, she took what was left and set up another gambling–et cetera house at 1000 East Whaley Street. This was the first un-shotgun house I'd ever lived in. It had electricity, three rooms and a kitchen, a well off the back porch, and an outhouse in the back. It was farther from the T & P station than our other house and didn't tremor as much when the trains went by. Best of all, it was only half a block from the corner liquor store.

Prohibition was ancient history, and the bootleggers who formerly dispensed homemade moonshine graduated to selling the cheap, packaged whiskey and wine. Emma was no exception. The liquor store man gave a good discount when it was bought by the case, and she doubled her money reselling it by the half-pint and quart. So after hours, all day Sundays, and during the games, it was bootlegging as usual. Even when the liquor store was still open, the gamblers would rather pay Emma a little more than have to leave the game to go get a bottle.

The liquor store was the pulpwood haulers' headquarters. Most of them lived across the Sabine River and came to town after cutting and hauling wood destined for the paper mills. Eighty percent were related either by blood or by marriage, and three or four would be part owners in the old, battered trucks. Every evening after work, the huge oak "council" tree at the back of the liquor store was surrounded by the old-model, beat-up, long-railed pulpwood trucks.

"Them ol pulpwood boys" looked like bodybuilders in overalls minus the shirts, and they were noted for hard work and paying their bills, especially their whiskey bills. The white store owner extended them liquor credit freely, cashed their checks, and even loaned them money. All they had to do was sign the book. They marched in and out of the store like ants, buying a half-pint at a time.

The cooking and gambling did it. As soon as they finished transacting business at the liquor store, the pulpwood haulers made a beeline for "Big Emma's." Every last one of them loved to gamble, and they lined the walls around the crap table as often as possible. Some were there so much it didn't seem like they'd ever left. Big Emma (they named her that) fed them and won their money. They didn't call her Big Emma because of size; it was more like an accolade for being the "top of the heap" whore.

They walked in heading straight for the kitchen to "jes help yoself." Emma had no set fee for the food. "When you git through, jes gimme somethin," she told them. They emerged as greasy around the mouth as a meat skin, pitched her a "fair price," and bought a half-pint. The haulers gambled and ate at the same time, keeping the dice so slippery Emma ofttimes had to stop the game to drop them into a glass of soapy water.

Just like with the railroad workers, when the pulpwood boys gathered, she sent for Allen. He lived in the Old Field section of town with the same woman he had been living with for years. Sometimes when I was sent to phone him, his old lady, Lucille, answered and I gave her the message. Or, if he answered, "Blue?" I'd say.

"Yeah?"

"This is Albert. Big Emma said to come git some'a this money."

Allen would come in a taxi. He was a good draw because he kept a pocketful of money all the time and the pulpwood boys wanted to beat him just because he didn't smell like pine resin. He stood out like a show horse in a stable full of mules at the crap table. They had on dirty overalls and he wore his customary tailor-made silk shirts and trousers. Nine times out of ten, their hopes of beating him were mere wishful thinking.

I'd seen him lots of times at the other house. He ignored me, and I did my best to stay out of his way. I liked to watch him gamble. He'd begin to sweat, take out his silk handkerchief, and meticulously place it between his neck and collar. He always rolled up his sleeves so the grime and kitchen grease the pulpwood boys smeared on Emma's old crap blanket nailed to the tabletop wouldn't get on his cuffs.

He was quick to squabble with them about their crap-table etiquette. "Man, don't be puttin that nasty-ass ashtray over heah, gittin all that shit on my shirt! Nasty, stankin, funky-dick muthafucka!"

While Emma was busy running the crap game, Salvador and I manned our designated posts. I covered the back door, handled the whiskey trade, and served as the official runner. Salvador generally sat on the front porch "out of the way," watching for the police.

Besides the hot tamale man, Salvador was the only other Mexican (I knew of) living in Longview. He kept mostly to himself and didn't participate in the games or ongoing hoopla of the gamblers. He drank his Canadian Club whiskey alone. Only occasionally would he take a drink with some of the others, but not before wiping the mouth of the bottle with his sleeve.

Emma was living the life of Riley. There was always a good crowd on hand, and she had even rented a nickel jukebox for the crap room. Pat was no distraction. Mama Joe still kept her and had moved just a few houses down the street. Emma had front and back door watchmen, was making lots of money, and whenever Salvador was out of pocket, she even turned a trick or two.

It happened again. Only Emma, Allen, and a white gambler called Blackie were left in the game. Emma backed off so Allen and Blackie could go "head-to-head." She pulled for Allen to take him and sat on pins waiting. When they finished, Allen was the winner.

Emma woke up all the broke, snoozing players so they could watch her play Allen. Salvador even left his post when she and Allen played head-to-head, but his interest wasn't in the game. He knew Allen was still her husband and didn't like the way she looked at him or touched his hand, jealously calling him her "sweet man."

The only rule about rolling and setting was "Go for whutcha know." It was teacher against pupil. Emma sat on the daybed with the crap table pulled up to her; Allen sat at his usual seat directly across the table. They went back and forth, all the while keeping it casual and friendly. Both rolled so smooth and easy that one die seldom stopped more than an inch ahead of the other. Emma had one distinct advantage; she gauged her rolls with the nails tacking the blanket down, just like she used to do with the cigarette burns.

Whenever they squared off to duel, she did everything to throw him off stride while he was shooting. "Give me another drank outta Emma's bottle, baby. Betcha don't bar it. Shoot 'em!" On and on with the rap. When he got set picking the dice up, she'd make him put them down somehow. "Hold 'em up there!" She'd grab his hand and pat it, offer him a drink, and just outright say, "Blue, put them dice down, baby."

Frustrated, he'd stop and throw her the dice. "Heah! When you git through playin wit 'em, give 'em back!"

She'd spit and blow on them, rub them between her thighs to hex them, and then toss them back. He'd miss. "Aw, gotdam! The mule throwed Rucker," she'd say and could hardly get the top screwed on the bottle fast enough.

They'd been going at it for hours, and, money-wise, they were about even. Emma called for a time-out. "Shit, Blue. Les stop an take a break an have a drank. Ain't you tired?"

"Hell yeah! I gotta git up an stretch my legs a minute. They dun damn near went to sleep."

She pushed the table away, went to the outhouse, checked on Salvador, and returned. "Hand me my bottle, baby," she said to me. Looking around the room, she shouted, "Resta y'all, *wake up! Wake up!* The house is on fire!"

That perked them up. "Give everbody a drank. Pass the bottle roun when Blue gits through. Git some water for 'em to chase it wit. Them nigguhs ain't useta drankin good whiskey," she added, referring to her personal bottle of "hockey-proof" Old Grand-Dad. She kept on, "Y'all wake up or you might miss somethin." I certainly didn't need any rousing. I was absorbed and watched every move they made. The others had to ask for the bottle three or four times before I heard them.

After seating herself back on the daybed and pulling the table close, she asked, "Blue, you bout ready?"

"Yeah, I'm ready," he told her, retaking his seat.

It was her shot. While rubbing the dice on the blanket, she said, "You know whut, Blue?"

"Whut?"

"I'm goin on an take you lak Grant took Richmond."

"Well, you won't be gittin no cherry. I been busted befo. Quit stallin an shoot the dice!"

"But I'm gon do it different this time, Blue. I'm gon make ten straight passes on yo ass befo I miss. Then I'm gon letcha shoot 'em one mo time, an it's good night, Irene."

After he took his shot and missed, he sang, "You got me!"

"An you the one taught me."

He never beat her. When their game was over, she'd throw him ten or fifteen dollars so he wouldn't leave broke.

They were good gambling friends, but he never ever slept with her. That's where he drew the line, content with just their gambling friendship developed over the years. It never failed, though; when the house cleared and we finished cleaning up, Salvador started his nagging, "Goddamme, Eemma, you thinkee I'm a goddamme suckum [sucker]. I no fuckin suckum. I see you make them fuckin goo-goo eyes to you goddamme sweet man."

"Whut the hell you talkin bout, Sabbado?"

"Eemma, you know goddamme well whut I talkee. Allen, you goddamme sweet man. I'm the goddamme man to theese fuckin house. I hangee my goddamme hat over here, not you fuckin sweet man!" He was way off base, as usual. She was tricking with Mr. Albert, definitely not Allen.

Disgusted, she said, "Aw, Mes'kin, fuck you! I'm tired. I don't wanna hear all that shit. Go lay down somewhere an git outta my face."

"Goddamme, Eemma, didn't I told for you? You leessen to my voice! I'm the goddamme man . . ."

I was busy as a cat covering up shit, keeping a lookout at the back door, and selling whiskey to the players. On weekends, Emma's bedroom at the front of the house became the trick room whenever the whores needed it. I had already rented it out twice and waited for Octavie to get through so I could clean it up quickly. Ida was in the wings.

It was midday Saturday, payday. The crap room was humming. The pulpwood haulers, Allen, two or three crapshooters from across town, and some white railroad workers all jammed around the table, betting hot and heavy. Emma had finished all the cooking earlier and was smack-dab in the middle of the action. All the bases were covered. Salvador was at his usual post in the front; I was taking care of all the other house business.

By late afternoon there was a lull in the action because several of the pulpwood haulers (the heaviest losers) left for the liquor store to borrow some money. The white gamblers were gone as well. Nobody was shooting craps, and the gamblers were just sitting around waiting and bullshitting.

Since there was no game going on, Salvador joined the revelry in the crap room. Departing from his normal aloofness, he stood against the wall drinking and laughing his head off at their "nigguh-whitefolks" jokes. They bullshitted about everything, from the way they each looked to the size of their peckers. Oscar especially enjoyed teasing Emma and said, "Lemme axe you sump'n, Big Emma. How on earth didja end up wit a pepper belly? Frum whut I heard, they screws lak rabbits, ninety miles a minute," he joked. They all laughed—except Salvador.

"Fuck you! You black-ass cheeken-sheet sonaveech!" Salvador shouted.

"Fuck you back, Mes'kin! If you don't wanna hear whut we talkin bout, carry yo Mes'kin ass on somewhere else. You stand over dere an laugh yo ass off at everthang somebody say bout somebody else, but when somebody say sump'n bout a Mes'kin, you git mad."

"Leessen, you sonaveech, you no talkee to me! I talkee to you! I'm the goddamme man to theese house!" he yelled, moving in Oscar's direction.

Oscar rose quickly from the daybed, ready to rumble. Some of the others held them apart. Throughout the momentary fiasco Allen stayed in his seat at the table, casually playing with the dice. "Say, Oscar, let Sabbado alone, man. An you, Mes'kin, you oughta take yo ass somewhere an set down."

Hotheaded and more than ready for a piece of Allen's ass, Salvador broke the grasp of the restrainers and attacked. He forced Allen into the crap table, jamming it against Emma and hemming her in on the daybed. Though Allen outweighed him by at least forty pounds, Salvador had the advantage as they grappled with each other atop the table. Allen was fighting with all his might to get him off, but Salvador was fighting equally hard to retain his position.

One of the two-by-four legs gave way, and table and all crashed to the floor. This jarred them apart momentarily. Allen got to his feet first and landed a clean blow to Salvador's face. Salvador reeled backward toward the kitchen entrance.

Both were straight-up slugging it out in the kitchen. Allen's heavier blows were doing the most damage. He knocked Salvador back seven or eight feet into the icebox. Emma rushed in, but Allen shoved her back through the doorway and quickly pulled out the .38 long-barreled revolver from his waistband. Before Salvador regained his bearings, *bang!* The scent of gunpowder filled the small room.

Still on his feet, Salvador staggered and slumped against the icebox. With blood pouring between his fingers, he held his head. "Goddamme, Allen, you sonaveech! You shoot me!"

"An that ain't all, Mes'kin. I'm fitna shoot you again!" Like a flash, Salvador ducked and rushed Allen a fraction before he squeezed the trigger. The bullet missed.

He bear-hugged Allen and came out of nowhere with a hunting knife, ripping him from the left shoulder blade all the way down to his hip bone. Allen hit him repeatedly with the gun barrel and managed to get elbow room for another shot. With his left arm tucked against his wounded side, he raised the .38 to fire again.

The head wound had weakened Salvador, and he was about to drop. Allen squeezed the trigger. *Click! Click! . . . Click, click, click, click!* He wheeled and walked out of the house, heading down the back trail.

Emma followed him out the door. "Blue, you hurt! Don't leave. Somebody dun called the ambulance. It'll be here any minute."

But Allen kept walking. Salvador had collapsed on the kitchen floor. Emma got a towel and attended him until the ambulance arrived. Allen got to the hospital on his own. I heard it took nearly two hundred stitches to sew him up. Hardheaded Salvador returned home that night. Miraculously, the bullet had ricocheted off his skull and come out near his temple. All he had was a headache and a swollen face.

As soon as Salvador recovered from his minor gunshot wound, he started blaming "Eemma" for what happened. "Eeet's all you goddamme fault, Eemma! You sent off for you goddamme sweet man!" But that was the case no more. Allen no longer honored the calls and quit coming to the house.

Emma and Salvador began fighting like cats and dogs. He soon discovered that when he drank too much he couldn't whip her, so he changed the course of things and started faking it. She would still get drunk, and that's when he would make his move.

I was so familiar with the routine I cautioned her not to drink so much. "Emma, you can't fight when you drunk."

But all I got was a customary "Jes hand me my bottle. I don't need you tellin me shit! Hell, I ain't drunk!" Followed by "You stay outta me an my o' man's bizness! I don't need no help frum you!"

Once she got started, the whiskey made her really blow it out. "I ain't scared uv no muthafucka on earth! Specially Sabbado!" All the while, he sat on the old metal trunk over in the corner of the crap room with his head down, feigning a drunken sleep and taking it all in. "I kin whup a whole cow pen fulla Mes'kins lak him in my underskirt an never show my ass!"

Unfortunately, this claim didn't hold true when she was drunk. He'd beat the dog shit out of her, but she sternly ordered me not to interfere. Most of the time I left, only to return to find her with a black eye and busted lip.

She put him out of commission for a while, though. They got drunk "together" and went to bed. Salvador waited until she fell asleep. He got up, put on his pants, and went behind the headboard. Reaching his arms through the iron railings, he got a choke hold around her neck. She woke up struggling and reached her hands through the rails, frantically trying to break the hold. She grabbed the first thing she touched, which happened to be his balls. Using her long fingernails, she ripped his nutsack. When she let go he fell to the floor, his trouser fly covered with blood. I talked her out of chopping off his head, or anything else, with the hatchet.

I was back in school but absent most of the time because they fought and stayed drunk so much. When I came home from school one afternoon she told me, "That old white daddy uv yo's died. They havin his funeral today."

"We goin?"

"Hell naw. His wife would shit a green egg if we showed up at First Baptist."

"I got to go change," I told her, heading for my room.

"Where you goin?"

I just kept walking, changed my clothes, and slipped away to the church. Even if I was wrong as two left shoes, I had to be there. I owed him that much. After all, he was my father.

I was practically running the house, and it even spilled over into the crap games. My big chance came after Emma and Salvador started arguing while the game was in progress. For fear of the gamblers leaving, Emma put me in charge so they could go in their room and finish the fight.

In many ways, I was better than she was. I had the "rollll" down to a T and controlled the dice better, knew how to gauge them in accordance with the nail heads, and wasn't drunk. The gamblers didn't hesitate when I took the game over. I had been around them so long I was viewed as a regular player. Besides, "money's money," young or old. When Emma sobered up, I turned the money I'd won over to her.

Emma was so busy trying to keep the licks off her ass, mine was being spared. When she got whiskey mean and missed a point on the dice, I still got my "jinky peckerwood-lookin ass" driven from the crap room; but I no longer quivered when she "buked" me, and I bit my lip to hold back the seething anger and to keep from lashing out at her.

Her fighting with Salvador had given the house a bad name; it was losing money. After the police were summoned several times to quell things, the gamblers got scared to come for fear of being arrested themselves. Now we were lucky to have three or four people at the house on weekends.

It was another Saturday, and I'd been up since early dawn getting things ready, just in case. I scrubbed the floors with Eagle lye (minus the piss) and cleaned up the crap room from last night's minor activity while Emma and Salvador were still in their room. With all the preparations taken care of, I left to round up some players. I walked down to the liquor store council tree, where the pulpwood haulers were parked, and told them, "There sho is a good game goin at the house."

Two or three interrupted their drinking and said, "When we finish takin care uv bizness, we might come by." I knew they probably wouldn't.

After leaving them I headed for the Terminal Cafe at the train station to give the same message to any potential players who might be there. I made all my Junction rounds to the places where the gamblers hung out before going back home.

I heard the low, muffled scuffling as soon as I stepped up on the back porch. When I walked through the kitchen and entered the crap room, I saw that Salvador had Emma pinned in the corner next to the trunk. He was choking her so hard his hands and arms trembled. The fight had gone out of her and she was barely struggling.

I rushed over and positioned myself so she could see my face. "Emma, you want me to help you?" She couldn't talk, but she motioned her eyes up and down for a yes.

We had a potbellied, wood-burning stove in the crap room and kept the wood stacked on the back porch. I ran out and got a big stick, ran back, and hit Salvador just above the ear. He released his hold, and Emma sank to the floor. The first blow stunned him. I got in another before he directed his attention to me, which was just what I wanted. I faded him off to give her a chance to catch her breath.

As soon as she got herself together, she jumped him from behind. Emma wasn't drunk this time, and Salvador was no match for both of us. Fighting savagely, he managed to raise the lid on the old metal trunk where he kept all his tools. I knew about the house's major weapon that was kept inside. He was going for the white-handled hatchet!

Emma slammed the lid down on his arm and plopped her two-hundred-plus pounds on top of the trunk. Salvador let out an agonized shriek. When he screamed, Emma looked at me and asked, "Is I got 'em?" More excitedly, "Tell me, *is I got this muthafucka?*"

"Yes mam, I bleeve you got 'em."

"Don't *bleeve* nothin. Tell me, is I *got* 'em?"

"You got 'em, Emma!"

"Thas all I wanna know."

Salvador's face grimaced with pain. "Goddamme, Eemma! Geet you big ass up! You brokee my fuckin arm!"

"You don't say?" she said and started bouncing up and down as he groaned. She was winning one for a change, and how sweet it was to be bullyragging him. "You know whut, Mes'kin? I been waitin a long, long time for this day."

"Goddamme, Eemma, you brokee my fuckin arm!" He shouted and squirmed, vainly trying to free his arm.

"I know gotdam well I am," she said unconcerned, "an thas not all I'm gon do." Then she ordered me, "Come here, baby."

"Yeah, Emma."

"You thank you kin hold this lid down if I git up off it? Be sho now! Set down on it an see." I added my skinny ninety pounds on the trunk lid along with her.

Salvador cried out, "I no heetcha no mas, Eemma!" and moaned, "Oooohh!"

"Emma!" I said concerned. "I don't thank I kin hold it down sittin on it. Lemme stand up so I kin brace my hands on the ceilin." I stood up and got into position. With my palms pushing against the ceiling, I told her, "I kin hold it now, Emma. Git up any time you ready!"

"Make sho you got it now! I'm fixin to git off."

"I got it," I reassured her.

"Don't tell no dirty!" She slowly started wiggling off the lid. Looking up at me, she said, "Be sho you got it now! I'm gittin off."

"I got the muthafucka! Go 'head an git off."

"Okay, I'm gittin *all* the way off," she told me and finally let her feet touch the floor. Satisfied that I had him under control, she taunted, "Awww, gotdam! Gotcha at last, ain't I? You know whut I'm fixin to do to yo ass? Betcha can't even guess, kin ya?" Pausing to look up, she asked me, "You still got 'em?"

"Yes mam, Emma."

Sugar Ray Robinson would have loved the footwork she put down. Moving and circling around Salvador, she jabbed and shadowboxed, stopping only to put her hands on her hips and shake her booty in his face. Finished with her roadwork, she let him have a fist right in the kisser. "Maybe that'll stop some uv that ol mouth uv yo's." Then back to the show, she put her head right down in his face. "Here, hit this, muthafucka! I know you wanna hit me. Why don'tcha? Oh, don't wanna fight now, huh."

Using her fist like a sledgehammer, she hit him again. "C'mon, hit me back! You know whut I oughta do? I oughta git that stove poker an ram it up yo ass. But I know you wouldn't lak that," she said sarcastically, "so I'm jes gon give you a good ass whuppin instead. How's that?" *Pow!* "You still got 'em?"

"I got 'em."

She wound her arm up like a pitcher and used the knuckle side of her fist like a club to pummel blow after blow on top of his head, only stopping to reconfirm "You still got 'em?"

She hit him so many times her hand was swelling. "Stop hittin 'em on his head, Emma. You gon break yo damn hand!" I warned.

"Thas awright. I wanna break it on his ol hard head!" She pounded him again. *Pow!* "Whew! I dun jesta bout give out whuppin this Mes'kin's ass," she declared, adding, "but it sho wuz a lot uv fun, even if I did fuck up my hand. Look at it," she said pitifully, holding it up with her other hand for me to get a better look. It was swollen to twice its size.

"Whut we gon do wit 'em now, Emma?" I was getting tired of straining to keep the trunk lid down.

"Hold 'em till I git outta the house. When you hear me callin, git down an run." A minute or two later she yelled out, "Any time! Let the muthafucka go when you git ready!"

I jumped off the trunk and dashed out the back door. Soon as I got outside, I heard "Pssst! Here I am over here." She was standing at the corner of the house. "I got some bricks piled up so when that sonuvabitch comes out, les bombard his ass."

Salvador emerged carrying the hatchet and looking for us. When he came around the corner of the house, I let go with an "alley apple" that caught him dead in the chest. I was putting some Satchel Paige shit on his ass, and all he could do was duck. He dropped the hatchet and took off. We had him on the run!

Victory in sight, I fired brick after brick as he fled down East Whaley Street. But with Emma's help, he was on the verge of making a drastic comeback. She was running halfway to him and rolling the bricks like bowling balls. Every time I zoomed one at him, I had to duck because he stopped running and was returning the fire. Like a shortstop, he scooped up the bricks she rolled and hurled them back at me. "Dammit, Emma!" I shouted after a near miss. "Quit chunkin! You feedin 'em ammunition!"

When she stopped helping, I started winning again. Salvador took off down the street, probably heading for the border. "We got 'em!" she boasted, as if she had really blasted him with those bricks.

"Damn, Emma! You gon git us killed one uv these days!"

6

Even though Emma had successfully discarded the thorn in her side, the stigma from her stormy relationship with Salvador lingered stronger than ever. Heretofore, our white neighbors had not complained at all about the gambling, boozing, or any of the other things that went on at Big Emma's place. But with all the hell-raising she and Salvador did, they started calling the police at the slightest disturbance.

Now, practically every time a patrol car came down our street, they stopped by to "look in" on us. The heat was on, and the enterprise steadily declined. Hardly anybody came to the house to gamble anymore. Since the success of the bootlegging business largely depended on the gambling crowd, it had to be abandoned. There was no money coming in, and it was back to basics, but with a different twist.

Emma could no longer get all dolled up, go uptown, and come back with a string of tricks following her. She'd gotten too fat. Now, instead of tricks catching her, "we" caught them. I hardly went to school and pulled duty on the front porch, alerting her to any potential customer passing by. My stomach always knotted up when I spotted one and summoned her.

It was freezing cold outside, and the lone crepe myrtle in the yard was weighed down with icicles. I woke up early and went over behind Ben E. Keith's produce house to hustle some kindling wood. I had a good fire going in the crap room when Emma came in and joined me.

"*Brrrrr!* Gotdam, it's colder than a well digger's ass in Butte, Montana!" she exclaimed, backing up to the potbellied stove. "How long you been up?"

"A priddy long time."

"You ain't goin to school?"

"Nawww, I didn't wanna go."

I neglected to tell her "*Never* no mo." I fought on the way to school and on the way home. Nearly everybody in Longview knew our business, and that included their children. Some kid was always talking bad about Emma and me. "Yo mama laks white mens. You ain't nothin but a peckerwood. You half white."

I also didn't mention that I beat up Willie Joseph at school with a broom handle for calling her a whore. And that I got a whipping for it and got expelled for three days. She might not have given a damn, but I wasn't taking any "Rayfield chances" (Rayfield would take a chance on anything). I wondered about what it was going to be like for Pat when she started school next year. If they picked on her like they did me, I'd be fighting all the time.

We huddled around the stove in silence until, "Emma?"

"Whut?"

"I don't thank no tricks is comin by this mornin. Do you?"

"Never kin tell. Men buy pussy when it's cold jes lak they do when it's hot. Ain't I got a bottle layin roun somewhere?"

"Yes mam, I know where it's at."

"Go git it."

I returned with the near pint, and she took a big swig. "Damn! I kin see now. Thas whut I needed wuz a eye-opener." She was in a decent humor in spite of our wretched condition.

"Emma, since there ain't nothin stirrin, tell me bout you an Aunt El some mo. Where'd y'all go afta y'all caught that train?"

She took another drink and cleared her throat. "We rode that muthafucka all the way to Dallas. Did I ever tell you El damn near fell off when we caught it?"

"No mam."

"Hell, for a minute I didn't thank we wuz gon make it."

"Whut happen?"

"I caught the damn thang priddy good, but when El hopped it, she missed wit one uv her feet. I held her on till it slowed down in Mineola," Emma reminisced, "but we made it. When we got to Dallas, we stayed wit Sally B for a while. Boy, when her an Bama tole us bout Duck bein dead, I got me a bottle an celebrated. I wisht I knowed where that hateful old bitch wuz buried. I'd go shit on her grave! I don't know how El let 'em talk her into stayin. She got her a little place in Frogtown. Soon as I made me some money an put a few rags together, I left."

"Then whut?"

"Then I jes went everwhere. If I heard bout a town where money could be made, I went. First place wuz Fort Worth. Then"—she paused to reflect—"I left there an went to San Antonio, then down to Corpus Christi." She added, "Thas a priddy place."

"Whut's it lak?"

"Gotta ocean an white, sandy beaches, real priddy. Then back to San Antonio an on out to El Paso. Since I wuz so close to Mexico, I said whut the fuck an crossed over. Thas how I met Sabbado. You know the rest uv it." Taking another drink, she said, "You oughta, I dun tole it to you a dozen times."

After a silence I asked the big question I had wanted to ask. "Emma, how come you didn't come back an git me?"

Her jawbone stiffened, indicating that one had gotten under her skin. I didn't give a damn, I wanted it to. "I'm here now, ain't I? I didn't hafta come back at all!"

"Yeah, guess not . . . I'm goin down on the streets."

"You didn't ask me."

"I ain't gotta ask nobody shit!" I grabbed my jacket and headed out the front door.

"Don't forgit who's payin the rent, *Mister* Smart-Ass!"

"Yeah, *both* uv us!" I shot back, slipped on some ice on the porch steps, and fell on my ass.

I stayed gone a few days, needing to clear my head and think. I hated to admit it, but she was right. She could have just kept on going. I cooled off and returned home in a better frame of mind. "Emma, I got a idea how I kin help make us some money," I told her when it was just the two of us.

"Doin whut?"

"Shinin shoes. I could make us a lotta money shinin shoes, specially when them troop trains stop over at the station. Even when they ain't no troop train, they's always some soldiers roun the station. I been wantin to do it, I jes hadn't said nothin to you bout it.

"I saved up enuff money to git whut I need. I kin git two cans uv black, two cans uv brown, an two cans uv tan shoe polish, a brown an black brush an three shine rags for three dollars at Shivers. An I kin make a shine box myself. Whutta you thank? Kin I do it?"

After taking another gulp, she said, "I don't care. Don't git in the way over there. See if you kin lead some'a them soldiers back over here."

I ran to Ben E. Keith's and relieved them of two of their sturdiest-looking fruit crates. Leaving them on the back porch, I rushed into the house and got the hatchet. After about two steady hours of carpentry, I had beaten those crates apart and put together a good-looking shine box. I got one of Salvador's belts and attached it to the box for a shoulder strap.

Only one thing was missing; I had to hustle some paint. The paint store uptown was just the place. They threw paint cans out back; maybe one of them would have enough. I was right and, using a piece of cardboard, painted my shine box green. On the way back home, I stopped by Shivers Drugstore and picked up my supplies.

The next day at the train station I made over seven dollars. When the troop trains stopped to let the soldiers take a break, I was right there with my shine box. I even had one twenty-dollar day after I learned how to pop those shine rags. I gave all the money to Emma to help make ends meet. Even on the occasional days that I went to school, I took along my shine box. After school, I headed straight for the train station.

Meanwhile, in an effort to get the gambling going again, Emma started talking to the police more and more when they stopped by. It didn't take her long to convince them that she knew about all the stealing going on in town. "Some'a them ol thievin nigguhs is always brangin somethin hot by here to sell or hock. I kin git y'all they names," she offered. That is, if they would cut her some slack.

One day an officer came alone. After he finished tricking and was about to leave, he said, "Emma, if you hear anythang about that Shivers Drugstore break-in, you be sure an let me know, now."

"Oh yessir, Mr. Buster, I sho will."

She had already given them a few tips on some people and was a "reliable" snitch. Not only did she snitch on thieves but she also snitched on her gambling and bootlegging competitors. She didn't view it as snitching. "I'm lookin out for us," she told me. "Fuck them nigguhs." When things got slow and she figured the crowd was over at so-and-so's house, she'd call the police and tell them a fight was going on over there so the cops would show up and scare everybody away.

The gamblers drifted back, but not in numbers. Most of them still took their chances at one of the other places. Emma never was big on keeping secrets, and after the police started coming to our house, everybody knew she was snitching. The gamblers kept on gambling while she talked to the cops in the next room. After the conference and when she returned to the game, a player would ask, "Whut's that all bout, Big Emma? Is they gon 'rest anybody? Cuz if they is, I'm leavin now!" he'd say, ready to break and run.

"Naw," she'd say, "don't y'all worry bout nothin. They ain't comin by here to do nothin but pick up they money." She'd be lying through her teeth. Bragging, "Tell me how many nigguhs' houses could y'all be gamblin in an the police come an don't take nobody to jail? Thas one thang y'all don't hafta worry bout at Big Emma's place. Y'all ain't gon hafta pay no fines."

Word spread like poison ivy, and the other bootlegging and gambling operators hated us. Me, because they figured if I knew they had a game going on, I'd tell Emma and she would call the cops on them. They were dead wrong—I hated her snitching. When they saw me coming, they'd warn, "Y'all betta raise up. Heah come ol Big Emma's boy."

Seemed like every day a different policeman came to the house. When they asked Emma questions she knew nothing about, she pretended that she did just to stay in their good graces. When this wasn't working, she quickly changed the subject to get them interested in "somethin else."

Now whenever we had a game at the house, there was no need to stand guard at the door. When the police came, I didn't even bother to announce it. They just walked through to the crap room and called her into the other room. I felt as tall as a worm.

School had turned out, and I rushed off the campus to get to my shoeshining job. After waiting for the traffic so we could cross over busy Highway 80, I, along with a hundred other kids, made the mad dash for safety.

I saw a patrol car parked across the highway while we were waiting. When we got to the other side, one of the policemen hollered from his window, "Hey you!" We all stopped and looked quizzically at one another. "You wit the shine box, git over heah!"

The other kids were suuure looking now, as I walked up to the car. "Yessir?" I didn't know these two.

"You Big Emma's boy?"

"Yessir."

"Git in, we wanna talk to you."

"Bout whut?" I asked as I crawled into the backseat.

"Bout that shoe polish you got thar," he said as we drove away.

"Whut bout it?" I asked, completely dumbfounded.

"Whar'd you git it?" the other officer asked.

"At Shivers Drugstore."

"Thas whut we wanna talk to you bout."

I knew the way to the jailhouse, and we weren't heading in that direction. "Where y'all takin me?"

"Aw, we jes gonna run out heah a little ways so's we kin talk in private." After we crossed the Sabine River, they turned off on a side road and stopped the car. "Git out!" they commanded. As we stood by the car, they told me, "Look, now, you kin save yoreself a whooole lot uv trouble, boy, an us too, if you jes tell us who you got it frum."

"I dun tole y'all. I bought it at Shivers Drugstore."

"Lissen, boy! Don't be a-standin thar lyin to us! We know whar the goddamn shit come frum!"

"I'm tellin y'all the truth! I bought it at the drugstore. I paid three dollars for all this stuff, my brushes an rags too."

One of them slapped me across the face, and I fell down. "You quit yore lyin, boy! Big Emma dun told us some nigguh come by y'all's house wit two or three cartons uv polish an you bought it frum him! Tell us who it wuz!"

The inside of my jaw was bleeding, and I started crying. "No sir, I didn't. I ain't bought nothin frum nobody but—"

The officer who slapped me reached down and jerked me up. With one hand he held me so we were face-to-face. "Boy, I'm tired uv lissenin to you lyin. Real tired. You read me?"

I trembled out, "Yessir, but I ain't lyin."

He looked at the other officer. "Big Emma said he wuz gon deny ever bit uv it. Boy, you callin yore mama a liar?"

"No sir . . . I mean yessir . . . well—"

"Git the belt outta the car pocket."

While one of them held my face down on the hood, the other dropped my britches and strapped my bare ass. Pitching and squirming, I twisted my face to one side and cried out, "Ask Mr. Shivers! Ask Mr. Shivers! He'll tell y'all!"

After two more licks they decided to go to the drugstore. In the backseat, I clutched my shine box in my lap and cried all the way. "Boy, you hush that shit up back thar. If yore lyin to us, I'm gon give you a lot worse'n 'at!"

They followed me into the drugstore, and I pointed out the man who sold me the polish. He confirmed it without hesitation. Satisfied, they left.

When I walked into the house, Emma wouldn't look me in the face. She knew. "Emma, why? You know I didn't buy nothin frum no nigguh. How come you tell 'em that an make 'em whup me?"

"Aw, you'll git over it. That wuzn't yo first ass whuppin an it won't be yo last. G'on outta here an leave me alone!" I didn't move fast enough to suit her. She grabbed an empty whiskey bottle off the crap table and threw it at me. I ducked, and it shattered against the wall. "I tole you to git yo gotdam ass on outta here!" she fumed.

I ran out of the house and stopped when I got to a tree. I pulled the strap off my shoulder and smashed the shine box to smithereens against the tall pine, cursing her with each blow. I didn't bother to pick up the polish.

I cried all the way to Miss Bertha's house, where I saw Floyd in the yard. "Hi," I shouted.

"Hey."

"Whutcha doin?"

"Nothin, we dun got all the washin hung up."

I glanced at the two drooping clotheslines heavy laden with wash-board-scrubbed clothes. "Wanna go to the picture show wit me? I'll pay yo way."

"Yeah! Lemme go axe Grammaw."

Miss Bertha gave him permission, and we hit the railroad tracks heading for town. After I'd watched the Tim McCoy cowboy movie for the third time and gotten so excited when he had a shoot-out with the bad guys I swallowed my jawbone breaker and nearly choked to death, the shine-box incident faded off somewhere into the back of my mind.

Friday, business as usual; we were getting ready for the weekend. I had taken care of the floor scrubbing, and Emma was in the kitchen cooking. I was in her room making up the bed and heard a knock on the front door.

I hurried to answer it. "Yessir," I said, unhooking the screen.

He looked at me for a moment or two. "Is this where Emma Barnes stay?"

"Yessir. Well, her name's Emma Sample now."

"Is you her boy?"

"Yessir."

"Is she at home?"

"Yessir, she's here."

"Would you tell her somebody at the door to see her?"

He wasn't a regular customer. I had never seen the elderly, light-skinned colored man before, but he might be a trick. I sure didn't want to let him get away—Emma would kill me. "You wanna come in an wait till I go git her?"

"No," he said politely, "I'll jes wait out heah."

I went to the kitchen. "Emma, a man's at the door to see you."

She was busy chopping a cabbage and didn't look up. "Who is it?"

"I don't know. Ain't never seen him befo."

"Whut do he want?"

"He didn't say. He jes ast if you live here an tole me to come gitcha."

She laid the butcher knife down. "I sho hope it's somebody wit some money," she said and hurried out of the kitchen. With me right behind, she asked, "You sho you don't know who it is?"

"Yes'm."

When she got to the screen door, I heard "Yeah, whut do . . . *You gotdam low-down sonuvabitch!*" She spat venom at the stranger. Clenching her fists so tight the veins in her hands looked like big macaroni, she screamed, "*Whut you doin on my porch? You gotdam sorry muthafucka you! You kilt my mama!*"

The old man stood, head hung low, not saying a word.

"*Why, the very idea, you come draggin yo sorry ass up to my front door! You muthafucka! You don't know whut you put me through in my gotdam life! You took everthang away frum me!*"

She flung the screen door open, almost knocking him down. His hat fell off, and she kicked it off the porch. "*Git! yo muthafuckin ass offa my gotdam porch!"* she yelled, shoving him down the steps. *"If I ever lay eyes on you again, I'll kill . . .* you." Her voice broke. The tears began pouring down profusely. She cried so hard she could hardly utter "You muthafucka you." She followed him down the street, throwing rocks at him.

"Who wuz that, Emma?" I'd figured it out but asked anyway.

"My ol chickenshit daddy. I oughta harked and spit right in his muthafuckin face!"

She headed straight to her fifth of Old Grand-Dad, knocked it halfway, returned to the kitchen, and started singing in perfect diction in her Sarah Vaughan–esque voice.

> Beautiful Hula, down in dreamy Honolulu,
> Dear, I'm feeling so peculiar
> Since I first met . . . you
> In a moonlit garden fair,
> Cupid, he is wandering there
> Waiting and dreaming in a garden of roses;
> Sometime, in the bright Hawaiian sunshine,
> Dear, I'm trying to make you all mine
> And I'll come back someday
> And we'll fly away
> My Hawaiian butterfly.

Just as if nothing had happened.

Pat would be starting school in September without a bodyguard. I hadn't been back since Wallace Clark called me "jailbird" at recess and I knocked out one of his front teeth. He ran and told Mr. Mason, who promised me a whipping when we returned to the classroom.

After we were seated, Mr. Mason called me up to his desk. Dangling the wide razorstrap in his hand menacingly, he ordered, "Bend

over, boy! I'm gon break you up frum all this fightin." Everybody
was quiet and the loud *whack! whack!* echoing of the strap on my
butt filled the room. The stinging pains grew and I bit deeper into
my lip. I wasn't going to cry with all those kids looking at me. This
seemed to infuriate Mr. Mason, who was determined to make me
cry out. Each time he hit me, he tiptoed for more leverage. After
about a dozen hard licks, he said, "Git on back to yo seat. Soon as I
rest my arm, I'm gon give you some mo."

All the kids snickered. I sat at my desk and took the Boy Scout
pocketknife out of my overalls and opened the big blade. Mr. Mason
summoned me for an encore. When I bent over this time, I gigged
him in the thigh and fled.

I told Emma I wasn't "never" going back to school. She didn't
ask why and just said, "If you wanna grow up wit no schoolin lak
me, thas yo bizness."

Gambling had fallen off during the past weekend due to several
raids at different joints around town. The new sheriff was trying to
put everyone out of business. Emma was feeling the crunch too, and
her fleeting usefulness no longer excluded her from the top ten list.

Hustling was at a standstill, suckers had been sucked up, and tricks
had been pretty slow over the past few days. Nubby, one of Emma's
die-hard regulars, hadn't been around yet, and I was sitting on the
front porch watching for him. He was a one-handed white man who
got some money for getting his other hand cut off in a sawmill accident. I think he was spending as much of it as he could on colored
pussy and whiskey. I couldn't believe Emma let him touch her with
that nub. Just the thought of it gave me the "all overs" (shudders).
If we missed him, he kept going around the block and coming back
by until one of us flagged him down.

I saw my pal Floyd walk around the corner. He had a big, shit-
eating grin on his face as he came up on the porch and sat down beside
me. "Hey," he greeted, handing me the shoe box he was carrying.

"Hi," I said, examining the box. "Whut's in it? Shoes?"

"Open it an see."

I ripped off the lid and my mouth flew open. Two pearl-handled, nickel-plated, Gene Autry cap pistols with a braided holster!

"You kin have 'em," Floyd told me, grinning like a mule eating briars.

"Where'd you git 'em?"

"I buyed 'em," he replied, brimming with pride.

"They sho must uv cost lots," I said as I fumbled with the buckle adjustment.

"They did, but I don't care." Voicing his excitement, he went on, "I got heaps uv money."

With the cap pistols strapped on and practicing my quick draw, I asked, "How much you got?" He ran his hand into his pocket and pulled out a wad of bills. "Damn, Floyd! Where'd you git all that money?"

"Thas awright where I got it frum, I got it. An I got some mo hid. Wanna go to the picture show wit me? I'm payin."

"Yeah, lemme go tell Emma." I found her in the kitchen washing dishes. "Emma, look whut Floyd brung me," I said, adding, "He got a whole lotsa money an we goin to the—"

Her eyes lit up like a slot machine. "Where'd he git all that money?"

"I don't know," I told her, shrugging my shoulders. "He won't tell me."

"Where is he?"

"Waitin on the porch."

She began drying her hands and heading for the front door. "Floyd, baby, come on in the house," she said, holding the screen open. "Let Big Emma see all that money you got." Floyd, acting more like a five-year-old than fifteen, was grinning from ear to ear as he showed her the roll of bills. "Big Emma got somethin she wanna show you, Floyd, honey." Looking at me, she said, "You go on back out on the porch." When I heard the door to her room close, my heart sank. I knew the rest.

Ten or fifteen minutes later Floyd came out, still buttoning his overalls with sweat rolling off his forehead. "You ready to go to the show?" he asked sheepishly.

"Naw! G'on. I ain't goin," I said angrily and brushed past him into the house. I stopped at Emma's doorway, just looking at her and trembling all over.

"Don'tcha be standin there turnin that peckerwood nose up at me! Money's money. He's yo friend. He ain't shit to me. He's jes another nigguh."

I stormed out the back door and ended up at the T & P pond. With my feet in the water, I sat watching the dragonflies skitter across the top, wondering how they kept from sinking. I unbuckled my holster belt and threw the whole thing at them damn skiddy-hoppers.

I found out later Floyd took the money from the grocery store where he worked as a porter. The manager had left the safe open and Floyd just helped himself. The manager called the police and, aside from what Emma took him for and the pistols at the bottom of the pond, got most of it back. He wouldn't press charges and was quite satisfied with the strapping Miss Bertha gave Floyd in the presence of the police. The manager even let him keep his job, but he sure lost his picture show pal.

Instead of things getting better after we ran Salvador off, they steadily got worse and went from sugar to shit. Everything was on a downhill slide. Emma always had to have an "o' man" around the house and moved in a new one—Amos Washington. Round two. He walked in the door kicking her ass and kept her cowered down. He was the only man I ever knew her to have that she was deathly afraid of, but I stayed out of it, having been warned repeatedly by her about "fuckin in me an my o' man's bizness. I don't need none uv yo gotdam help!" she would say, almost falling down from too much drink.

I learned the hard way to obey her request because sometimes when it got way out of hand and I couldn't take how he was beating her, I said, "Don't hit her no mo, Amos." Even in the heat of battle, she turned on me and cussed me out. So I left, heading down on the streets, and would be gone a few days. When I came back home, I saw her beautiful face erased with bulging black eyes and busted lips that he didn't give time to heal.

Sunday afternoon, nothing much was jumping on the streets, so I headed back to the Junction. I stopped at the Star Cafe and got an order of chicken giblets and rice. I was sitting at the counter eating when Percy stepped inside and saw me. "Say, man, I jes passed yo mama's house an it sho sound lak some bad shit goin down in there. Sound lak they gittin it on hot an heavy. I could hear Big Emma hollerin to the toppa the roof."

I left in a hurry. As I approached the house I heard her begging, "Amos, please don't kill me." I went inside and eased her bedroom door open. She was on the floor, bloody as a beef, with only her panties and bra on. Amos had her by the hair with her head pulled back, holding the neck of a broken whiskey bottle to her throat, threatening to kill her. I presumed he had hit her with it, because blood was pouring from her head. Neither saw me.

I ran to the backyard, got the hoe, hurried back, and eased her door open. Tiptoeing up behind him, I laid a good lick on his shoulder and another on his arm. He released her and came after me with the broken bottle. Chopping and hacking at him, I landed a couple more good ones as I backed out of the front door onto the porch. Almost as drunk as Emma, he staggered down the street and out of sight.

Somebody had called the police. They picked up Amos and took him to jail, then came to the house and arrested me. Emma went to the hospital and got her head stitched up. When Amos went before the judge, they charged him with assault and battery along with disturbing the peace and fined him $38.50. The judge charged me with assault and fined me $15.00.

The next day Emma came to the jailhouse with her head bandaged. Old man Buster Wells, who had been tricking with Emma for years, brought her up on the elevator to the cells. After he unlocked and opened the big steel door to the cellblock, I heard her say, "Lemme have my baby outta there. Emma's here, baby," she said, talking loud, showing off.

Awright, I thought, *I'm gittin outta this muthafucka*. With a grin plastered across my face, I moved away from the cell-door window.

Waiting. I heard Mr. Buster's ring of keys rattling and went back to the window to see what was taking so long.

"C'mon outta there, Amos," I heard Mr. Buster say. "There's a purdy woman out heah to see you."

The three of them walked right past my cell on their way out. My eyes were riveted on Emma. She never even glanced my way, didn't even have the decency to say, "Thank you, dog, for savin my life." As I stood frozen, watching her leave, my knees weakened and I had to hold on to the window bars to keep from sinking to the floor. I grew dizzy with anger and then everything shut down.

She broke my heart so many times. She beat me, she left me, she fucked Floyd; but it was this moment I learned I could hate her— my enlightenment. Five days I stayed in jail to lay out my fine at three-dollars-a-day credit. Even after that, my love for her overrode the rumbling volcano inside me and I hung on for more. Amos left Longview for Spokane. Good riddance! I had outlasted another one.

Over the past month the weekend gambling had been running hot and cold. The police were raiding other places pretty regularly, and the crowds had drifted back our way. This was a live weekend; the house was full. I'd gone to the liquor store earlier and gotten a case of wine and half-pints on credit and was selling it hand over fist.

Emma was surrounded at the crap table, constantly taking big swigs out of "her" bottle. She was missing a lot of cuts out of the bets because she was arguing and bragging with the gamblers.

During one of my passes through the crap room, I heard Herman telling her, "Naw you don't, Big Emma. You don't wanna be fuckin wit me. No way, shape, form, or fashion."

"Shit, nigguh!" she snarled back. "I had my own brother kilt. Whut makes you thank I won't fuck wit you?"

Whenever she got whiskey mean and told somebody that, it made me cringe, and usually a hush fell over the game. This time was no exception. After the brief silence, another player spoke up.

"Say, Big Emma, y'all cut out all the shit. I ain't won a bet since y'all been jaw jekin."

I was with a customer when she called, "Baby, come here when you git through."

I nudged past the gamblers standing around the table. "Yeah, Emma?"

"These gotdam nigguhs dun gathered up all the change outta the game and crammed it in they pockets. Run down an git me a rolla nickels right quick," she said, handing me the two dollars. "An don't you tarry! I need 'em."

I trotted everywhere I went, but since this was a hurry-up deal I left running at full speed for the liquor store and headed back faster than Jesse Owens. As I came streaking past the outhouse on the back trail, my hand hit my thigh and the roll of nickels sailed into the darkness. I put on the brakes and ran back to the spot where I thought the roll landed.

I spent what seemed like an hour crawling around and uprooting every blade of johnsongrass. Two of the gamblers leaving the game saw me crawling around. Hawk Shaw asked, "Whutcha doin, man?"

"I lost a rolla nickels."

They volunteered to help. Before long Hawk Shaw said, "Come on, man. We gotta go. We can't find nothin dark as it is out heah." I kept on looking for a while longer but gave up. I suspected Hawk Shaw had found the nickels when he abruptly withdrew their services.

I went into the crap room and walked to the table. Emma glanced up and asked, "Where's my change? Hand it here!" Not getting the nickels, she looked up again. "Whut you dun?"

I squeezed out, "Emma, I lost the nickels."

Busy placing a bet, she didn't hear me and demanded, "Hand me my gotdam change!"

"I lost the nickels. I wuz comin aroun the trail runnin an my han—"

"You jinky peckerwood muthafucka!" She pushed the table back and came at me. When she got within striking distance, she hit me in the mouth with her fist, knocking me into the corner by the jukebox. I slunk to the floor. Blood was running out of my mouth, and my tongue quickly detected the loose front tooth.

Emma sat down on the daybed and pulled the table back up to her, casually asking, "Whose shot is it, baby?"

Still dazed, I stood up and wobbled into my room, grabbed my navy jacket, and left.

7

Twelve years old and I was on my own again. Only this time, it was me catching the freight out of town. I cut behind Ben E. Keith's and stayed on the tracks until I got to the trestle and sat down underneath. When the freight train waiting back at the station blew its clearance whistle, I wiped away my tears and got ready. The big engine spun its wheels to get a starting grip to pull the long line of boxcars. It began rumbling slowly in my direction. Crouching in the weeds beside the tracks until the engine lumbered past, I waited until about twenty cars went by, picked out an empty one, and hopped aboard.

I'd learned about catching trains from Lonzo. In his drunken stupors he had talked about hoboing and being a brakeman until he would keel over backward. He told me what the whistles meant, which end of the car to catch, all the brakeman hand signals, about the signal lights, how to brace the gondola from the inside so nobody could lock it from the outside, how to read the destination markings on the sides of the cars and oil tankers, how to ride the rails (riding underneath the boxcar on two rods), which way to face when on top, how to make a train slow down, how to stop it, et cetera, et cetera, et cetera.

When the freight came to a stop, I jumped out of the boxcar and made a dash for the underbrush. The "knob knockers" were already walking down the tracks inspecting the long string of cars for hoboes while the train waited. After the passenger train whizzed by, the freight whistle sounded for clearance up ahead, the signal lights went from red to green, and it slowly started pulling off.

I left my hiding place and jumped back on. When it was running fast again, I fell asleep. I woke up and looked out of the open door and saw signs along the highway indicating Little Rock wasn't far away. While the train was stopped in the Little Rock freight yard, I got off to hustle some grub, made my way to the highway, and started walking. I wandered about a mile from the freight yard and came to a small country store. Approaching the entrance, I wondered what to buy with the thirty-five cents I had in my pocket. I settled for a dime's worth of bologna, a dime's worth of block cheese, and a nickel box of crackers. After paying I asked for an empty jug that I could fill with water and stole an onion on my way out.

I ran back to the underbrush near the tracks, ate, and waited. Watching from my hiding place, I saw them switch engines. This was as far as old Texas & Pacific was going; a Cotton Belt engine was hooked on. When the engineer blew the whistle for takeoff, I climbed aboard. I had no idea where the train was headed and didn't care, just as long as it was far, far away from Longview . . . and Emma.

Lonzo didn't lie when he told me the Cotton Belt was the fastest freight line. The train was going much faster now, as if it had to be somewhere and was already late. Every time it neared a railroad crossing the engineer started the old whistle to moaning, and I rushed to stand in the open doorway to wave at the car passengers as we streaked by.

It sidetracked for a few minutes in Memphis to let another train have the right-of-way and took off again. Knoxville, Richmond, and on to Baltimore. I had to do some hustling in a hurry. That bologna, cheese, and crackers had long since disappeared, and my belly talked in growls.

I looked pretty grimy when I stepped inside the small cafe in the colored part of town and took a seat at the counter. There wasn't a thing on the homemade menu tacked to the wall I could get for a dime. I ordered a twenty-five-cent hamburger "to eat here" and bought a package of pigskins to munch on while I waited. The cook brought the hamburger and sat it down in front of me and went back to the kitchen. He'd collect for it after I finished. I caught him not looking, wrapped the hamburger in the napkin, and hit the door running. He came to the door shouting something, but I was long gone.

I bummed around town, sleeping here and there, until I started hanging around Miss Lizzie's place, running errands. She had six rooms upstairs and rented them out for transient trade. With servicemen everywhere, her rooms were rarely unoccupied. I worked my way from errand boy to cleaning up the rooms behind the whores. For this she paid me five dollars a week and board, and anything I could hustle short of stealing from her military trade.

Miss Lizzie's place was safe because she actually did palm-grease the police to let her operate her bawdy house. They only came by to collect their dough. With that in mind, I kept a crap game going out in the backyard after I got off work and kept all the neighborhood boys broke. Sometimes, my little crap game attracted grown-ups. They'd shoot for nickels and dimes with us for a while, but then invariably raise the stakes. That's when I really "rolllled" the craps.

After losing more than expected in what started out as a nickel-and-dime kid crap game, one of the men would ask, "Where'd you learn how to shoot craps lak that, boy?"

"I don't *know* how to shoot 'em, sir. I'm jes lucky."

With some good jeans and tennis shoes, a new multibladed pocket-knife, and some jingle in my pockets, it was time to move on. I still hadn't seen any of the places and things in Lonzo's stories. I headed for the railroad tracks. Each time I looked behind me I saw swirling dark clouds forming en masse. After walking a couple hours, I spotted a switch tower in the distance. The law of riding trains—"train people don't lak hoboes"—shot through my head as I climbed the outer steel ladder to the upper platform.

I rapped on the window with my knuckles. The big-bellied white man inside had on earphones and didn't hear my knock. I opened the door, went inside, and pulled off my cap, waiting for him to turn his chair around and see me. Startled, he hurriedly removed his headgear. "Damn, kid, you scared the bejesus out of me! What can I do for you?"

"Would you give me a drink uv water, please?"

Pointing to the glass jug turned upside down, feeding the fountain, he offered, "Grab you one of those paper cups and help yourself."

"Thank you." I pulled a coned cup from the dispenser and swigged down four cupfuls before stopping. "Sho looks lak we gon git some rain."

"Yep, sure does. Where you headed?"

"New York," I told him and whipped out my much used death-message telegram: `Come home quick. Stop. Grandma sinking fast. Stop. Grandpa.`

Raising his eyes from the telegram, the switchman said, "Gee, kid, I'm sorry to hear that." Luckily, he hadn't noticed the eight-month-old date at the heading.

"I got to git home, mister," I murmured, faking sadness. Then I asked the question nobody asks the switchman, "Kin you tell me which set uv these tracks I need to be on to ketch a train goin east?"

"You know I'm not supposed to do this," he said, walked to the window, and beckoned, "Come here. Get on those tracks heading straight up there toward that gap. There'll be one through here in about"—he took out his big Elgin pocket watch—"four hours from now. She gets here around midnight, but I don't advise you to try and catch that one."

"Why?"

"It's an express hauling frozen meat. He's pulling a lot of refrigerated cars and don't be doing nothing but kicking up dust when he comes by here. If I was you, I wouldn't try to catch that one, too dangerous. I'd wait for the one that comes through about six in the morning. I think you'd have a better chance."

"Yessir, I 'preciate you tellin me that, but I got to ketch this one."

"Well, kid"—he was so friendly I couldn't believe he was a railroad man and I was hoboing—"if you're dead set on catching it, walk on down the tracks about three or four miles. You'll come to a deep curve. I expect it might slow down long enough rounding that curve so you can give her a try." I thanked him and left.

A full moon that came out of nowhere rose over my back as I walked down the tracks, my shadow dancing ahead of me. Every so often, a dark cloud zipped across its glowing face, according to Miss Bertha a sure sign it was going to rain. I hoped not. I had no idea how much farther I had to go before I got to the curve the switchman had described. After about thirty more minutes of hard walking, I heard thunder rumbling and tightened my gait. All I saw up ahead was this long set of tracks going straight through the middle of nowhere.

The wind picked up, got cooler, and was blowing much stronger. The moon disappeared and darkness swallowed me. Looking over my shoulder, I saw jagged streaks lighting up the black skies. I could smell the rain coming and quickened my step as the flashes chased me. I knew it was getting closer because the crackling and peals of thunder boomed so soon afterward. Before long, the thundering light show lit up the entire sky.

I trotted along the crossties until a bolt struck the tracks behind me. Like a huge Fourth of July sparkler, it was walking them right toward me, sparks flying! I had heard stories in the hobo jungles about how lightning walked the tracks. It was pouring down now, and I was running my heart out. The embankment was too high to jump off; I had no choice but to outrun it. When I looked back I saw smoke rising from where it had fizzled out. Shaking like a leaf, I was cold and soaked to the bone by the time the storm passed over.

That chickenshit moon ventured back out and showed its grinning face. Up ahead, a trestle. I was glad to unwind and squatted with my back against the pilings. Quickly, I dozed off. How long I slept I didn't know, but way over in the still of the night I thought I heard the faint sound of a train whistle. How far away it was, I couldn't tell. I had to wait for another blow before I could make a decent guess. I heard it again and realized what it was, a manifest express. I never rode a manifest before. A chill ran up my spine because I knew they went much, much faster. "Well, shit," I said as I made my way back up the embankment to the tracks, hoping to get to that curve.

Way after while the whistle blew again. I began to trot. I knew I had walked and trotted at least three miles but hadn't come to a curve yet. Maybe the old guy had miscalculated. The next time it blew, I put it in high gear. I could tell by the whistle the engineer was asking for clearance up and down the line. It blew once more and I guessed it to be a few miles behind me.

A couple hundred yards ahead, the curve! I felt the tracks vibrating and turned around to see if the train was in sight. I didn't see it but knew it wouldn't be long. The next time I looked behind me, I saw its headlight flashing. I slid down the embankment, crouching close to the ground so the engineer, fireman, and railroad dicks wouldn't see me in the spotlight when the engine went past. As soon as it did, I crawled up the embankment and picked out a boxcar in the middle that I was going to catch.

I summoned all of my freight-catching know-how and got ready to make my catch. About twenty boxcars passed me, and I locked in on the middle one. When it got fifty feet from me, I took off running alongside the train. As soon as it caught up with me, I grabbed the handrail just as the train was bending the curve. *Wrong!* After all his instructions on how to catch a train the "right way," Lonzo would have disowned me if he saw what I did.

I should have caught the boxcar a little *before* it got to the curve or a little *after*. That way, the wind wouldn't have me blowing in the breeze as straight as one of the stiff, starched shirts on Miss Bertha's clothesline. After the train picked up speed coming out of the curve, the force of the wind had me and I couldn't pull myself to the boxcar to put my feet on the iron stirrup. I was hanging on, waving like the Texas flag, and felt my strength slipping away. It's a motherfucker when you have to turn something loose that you can't afford to, but I had to let it go.

Slung out into the night, all I could do was shut my eyes and hope for the best. There was no need of looking—I was completely airborne and couldn't dodge shit! When I hit the ground—*boom!*—I rolled down the steep embankment, tumbling for what seemed like forever through the underbrush, coming to a stop at the bottom. I shook my head and shouted, "Fuck!" The cuts on my face were stinging, as were both gashed elbows. I felt myself—ripped pants, knees gritty, minor nicks and scrapes. After realizing every bone in my body wasn't broken, I didn't have any time to lose. The train was passing me by.

I clawed and crawled my way up the embankment more determined than ever. Through gritted teeth, I vowed, "I'm ketchin you, you bad muthafucka." That catch I made redeemed me with Lonzo and elevated me to true hobodom. I knew from then on I could catch a freight with the best of them, just *not* in the fucking curve! After all this shit to catch the damn thing, I didn't even know where it was going. I took off my belt, strapped myself to it, and rode on.

I headed on up the Eastern Seaboard: Trenton, Newark, and finally New York City. It didn't take long for my money to run out. I started shining shoes in Grand Central Station by day and sleeping at one of Father Divine's flophouses in Harlem for a quarter a night. Each night the rows of cots were filled with derelicts, drunkards, and the run-of-the-mill down-and-outers. The shelter also provided one meal a day. When passing through the chow line, we were required to say "Peace, Father" before receiving a helping. Occasionally Father Divine, a black preacher followed by an entourage of "angels" (all attractive white women), paid a visit to the facility in the flesh.

I was so busy trying to survive I almost forgot about the Empire State Building and the Statue of Liberty. After about a year I came to realize the "Big Apple" was full of very private people who couldn't care less. I could hardly wait until winter was over so I could get back to hoboing. Soon as the weather broke I walked to the freight yard, hopped a train, and headed west. It was late spring and the railroad dicks were chasing me all over the Chicago freight yards because the train I had caught in Akron was loaded with military equipment. With the war raging in Europe and fearing possible sabotage, railroad security was on high alert and extra precautions were taken to keep the hoboes off. I had to sneak back that night to catch one.

Just this side of Omaha the train stopped and I headed for the bushes, following my nose to the smell of brewing coffee. Walking into the clearing I saw five colored hoboes crouched around the fire. "Hi," I said and gave them my best smile. Two or three nodded their heads. "How bout a shot uv y'all's java?"

"Sho, boy, c'mon an hep yosef." After I filled a tin can from the gallon bucket brewing in the middle of the fire, one of them asked, "Where you comin frum, boy?"

"Chicago," I told him, adding, "I wuz lucky to git outta there. Them dicks run me all over the place."

"Yeah," another said, "they priddy rough now on account uv the war. Where you headed?"

"West."

"Where west?"

"Jes west."

"Good thang you is, cuz it sho be hard hoboin through the South. They gotta dick name Texas Slim wekin twix Fort Worth an East Texas that ain't jes throwin hoboes off, he been shootin 'em left an right."

One of them got around to asking me, "You ever smoke any grass?"

"I kin roll it in the dark an light it on top uv a movin freight train," I said, accepting the joint that was passed. I took a long hit, held it in, and started coughing my head off. They cracked up laughing.

I made it to Omaha and joined up with a traveling carny. When it left Omaha, we headed back Midwest. We made Kansas, Oklahoma, Missouri, back to Nebraska, then on to southern Illinois, crossing the Mississippi and Big Muddy at least a dozen times. I did everything from hawking for the sideshows to operating the concessions. I stayed with the Smith Brothers show almost two years and, indeed, saw some of the places Lonzo had told me about.

The Huckleberry Finn in me gave call and I headed west once more. I caught a freight out of Illinois and left the carny behind. After a change of trains in St. Louis and another in Kansas City, I made connections with the Denver line. I climbed up inside the empty cattle car and squatted down in a corner. It was dark as a sack of black cats in there. The only light came when a flickering poked its way through the open door. The train had been running and "hollerin" steadily for what seemed about two hours.

There wasn't much to see in the darkness outside, except the green signal lights alongside the tracks. By watching the ground as it zoomed by, I could tell the "monkey motion" on that old engine was really churning, and the green lights beckoned "c'mon."

I pulled some of the ankle-deep, loose hay up under me to soften the hard floor. My belly said it was time to knock out that last can of sardines I had in my back pocket. I took out my all-purpose hobo pocketknife and began opening them up.

A flash from a passing car's headlights shot through, and I saw movement at the other end. My heart almost jumped out of my chest as I squinted to make sure I saw what I thought I saw. The harder I looked the clearer the outline became. The large, shadowy figure sat up and started brushing off the hay. I closed the can opener, opened the big blade, and slid the knife just underneath my sleeve.

Standing up and walking over to the doorway, the tall man harked and spat out the door several times. In a gruff voice, he said, "I saw you when you got on way back yonder. Got any idee whar we at?"

"Nope," I said, knowing by his voice he was a white man.

He walked toward me and stopped a few feet away, his body swaying to the rocking of the train. "How bout a taste uv them sardines?" He was so close I smelled the stale booze from his clothes.

"I jes got enuff for myself," I told him, all the while easing the knife into my hand, ready to fight to the death over a funky nickel can of sardines.

"Oh, yeah? Well, if thas the way you gon act, you little shit, I'll take the whole fuckin can!"

He lunged and stepped right off into hell. I let him have the full force of the blade. He doubled up in pain, clutching his groin and cursing. He backed away toward the open door. I leaped and threw my shoulder against him as hard as I could. Out the door he went. He rolled and tumbled into the weeds. I watched until the caboose passed the spot I last saw him. After that, I hardly slept the rest of the trip to California.

At night the Golden Gate Bridge was everything Lonzo said it was: "It looks lak a diamond [whistle] neckalis stretched 'cross the [whistle] ocean."

I had learned how to pick pockets while traveling with the Smith Brothers show, so the Alameda Race Track became one of my regular stomping grounds. Armed with a single-edge razor blade, I stood at the rail. When the horses came into the far turn and headed for home, the excitement grew. While the men jumped up and down rooting for their horses to win, I cut their back pockets with the blade.

When I made one of my better cuts, the billfold almost dropped into my hand. By the time the horses crossed the finish line, I could collect two or three billfolds. There were eight races today. That meant mucho crowds and mucho bucks. When the races started, I went to work. I had a feeling it would be a good day at the tracks.

During the third race, while pretending to watch, I accidentally cut the wrong pocket of the guy next to me. He let out a painful yell, looked at me, and pointed his finger, hollering, "I've been cut! This guy's trying to rob me!"

I took off through the crowd, pointing up ahead and shouting, "Hey, somebody! Stop that guy! Stop that guy!" My racetrack pickpocketing had to be abandoned. The one thing I didn't want was to get busted, and, so far, I'd been extremely lucky.

Lady Luck was still on my side. An older woman, Gladys, living at the same rooming house I did in Chabot Terrace, took note of my worldly ways and youthful good looks. One day she commented on "what pretty eyes" I had. Having learned from Emma what to say and how to say it, I took her advice: "Don't be no fool. If a woman got somethin else to give you 'sides pussy, take it."

Gladys placed me under her ever-loving wing. All I had to do was provide her with loving and let her show me off. She provided the rest. Attractive at thirty-five, she was a recent divorcée whose ex–old man was pretty well off. She took him to the cleaners and was living there until her house was ready in Vallejo. When she moved, I moved in with her.

I'd been around whores all my life and viewed women as either trickees or potential tricks. I stayed with her over a year, not "hittin a lick at a snake" as Aunt El would say, until the call of the wild hit me again. In the dead of night as Gladys lay sleeping, I got up and put on my traveling clothes, took half the money from her purse, and eased out the door.

In the glow of dawn I caught a freight to L.A. Working at odd jobs got boring. I became restless and decided to head for home. I hooked a freight and took off for Texas. I made good connections in Phoenix and Tucson. I took the Missouri Pacific (MoPac) out of El Paso going east. I hopped off on the outskirts of Dallas.

I bilked the wrong people in North Dallas with the dice one night. I wore their asses to a frazzle with my smooth roll until they figured out they didn't have a Chinaman's chance, and I had to leave running. It was late. I took a Rayfield chance and headed for Frogtown, the shantytown where Emma said Aunt Elzado lived. I asked around and found her. When I knocked on her flimsy front door, ducks started quacking like crazy inside. The lamp came on. "Who is it?" I knew it was her.

Trying to talk over the quacking, I said, "It's Albert, Aunt El."

"Emma's Albert?"

"Yes mam."

"I'm comin, baby," she said and the lamp went up another notch.

She opened the door. Disheveled, with wild plaits haloing her head, she gave me a big hug and said, "You look so good, all growed up an everthang. I'm glad you fount me." She looked the worse for the wear, and the mileage was beginning to show. A flock of quacking ducks flapping their wings were going wild behind her. "C'mon in, baby. You muthafuckas git out the fuckin way an hush!" she yelled to the ducks. Obeying like dogs, they quieted down and waddled away. I stepped in a big pile of duck shit as soon as I entered the door.

Leading me toward the only thing in the little room to sit on, her squeaky bed, she grumbled, "Muthafuckas dun stole everthang I own. Thas the reason I got these gotdam ducks an a butcher knife ready for they ass." We sat down, and the bedsprings squeaked loudly. "Baby, reach under the pillow an git my stuff," she said. I handed her the half-pint.

She took a swallow, coughed a little bit, and wiped her mouth. "How's yo mama?" No response. "When's the last time you seen her?" No response. "Well, I kin see we ain't goin nowhere wit this shit. Emma's my sister an I love her, but I never lak'd the way she treated you. Jes wudn't right. Well, you stay wit Aunt El awhile, baby. I be glad to have yo company. Now, tell Aunt El, whut brangs you to Dallas?"

"I'm jes passin through, Aunt El. I hustled the wrong bunch in North Dallas an had to run for it. I headed for Frogtown to see if you wuz still—"

A knock on the front door interrupted. The ducks began quacking and flapping their wings. I crawled underneath the bed as she went to the door and opened it. I could see the man's muddy boots, her bare feet, and lots of duck feet standing there. I heard him say something about "poonté."

"Naw, no poonté tonight."

He shouted, "Poonté!"

Right back, "Gotdam muthafucka, I tole you I ain't sellin none tonight! You *comprendo* that?" He mumbled something in Spanish. "Cuz it's *my* fuckin pussy, thas why!" she shouted, slamming the door in his face. "Gotdam crazy-ass Mes'kin," she grumbled on her way back to the bed. She sat down and the springs squeaked. Dropping her head between her legs, she looked under the bed at me. "You awright under there, baby?"

"Yes mam. Why don't you go on back to bed, Aunt El. I be awright under here." The lamp went out. Within a few minutes so did Aunt Elzado . . . and the ducks.

I was awakened by a rooster crowing and crawled out from under her bed. The ducks quacked their asses off, but Aunt Elzado was hungover and didn't even stir. I took a hundred-dollar bill from my money belt and eased it under her pillow next to her bottle.

I headed for the railroad tracks, scraped duck shit off the bottoms of my Stacy Adams wing tips on the rails, walked on across, and saw my next ride coming. The wind whispered, Longview called, pulling me back like a horseshoe to a magnet. I hopped my first diesel-driven train, the Cotton Belt route. Then I realized after I settled down in the boxcar that the Cotton Belt didn't go to Longview, close as it went was Tyler, thirty-two miles away.

It was midday when the train stopped in Tyler. I hurried out of the freight yard and found my way to a joint in the colored part of town. In a matter of hours I was in a fight and in jail for assault with intent to kill. When I went before the judge, he asked, "How old are you, boy?"

"Eighteen."

"For tearing up them people's place and breaking that nigguh's nose, I'm giving you a choice. You can take a jail sentence and I'll put the key around a jackrabbit's neck, or you can join the Army." With a rap sheet longer than two dollars' worth of link sausage, I decided to hell with that rabbit. A deputy marched me from the courthouse to the recruiting office.

With a lot of help from the recruiting officer, who looked over my shoulder and guided my hand to enough correct answers on the entry test, two days later I was in Fort Riley, Kansas. Boot camp was a breeze. Unlike the majority of pimply-faced rookie soldiers away from home for the first time, I was street tough and had been hoboing around the country, in and out of jail. After basic training and breaking everybody in the barracks shooting craps in the shower stalls, I got my first furlough and caught the Greyhound for Longview.

Instead of taking a cab from the bus station, I gambled that Emma hadn't moved and decided to walk the six blocks. I felt like a million bucks. My adrenaline was pumping, and I could hardly wait for everyone to see me in my soldier suit. At five-foot-eight and a solid 142 pounds, I was a svelte welterweight, muscular, with a good set of shoulders and a smooth, confident gait. My boot-camp haircut had grown out a little, and tiny dark brown curls covered my head. With the cotton broker's blue eyes and Anglo facial features, I was often mistaken for Italian or Puerto Rican. I was asked many times "what" I was, placing me in a position to choose for the occasion. I crossed the line back and forth and drank the wines of many vineyards.

After covering the five blocks to the Junction, I walked into the corner liquor store. I was surprised not to see any of the pulpwood trucks parked in the rear until I looked at my watch. It was only two thirty, too early. "Hi, Mr. Milton," I greeted.

"Hi. What'll it be?" Taking a better look, he asked, "Say, ain't you Emma's boy?"

"Thas right."

"Damn, boy, it's good to see you." He extended his hand to shake. "How've you been?"

"Jes fine," I answered as he pumped my hand.

"Well," he said, "you sure ain't the scrawny little kid you used to be. Looks like the service agrees with you. What'll you be havin today, Albert?"

"Lemme have two quarts uv Old Grand-Dad."

"Bet you're gittin this for her, ain'tcha?" he said while reaching on the shelf.

"Yeah. Do she still live up the street?"

"Yep, same place," he told me. "Seems like I recall her and Pat in earlier. Yep, they were," he said with certainty. "They were gittin ready for the weekend," he went on, winking his eye. "Be needin anything else?"

"Naw, thas all for now."

"That'll be twelve dollars and sixty cents," he said while putting the bottles in sacks.

I paid him and stuffed the sacks in my duffel bag. "Be seein you, Mr. Milton."

"Take care now. Come back in to see me."

"I will."

With only a half block to go, I stopped to wipe the dust off my spit-shined paratrooper boots, fix my cap, and square my shoulders. I could see the house. It looked pretty good with a fresh coat of white paint. It even had a new front porch. I saw Pat and another girl playing in the front yard and quickened my step. Pat saw me and let out a squeal. "Oh! Bubba, it's you!" she cried, throwing her arms around my neck.

"It's me, all right." Holding her away from me, I said, "Damn, lemme take a look atcha. You nearly tall as me! I can't believe how you growed up so fast. Whut you doin over here?" I asked.

"I live here."

"You do? Where's Mama Joe?"

"She died three years ago."

"She did?"

"Yeah, when she got sick she wouldn't go to the hospital at first, lak I tried to git her to. When she did go, it wuz too late. I been here wit Mama ever since." Looking around at her playmate, Pat said, "Girl, I'm sorry. I'm so glad to see him I forgot. Bubba, this is my friend Betty Carol. She live next door."

"How you, Betty Carol?"

She almost blushed right down through the ground. "Hi," she managed, then got the young girl giggles.

Pat admonished her teasingly, "Betty Carol, stop actin so crazy, girl."

"Where's Emma?" I asked.

"In the house. Betty Carol, wait for me. I'm goin in the house wit Bubba. I be back in a minute." Walking toward the porch steps, she said, "Bubba, boy, you sho look good." Snickering, she went on, "Didja see the way Betty Carol wuz checkin you out?"

Chuckling, I said, "Yeah, I saw her."

"How come you didn't let us know you wuz comin?"

"I wanted to surprise y'all."

I dropped my duffel bag in the hall and followed Pat through my old room into the crap room. Emma wasn't at her usual station. Jake was running the game. "She must be in the kitchen," Pat surmised. The ten or fifteen players gathered around the crap table hardly noticed us passing through. She wasn't in the kitchen either. "She must be in her bedroom, Bubba." When we walked back out of the crap room into my old room, Pat paused. "I got yo room."

"I kin see that." I said jokingly, "Looks lak a girl's room. But how do you sleep with all the noise in the crap room?"

"Same way you useta. I close the door an go to bed."

"That ain't the way I did it."

"How'd you do it then?"

"I didn't go to bed till the game was over."

"Well, I can't stay up lak that. Mama makes me go to bed."

I stopped in the hall to get the sacks out of my duffel bag. "Say," I whispered, "why don'tcha go on back an play with Betty Carol. I wanna go in by myself an really surprise her."

"Okay," she whispered back, "but don'tcha go off nowhere."

"I won't," I assured her as she tipped down the hall.

I knocked on the door. "C'mon, it ain't locked." I pushed it open. She was lying across the bed. Without looking to see who it was, she asked, "Whut is it?" I didn't answer. She turned her head toward me, wiping away the tears. "My God, is that you, baby?"

"It's me, Emma."

She rushed to hug me. "Damn! Let Emma gitta good look atcha. How long you been in the Army?"

"A couple months."

"Do Pat know you here?"

"Yeah, I talked to her out in the yard."

"Damn, you sho look good in yo uniform. Look lak it wuz melted an poured on you." She squeezed my arms. "An muscles too."

Smiling, I told her, "I got a few."

"Set down, set down," she said, leading me toward the bed. "I can't git over how good you look!"

"Sorry I can't say the same for you," I replied, inoffensively.

"Yeah, I know." Seeing the two sacks in my hands, she asked, "Whut'd you brang me?"

"Aw, I stopped by Mr. Milton's an picked up two OGDs."

"Well, bust one. I kin sho use a good drank right bout now."

"Whut's the matter?" I broke the seal and passed it to her.

"Whut's the matter?" She took a swig and wiped her mouth. "Pat didn't tell you?"

"Tell me whut?"

Her eyes quickly refilled with tears. "Blue's dead."

"Whut? When?" I asked in amazement, handing my handkerchief to her.

After drying her eyes, honking her nose, and another long snort, she said, "Two days ago. Died right out there on the front porch, bless his heart." Biting her lip in a vain attempt to stop the flow of tears, she went on, "He wuz tryin his best to make it back to Emma."

Astonished, I asked, "On the front porch?" I repeated it more for myself than for her. "How'd it happen?"

"Wuzn't long afta you left an Blue started comin to the house again. Thangs picked up afta the war an he wuz over here much as he wuz at home. When the game wuz over an everbody wuz gone, I got out my bottle an me an him would jes set an talk. We'd been doin that for a long time. Finally got roun to sayin we still loved each other. We jes sorta left it hangin, cuz neither uv us didn't have no ready answers for whut we oughta do bout it.

"Wednesday, I had a house full uv folks. The roundhouse bunch got paid off, an I sent for Blue. We gambled all night, on into the next mornin. Both uv us wuz so damn tired when the game wuz over, we come in here an jes fell out 'cross the bed an went to sleep. I woke up bout noon, eased off the bed, an went in the kitchen.

"I wuz almost through cookin by the time he got up an made it back to the crap room. He looked so priddy wit his clothes all rumpled up an needin a shave. We knocked out all the Old Grand-Dad the night befo so all I had for a eye-opener wuz a fifth uv vodka. I got him a glass an put the bottle on the table. We kilt it in bout a hour. I dished us up a plate an we set at the crap table eatin an talkin.

"We made up our minds we wuz goin back together. When he said thas whut he wanted to do, I couldn't keep my hands off him. My mouth wuz greasy, but I kissed him anyhow, got grease all on his silk shirt. He didn't give a damn. I hadn't seen Blue that happy in a long time. He said it wuzn't no use to keep puttin it off. Soon as we got through eatin, he wuz goin home to git his clothes.

"We walked an hugged up to the door. When the taxi come, he kissed me an said, 'I be back afta while.' Afta he left, you could hear me singin frum here to the courthouse. Pat wuz next door playin wit Betty Carol, an I didn't know whut to do wit myself. I wuz goin crazy waitin. I filled up my washtubs an started washin clothes. That Pat keeps me washin all the time, but she's sho a big help. I bet I made a dozen trips lookin out the door to see if he wuz comin. I thought he must be havin hell gittin away frum his old lady.

"I wuz out on the back porch washin an thought I heard somethin, but wuzn't sho. All uv a sudden I had a real funny feelin, lak spiders crawlin all over me. I come through the house runnin. When I got to the screen an seen him layin on his side, I thought he wuz takin a nap.

"I walked on the porch an knelt down 'side 'em. I said, 'Blue! Blue! Whut's the matter, baby? C'mon, wake up, Blue. Let Emma help you in the house.' Bless his sweet heart, he wuz holdin his priddy clothes in his arms. I turnt him over on his back an saw my baby's face. My heart . . . seem lak it jes shut down . . . lak it wuzn't gon beat no mo. I set down an lifted his head up an put it in my lap. I . . . didn't know . . . whut else to do." Her head drooped with each agonized word. The rush of tears splattered off the near-empty bottle cradled in her lap. With a deep sigh, she went on, "I don't know how long

I set there rockin an holdin him befo the ambulance come. Don't even know who called 'em."

"Whut killed 'em?" I asked dumbfounded.

"The doctor said afta he dun one uv them thangs on 'em . . . au . . . au—"

"Autopsy?"

"Yeah, he say that vodka jes recooked them cabbage an ham hocks in his stomach. That acid spread through 'em so fast it made 'em deathly sick an helpless. The doctor say it wuz 'a cute indigestion.' I tole him I drunk an ate the same thang Blue did, an that I drunk most'a that vodka myself. He tole me everbody's system ain't the same. He say Blue would prob'ly be alive today if he jes stuck his finger down his throat. Bless his heart, he wuz jes too sick to do it. Damn," she said, wiping her tears, and reached for the bottle. After a big gulp, she asked, "Whut time you got, baby?"

Looking at the Bulova I'd won in the barracks latrine, I told her, "Ten after four."

"Shit! I didn't know it wuz that late. I wuz spose to be at the undertakers at three," she said and stood up.

"Who got the body?"

"Nobody but the best, Swifty."

"When's the funeral?"

"Well, I don't know right now. They got in touch wit his sister in California an I'm waitin on her to git here."

"You thank she comin?"

"Aw, yeah, she'll be here. You wanna go down there to see 'em wit me?"

"Have they got 'em laid out?"

"Naw, he ain't dressed yet. Swifty's got 'em back in the cold room," she said, looking in the mirror and fixing her hair.

"I'll wait till he gits some clothes on," I told her. "'Sides, I wanna spend some time with Pat."

"Suit yoself, baby. I gotta go." Leaving out the front door, she said, "Why don'tcha git us another bottle while I'm gone?"

I glanced out the window and saw Pat on the porch by herself. I went out and sat down on the steps. She came over and sat beside me. "Thas kinda weird bout Allen, ain't it?" I asked.

"Yeah, sho wuz. I wuz over to Betty Carol's house when it happen. Mama be down to that undertaker parlor four or five times, jes lookin at 'em. Tried to git me to go down there wit her. I said *no way*. I'm scared uv dead peoples. You scared uv 'em, Bubba?"

"Naw, but I don't wanna see none buck naked. How long do she generally stay down there?"

"No tellin. Sometimes a priddy long time."

"Say, whut all do you do roun the house?"

"Aw, I help wit the cleanin up an cookin, watch for the police, run errands. Stuff lak that."

"You do go to school, don'tcha?"

"Sho, Bubba. I'm in the sixth grade, least I will be when it starts again."

"Do you lak it?"

"I hate it."

"I felt the same way when I wuz goin. But you need some so you kin git a job when you grown."

"Aw, I know, Bubba, but I still hate it. I wisht I didn't hafta go at all. By the way, I heard bout whutcha dun to that teacher."

"Do the kids pick on you?"

"Naw, they know I'll tell my big brother on 'em if they do," she kidded.

"Do you ever hear anything frum George?"

"Not since Christmas, when he sent me them two old funny-lookin sweaters. Look lak he bought 'em for somebody's grammaw instead'a me."

"Where's he at?"

"California, somewhere. Bubba, where all you been? I mean, befo you got in the Army."

"Lotsa places. New York, Baltimore, Philadelphia, jes about all the Midwest states, California, Little Rock, you name it."

"How'd you git to all them places?"

"Hoboed. Lemme ask you somethin. Do you git many whuppins?"

"Nawww, Mama ain't never whupped me. She cuss me out sometimes, but thas bout all."

"Well, if she ever tries to, you run."

"Don't worry, I will. I know how she is when she gits to drankin. Thas when I stay outta her way."

"None'a them old crap nigguhs don't mess with you, do they?"

"Nawww, if Mama wuz to ketch one uv 'em meddlin me, she'd run his ass 'way frum here."

"Don't make no difference. Jes keep yo head where yo ass is. You a big girl now. So watch yo step, know whut I mean?"

"I know whut you mean, Bubba. I am."

The taxi pulled up; Emma was back. "Let's talk some mo later, okay?"

"Okay, Bubba."

I smiled and handed her a ten. "Buy you somethin."

Emma stopped in the yard. "You been in the game yet?"

"Naw, I was waitin on you to come back."

"Well, I'm back an jesta bout ready. Whut you an Pat been doin?"

"Jes sittin out here talkin."

"Didja go down to the liquor store?"

"Not yet."

As we were walking down the street, she asked, "Where in the world you been all this time?"

"All over."

"How?"

"Hoboin most'a the time, 'cept when I wuz travelin with a carnival."

"A carnival? Whut on earth . . . ?"

"Aw, I used to stick my head through a hole an let 'em chunk balls at me."

Since I was buying I thought about it a few seconds and decided I didn't want to be running back and forth to the liquor store all night. "Mr. Milton, why don'tcha let us have two."

"That'll be twelve sixty, and let's see, half of that would come to six thirty. Emma, yours is on the house, and I'm sorry to hear about Blue." Shaking his head, he added, "Too bad."

"Thank you, Mr. Milton," she said.

"Think nothing of it. Hell, Blue was all right."

"Yeah, he sho wuz. Thanks again for the bottle. C'mon, baby, we betta git on back befo Jake pockets *all* my gotdam money."

"Y'all hurry back now."

"Awww, I'll *be* back," Emma emphasized. "An if anybody come by here lookin for somethin, be sho an tell 'em where Big Emma's at."

"I'll suuure do it."

When we walked up on the porch, Emma said, "Pat, it's still early. Why don'tcha go see if Betty Carol kin play?" That was right down Pat's alley, and she left running. Emma stopped by her room, hid one of the quarts under her mattress, and we headed for the crap room.

We waited at the table for the current shooter to "fall off" (finish his turn). When he did, Emma said, "Jake, I'll take it now."

The disruption of moving the table to let Jake out and her in afforded a piss break for some of the crowd, and left their spaces up for grabs. I positioned myself at the table across from Emma. While she squared up the cut money with Jake, three more gamblers left the table and were on the prowl in the kitchen.

One of them came back to the door. "Big Emma?"

"Yeah, baby, whut is it?"

"When you cook these beans an pig feets an stuff?"

"Yestiddy. It's good. Find y'all some pots an warm up anythang y'all kin find. Help y'all's self." Talking low, pretending not to want those in the kitchen to hear, Emma said, "I wuz thankin bout grabbin me one'a them feet afta while, but I kin forgit it now. Them long-mouthed wolves'll eat up ever last thang in there 'ceptin my pots an pans."

The gamblers around the crap table began laughing at her, and she really put on a show. "When these nigguhs git hongry, they even eats up all the lard out the bucket. They crawls roun under the kitchen table worse'n them roaches an finds the sack uv potatoes, eats 'em skins an all."

One of the kitcheneers overheard. "We hear you talkin bout us in there, Big Emma," he said and laughed.

"Naw I wudn't, baby. Not me. You know Big Emma wouldn't do a thang lak that. Don't pay me no mind. Jes go right ahead an help y'all's self."

"You needn't worry, we is."

"Y'all know whut I did?" she asked, speaking low again. "I went down to Kerns Bakery an bought twenny-seven loafs uv day-old bread, come back an cooked a big pot uv neck bones"—she paused to take a swig—"five pounds uv 'em. An a four-pound sack'a navy beans. Alla y'all dun ate my cookin an know I love hot pepper."

The listeners nodded, and she continued, "I don't cook without it. I cut up at least a dozen fresh cayennes an crumbled a half pack uv the dried ones. I said I'm jes gon see. Them fuckin beans an neck bones wuz so hot you couldn't stand close to the pots. Did that stop 'em? Why, hell naw. I bleeve these nigguhs' mouths is made outta iron. They'll eat wood . . . anythang." She could make a dog laugh when she started hurrahing.

Snickering at herself, she kept on, "Some uv them nigguhs got broke, went to ramblin roun in the kitchen, an found them beans an neck bones. Shit, they ate the meat an chewed them bones up into sawdust. An jes turnt them beans up an drunk 'em lak lemonade. An ate up them twenny-seven loafs uv bread an come back in here wit sweat pourin off 'em. I tole Ollie he sho bet not shit in them woods an start no fire!"

When the laughter subsided a bit, Percy said, "She ain't lyin. I wuz one uv 'em. Man, I tell you, them wuz the hottest muthafuckas I ever tried to eat. Only way we could halfway cool our moufs off wuz wit that bread. Shit, man, I betcha I drunk up two buckets uv water. Look lak steam wuz comin outta my ears."

Emma interrupted the break in the action. "Hey, y'all in the kitchen, brang y'all's plates on in here. We kin make room." They came marching out, plates in hand. "Y'all move roun a lil bit, baby, an let 'em git in here. Jake, look out back an see if them nigguhs is through peein. Tell 'em quit playin wit they selfs an git on back in here.

"You nigguhs eatin, keep y'all's plates outta the way so the dice won't hit 'em. An, baby, befo y'all shoot, don't wipe y'all's greasy hands on my blanket neither. Use that dishrag hangin in the kitchen. Whose shot is it?" She still didn't miss a beat.

It was Percy's shot, three shooters ahead of me. My turn came. "Twenty, I shoot."

Randall faded me. "Shoot 'em."

Emma watched closely as I picked them up. She saw me set the dice. I had never developed her famous Hudson shot but had my own style of concealing my setting motion. Locking the two aces in the middle "on the come out" (first roll) prevented me from rolling eleven (winner), but it eliminated the possibility, providing I controlled them, of rolling two, three, or twelve (craps). With the two aces in the middle, I provided myself the chance to roll four-trey seven and five-deuce seven, both winners. If that didn't happen, I'd catch a point (four, five, six, eight, nine, or ten).

I gave the fake shake and rolled them across the blanket. Five for a point. "I bet I bar it for twenty."

The fader Randall called, "Bet."

Looking around the table, I said, "Bar it on you, Claude, for this twenty."

Claude called the bet.

The "bar points" (four, five, nine, and ten) are cakewalks if you know the combinations and can roll the dice so they tumble in the same direction. As I placed my bets, I quickly surveyed the positions of the dice on the table, anticipating the combination for five. I joined them together smoothly, placing the trey from one in the middle against the deuce from the other. This rules out missing five with the four-trey seven or five-deuce seven. (Both losers after you catch a point.)

The only seven left I could roll was six-ace, and if I missed five with the six-ace seven, that was the bar. (You don't win or lose the side bets—you "draw down.") I'd lose the "fade" (what I shot originally), but I'd break even on the side bets. When shooting for any of the bar points, the six-ace seven is a key factor. If I missed a bar point, that was the seven to do it with.

But if I rolled five again before I rolled the six-ace seven, that would be a winner all around. With a trey and a deuce locked in the middle, two sevens are eliminated and the only one left is the bar. With the three-two combination in the middle, I'd have two ways to roll five: four-one and three-two—two to one odds in my favor.

For the moment, I couldn't think of any place on earth I'd rather be than across the crap table from Big Emma with five for a point. I loved to bet on it and shoot for it. Double-checking around the table to make sure all my bets were covered, I started into motion.

Emma reached across the table and blocked my arm's path. "Jes hold whutcha got, baby," she told me, referring to the three-two combination I held locked in the middle, "an let Emma try to git a bet on. Thirty dollars he bar it. Bar five for thirty!" Poised and waiting, I *knew* I was going to make five, never giving a thought to the six-ace seven. Somebody covered her bet and I went into motion once more.

Emma was right, I had developed a sensitive touch from all the years of practicing with my peewees. That's the size I cut my eyeteeth on, nowadays the size most commonly used. I held the two small dice between my index and little fingers, cupping them against my palm with the two middle fingers, using my thumb for concealment and added balance. This allowed the dice to be only slightly ajar when shaking.

My "fake shake" merely clucked them against each other. What's in the middle stays in the middle. With a guiding follow-through with my thumb at the time of release, I let go. They took off across the blanket side by side like a pair of Dalmatians. At the crack of my "whip" (snapped my fingers), I hollered, "Oh, Fantail Fanny!" They stopped right in front of Emma on four-ace.

"Five!" she exclaimed. "He jumped it" (making the point on the first roll).

That struck a chord. Randall wanted to fade again. "Whutcha shootin?"

"Shoot the forty," I replied.

"I gotcha," he said, counting his money down on the table. "Let 'em take wings an fly."

Emma bet "I do" again.

I rolled four-trey seven on the come out, a winner.

"Damn!" Randall exclaimed. After picking up the dice and blowing on them for good luck, he said, "Let 'em shoot again. I'll fade anybody three times." Knocking the dice over in my direction, he told me, "Shake up an brang 'em on."

I picked them up, locking the two aces in the middle. "I'm shakin 'em," I said, holding the dice over to his ear. "I know you hear that. They sound lak a nest uv rattlesnakes." I sent them sailing again, caught eight for a point. Damn near all the gamblers at the table wanted to bet against me on eight.

When I finished covering all the side bets, I had close to two hundred dollars riding on eight. Emma had sixty saying that I'd make it. I made six rolls and hit it with two fours. I had their noses wide open.

Two or three different ones said, "Let 'em shoot, I got 'em," all to no avail. Randall still had the choice since he'd been fading me from the beginning.

"Whutcha shootin now?" Randall asked.

"Forty."

"I'm gon fade you one mo time, then the devil kin. Shoot 'em."

I caught six for a point and made it after a few rolls. Big Herman faded me for thirty dollars. I rolled another seven on the come out. Next roll, I caught four for a point and loaded up on bets again. Second roll, I made it with trey-ace.

That one stung. Walter said, "Damn! This nigguh ain't missed nothin."

Emma bet with me every time. I made nine straight passes before I fell off. When the dice got back to my turn again, I rolled three sevens on the come out, caught four for a point twice, and made it with trey-ace both times. The players began to draw back, folding their arms.

Ralph spoke up. "Hell, some'a y'all fade 'em. I jes had 'em."

I couldn't get faded.

This caused a standstill in the action until Emma brought out her bottle. "Here, baby," she said, handing it to me, "take a drank an pass it roun to these po devils. Y'all gitcha a swallow uv that good whiskey." Barnstorming, she went on, "Take the rags outta y'all's asses an gamble. Tell y'all whut, I ain't gon shoot no mo. I'm jes gon back up an side-bet." Giving me the green light, she said, "Go 'head, baby, do yo stuff."

I tried again to get faded. "Forty dollars I shoot."

They stirred uneasily. In order to get any more action, I knew I would have to resort to proposition gambling, commonly known as "sucker bettin." I picked a point on the dice (four, five, six, eight, nine, or ten) and bet that I would roll it a certain way. If I rolled it any other way or rolled *any* seven in the process, I lost.

"Awright," I said, "I know y'all waitin on somethin dead. Instead'a forty dollars I shoot, forty dollars the dice make four with two deuces."

"Shit," Jake said, putting his money down, "I'll jump off a airplane to bet ginst that. I don't care if you is Big Emma's boy. Shoot 'em," he said confidently.

Emma knew that either I was crazy to make such a wager or I really knew how to shoot the shit out of a pair of craps. I slowed it down, rubbing on the dice, waiting for her to place her bet. She was hesitating because she would *never* make such a dicey bet. "Forty mo he do," she announced. Walter quickly covered her bet.

Making four with two deuces sounded gloomy until I did away with one of the fours and set the trey-ace in the middle with the two deuces on the bottom. With this combination in the middle, the only seven left is five-deuce and a hurting four, trey-ace, narrowing the odds from four to one against to two to one against. Good, consistent rolling and a bit of luck make it about even.

I knew the distance I could roll the dice before they'd start to run ahead of each other, and had a mental picture of how far they should roll to allow the two deuces on the bottom enough turns to settle on the top. I used to practice this shot by sticking the dice together with a little dab of spit. That way, I could see how far they'd roll before breaking apart.

Control is the key, releasing them with just the right push and dash of follow-through so that before they reached the predetermined distance, they'd put on the brakes like Tim McCoy's horse sliding to a halt. I did it three times in a row, doubling the bet each time. Emma did the same thing betting on the side.

"Damn, Emma! This nigguh's worse'n Wizard Ganzi!" Jake exclaimed. "An that nigguh kin throw a pair uv craps clean 'cross the roof uv a house an tell you whut they gon land on on the other side!"

"He's a chip off the old block. I taught him everthang he know," she said proudly. "Shit, me an that boy been down the road together. Ain't we, baby?"

"Yeah, Emma."

What an honor to even be mentioned in the same crapshooting breath with Wizard Ganzi, a craps master who could "shoot the dots off" a pair of dice. He put so much English on them you could hear them humming when they zoomed down the blanket and stopped on the right numbers, as if being pulled by invisible strings. Even Emma didn't fade Ganzi. Whenever he came to our house, he had to bet the "straight make" on all bar points. Hardly anybody who knew him would bet against him.

Jake broke the interlude. "Say, Big Emma, ain'tcha got another bottle stashed somewhere? Many licks this nigguh dun hit me, I could drank a gallon."

Acie joined in. "Hell yeah, Big Emma. Go git da bottle." Looking around at the others, he asked, "Ain't y'all tired?" As they nodded, he added, "I didn't hafta axe y'all if you wuz broke. Big Emma's boy took care uv dat."

Emma told Acie, "Stick yo head inside the door an see if Pat's still up."

After doing so, he reported, "Reckon not, Big Emma. Ain't no light on in dere."

"Well, tiptoe on through. Go in my room an look under my mattress an git it."

The game was over. I finished counting my money and had won $640. I tossed a hundred to Emma for the "wear and tear." The rest of the night we just sat around bullshitting. I asked about Lonzo. "I wanna see 'em befo I go back an buy 'em a drink."

"That old drunk?" Emma snapped.

"Don't call 'em that," I replied.

Leroy said, "Lonzo been dead over four years."

"Damn!" I exclaimed. "Everbody I hear about is dead."

"Yeah," said Pee Wee, "they been drappin lak flies."

Walter added, "Slim Linzy dead too."

"How'd *he* die?" I asked.

"Accident. Slip an fell goin up the gangplank into one uv them boxcars wit a crosstie on his shoulder. Fell on his neck an broke it."

"I'll be damn!" I said. "An he'd been loadin 'em a thousand years. I used to lak to watch Slim eat fish an gamble. When he got about half-drunk, he'd lean back against that wall, put one uv Emma's fried perch in his mouth, an close his eyes." Everybody was laughing at my kind remembrances. "He wouldn't leave nothin but the skeleton. Whenever his shot came, he'd open his eyes right on cue. Emma'd wind up cussin 'em out for fish-greasin the dice if he made a point an she had him faded." Looking over to the wall, I added, "That wuz his favorite spot over there."

"Yeah," Emma said, "jes lak that wuz Blue's favorite spot you in."

"Say, Big Emma, tell us that toast you say all the time befo this bottle run out," Jake requested.

"Okay." In toast gesture she held the bottle up over the center of the table.

Whiskey, oh whiskey, gotdam yo soul.
You caused me to spend both silver an gold.

We wrestled an tussled an you throwed me in the ditch.
But I'm gon try you one mo time,
You red-eyed sonuvabitch. Snakeshit.

And the whiskey took a long trip down her throat.

I had heard enough bullshit and obituaries. It was Saturday night, time to see the town and some of my old cronies. "Check y'all later," I told them, then headed down on the streets to my old stomping grounds.

8

The next day Allen's sister arrived. She came to the house in a taxi. After they finished hugging and greeting, she told Emma, "I went straight to Lucille's from the bus station. Didn't take her long to send me to you," she kidded.

"You should'a come here in the first place."

"Well, I would have but her and Allen's address was on the telegram. Before I go any further, let me apologize for not being here sooner. I had a little difficulty putting the traveling money together on such short notice," she said, embarrassed.

"I understand, Effie," Emma commented.

As she was being seated, Effie said, "Emma, tell me what on earth happened to my brother."

"Blue died right out there on the front porch . . ."

Effie cried through the whole story. Shaking her head in disbelief, she moaned, "Oh my God, what a shame."

As I sat in the room listening to them talk, I could definitely see the resemblance of this fiftyish prim and proper lady to Allen. They had the same deep black coffee-grounds complexion, maybe she was just a shade lighter, and very similar facial features. There would be no mistaking them as siblings. Except for her sounding like a white woman with a heavy California accent, even their voice tones were alike.

The conversation took a direction that let me know they went back a long way together when Effie said, "Emma, don't tell me this is that pretty baby all grown up."

"Thas him."

"Gee, it just doesn't seem like I've been gone that long. When James and I moved to California, he wasn't more than two years old. How old are you now, young man?"

To sound as old as I could, I replied, "Goin on nineteen."

"Effie, I got a girl too," Emma said. Then she asked me, "Didja see Pat out there anywhere?"

"Yeah, she's over at Betty Carol's playin."

"Oh, that's all right, Emma. Don't take her away from her friend. I've got to be going pretty soon so I can take a bath and clean myself up some. How old is your daughter?"

"She'll be twelve this comin August. You got any?"

"No, I haven't been so blessed."

"Have you got any place to stay?"

"Oh, yes. I stopped and got a room at the hotel on my way over here. Emma, this is as good a time as any to talk business, and if I don't ask I won't know. Who's handling the arrangements, you or Lucille?"

"I am. I'm takin care uv everthang."

"How is Lucille taking all this? I mean, you handling everything and all."

"How she takes it is her bizness. I'm still his legal wife. Everthang he had, he left it to me. All his social security, everthang. Lucille didn't git shit."

"Did he have a policy to cover the funeral expenses?"

"Yeah."

"Is it enough to cover everything? I have to ask you because I hadn't heard from either Allen or Lucille in over three years. So, I don't know about their financial situation."

"Effie, don't worry. When the insurance man tole me I wuz gon git a check for thirty-five hundred dollars, I went straight to Swifty an tole 'em to give Blue the works."

"That sure takes a load off my mind," Effie said, "because money-wise, there isn't a thing I can do. I've been in financial trials ever since James died a year and a half ago. It's not easy for a woman my age to find work that pays a decent wage. I've been barely able to make it. Everything's so terribly expensive in California, you know. I'm just hanging on by my fingernails."

"Well, why don'tcha let go?" Emma capped back, sick of Effie's down-in-the-mouth shit.

Effie broke the awkward silence. "When do you plan to have the funeral?"

"Whut about tomorrow? I know Blue's ready to git outta that cold storage. An you prob'ly wanna be gittin on back as soon as you kin, don'tcha?"

"Well, yes. I only have enough money to stay a couple of days."

"Awright, we'll have it tomorrow then. All I gotta do is let the preacher know."

"Oh . . . you're having it in a church? Which one?"

"Galilee Baptist. Let's say two thirty. You know where it's at, don'tcha?"

"Yes, I remember. Emma, you're so sweet to be doing all this. Is there anything I can do?"

"Naw, Effie. He wuz my man. I'll do it."

"Are you expecting a large crowd of people to attend? Reason I asked, there isn't much notification time."

"There'll be a few."

I was asked to call a taxi for Effie. I ran to the cafe to use the outside pay phone and returned. Standing and smoothing down her dress, Effie said, "Emma, except for the extra pounds, you haven't changed a bit."

"You ain't neither, Effie . . . 'cept for the extra pounds."

"After I take a bath and rest a little bit, I'm going over to the funeral home and sit with Brother awhile."

"You can't do that yet. Swifty got some stuff smeared all over 'em to keep 'em lookin fresh for the funeral. I know Blue'll be glad to git that shit off."

Hearing the taxi's honk, Effie said, "Well, Emma, I'm going to my hotel room and cry some more. I still can't believe it, the only brother I had."

"Yeah, I know. He wuz one uv a kind."

"Okay, Emma, I'll be seeing you. And nice seeing you too, young man."

"Nice meetin you, Miss Effie."

Soon as Effie's cab pulled off, Emma said, "Damn, I got a lot uv thangs to do. Baby, I hate to bother you again, but will you go call me a cab? I didn't wanna ride in that one wit her. I wuz tired uv lissenin to her shit. All that slut wuz inerested in wuz if it wuz gon cost her anythang."

I had to explain to the taxi dispatcher, "Yes, one came, picked up a passenger, an now we want another." It arrived shortly, and Emma hightailed it.

The next day at two o'clock, Swifty came to the house and picked up the "family" (Emma, Pat, and me) in the company limo. The church was located in Allen's neck of the woods, the Old Field, a predominantly colored neighborhood. All decked out in "tie an tails," spats and white gloves, Swifty escorted us inside. It was packed! I found out later that Emma had paid somebody to drive around where the street hustlers hung out, blaring the time and place of his funeral over a loudspeaker. The street people heeded the call, dressed up in their finery, and turned out en masse to bid farewell to one of their own.

Swifty led us down the aisle to the front bench in the church. Emma took the first seat, then I, then Pat. A short while later he escorted Effie to her seat beside Pat. Lucille, eyes straight ahead, sat on the front bench across the aisle.

Even with all the windows and doors open, the early summer afternoon had the church steaming hot. People fanned themselves frantically with complimentary Citizens Funeral Home hand fans. The soft, low playing of the organist was almost drowned out by the appraising ooohs and aaahs from the spectators as the casket was rolled down the aisle.

When Swifty and his attendants rolled it past us and placed it in front of our bench, I could understand their exclamations. The expensive mouse-gray casket, adorned with full-length high-polished stainless-steel handles, was a showstopper. The eggshell, fluffed crepe lining matched perfectly with the spray of white carnations that lay on the top. It was a stylish, befitting send-off, symbolic of his flair for imported hats and tailor-made clothes.

I don't know if Emma bought all the flowers, but the front was full. Emma leaned over to me. "Ain't that casket a knockout? Swifty say it's stainless steel an won't leak. Wudn't nothin too good for Blue. These nigguhs be talkin bout this funeral for the next twenny years," she whispered just before the music stopped.

The preacher positioned himself behind the pulpit, read a long verse from Isaiah, and commented, "The Lawd giveth and the Lawd taketh away. The Lawd blessed Allen Sample with forty-five years on this earth and decided it was time to take him on home. Allen Sample has paid the debt we all got to pay."

He turned things over to Swifty, who walked up front to escort the immediate family to the casket. Effie was first, lingering awhile and weeping. Swifty assisted her back. Pat had agreed earlier to go up with me, but when the time came she wouldn't budge.

I looked at him. Except for the mingling gray hair and longer sideburns, Allen's appearance hadn't changed much since I'd seen him last. The collar of his white silk shirt was meticulously folded back over the top of his steel-gray suit jacket collar. The way Emma said she liked to see him wear it.

Swifty reached for Emma's arm to assist her. She snatched it away from him. "I don't need *nobody* to help me git to Blue!" Rising slowly and smoothing down her black chiffon dress, she cast a "Blue always b'longed to me" look at Lucille.

Immediately she reached over into the casket and began straightening his clothes and cooing to him. "Here I am again, baby," she said, the tears streaming down her face. "Looks lak this is the last time I'm gon git ta see you." You could hear a pin drop. "Emma's dun come far as she kin go. I loved you hard as I could, Blue . . . you knows that," she told him, bending over the casket and placing a kiss on his lips. "I'm sho gon miss you, but Emma'll ketch up wit you again someday . . . somewhere down the line." She kissed him again, caressed her tears off his face, and came back to her place on the bench.

After a few moments of silence Swifty raised his hands. The others rose and started filing past the casket. Every time a hustler passed the casket, he or she dropped a dollar bill in it. I leaned over and whispered to Emma, "Why are they doin that?"

"Thas the way hustlers do good hustlers."

After everybody passed the casket and viewed the body, just before Swifty closed the lid, I rushed up and put in my crumpled dollar bill.

On our way back from the burial, Emma said, "Let us out right here, Swifty," as we passed the corner liquor store. He made a U-turn, pulling to a stop under the canopy in the driveway. We got out. Emma walked around to Swifty's side. "Thanks, Swifty. You sho dun a good job on Blue."

"Thank you, Miz Emma. If I kin be uv service to you in any way, now or in the future, please, mam, don't hesitate to call."

"Yeah, well, I ain't plannin on callin you again no time soon." Flashing his ever-ready smile, he thanked her once more and drove away. After Emma told Mr. Milton about what a "good funeral" Allen had, we took our two quarts and left.

When we walked up in the yard, Sweetie, Ralph, Jake, Acie, and some of the other regulars, still dressed in their funeral rigs, waited on the porch. "Pat," Emma told her, "go pull yo Sunday dress off an put somethin else on. Damn," she said to the players on the porch, "y'all sho got back in a hurry."

"We didn't go out to the boneyard. We come on straight frum the church house," Jake responded. "Big Emma," he continued, "we been talkin bout it, an I wanna tell you sump'n, baby. You sho had Blue put away in grand style."

"He look so natchal," Ralph added. "Didn't even look dead."

"Yeah," Sweetie said, "he look lak he wuz gon open his eyes an smile at us. They say ol Swifty sho know his stuff."

Leading the way into the house, Emma stopped in the hall. "Here, Jake," she said, handing him the dice from her purse, "y'all go 'head an git started. I gotta duck somewhere an pee." She sped up, rushing through the house, headed for the outhouse in back. The other eight of us scurried for favorite spots around the crap table. By the time she returned, the game was well under way. She took over.

Nobody would fade me when my shot came. I passed my turn to the next shooter and started betting on the side. I had the same feeling Emma did about that: "I'd ruther be shootin at a bird than have the bird shootin at me."

She opened up one of the OGD bottles, drank a big swallow, and passed it around. By early evening I was just twenty dollars ahead. The Wizard Ganzi label they'd hung on me stuck like glue. Still nobody would fade me, and I was losing incentive in a game of "fade but can't shoot."

Emma didn't have her mind on the game *at all*. She was losing and drinking that hundred-proof like it was water. The game slowed down, matching the tempo of her lack of interest and enthusiasm. "Say, Big Emma, whutcha got to eat?" Sweetie asked.

"Nothin."

"Well, hell. When you gon cook sump'n?" he asked with customary expectations.

"Is you nigguhs *always* hongry?" she fired back, semiaggravated.

"Yeah!" Acie and Pee Wee chimed.

Nobody was betting anything. Walter was "playing" with the dice on the table. Looking up at the ceiling, he said, "Les see, I been over heah all day, when's the last time I et?" he said, rubbing his chin, feigning to remember.

"Awright, awright! I'll git up an cook somethin in a minute. My bottle's empty, an I ain't goin *nowhere* till I git another drank."

Walter ran his hand in his back pocket and pulled out a nearly full pint of Gordon's gin. Reaching it to her after uncapping it, he said, "Big Emma, I know this ain't yo drank, but you sho welcome to some uv it." Then he added, "Ain't nobody drunk out uv it but me."

"Hand it here," she commanded, taking the bottle and turning it up. After she drank, it was half-empty. "Percy, you the closest to the kitchen. Step in there, baby, an see if you kin find Big Emma a piece uv lemon, an brang the salt box."

"Okay, Big Emma."

He came back with it, and she salted the lemon, took a big suck-lick, frowned, and told Walter, "Now, hand me that bad-tastin muthafucka again. I'm ready for its ass now." When she took that next slug of gin, I said to myself, *Pull y'all's hats down tight. We goin round some mighty steep curves.*

"Jake, I'm gon leave my dice wit you. If y'all wanna play some mo, go 'head. But be sho an git my cuts. Y'all lemme out," she told us as she pushed and we pulled the table back. "Baby," she said, talking to me as she passed by, "go out there an see if you kin find Pat. Tell her I said come on in here an help me."

I walked out on the front porch. Not seeing her, I called, "Paaat! Paaat!" She came running out of what seemed to be her second home.

"Whutcha want, Bubba?"

"Emma wants you to come in the kitchen an help her."

"Oh, awright," she said angrily. Stomping up the porch steps, she complained, "Ever time we git to playin good, she calls me."

I followed her back through the house and stopped at the crap table to rejoin the "jaw jekin" session. I listened to my fill of bull and then went in the kitchen. "How y'all comin in here?" I asked. I was getting hungry too.

Emma didn't say a word as she cut up the two fryers. I knew why Pat wasn't talking. She was still mad. I stood watching until Emma looked around and said, "I miss Blue already. Don't you?"

"In a way," I replied without much sentiment.

"You never did lak him."

"He never did lak me frum the day I wuz born."

"I guess carryin his name aroun eighteen years don't mean nothin."

"Sho as hell don't, he wudn't my daddy. You could'a give me anybody's last name. He wuz jes another nigguh to me."

She gave me a hard look. "Whut time you got?"

"Eight forty-five."

"Run down to the liquor store an git me another bottle befo it close."

I said jokingly but meant it, "Emma, git somebody else to go. I don't work here no mo."

She turned away from the sink to face me, glaring that hateful stare that used to send icy shivers up and down my spine. Gripping the butcher knife tighter, she hollered, "Why you gotdam half-white sonuvabitch! Don'tcha talk back to me! You do whut I tell you! If it wudn't for yo muthafuckin ass, Blue—"

"I'm goin back in the crap room," I interrupted and turned to walk away.

She and Old Grand-Dad went on the attack, grabbed my arm, and spun me back around. "Don't walk yo peckerwo—"

The anger swept through me so suddenly I didn't have time to bite my lip. Retaliating, I yelled, "Don't you put yo muthafuckin hands on me!"

Pat screamed, "Bubba, no!"

The explosive blow to her jaw carried her two-hundred-plus pounds crashing into the refrigerator. She slid to the floor, still clutching the knife. "Don't never call me that no mo!" I demanded. Grabbing her wrist, I positioned the blade against her throat and shouted, "If you do, I'll kill you! It wuzn't my fuckin fault!"

I brushed past the onlookers in the doorway, got my duffel bag, and stormed out of the house, headed for the bus station. I felt like I had just committed the most shameful act of my life and didn't try to hold back the tears.

BREAK TIME

I broke restrictions—"All new personnel are restricted to the base for thirty days prior to eligibility for passes to town"—the same day

I arrived at Fort Bliss, my new base. Soon as I was located in my quarters and the corporal left, I left. I walked off the base, caught a taxi, and went to downtown El Paso. After reporting back three days later and getting my ass chewed out, I caught extra duty for thirty days cleaning the latrines. And I was re-restricted, this time to the company area. "One thing you better learn quick, Private Sample. I'm not gonna put up with any horseshit," my CO told me.

It took a week to get my gambling-bootlegging operations in full swing. I kept a hut full of drinkers and would-be gamblers nightly. My hut was the hottest spot in the company area. As soon as latrine inspection was over, I'd run half a mile to the off-limits liquor store, pick up four gallons of cheap wine, and resell it to the players for two bucks a half-canteen full. When it wasn't my shot and I took my time and measured it right, I could pour twelve half canteens from the $3.50-a-gallon wine. Since we were using my blanket in my hut with my dice, I cut the game for "wear and tear."

Even Sergeant Top, the company first sergeant, joined in the crap games when he had to pull weekend duty. He was a good bettor but didn't know how to gamble. On more than one occasion, he left my hut owing me as much as eight hundred dollars. Usually, he paid it back during the game. But the times when he couldn't or didn't pay up when due, I didn't pressure him. One hand washes the other; he covered for me at roll call and kept my name off the KP and guard duty rosters.

Five days prior to expiration of my area restriction period, I won seventeen hundred smackeroos! All that money started, as the old folks used to say, "burnin a hole" in my pocket. I sneaked out of the area, hailed a cab, and hooked it for town. Top took care of me as long as he could, but after eighteen days he had no choice but to declare me AWOL.

On the twentieth day I got arrested by the locals in El Paso for fighting in a bar. After checking with the base and being instructed to "hold," the locals turned me over to the two MPs. Top, with twenty-four years in the service and practically running the company, used his pull to persuade the CO to push for only a summary court-martial and thirty days in the stockade.

Rejoining the company after I pulled my sentence, I resumed my gambling-bootlegging operations right where I left off. Less than a month after I was released from the stockade, I won big again. I took off AWOL and went to Juárez, got with a señorita, bought some civilian clothes, and was shacking up. I'd been AWOL for twenty-seven days and didn't try to hide. I knew the MPs couldn't touch me in Mexico.

But good fortune breeds envy. Some of my compadres in my company saw me at the same bar several times and told Top. He came to Juárez and waited around in the bar until I finally showed up. "Sample," he said, "I can help you if you come back with me now. But, man, if you fuck around over here three more days, you're gonna be up for a general, which means at least ninety days in the stockade and possibly a BCD [bad conduct discharge]. If the CO recommends a general court-martial for you, there won't be much I can do."

He pleaded with me to go back with him, but I steadfastly refused. "Top, I ain't goin back with you. Tell you whut I'll do, I'll come back tomorrow."

After much dickering, he conceded. "Okay, Sample," he said, "I think I can hold things off one more day, but get your butt back tomorrow."As shithouse luck would have it, I got arrested that night in Mexico for assaulting a police officer and put in their no-top jail. I escaped, and three days after I promised Top I'd be there, I showed up at the base. I got a special court-martial, the middle rung on the military courts' ladder, and was sentenced to sixty days in the stockade and forfeiture of all pay except ten dollars. I'd hardly begun serving my sentence before I broke a fellow stockade inmate's face and got thrown in solitary for assault and battery.

With one summary and two special courts-martial under my belt, two and a half years later I had 150 days "bad time" (lost time in the stockade) to make up before I could get discharged. But, with a lot of help from Top when the time came, I managed to somehow slide out of there with a good discharge.

In 1952, not quite six months after being discharged, I was standing before a judge. "I sentence you, Albert Sample, to two years in the State Pen" for burglary . . .

Racehoss

9

. . . and I violated parole.

I was sent back to serve the six months remaining on the two years. In 1956 I was sentenced to twenty years for robbery to run concurrent with the thirty I got for robbery by assault. My mind was racing as the transfer truck, "Black Betty," slowly backed inside the gates of Retrieve, one of the twelve prison units constituting the Texas prison system.

This was it, "the burnin hell," the place that "gits yore heart right" I'd heard so much about when I served time at the Clemens Unit. Retrieve, formerly an all-white prison unit, had been repopulated a few years previously with the worst, most incorrigible black cons that were in the prison system. Most were multirecidivists serving heavy-duty sentences. That measly two years I pulled on Clemens was just a drop in the bucket compared to this new thirty-year package I was breaking the seal on in this plantation prison hulled out of the cotton-growing farmland fifty miles south of Houston.

While unloading off the back of the black van, I looked up and saw the numbers inscribed above the redbrick archway. The year 1934 leaped out at me. This widow-maker was born during the Great Depression, just like me. *Whut a coincidence*, I thought, *that wuz the same year I got "busted" for the first time when Emma went to jail for bootleggin.* Going to jail was fun and games back then, but as I stepped into this bastard world of the prison system, I knew growing up with Emma and the time I served on Clemens were just boot camp for what I was facing now.

Inside the building there were four separate "tanks" on the lower level and one on the upper level across from the inside picket post. It was late morning, and the field hands were still outside working. The tanks were empty, except for the building tenders.

The guard who brought the six of us in hollered up to the inside picket guard, "Boss, open up them Number Three an Two tanks. Put half uv these nigguhs in each one uv 'em."

I looked up and saw the soles of the picket guard's shoes as he walked around in the metal-caged picket overhead. He threw the levers, opening the tank doors. "Awright, you first three nigguhs," he said, pointing us out, "git in that Number Three tank. Rest uv you git across the hall in Number Two." After we were inside Number 3 tank, he hollered, "Got three new uns comin in, Ol Bull!"

As the broad-shouldered building tender walked toward the front of the tank, the long piece of chain hanging from his belt rattled noticeably. "Got 'em, boss," Bull hollered while the door was clicking shut. He told us our bunk and locker numbers, what time we'd be fed, and when the lights went out. Then he laid down the tank "laws": "Ain't gon be no loud talk an no two nigguhs settin on no one bunk. Don't nobody git offa yo bunk at night afta count time till you holler 'alley, boss' an gits a okay."

When he said that "alley, boss" part, it reminded me of the time I was five and had a bad cold. Emma carefully measured out two spoonfuls of castor oil into a cup with a little squeezed orange juice. As I was putting the cup up to my mouth, I pleaded with her not to make me take it. Just the smell was making me nauseous. She told me I'd better drink it and forget about the smell.

I turned the cup up and swallowed it, but it wouldn't stay down. I immediately vomited all over the kitchen floor. She grabbed me by my hair and pressed the butcher knife she'd used to halve the orange against my throat. She held it so tight it cut the skin. "Pick up that bottle an drank ever bit uv it, an you bet not waste a drop. If you utter, I'll pull yo gotdam peckerwood head off!" I gulped down the rest of it. She ordered me to get on my cot and "stay there."

In a very short time I needed to go to the outhouse. Since I wasn't supposed to get up, I hollered into the kitchen, "Emma, kin I go outside to do-do, please, mam?" My life hadn't changed much. Here I was having to get permission to take a shit again.

I tuned back in to hear Bull saying, "When dey rangs dat bell, be ready ta git y'all's asses outta dis tank."

Despite my color and size, he didn't hassle me. With that acquired jailhouse look recognized in any prison that says "Don't fuck with me," I entered Number 3 tank to spend the next thirty years. Bull knew if he started some shit, one of us would die; he saw it in my eyes. I didn't care how big he was.

The tank had three double-deck rows of bunks with twenty bunks each, and one with twenty-five. Bars that ran from the floor to the ceiling separated Number 3 tank from the one adjacent to it, Number 4. At the front of the tank sat an old-fashioned barber chair, a domino table, and silver painted lockers lining the front wall. In the back were a six-sprinkler shower stall, a urinal, and a long, eight-faucet face basin that doubled as the tank's drinking fountain. Instead of a mirror, an elongated piece of stainless steel hung above it. A row of eight doorless commodes, with those old-timey wooden seats regulating the flushing, faced the front of the tank.

About thirty minutes later the field workers came in for lunch. They were wet and muddy. Our clean, white clothes tattletaled we were new arrivals. Some made snide remarks as they rushed for the back to wash up. "Y'all won't be so priddy an white afta dat bell rangs."

Within a few minutes the picket boss pulled the tank door levers, and Bull hollered, "Les go eat!"

The Number 3 and 4 tank (east-side) cons single-filed into the mess hall along with the cons from the west-side tanks (Numbers 1 and 2). I quickly scanned the mess hall hoping to see someone I knew, but didn't. After passing the steam tables, we sat eight cons to a table.

While we ate, the building tenders slowly walked up and down the aisles—overseeing. No talking allowed and fifteen minutes to eat.

When the mess hall emptied and we returned to the tanks, the picket boss hollered down, "All you ol new nigguhs, come on up to the front," as he opened the Number 2 and 3 tank doors. The six of us stepped out into the area underneath the inside picket. The captain who was waiting there ordered us to line up against the wall. He sized us up, and I knew my light complexion made me stand out like a sore thumb against the blackdrop of the other five.

He told the first two men, who were both bigger than me, "Ketch that Number Three hoe, an you ketch that Number Five." I'd learned on Clemens that the higher the squad number, the better off you were. Judging my size against theirs, I figured I'd probably be put in Number 7 or 6 at least. On Clemens I'd been in Number 12 utility squad mending fences and putting in culverts, and had never done field work.

I was next. "You ain't all that big," he said, stepping in front of me, "but you wuz big enuff to rob them folks. Got you some big time this time, didn't you?"

"Yes suh."

"Well, I'm gonna put yore yaller ass whar you kin start doin some uv it. You ever been baptized, nigguh?"

"No suh."

"Welcome to the burnin hell. You fixin to git baptized in fire. When that Number One hoe comes out, you ketch it."

Back on the tank, one of the cons said, "Man, Cap'n Smooth put you in a baddd muthafucka! All them nigguhs is wild. An the lead-row nigguh they got, Ol Road Runner, runs wide open all day long. An Boss Deadeye is a sho-nuff number one driver. You betta be ready to hit the door runnin!"

Another added, "Boss Deadeye gon have a field day wit that lil nigguh."

The turnout bell sounded. I tensed.

"Lemme have 'em, boss," shouted Cap'n Smooth, who stood at the back door.

"Number One!" the inside picket boss hollered down, opening all of the lower tank doors.

The Number 1 hoe squad cons from all four tanks ran at full speed down the hall like a herd of buffaloes. Eight white bosses on horseback were waiting as we fled out the back door.

Cap'n Smooth counted us and hollered, "Got twenty-seven uv 'em, boss."

The boss with the patch over his eye rode up behind us and answered loudly, "Thas right! Ol Road Runner, y'all git some grubbin hoes an shovels."

By the time we got to the hoe rack, I was out of breath. I reached for a hoe and a con snatched it away from me. "Thas mine, man!"

I reached for another and a different con grabbed it. "Gimme dat hoe, man!"

When I got the same "thas mine" bullshit on my next grab, I hollered, "Man, fuck you! These things b'long to the gotdam state!" I ended up with a broken shovel with half a handle and half the blade missing.

As we left the hoe rack running behind Road Runner, Boss Dead-eye rode at our heels, yelling, "Gitcha goddamn asses offa this yard an on that turnrow," referring to one of the narrow roads that separate the acres in the field. "Go 'head!"

It didn't take much to figure out why they called the lead-row man Ol Road Runner. He was tall, skinny, and extremely long legged. He walked so fast the rest of us ran and trotted to keep up with him. His long "drag step" with his feet never leaving the ground made him look as if he were walking on a pair of skis.

We must have walked and run five miles down that muddy road behind him. The muscles in my legs cramped and the new brogans were killing my feet. Knowing this was just the beginning, I wondered if I wouldn't be better off dead. By the time we got to the "bottoms," my shirt was wringing wet. Road Runner never broke stride until we reached the place to "ketch in." I was glad to get there just so I could quit running.

Boss Deadeye stopped his horse and yelled, "You nigguhs ketch in heah an start diggin up them tree stumps. Git ever bit uv them roots outta thar." I began shoveling dirt like a salamander around one of the huge stumps. Even with one eye, Boss Deadeye quickly spotted my shovel-handling ineptitude. "Ol new nigguh, come heah!"

I stopped digging and dropped my shovel. I walked to within ten feet of where he sat astride his horse and pulled off my flop-down hat. *Everybody* knew this "rule." I'd learned that much on Clemens.

"Whut're you doin out heah 'thout sump'n ta wek wit?"

"Thas all—"

"Shet yore goddamn mouth! Aw, I know you thank you good as a white man. Yore kinda nigguhs don't aim ta do much wek. Ain't use to it lak them black uns is. Whar you come frum, nigguh?"

"I'm frum Longview, boss."

His next question, "Whut color is yore ol mammy?"

Before I knew it I told him she was white and my daddy was a colored man. I saw it in his one eye, he didn't like my answer worth a damn. Angered, he spat tobacco juice at me but missed. "You know whut, nigguh? You 'mind me uv a big pile uv yaller shit." Some of the cons in the squad started snickering. "Frum now on, I'm gonna call you Ol Shit-Colored Nigguh. When I call you that, you betta answer me." Leaning forward in his saddle, he asked, "Do you unnerstan that, nigguh?"

"Yes suh, boss, but that ain't my name." A hush fell over the squad.

"Why you goddamn, impudent, shit-colored maw-dicker!" He spurred his horse and tried repeatedly to hit me with the knotted end of the big rope tied to the horn of his saddle. With me avoiding him and his horse, we went around and around. Finally he gave up. Thoroughly aggravated, he said, "Gitcha goddamn ass back over yonder an git ta wek!"

Later, a con began to sing in the squad working next to ours. Another con urged him on, "Blow it outcha soul, nigguh." As the singing grew louder, I realized the cons in the next squad were cutting trees and hitting their axes in rhythm with the song. I listened to them and kept on digging.

We dug stumps and we dug stumps until "Dere it is, it's in da air!" Cap'n Smooth, who sat on a horse up ahead, had raised his hat, signaling that the workday was over. We rushed to line up behind Road Runner for the long run back to the building. I was on the back row in the squad, right under the nostrils of Deadeye's horse. Each time he snorted, he blew cold slobber on my back. He nudged us with his big head to keep us all bunched up and in line. I soon learned that if a con lagged behind while working or walking, that old horse would bite the shit out of him.

Seemed like I was running in slow motion. Boss Deadeye yelled, "You nigguhs betta git on to that house. Go 'head!" Road Runner laid his ears back and took off. He left us struggling to catch up as we trotted wearily behind him with the other seven squads behind us.

On the yard we stopped by the hoe rack to put away our tools, then took off again for the back gate. Boss Deadeye rode over to the outside picket and dismounted. He hung his pistol and shotgun on a hook tied to the end of a rope and the back-gate picket boss pulled his weapons up into the picket. We stood at the back-gate entrance behind Road Runner, eagerly awaiting the signal from Boss Deadeye to "go 'head."

Instead, he walked over to the side of the squad, evil-eyed me, and said, "Ol Shit-Colored Nigguh, come heah."

I didn't move. Cap'n Smooth came out of the small building beside the back gate. Deadeye walked toward him. "Cap'n, I got a ornery ol nigguh in my squad that laks to play deaf." Then he yelled, "Ol new nigguh, git yore goddamn ass over heah."

I stepped out, and the rest of my squad went through the back gate. Cap'n Smooth told me, "Stand over yonder," pointing toward the other side of the back gate. I was the first con cut out that evening.

Waiting by the gate, I saw all the other squads. Each one stopped at the back gate and waited for the "go 'head." They rushed through, stopped midway in the yard, stripped, and were searched by the waiting bosses. By the time the last squad went through, five of us were standing outside the fence, waiting.

After the back-gate boss strip-searched us and we had our clothes back on, Cap'n Smooth marched us into the building hallway. He yelled up to the inside picket boss, "Hand me down five pairs, boss."

When my turn came, I didn't drop my head and lower my eyes the way the others had done when he spoke to them. He didn't like that. After clamping the cuff on tight-tight, he ordered, "Put that wrist on the floor, nigguh!"

I got on my knees and placed my cuffed wrist on the floor. He stomped the cuff on even tighter and then backed me up against the iron bars that separated the mess hall from the inner hall. With one cuff clamped on my right wrist and my back against the bars, he took the unclosed cuff and looped it through the bars above my head. Then he told me to fold my left arm above my head while he clamped on the other cuff. When he finished, I was left hanging with my toes barely touching the floor. "You swoled up, but I'm gonna unpuff you."

After an hour or so, a couple of the cuff hangers started groaning. I bit my lip to keep from crying out too. I thought about what that lying boss told the captain, "All this nigguh's dun all day long is look up in the sky an count birds. Cap'n, I had to beg this nigguh to git him to go ta wek." The pains shot through my arms; I dug my teeth deeper into my bottom lip until I tasted the blood inside my mouth.

When the bell rang for supper, none of those who made it in would even look at us as they filed past to enter the mess hall. They looked straight ahead. As I smelled the food and listened to their spoons scraping the tin pans behind me, I thought about those big, thumbtack-size butter beans I'd passed over at lunch and wished I hadn't.

After "count time" (nine o'clock), the lights were dimmed inside the tanks and the hours crept by. I sure had to piss, but the con hanging next to me told me, "We git to piss when they lets us down. If you piss in yo britches, thas another hour."

"How long will they leave us hung up here?" I asked.

"They lets us down in time to eat an git ready to go to work."

Along about hour six, one of the hangers began moaning louder and louder, violently jerking and pulling against his cuffs. He frantically wiggled and twisted his body around until he was facing the bars. Using his foot to push against them, he reared back, pitching, straining, and pulling as hard as he could. Realizing he couldn't get loose, he bit into his wrists as if they were two chocolate éclairs, gnawing away like a coon with its foot caught in a steel trap.

The blood-splattered con hanging next to him pulled as far away as he could, and hollered and yelled for the picket boss. Looking down from his perch, the picket boss ordered the turnkey, "Run git a bucket an dash some water on them two crazy nigguhs down on the end." The dousing worked; the struggling con quit mutilating his wrists and contented himself with moaning and groaning out the night like the rest of us.

I was wide awake the whole time. Finally, the dim tank lights were turned back to bright. The picket boss handed down the cuff keys to the turnkey, who unlocked us from the bars. After the cuffs were removed, my arms dropped, my hands dangled, and my swollen wrists throbbed like a bad toothache.

The picket boss opened the door to my tank, and I headed straight for the back to take a piss and get a drink. I barely sat down on my bunk before a building tender shouted, "Les go eat!" That walk to the mess hall past the bars I had just hung on all night wasn't fast enough for me. I didn't want to look at that place of pain either. As I passed the steam table, I pointed to every food item on it.

"Oh my God, here we go again," I said under my breath when the turnout bell rang.

"Lemme have 'em, boss."

"Number One!"

We tore down the hall. The last man out the door got kicked in the ass by Cap'n Smooth. "Got twenty-seven uv 'em, boss!"

"Thas right, Cap'n." Then, "Go 'head! Git offa this goddamn yard!"

We were low-flying as we followed Road Runner down the turn-row. How could he possibly be in such a big hurry to get back to digging stumps? Every stride keeping up with him was torturous. When we reached the edge of the bottoms, it was like following a bloodhound. He headed straight through the woods to the same stumps we were digging around yesterday.

We started working. The other cons in the squad shied away. They surmised that I was on the boss's shit list after yesterday's episode. I dug around a stump by myself and managed to dig it out. I knew I couldn't just stand around, so I got in a hole with a crew and started digging. Nobody said a word as we dug and dug.

There had been a slight drizzle when we left the building. Now, icy pellets dropped. Thirty minutes later Cap'n Smooth knocked us off. When we got to the turnrow, Boss Deadeye made us take off our brogans so we wouldn't "be a-wearin 'em out in the mud." We tied our shoelaces in a knot and hung the shoes around our necks.

Walking on the slick turnrows was like walking on wet glass. While we slid and half fell across the mud, that damned Road Runner, with his barefooted ass, was making two ski tracks straight down the middle of the turnrow. To stay on my feet, I walked in his tracks the way trucks follow trucks down a muddy road.

This time after the strip search, I made it back to the tank. Once inside the building, we tried to crowd through the tank door at the same time. The two on-duty building tenders yelled, "You nigguhs throw dem muddy clothes on dese sheets," which they had spread on the floor in the front of the tank. "Don't y'all be slangin dat fuckin mud all over dis gotdam flo!"

Freezing my balls off, all I wanted was to get to the shower. I had so much mud clogged between my toes, my feet looked like I was wearing a pair of grayish black flippers. So far, coming in the building first was the only good thing about being in the Number 1 hoe squad. After the shower I hurried to my bunk and put on the dry clothes the building tenders had placed on it. Picking up and delivering the field workers' clothes from the laundry was one of their main duties.

The hard walking and shoveling had my body aching all over. My palms and feet had blisters stacked on top of blisters. After I ate lunch, it was back to my bunk. For the first time since I arrived yesterday morning, I saw the full deck, all eighty-five of us together. I recognized the ten Number 1 hoe squad members in the tank, but saw no other familiar faces.

The tank was beginning to sound like the Cotton Club in Longview on Saturday night. Cons were laughing, bullshitting, grab-assing, and acting like they were having the time of their lives. None of them even looked tired, and I was near exhaustion. Hanging on the cuffs all night took it out of me. I heard some guys bragging about who was the fastest worker and who had the toughest bosses. The field work and the bosses were the general topics of most conversations.

The tank activities got into full swing. Several radios, each on a different station, were blaring. Some men were setting up cigarette-rolling operations, some were getting out their cards and dominoes. Dice shooting wasn't allowed because "nigguhs git too loud shootin dice." A few cons were diligently striking and blowing out wooden matches to glue together to make lamps and jewelry chests, leaving the air with a heavy smell of phosphor.

Everybody seemed to have an outlet. Some were reading the Bible, others wrote letters. The guy in the bunk across from mine was using a tin snuff can with holes punched in the top to scrape and sand the calluses on his feet. Three separate quartets were singing in the back near the commodes. Somebody was sitting on the ledge above the commodes beating "bongos" (tin buckets).

Two or three card games were in progress on the back bottom bunks, out of the sight of the inside picket boss. They played for cigarettes and Bugler tobacco in lieu of money. I sure wanted to get in a game, but I had no cigarettes with which to gamble.

I got in the shave line at the front of the tank. Ol Crip, the barber, was built like a question mark with a hump on his back. One leg was shorter than the other, causing him to limp and walk like the Hunchback of Notre Dame. He shaved cons and squabbled incessantly when too many got on the waiting bench. He acted irritated with each "customer" who sat down in the barber chair, and swished his razor like Zorro. When a freshly shaved con got up out of that chair, he was both bloody and lucky. Nobody dared squawk with Crip while he held a razor so close.

My turn came. Reluctantly, I eased into the chair and lay motionless when he let it back, and said not a mumbling word while he ripped his dull razor across my face. After that, I knew I had to make preparations to get my own shaving gear but quick! I went to the back of the tank and splashed some water on my face, looked in the stainless-steel "mirror," and couldn't see shit. But I didn't need one to know that I, too, displayed Crip's battle scars.

All of our heads were clean as cue balls. I had been scalped right before I left the "Walls Unit" in Huntsville and sure hated to think of Crip with those Triple O clippers on my head. Those hickeys and scars on the bald heads in the tank were reminders of his heavy hand.

Besides a razor, I needed a toothbrush and a box of soda. Hoboing around, I'd learned to make it with the bare basics. I knew the only way I was going to scuffle up on some cigarettes to buy my toiletries was to get in a card game, somehow. I knew how to "deal" cards almost as well as I could roll the dice. I sat down on one of the back bunks to watch the game and was sitting there about an hour when one of the building tenders called out, "Ol Kotch Tom, c'mon up to the front!"

He looked around at me and said, "Hey, man, stop my hand for me till I come back." He was gone about half an hour. When he returned he commented, "The bosses didn't want nothin, jes fuckin wit me."

I had won eighteen packs of cigarettes in his absence, and he gave me half. That was my start. When the game broke up about fifteen minutes before the chow bell rang, I was a winner again with twelve "decks uv squares" (packs of cigarettes), three packs of Bugler, and five sacks of Bull Durham. When I got off the con's bunk that I'd been gambling on, I felt obliged to give him a couple of packs for "wear and tear." At least I established one thing, I knew how to play cards. Word circulated in the tank, "That lil nigguh kin play."

After returning from supper, I got in the commissary line when the picket boss called it out. Even though I had no "cho-cho book" (scrip coupon book used in place of cash with denominations of one, five, ten, twenty-five, and fifty cents issued to those cons whose relatives sent money for them to the Inmate Trust Fund), I was in a position to barter at the commissary. I swapped one pack for a toothbrush, two for a razor and blades, and three for a lock for my locker.

When I got back to the tank, I asked Kotch Tom how I could scrounge a box of baking soda. He told me, "See Big Filet Mignon when he comes in frum the kitchen." With a name like that, it wasn't hard to spot him. I put in my order and paid him a pack.

Some cons were playing dominoes at the table up front. I walked over and was standing there watching when Kotch Tom came and stood beside me. He asked if I wanted to take the next down. I nodded. We waited for our turn since we were the next partners to play, and held our down until it was almost bedtime. The game had provided me the opportunity to get to meet some of the tank residents and establish another thing: I was a damn good domino player too.

The call went out, "Y'all git on 'em. Count time." I got on my bunk and awaited my first bunk count time on "the burnin hell." The lieutenant rushed into the tank counting two rows at a time as he walked briskly down one alleyway and up another. Big George, the other daytime building tender, was supposedly counting right behind him. After they made the final turn in the last row of bunks, Big George had a confused look on his face.

When they reached the front of the tank, the lieutenant hollered up to the inside picket boss, "Eighty-four uv 'em, boss." The boss acknowledged that he was right, and added that one was in the hospital. Big George looked relieved. The lieutenant entered Number 4 tank, repeating the process, and across the hall into Number 1 and 2 tanks.

Then he went upstairs. Number 5 tank upstairs (east side) housed the trusties—cons with "jobs" who worked without supervision. The auditorium (west side) bunked fifteen white cons kept segregated from us. The prison system hid them at this all-black unit for protection. Most were ex-policemen who would have been killed if sent to one of the units housing the white cons, but they were safe here.

We remained quiet and on our bunks until the head count was over. "Count's clear!" came the shout after the lieutenant, inside picket boss, and turnkey completed their calculations. All 415 of us, the figure I'd seen on the count board located on the wall at the bottom of the stairs, were accounted for.

The switch was thrown to dim the lights in the tanks to about a twenty-watt bulb's worth. Activities were at a standstill and we settled in for the night. It was hard to fall asleep and I had to piss anyway. "Alley, boss," I hollered. Several seconds later I got his okay. I walked about midway down the alley and heard a catcall whistle. I turned my head and looked straight into the eyes of the whistler. "Whut you got on yo mind, man?" I asked him.

He grinned and asked belligerently, "Whut diffunce do it make?"

Forty, the "night alley" (night building tender), was in back cleaning up and overheard our conversation. He yelled up the alley, "Y'all betta git down on dat bullshit. An Ol Rag, you betta take yo ass to sleep an let dat new nigguh 'lone."

I continued on my way toward the back. Rag whistled again. I didn't stop. I knew my future in the tank was on the line. I walked over to the row of commodes and picked up half of one of the broken wooden seat lids. I concealed it beside my leg and walked back up the aisle. When I was even with his bunk, I smashed him on the head with the edged side.

He hollered like a stuck pig—couldn't whistle anymore—and struggled to get out of my reach. I hit him with the flat side right above his ear. That lick sounded like somebody fired a .22 pistol in the tank. He fled down the alley to the back with me in hot pursuit.

Forty rushed up to us and blocked my pathway. "Say, man," he said without malice, "don't hit 'em no mo. Lemme hannel it."

I stopped. Forty went over to Rag and looked at his head. Then he hollered up to the picket boss, "Got one comin out, boss. Needs to go up to the hosspital an see Doc Cateye." He followed Rag to the front of the tank.

When they got to the door, the boss looked down from his lofty perch. "Goddamn, Ol Forty, whut happened to that ol nigguh?"

"Wudn't nothin, boss. He jes had a nightmare an fell off his bunk."

Seeing all the blood on Rag's head, the boss, apparently an old-timer on the job, quipped, "I thought that nigguh slept on one uv them bottom bunks."

"Yes suh, boss, he do."

"He must'a dreamt he fell off a fuckin skyscrapah," the boss joked as Rag made his way upstairs to the hospital.

The following morning the sleet was still coming down, and we didn't turn out. As soon as we returned from breakfast, the card and domino games got started. Kotch Tom was busy setting up a card game on one of the back bunks. While I sat on my bunk trying to catch a name here and there, the tank door opened to let Big Filet Mignon back in after his breakfast shift. A little later he walked over and handed me the box of soda. I went to the back and brushed my teeth, then got my cigarettes out and got in one of the card games.

It amazed me that so many cons in the game knew little or nothing about gambling and were just killing time. With that advantage it was easy to get away with cheating, so occasionally I stole a card or two. I was deeply involved in the game when Big George yelled out, "All you ol thangs, come on up heah to da front an unlock dese lockers. Git ready for shakedown!"

There was a mad scramble to the front of the tank and the sound of unlocking locks could be heard throughout. I asked somebody, "How long do it take?"

"Long as dey wants it ta take," he answered, adding, "It give da bosses sump'n ta do when we lays in."

Big George did a follow-up. "Don't y'all take nothin outta dis tank to dat mess hall, 'ceptin yo ass, da clothes on yo back, an yo brogues."

As we filed out of the tank, I saw that "everybody" was there. All the field bosses, the captain, lieutenant, and dog sergeant were standing underneath the picket waiting for us to empty out. The captain split the bosses up into two groups. One group took the west-side tanks and the other took the east side. The captain and lieutenant went upstairs to "check out" the auditorium, where the white cons lived, and the dog sergeant took the trusty tank.

The three-hundred-plus of us lower-tank inhabitants filed into the mess hall and took our seats at the tables. All the cons were there, except the trusties still out working and the whites. We sat quietly as the banging of the lockers and bosses' voices filled the mess hall like hollow sounds coming from an empty barn. The bosses carried on a lot of bullshit with one another and seemed to enjoy ransacking the tanks.

Two bosses remained in the mess hall with us, walking up and down the small aisles that separated the tables. Watching. Every so often, a con was called out and wouldn't return. Instead, he stood underneath the inside picket until the shakedown was completed. After a good three hours, the order came from the captain for us to reenter the tanks. By this time, at least twenty cons were standing under the picket.

We stripped in the mess hall and slowly filed into the area underneath the picket, where the bosses waited to squeeze-search our shirts and pants and inspect our brogans before we went back into the tanks. After the clothes search, it was the "bend over and spread yore cheeks" part. Some of the comments those bosses made were rib splitters, and I could hardly keep from laughing as I waited my turn. "Hey, boss, take a look at this un. This ol nigguh's asshole looks lak a burnt-out stump."

Another said, "Looks lak this heah nigguh had a complete overhaul, cuz all his bushins, rangs, an inserts is a-missin. Big as this nigguh's asshole is, I betcha he couldn't shit in a number three washtub."

My turn came. "Well, looka heah, heah's one'a them white nigguhs!" one said, looking at one of the older bosses. "Boss Harper, is this heah one'a them nigguh babies uv yourn?" He kept on, "Say, has Boss Harper ever told y'all bout how many nigguh gals he's dun screwed? An how many uv 'em he knocked up?"

Another said, "As a matter uv fact, if I recollect it wuz fifteen uv 'em." They were all laughing and teasing him so much that little attention was given to me as I bent over.

We filed past the two cardboard boxes filled with contraband sitting under the inside picket. While we were busy dressing in the tanks, the warden, Big Devil as he was called by the cons, held court in the hallway. He made each con reach into the boxes of confiscated items and pick out what belonged to him. Sometimes it was crude-looking knives made out of spoons and forks, clubs, chains, lengths of iron pipe, hand-drawn fuck books, or a scrapbook of female mannequins from mail-order catalogs.

Each was sentenced according to the importance Big Devil placed on the contraband item. Those with the weapons got the lighter punishment and were made to stand on the soda water boxes (wooden cases) for several hours. Those with the forbidden jack-off materials were sentenced to hang on the cuffs all night long.

Kotch Tom was one of those who got the cuffs. They found a photograph of a white woman in his locker. I later learned that it was a picture of his wife, and that he was doing a life sentence for killing a white bus driver in Houston. The way I heard it was he had boarded a bus in Fifth Ward, a predominately black ghetto, with his German wife, whom he met and married while in the Army overseas. The bus driver allegedly stopped the bus and demanded that he not sit in the seat next to the white woman. When Kotch Tom told him she was his wife, the bus driver slapped him. Kotch Tom pulled out a pocketknife and stabbed him to death.

As count time neared, Crip and Big George gathered up their mops, brooms, and buckets from the back, signaling that it was time to get on our bunks so they could clean up. They had soapsuds a foot deep all over the tank floor. One was spreading it with a mop while the other was following behind scrubbing with a scrub broom. In twenty minutes they had water-hosed the entire brick floor and herded all the suds down a six-inch drain in the center.

Each time the inside picket boss who the cons nicknamed

Wise-Em-Up paused to look down into the tanks, he'd holler, "You ol wild-assed nigguhs betta git down on it! Some'a you ol sorry-assed thangs gonna hafta talk ta that warden in the mornin." He did that periodically with each tank, whether it was quiet or not. Two or three cons were in the back using the commodes. "Awright, some'a you ol wild-assed nigguhs keep on millin roun back thar an yore gonna hafta talk ta that warden in the mornin."

After count time I tried to go to sleep. I would soon discover that at any given time during any given hour on any given night, I could turn over in my bunk, open my eyes, look around, and see some other con with his eyes open too. Sleep was hard to come by until I got accustomed to the night life in the tank. Eighty-five men compacted together for every offense conceivable, including murder; so there were many troubled consciences. Cons having nightmares, screaming out, crying, and moaning all through the night made sound sleep practically impossible.

I finally dozed off, only to be awakened by a bone-chilling scream. Earlier that day I had overheard Big George and one of the new cons who rode down on Black Betty with me having some words. I heard the new con tell him, "I don't play that shit."

Big George walked up on him while he was sitting on one of the commodes and hit him across the back with the piece of chain he wore on his belt. After the scream Big George shouted, "Git yo gotdam ass up under one'a dem bunks befo I kill you!"

Hearing the commotion, Boss Wise-Em-Up hollered down his customary threat. Big George yelled up to him, "Brangin one out, boss. I got one'a dem smart-ass nigguhs in heah."

Wise-Em-Up let the victim out of the tank and made him sit in the hall under the picket for the rest of the night. His groaning joined with that of the others who were being punished out in the hallway.

Shortly after wake-up time the doors under the picket, which led from the guards' barbershop, were opened by the turnkey. The captain came through and walked over to the new con, who stood up and showed the chain marks on his back. The inside picket shifts had changed. Boss "Humpy" was on duty. He told Cap'n Smooth that he had been told this con created a disturbance on the tank and Big George had to put him out. Since it involved a building tender, no questions were asked.

Cap'n Smooth told the turnkey to get a soda water box and place it upright on the floor, then ordered the new con to get up on it. After a couple of tries and falling off, the captain told him he'd put him in the pisser if he didn't get his "goat-smellin ass up on that soda water box an stay thar." Finally, the con was able to maintain his balance on the upright box and began serving out his official punishment. Those hanging on the cuffs were let go so they could eat and catch out.

I thought to hell with the new con, that was his problem. But I had already made up my mind about Big George. If he ever fucked with me, I was going to kill him. I didn't know how since I hadn't procured a weapon yet; but if he ever crossed the line, he was one bastard I would kill in a heartbeat. Building tenders had the power to whup you if you let them, kill you if you let them, or snitch on you and get you killed for another con.

Each passing month I was doing better and better keeping up with Road Runner on the turnrow and learning how to "wek." When we weren't cutting down trees, underbrushing in the woods, and grubbing stumps, we were on the yard using wedges to bust logs for the furnaces. Then to the muddy garden, crawling on our knees picking the half-frozen spinach. Road Runner could crawl damn near as fast as he could walk. His knees must have been made out of stone because he never complained like the rest of us.

When it was too wet and cold for these jobs, we got our "aggies" (hoes) and headed for Oyster Creek, which ran right through the middle of Retrieve, to flatweed along the creek banks. There was always some con in the squad who got out into the cold water to hoe all the weeds. Seeing this, Boss Deadeye would start riding his horse all along the bank, crowding us up to make sure that we got knee-deep out into the frigid water, hollering, "You maw-dickers git yore asses off in that crik lak that nigguh's doin!"

As soon as we finished the Oyster Creek banks, it was on to the shit ditches and all the shit they caused. It usually took a week to clean the two sewer ditches that snaked their way from one side of the prison unit to the other. Squads worked on both sides of a ditch, hoeing everything on the way down to the middle of the shit stream, and pulled the muddy grass and weeds back up the slope to spread it out on the turnrow to dry.

It never failed. When two squads met in the bottom of the ditch face-to-face and started splashing shit on each other, the battle began. After the fighting, everybody left the ditch covered. We'd get back in line beside one another and stink it through the day. The bosses drove and pushed us relentlessly to get finished. They hated to ride behind us. "Y'all's goat-smellin asses is stagnatin these hosses." True or not, the horses were their unruliest when we worked the shit ditches; but so were we.

After a day of battling in the shit ditches, I was so tired I could hardly keep my eyes open. I waited until some of the traffic cleared in the back so I could get to a sink and wash the shit off my brogans. Count time over, I was trying to doze off when I saw a head bob up at the end of a con's bunk. The next minute I looked, he was way over at the other end of the tank. Then he darted closer to my bunk. I asked Beer Belly in the bunk across from me, "Who is that muthafucka?"

"Das Ol Toe Sucker, man. He loves to suck toes." I immediately turned my feet up under my ass. "He ain't got no teefs in front. Some nigguh in heah dun kicked 'em out. Waked up wit dat muthafucka slurpin on his damn toe."

Even as grueling as the work was in the squad, I'd rather do it than work in the kitchen. They worked seven days a week, rain or shine. The kitchen flunkies were the first ones out in the mornings and the last ones to get back in the tanks at night. Between meals, they hosed down and scrubbed the mess hall.

News quickly circulated in the tank one Sunday afternoon that

Big Filet Mignon got busted. He could slip those pork chop and steak sandwiches off the guards' stove and out of the kitchen right under the guard's nose. He wrapped them in some dishrags and tied the bundle to his nutsack. No guard was going to feel underneath there when frisking the flunkies and cooks.

It happened right before the evening meal. We were having baked ham for supper, but the meal was held up because one of the hams was missing. Big Filet Mignon had swiped one from the oven, took it back to the vegetable room, and hid it in one of the vegetable bins to let it cool.

When it cooled to his liking, he deboned it, propped it up on a table, and made love to it—pineapple rings and all! He got carried away and began calling it affectionate names out loud, "Oh! Bessie May, you sweet thang. Oh! Bessie May, tell me it's good to you. Oh, baby-eeeee!"

The mess steward (Cap'n "Foots") and some of the kitchen crew heard him and went to investigate. They said Cap'n Foots walked right up behind him while he was "humpin dat ham."

Cap'n Foots brought him out of the kitchen and stood him under the inside picket to await Big Devil's arrival for sentencing. After word filtered through the tanks why he was busted, we threw cups of hot water and even our brogans through the bars at him. Everybody was furious with him for making us potential secondhand dicksuckers.

The inside picket boss hollered for the captain. "Cap'n, Cap'n, you betta come move this rotten bastard away frum under this picket afore some uv these ol nigguhs knock hell outta him."

When Big Devil arrived, he and Cap'n Foots took Big Filet Mignon back through the kitchen, headed for the pisser. Big Devil cursed him every step of the way. "Why you goddamn low-down sonuvabitch! I'll bet you been a-fuckin that meat ever since you been heah! Ain'tcha?"

"Naw suh, Warden. I swears thas the first time I ever dun it."

"Shet yore goddamn lyin mouth, you rotten bastard!" *Smack!*

Big Filet Mignon stayed in solitary overnight and was shipped away on Black Betty the very next day. Nobody touched the ham that evening. He taught us a lesson—don't eat the fuckin ham.

10

Ol Doc Cateye, serving 460 years, had been running the hospital "forever." However, recently he had inherited a medical officer who was hired on with the rank of lieutenant to take over the helm. Lieutenant Maulden had spent a few years in the Navy and supposedly worked in the ship's sick bay. His experience and training must have been superb, since he acted well prepared for the tremendous responsibility now resting upon his narrow shoulders.

The hospital upstairs at the rear of the trusty tank consisted of four bunks, which were rarely occupied. It required near death to lie on one of those bunks. Besides Doc Cateye, Lieutenant Maulden would also supervise the convict dentist, Ol Nolan. Now that he commanded his own hospital and medical staff, the lieutenant was finally in the upper echelons of medical practitioners.

Lieutenant Maulden stood about five-foot-six, was forty-plus years old, had a fat beer belly, and wore his britches anchored down off the low part of his hips. There was so much slack in the seat that his pockets waved when he walked. When he listened to a con's ailment, he was very cautious not to stand too close. He'd stare at the con through the bars in a trancelike state while smoking his pipe. Every so often, he'd kick out a puff of smoke and nod his head. When the con finished, the lieutenant would give his diagnosis in long, rambling medical terminology.

Regardless of the illness, the medication was always the same. If the problem was from the waist upward, Maulden prescribed aspirins. If it was from the waist down, he prescribed Doc Cateye's "jet juice" (a special concoction of castor oil, mineral oil, Epsom salt, a little sugar, a little dab of quinine, and either grape or strawberry food coloring).

Doc Cateye had convinced Lieutenant Maulden, the warden, and half the convict population that his nostrum really worked and could cure everything from the flu to epilepsy. After drinking a cupful, the con spent the rest of that day or night on the commode. We all knew not to drink it when going to the field because there was no way the bosses would let anybody stop working ten times a day to "git on the job."

Every night after we finished supper, the medical duet appeared at the tank doors and hollered out, "Medicine line!" It sounded like they were racing to see who could say it first. Cateye carried the little medicine tray and kept it neatly arranged with cotton balls, a bottle of aspirins, a jar of Mentholatum, and a bottle of Mercurochrome. He also had Whitfield's ointment, which cons put on the calluses of their feet. They had to be careful because that ointment burned like acid.

Lieutenant Maulden watched over Doc Cateye like a resident physician as Cateye issued the medication through the bars. And did Cateye ever resent his new intern status! After all, he'd only been the "Doc" for a measly twenty-one years before he became the lieutenant's assistant.

Occasionally when Cateye would be busily waiting on two or three patients at the same time, the lieutenant shook out a couple of aspirins or whatever and handed them out. He certainly didn't want any of us to think he minded touching fingers with a black con as he handed out the medication. To him "a patient is a patient, regardless of race, creed, color, religion, or national origin."

Only thing contradictory to his equality stand was the way he treated the fifteen white "hideaway" cons. They went directly to the hospital to receive their medication instead of having it poked through the bars to them. And they didn't need a 102-degree temperature to get a lay-in either. All they had to do was say they were sick; their word was good enough for him.

The black cons didn't want the lieutenant handing them medication from Doc Cateye's little tray anymore, anyhow. He had scared most of them away. Unwittingly, he almost single-handedly broke up all the homosexual activities on the entire camp. Hospital business suddenly picked up, but even then, Doc Cateye came up with the prognosis for the epidemic.

The breakout occurred because of Maulden's inability to differentiate the Whitfield's ointment from the petroleum jelly. Granted, they are both alike in clearness, but they certainly smell different. Of course, Lieutenant Maulden wouldn't smell the jars because doing so might make it appear that he didn't know his medicine. Except for smelling, it's difficult to tell them apart, especially for the trained, infallible medical eye of Maulden.

He inadvertently gave some cons the Whitfield's ointment instead of the requested petroleum jelly. Needless to say, all the cons in the tank and the inside picket boss knew for certain some screwing was going on in Number 3 tank that night. One of the Whitfield's ointment recipients, Ol Mus Havit, had gotten with his partner and paired off under a bunk. That ointment got hot, and all of a sudden a loud howl was heard, "Whew! Say, man, git up offa me! My ass is on fire! Oh! Gotdam!"

They came out from underneath the bunk like two mad bulls. The culprits were put out of the tank by the building tenders, and the inside picket boss made them sit under the picket all night without allowing either to wash it off. I bet they would have been glad to sit in something wet and cool, even the stinking shit ditches.

With two bars on his shirt collar now, Captain Maulden ventured downstairs to the tanks without Doc Cateye at his side. He must have thought there was a need for him to come down alone every so often to establish that he was the man with the fuzzy balls and not Doc Cateye. He wanted the cons to get used to the idea that everything having to do with medication, lay-ins, or the hospital in general had to be coordinated through him and him alone.

It seemed the classification committee made another terrible miscalculation when they sent a "gnat liver" (young) first offender to serve his measly two-year sentence at the burnin hell. There weren't many young cons on our camp, and even fewer serving under ten years unless they had screwed up on one of the other camps. If that was the case, they were reassigned to Retrieve to help rid them of whatever "adjustment problems" they were experiencing. However, they were already pretty tough cookies by the time they got here.

Yet, here the new con stood pitifully, like the Pope in the middle of hell. When Black Betty dropped him off at the back gate, the boss brought him in the building and stood him underneath the picket to await his tank assignment. The "goon squad" (building tenders) crowded up to the bars and hung on them like apes, shouting obscenities at the "new one." They acted like a bunch of dogs over a bitch in heat. Their clamoring worsened when Cap'n Smooth showed up.

One started begging, "Please, Cap'n, put 'em on my tank. If y'all put 'em in heah wit me, I swear I'll pick a bale a day."

Then another, "Cap'n, you knows I been heah a long time, pleeze, Cap'n, have mercy. Pleeze, lemme have 'em."

Still another, "Cap'n, if y'all put 'em in heah, y'all sho won't have no troubles wit dat nigguh. I keep it so slick twixt his legs he won't be able ta walk for runnin," he remarked blatantly.

"You nigguhs dry up them ol mouths an git back away frum them bars! You sonsabitches act lak you ain't never had no boar pussy befo. Hell, this heah ain't the first little ol mare nigguh y'all dun seed." He continued, "I ain't gonna tell you sonsabitches no more ta git down on that ol head runnin!"

After they quieted down, Cap'n Smooth asked the new con, "Nigguh, if I wuz to letcha choose the tank you want frum one to four, which'un you'd choose?"

Mumbling, "It don't make no difference."

Sarcastically, "You mean it don't matter who fucks you in yore ass?"

In a voice reeked with fear, "Captain, sir, I ain't no punk, sir. I jes wanna do my time an git away frum heah." This was a whole lot easier said than done.

"Hey, y'all hear that? This nigguh claims he ain't no gal-boy. Whutta you thank about that, Ol Trigger Bill? You bleeve this little ol nigguh's tellin me the truth?"

Trigger Bill was the building tender on Number 2 tank begging to have the new con put in with him. After being singled out, he looked down and started shuffling his feet and grinning like a mule eating briars. "I don't know, Cap'n, suh," he said sheepishly, "jes whutevah y'all say."

"Tell you whut I'm gonna do. Since you ain't no bigger'n a piss ant an wouldn't last long as a fart in a windstorm in that field, I'm gonna put yore scrawny little ass in the kitchen. Now, I hafta pick a tank fer you since I can't gitcha to do it." Turning to the bar apes, he said, "I'll put this little ol nigguh on the nigguh's tank whut comes up wit the best name fer 'em."

The vultures began hollering out name after name. "Betty Grable, name 'em Betty Grable, Cap'n." That got a sharp stare from Cap'n Smooth.

"Name 'em Sweet Meat, Cap'n," another shouted.

"Cap'n, bein dat y'all dun put 'em in da kitchen, name 'em Ol Dumplin," Bull rendered.

Cap'n Smooth liked that name, so Ol Dumplin it was. The picket boss threw the lever and the door opened. Clutching onto his few personal belongings tightly, Dumplin noticeably flinched when the big steel door slammed shut behind him.

Bull, nicknamed for his brawny wide chest and beefy arms, was an imposing figure as he stood waiting. The two daggers and trace chain hanging from his homemade belt were a daunting sight. No sooner had the door closed than Bull made his move. "You kin put yo stuff in my locker so nobody won't steal it. An you kin use anythang in it. I'm gon hep you till you git settled in."

Next, Bull got permission from the picket boss to go to the laundry to get some sheets for the new con. All a building tender had to do to get out of the tank was ask. They received preferential treatment and were privileged to possess overt weapons. They were the policemen of the tanks. Under the guise of enforcing the "rules," their brutal behavior was tolerated by the prison hierarchy, from the warden on down to the lowly bosses. Their gang rapes, beatings, and harassment of weaker cons were ignored and their versions of what happened in the tanks were readily accepted.

Bull used his power position, promised to pay cigarettes or whatever, and soon returned from the laundry with a mattress cover, pillowcase, and *two* neatly starched and pressed sheets. Unlike the rest of us, Dumplin would be sleeping on a sheet instead of the stiff ducking mattress cover.

"I'm gon look out for you," Bull said as he slow-eyed Dumplin's physique. "If any uv dese nigguhs fuck witcha, jes lemme know." Lavishing his concerns, he went on, "Betta put yo brogues on cuz dey's gon call you in a few minutes so you kin go ta wek in dat kitchen."

Just like he suggested, Dumplin sat on Bull's bunk and changed from his free-world shoes to his brogans. He followed Bull's lead like a lamb being led to the slaughter. Bull was a pro when it came to conning new cons.

It wasn't long before the call came from Cap'n Foots, "Boss, lemme have that new nigguh outta thar."

The boss opened the door. "Ol Bull, gimme that new nigguh. That Cap'n wants 'em in the kitchen."

When Dumplin stepped out, Bull stepped out behind him and hollered up to the picket boss, "Comin out wit 'em, boss. I needs ta see da cap'n."

He said this to back up what he'd been shooting Dumplin about being heavy with Foots and talking to him on his behalf. Cap'n Foots sent the new con on to the kitchen before asking Bull what he wanted. Bull knew that was the way it would go down and had timed it perfectly. Dumplin was gone now and wouldn't hear him tell Cap'n Foots, "Cap'n, suh, we's outta toilet paper."

As soon as Dumplin finished his shift in the kitchen and came back in the tank, Bull met him at the door and led him to his bunk in the back. Bull sat down beside him and began making his demands for payback. Dumplin responded, "Man, I thought me an you wuz awright, that you wuz my friend. I ain't doin but two years an I don't wanna git involved in no stuff lak that."

Bull got more aggressive, "Muthafucka, you dun smoked up my tight rolls, et up my stuff, used my fuckin locker, an I'm even out dere gittin down to da man for yo ass. Whut you mean you ain't gon do nothin? Nigguh, jes for dat, you gon suck my dick!"

With no forewarning Bull punched him in the eye, knocking him clear over to the next row of bunks. Before Dumplin could get up, Bull's brogan caught him in the short ribs, preventing any outcry. Bull fiercely stomped him while Big George blocked the alleyway so the picket boss couldn't see. They didn't want to involve him as a witness. That way if any inquiry was made, it was their word against Dumplin's.

After Bull tired of his kicking assault, he got some water from the basin, dashed it on Dumplin's face, and jerked him up by his shirt collar. "Nigguh, you gon suck my dick!" he bellowed while pulling out his prick and forcing it into Dumplin's bloody mouth.

Nearly every night after Dumplin pulled his shift, Bull lay on his bunk in the back and forced the young con to play with his pecker until he raised a hard. Then he'd make Dumplin suck him off while anybody in the tank who wanted to looked on. Bull mistreated him until it was hard to stomach, but it wasn't my fight. This wasn't a place to lend a helping hand and say, "Man, don't do him like that."

After work one night, Dumplin came back to the tank and took his shower as Bull waited for him. He went up front and put his toilet articles into his locker, obediently returning to Bull's bunk to begin the nightly ritual.

The same scene had been played with such sickening regularity that most of the cons now paid little or no attention to it. He played with Bull's pecker until it got good and hard. All of a sudden, Bull let out a bloodcurdling yell. His long black peter was lying on the floor in the alleyway, and looked like it was breathing. Dumplin had cut it off with a razor blade.

Bull went running up the alleyway toward the front of the tank, hollering every step of the way. He climbed up on the bars to get the attention of the picket boss, who was pacing around in the picket, cracking and eating pecans. "Boss, boss! Hep me! Dat nigguh dun cut my dick off!"

Boss Humpy angrily yelled back, "Nigguh, gitcha goddamn ass down offa them bars an quit a-skeetin 'at blood in heah all over this fuckin flo!"

"Boss! Lookit whut dat crazy nigguh dun ta me!"

"Hell, nigguh, I don't wanna look at it. Now, I dun tole you to gitcha goddamn ass down frum heah! I don't give a damn if he chopped yore nuts off! Aim that goddamn thang the other way!" Trying to coax him down, he went on, "If ya git down frum thar, I'll call fer Cap'n Maulden."

After Bull descended, Boss Humpy hollered across to the hospital, "Cap'n Maulden, you an Ol Cateye betta come on down heah. I got a ol nigguh wit his dick cut off. Cap'n, kin y'all hurry? This sonuvabitch is a-bleedin all over everthang."

Ol Bull damn near bled to death before they arrived and took him upstairs. He left a trail of blood behind as they went. A trail the turnkey hurried to erase with his mop. From the hospital we heard Bull's hollering. "Lawd! Ham mercy, Jesus! Oh Lawd! Oooh! Jesus! Jesus! Jesus! *Oooh! Jesus!*"

Forty was on the back bunk playing cards and deadpanned, "Dat nigguh didn't know shit bout Jesus till he lost his dick." The other players cracked up.

It took a while for the "healers" to get him quiet. An hour had passed before Captain Maulden and Doc Cateye reappeared at the tank door. Proudly displaying his bloodstained doctor's smock, Captain Maulden called out, "Ol Forty, will you come on up here to the front? I need to talk with you a minute."

Forty was the only building tender on the east-side tanks who treated everybody pretty decently. He didn't participate in the gang beatings and wasn't viewed by the cons as a bona fide member of the goon squad. He got punished many times because the other goons badmouthed him to the warden. About all he liked to do was gamble. So when Captain Maulden called him to the front, he interrupted Forty's card playing.

"Yassuh, Cap'n?" Forty answered with a frown on his face.

"Ol Forty, I suppose you know what happened a while ago to Ol Bull."

"Yassuh."

After shooting up a puff of smoke from his pipe, "Well, what I need to ask you is this, ahem," he said, clearing his throat. "You wouldn't happen to know if Ol Bull's penis is still layin roun back there, wouldja?"

"His whut, Cap'n?" Forty responded, glancing at Doc Cateye.

"Reason I'm askin is I, we, might be able to save it for that ol boy."

"Yassuh, I reckon it's still back dere somewhere, Cap'n. Ain't nobody moved it as I knows uv."

True. We were just stepping over and around the nasty-looking thing and laughing, especially after Beer Belly said, "Dat muthafucka look lak a dyin fish gulpin for air."

"Well, I tell you what I want you to do. Go on back there and get it and bring it up here so me and Cateye can have a look at it. We just might be able to save it, but we gotta work fast. I'd hate to see that ol boy go through the resta his life without a stick to fight with."

"Cap'n, suh, I ain't tryin ta be smart witcha or nothin, but, Cap'n, suh, I been in heah over sixteen calendars an ain't nobody never sent me ta go fetch another nigguh's dick."

Doc Cateye toyed nervously with his stethoscope as he watched the captain continue to hog the spotlight. "Now, Ol Forty," Captain Maulden continued, "I admit this might be a bit unusual, but it ain't every day that some nig—"—pause—"poor fellow goes and gits his lifeline whacked off. How'd you feel if it was yours laying back there? Just think about it, Ol Forty. Let's work together on this thing. Now, go on back there and git it so we can have a look. Don't force me to pull rank on you," he urged.

"Yassuh," Forty yielded.

Forty was cussing under his breath as he sullenly walked down the aisle. "Gotdam muthafucka wants me ta go git a nigguh's dick. Shit, I sho be glad when I git the fuck outta dis muthafucka." He went to the back where the mops and brooms were kept. He got a broom and began sweeping the severed sex organ up the alley. More than once it rolled underneath a bunk, and he had to get down on his knees to reach it with the broom. He was having hell keeping Bull's lollipop rolling in the right direction.

After a lengthy ordeal, he rolled Bull's gritty prick up to the bars. While the healers bent down to scrutinize the seven- or eight-inch piece of meat, Forty leaned on his broom and looked off into the distance, totally unconcerned.

Captain Maulden broke the silence. "Roll it over for me, would you, Ol Forty?" Looking at his able-bodied assistant, he asked, "What do you think? Think we can make it work?"

Cateye, still making his own medical observation, said in his high-pitched southern drawl, "Well, Cap'n, I don't rightly know, might be worth a try."

"Goddamn, that ol boy sure was blessed! Here, Cateye, take a look at it through this magnifyin glass." When Cateye finished, Captain Maulden asked, "You wanna look at it, Ol Forty?" offering him the magnifying glass.

"No suh!" Forty quickly rejected.

"I'll bet he had a lot of fun with that thing."

"Yassuh, Cap'n," Forty agreed, "I 'magine he did. But it's sho over now."

After much deliberation, Captain Maulden said, "Tell you what, Cateye, why don'tcha run back upstairs and take another good look at the other end of this thing, and see what you think."

Cateye ran upstairs. Before long, he was skipping steps as he came back down quickly. "Cap'n, I don't thank whut you got in mind is gon wek atall."

"Why not? Why won't it work?"

Cateye went on, "Well, Cap'n, the other end uv Ol Bull's dick . . .

excuse me, Cap'n, penis, shrunk lak a vine afta we sewed it up. But this part heah is still so big an hard, I doubt if we kin match 'em back. 'Sides, it's too heavy."

Captain Maulden's face flushed and clearly registered disappointment. He wasn't going to get to practice his surgical skills on Ol Bull's pecker replant.

As the two stood up and shook their heads in dismay, Forty interrupted, "Er . . . pardon me, Cap'n, suh. Now dat y'all ain't gon use dis dead peter, whut y'all want me ta do wit it?"

"Well, tell you what, Ol Forty. Just take it on back there and get rid of the damn thing." Captain Maulden's last action before closing the matter was to snap his fingers in disgust and say, "Damn! It's a damn shame, that's what it is, a damn shame." As he turned and walked back up the stairs, he continued, "What a waste."

Forty began sweeping Bull's "remains" down the alleyway. When he reached his destination, he got the dustpan from behind the big green trash barrel and swept Ol Bull's once precious cargo onto it. Walking carefully so he wouldn't spill it, Forty dropped the contents into the commode, mashed his foot down on the lid, and *swoosh!* away it went, off to the shit ditches en route to Oyster Creek.

The next day Black Betty came, and a neutered Bull was transferred to the Walls to the "sho nuff" hospital. He didn't return after that. We heard a few years later he made parole. He certainly left prison with a lot less than he came in with.

As for Dumplin, Big Devil decided he should do his two-year sentence "flat." This meant instead of getting out in the normal fourteen months and twelve days, the equivalent of two years with good time, he would serve the full two calendar years. After the de-dickatashun, even though his mouth may still have been dirty, Dumplin could pull his shift in the kitchen, return to the tank, and get on his bunk without anybody bothering him. Not even a little bit! He had earned his right to sleep in hell.

*   *   *

After a few months, my body had toughened to the work. I could do the different jobs well enough to keep up, and the cons in the squad had accepted my presence. I was a bona fide hoe-carrying shit-ditch fighter. Boss Deadeye even let up a little. After I got cursed out about it, I learned not to look at him when he removed his patch to wipe the sweat away with his bandanna. He got madder than hell when any of us caught a glimpse of his "dead" eye.

When we cut trees in the bottoms that lay along the banks of the big Brazos River, we sounded like a bunch of woodpeckers. We dug the blades of our axes into the trunks of the huge sweet gum trees while the bosses sat lazily on their mounts. Both men and horses were half dozing in the warm, wintry sun creeping down through the dense, tall timbers. Their tranquil nodding allowed members of the tree-cutting foursomes to take turns standing behind the trees for a few minutes' rest while the other three cutters in their crews kept up the lick.

Those old bosses had been listening to the sound of those axes for so long, they could almost tell when all the axes weren't hitting. The horses were no dummies either. They knew how to get out of the way when one of those big trees was falling. Of course, sometimes we did get lucky when a horse and boss were napping so serenely neither reacted quickly enough to avoid getting brush-whipped by a falling tree everybody "forgot" to yell "*Tim-berrrr*" for.

Huge brush fires were burning all along the massive clearing we left behind. We continued plodding through the dense underbrush native to the Brazos River bottoms, felling tree after tree. After the ax teams cut down "enuff" trees and the brush pullers finished their tree-trimming work, the ax teams pulled back and began cutting the trees into sections for the sawmill. Whenever Big Louzanna got on a fallen tree, he took the "butt cut" (the largest part of the tree trunk). He and three other cutters perched themselves atop the thirty-footer and began chopping away at each section.

A couple of squads away, Lil Alfonso, a lifer, started up a river song, "Black Betty's in the bottoms, let yo hammer rang. Black Betty's in the bottoms, let yo hammer rang." Little by little we began to join in. Our ax licks harmonized more and more as we cut with a steady rhythm to the beat of the song. "Black Betty's in the bottoms, let yo hammer rang, let yo hammer, hammer rang. Great God Amighty! Let yo hammer rang. They ain't gon be no jackin [brushing chips out of the way before continuing to cut the tree down—used as a rest break] till we hear the butt cuts crackin."

By now, I knew the work songs and sang along with the two-hundred-con choir. We echoed back, "Let yo hammer, hammer rang, great God Amigh—ty! Let yo hammer rang."

"I wanna drank o' water."

"Let yo hammer, hammer rang."

"I want a drank o' water."

"Let yo ham-mer rang."

"I don't wanna drank it."

"Let yo ham-mer rang."

"I wanna spit it on my hammer, cuz my hammer's strikin fi-re!"

All of us sang and cut in a frenzy to keep up with the beat. Working much faster now, we had a steady flow of chips flying as we chiseled deeper and deeper into those about-to-become logs.

Over all the chopping and singing, Big Louzanna cut loose with "Roberta" and "Loucindy," slowing everything down. His *booming*, heavy baritone voice completely drowned Lil Alfonso's lead. By the time he let go with the second heavy moan, "Oh! Roberta! Roberta! won'tcha come by heah," the choir switched over and joined in with him. Humming and moaning the background, we slowed our axes to half the previous pace to keep beat with Big Louzanna's ax and began to "rock" in the bottoms.

"I got a woman in Georgia, an I got a woman in Alabam. Dey both jes as sweet as dey kin be. Sweet as dey kin be. But neither one uv 'em will ever see po me," he led.

"See po me, see po me."

"But dat woman in Alabam, hot ta mighty gotdam."

"Hot ta mighty gotdam, hot ta mighty gotdam. Sweet lak black-berry jam."

He sang the lead with such melancholy, it almost brought tears to my eyes. Then he'd go right into "Loucindy."

"Oooh! Loucindy! Loucindy! won'tcha come by heah. Oooh! Loucindy, won'tcha come by heah. An let me rock you mama whilst yo man ain't heah."

"Hot ta mighty God knows, hot ta mighty God knows."

"Now I ain't never been ta Houston, but I been tole. Never been ta Houston, but I been tole. . . . The women in dat Houston town got some sweet jelly roll."

"Sweet jelly roll! Dey got some sweet jelly roll!"

"Dey say dat when dey walks, dey reels an rocks behind! Now ain't that enuff ta worry a convict's mindddd."

"A convict's mind."

"Oh, Loucindy! won'tcha come by heah, an let me rock you, mama, whilst yo man ain't heah. It rangs lak silver an it shines lak gold."

"Rangs lak silver an it shines lak gold."

"But the price uv my hammer ain't never been tole."

"Ain't never been tole."

We all sang the last stanza together.

"So les raise 'em up together, an then drop 'em on downnnn! Dey can't tell the diffunce when the sun goes downnn! Dey can't tell the diffunce when the sun goes downn."

Singing very low now, we faded out.

"When the sun goes down. When the sun goes down. When the sun goes downnn."

Every ax was hitting in rhythm. Boss Deadeye sat on his horse, contented. "When them ol nigguhs is sangin, everthang's awright," he declared. I doubt, though, if he understood the song. Two hundred cons in those godforsaken woods, all hitting with Big Lou. With his shotgun laid across his arm, he listened as we sang and sang.

11

Spring had sprung. Oh, spring! And with it, Boss Deadeye's field of agitation bloomed. "You goddamn, shit-eatin sonsabitches! Move them goddamn rows on away frum heah! Goddamn rotten-assed bastards, wanna jes drag them ol asses roun. Don't wanna do no wek. But I tell you maw-dickers one damn thang, y'all goddamn sho won't eat no seppa tonight. Y'all goddamn sho gonna miss that ol hog an bread. Jes come on back heah ever goddamn one'a y'all, an ketch in on the end uv them rows an start 'em over again.

"Aw, I know you sonsabitches wanna go down through thar buck-jumpin an leavin half a them goddamn weeds! I spose you rotten bastards is leavin that fuckin grass fer me ta git! I wants four stalks to a hill [thinning the row—leaving four cotton stalks to a group a hoe blade apart]. An I wants ever fuckin blade uv grass out uv that man's cotton. Not some uv it, ever fuckin blade uv it!"

Then he singled out a slower worker. "Aw, I know you don't wanna do nothin 'sociated wit wek. You got yore fuckin mind on that ol nappy-head, snuff-drippin whore you lef out thar in that free world. Ain't no needa thankin bout her cuz some other mule-dickted nigguh's bogged up to his belly in her rat now. An she damn sho ain't thankin bout yore rotten black ass. Aw, I know you don't lak it bout some other nigguh fuckin yore ol whore. I might even drap by her house this Sadday night mysef."

On and on, "I know you wanna hit that goddamn Brazie. Well, I

tell you whut, why don'tcha hit it? I ain't lookin atcha. This ol raggedy
shotgun ain't even loaded. Hell, only reason I tote it is so I kin fan
away some'a these goddamn gnats. Go 'head!"

Knowing we were hot and thirsty, he'd say, "Water nigguh! Brang
me some water." We could hear the ice rattling in the gallon syrup
bucket each time Water Boy Brown hopped over the freshly chopped
cotton rows. After Boss Deadeye drank, rinsed his mouth, and spat
water on the ground, he dismounted and poured it down. The horse
pissed too.

He got the kerosene-soaked rag from his saddlebag and wiped
around the horse's eyes and underneath his belly to help keep away
the gnats, flies, and mosquitoes. After completing his pissing and
horse-wiping ritual, he got back in the saddle and picked up his
agitating rhetoric right where he left off. All day long, every day.

Spring was almost over and so was cotton-chopping time. Hal-
lelujah! The next phase in the work cycle was picking the white
gold. I kept hearing the cons in the tank talking about the hog law
so much until one night I asked Beer Belly, who was in Number 4
squad, what it meant. He was a talker, and began his explanation by
saying that Cap'n Smooth decided who made it through the back
gate every evening based on how much cotton each con picked that
day. The weights were recorded in the hog law book. If a con didn't
pick "enuff" he didn't eat. Besides missing the evening meal, he hung
on the cuffs or spent time in the pisser.

Beer Belly told me cons tried everything to beat the hog law
during cotton-picking season. "Dey piss on the ground, make big
mud balls an cover 'em wit cotton an throw 'em in dey sacks. One
time a nigguh weighed up Big Devil's dog in his sack," he recounted,
chuckling. "He let 'em out on the way to the dump sheets." He went
on to say Cap'n Smooth even based his decision to punish on the
condition of the cotton. If it was "dirty," it was the cuffs. A mud ball
brought an ass whipping and the pisser.

From what Beer Belly said, cotton was picked on an average in the
"bull" squads, Numbers 1, 2, and 3. "Ta keep frum gittin punished,

you hafta stay within fifty pounds uv whutever the highest weight in the squad wuz for dat day. Dey puts the high rollers in dem three squads. Dey even sews three extra foots onto dey cotton sacks so dey kin hole mo." I damn sure wasn't a "high roller" and began to worry about the hog law book.

"You know whut? We be sendin so much cotton to dat gin over at the Ramsey camp, dey runs outta storage space an dey sends word back by the truck drivers ta tell us ta hold up for a while. Thas when we git some rest. Sometimes we set rat down on our sacks in the middle uv the fields for nelly a hour ta give the gin a chance ta ketch back up wit us." He went on to say Numbers 4, 5, and 6 squads didn't have to pick as much as Numbers 1, 2, and 3. And the "pull-dos" (older cons with a physical disability, e.g., a finger missing, a limp) in Numbers 7 and 8 picked less than all the squads. He added, "Don't be fooled cuz some'a dem ol fuckers kin pick a whole lotsa cotton.

"Durin pickin time we weks seven days a week. We gits a short half on Sunday, knocks off roun three. You sho do hafta watch yo cotton, cuz dem nigguhs'll sho try ta steal it. Dey has mo fights out dere bout dat den a liddle bit. Specially when we leaves our sacks on the ends ta come in ta eat. When we git back, nigguhs start grabbin the fullest-lookin sacks dey kin find. Cap'n Smooth say ain't no such thang as a nigguh whut can't pick cotton—an a whole bunch uv it.

"An, man, dey haves dat field s'rounded! Dat high rider [additional field guard armed with a rifle who watches the squads from a distance] be settin off over yonder wit dat .30-30, an Buzzard, the dog sergeant, brangs four packs [four dogs to a pack] uv dem ol skinny hounds to the fields 'stead uv the usual two packs. He pistol-whups his hoss, so whut he thanks bout us ain't shit. Dem dogs an the dog boys who hannel 'em be layin off to the side under a tree in the cool, jes waitin for some nigguh ta run off. Dem ol dogs is so po, don't look lak dey could run fifty foots. Hell, all dey feeds 'em is cone bread an blue john [watery, blue-colored fat-free milk], but dem bastards'll run a nigguh long as Luke run John."

Beer Belly hardly paused to catch his breath. "Dey got one name Ol Rattler, who got two open-face crowns on his front teefs, a reward for trackin down convicts. One time dey wuz runnin a nigguh, an all the rest uv dem ol dogs had give up on the trail. But Ol Rattler wouldn't quit. He kep on sniffin for two days an nights. The track led 'em to the airport. When Ol Rattler got dere, he sot rat down in the middle uv the runway, looked up in the air howlin, an pointed to the sky wit one uv his front foots. Dey checked whut airplant jes lef. When it landed in Memphus an dat nigguh stepped off, dey grabbed him an brung his ass back. So don't even thank bout leavin cuz dey ain't bout ta lose no nigguhs come cotton-pickin time. We needs all the hep we got."

After he finished his tall dog tale, I asked, "Kin you pick good?"

"I picks enuff ta make it through the back gate. I can't 'ford not to," he joked while patting his big belly.

"I ain't never picked cotton befo."

"Aw shit, well, you sho ain't got no bizness in One Hoe. All dem nigguhs is some cotton-pickin muthafuckas. You miss enuff meals, you gon learn or you gon starve. Das why dey calls it the hog law, cuz it mess witcha meat an bread. But thas awright, you needn't worry. You'll git use to it."

"I hope so."

"You be surprised how much dem miss-meal cramps make a nigguh's cotton weights go up."

The constant humming of sewing machines operated by the night laundry crew could be heard all through the night. They were sewing on the three-foot extensions to the bull squads' sacks. As I lay on my bunk with my hands folded under my head, I became very anxious anticipating the morrow's coming. When the dim ceiling lights gave way to the glare of the hundred-watt bulbs, it was still pitch black outside.

"Chow time, les go eat!" We rushed to finish in the allotted fifteen minutes. Back on the tank I got a long drink at the sink, grabbed my hat from underneath my mattress, and went to the front to be closer to the tank door.

Someone over in Number 4 tank hollered, "Heah they come," referring to Cap'n Smooth and his entourage, Lieutenant Sundown and Sergeant Buzzard. The front office could be seen from the Number 4 tank windows. Thirty seconds later "Big Tom" (the turnout bell) rang and the tank doors opened. This time, instead of Cap'n Smooth waiting at the end of the hall by the back door to count us as we went streaking by, he stood underneath the inside picket.

"Whenever you nigguhs git outta that back door, I want ever squad to stop by in front uv 'at laundry, an ever nigguh gitta sack! First nigguh I ketch 'thout a sack when we git to 'at field is gon git sump'n dun to his goat-smellin ass," he said and strutted down the hall to take his position at the back door. Aiming his voice back up the corridor, he called, "Lemme have 'em, boss!"

"Number One!"

We hit the yard following Road Runner to the bundles of neatly stacked cotton sacks piled on the ground in front of the laundry. He grabbed a sack from the first pile and took off. The rest of us followed suit. Boss Deadeye was loping his horse to keep up as we sailed through the back gate. "Go 'head!"

Ol Sol was just showing its huge orange face over the eastern horizon by the time we crossed the main turnrow. As far as the eye could see was row after row of blossoming cotton bolls. It looked like an endless plain of freshly popped popcorn. We turned off the main turnrow, which led into the camp, onto the Williamson turnrow. Each squad stayed about twenty-five yards behind the next. We trotted straight down the Williamson turnrow to catch our sets of rows. The rest of the field workforce would string out to catch theirs after we did.

"Count off twenny-seven rows, Ol Chinaman," Boss Deadeye hollered to our tail-row man, who worked the last row and was responsible for spotting and counting off rows. Chinaman began to step them off, calling out the number of each as he went. As soon as he hollered out the number, the con who had been assigned that number got on it and began picking. "You sonsabitches ketch 'em goddamn rows an gitcha maw-dickin asses offa this turnrow!"

I caught cotton row number fourteen. By the time I picked the cotton from two stalks, the rest of the squad were already twenty or thirty feet ahead of me. I raised my head up for a moment and couldn't even see the end of my row, it was so long. The squad was continuously moving ahead of and away from me.

My row was in the "swing" (middle of the squad) and the worst place to be. That's where the bosses ride while watching the squads work. Boss Deadeye was walking his horse right beside me. Out of the corner of my eye, I saw him leaning forward in his saddle, eyeballing my every move as I carefully plucked each boll from the stalks. The faster I tried to pick it, the more I dropped. The more I dropped, the more time I wasted trying to get all the dirt, leaves, stems, and sticks out before putting it in my sack. Deadeye was so close I heard the crying of his saddle each time he shifted positions.

"Ol Cap Rock," Deadeye hollered, "hit this sorry bastard's row a lick up thar an hep him git the end uv his sack off 'is goddamn turnrow."

Cap Rock was the push-row man and worked the second row in the squad. He picked up his sack, walked across the twelve rows, and started picking cotton ahead of me on my row.

Then Deadeye started on me. "Nigguh, you betta go to feedin 'at bag an movin them shit scratchers lak you aim to do sump'n! Aw, I know a-pickin cotton's neath yore style. I betcha a few weeks in 'at pisser jes might hep you tighten yore sorry ass up a notch."

It was open season on my row for Cap Rock, who picked a long strip and went back to his row. I finally picked my way up to the cottonless stalks he left. Just to be able to walk down the middle of the rows and straighten my back up for a minute was a blessed relief. When I leaned back down, I rested one elbow on my knee while I picked to take some of the strain off my back. The skip Cap Rock had picked in my row caught me up with the squad momentarily, but in no time I had fallen way behind again.

It wasn't long before some of the cons in my squad yelled for Water Boy Brown to bring them another sack. He brought an armload from the water wagon. Those pickers who needed them got out of their full sacks, tied knots in the strap parts, and with green cotton bolls marked their prison names on them. Water Boy Brown draped the full ones over his water wagon and hauled them off to the scales. Most of the squad had filled up a sack, and the other few, excluding me, would be getting a new one in a very short time.

About an hour later, Deadeye hollered, "Awright, Ol Road Runner, y'all raise 'em up an head on to them scales."

We picked up our sacks, slung them across our shoulders, and ran behind Road Runner down several turnrows. We crossed over quite a few more before reaching the area where the scales had been set up. Huge sheets were spread out on the turnrow for us to dump our cotton onto after our sacks had been weighed.

The sheets would be tied up, loaded onto trucks, and hauled to the gin over on the Ramsey Unit. By the time we reached the scales, I was out of breath from the long run. The full sacks were waiting on the turnrow. Road Runner hung his two stovepipe-looking sacks on the scales first. After the scale man hooked the rope around them, he hoisted the load so the sacks didn't touch the ground.

Cap'n Smooth hollered out his weight, "He's got two thirty-five." He continued to call out the weights of the pickers as their sacks were hung on the scales and a convict weight keeper logged them. After emptying, they went to the water wagon, got a drink, and waited for the rest of us to weigh up.

"He's got two thirty, he's got two fifteen, he's got two twenty, he's got one ninety-five." Cap'n Smooth stopped and commented when the weight dropped under two hundred pounds. "Nigguh, you betta take yore goddamn ass to wek an quit a-draggin roun 'fore I do sump'n to you." Then to Boss Deadeye, "You gon hafta put this rotten bastard to wek, cuz I bleeve the sonuvabitch dun laid the hammer down, jes flat dun quit." Everything stopped until he finished preaching his sermon about the low weights.

As I sat on my sack waiting my turn, I felt like jumping up and running right out across the field. To hell with the .30-30 and the bloodhounds. The weight keeper called my number. Cap'n Smooth looked at me as if I had spit in his face when I stepped to the scales dragging my sack. Beer Belly's words rang loud and clear as I hung it up.

Cap'n Smooth hollered, "Forty pounds! Kin you bleeve it? Forty fuckin pounds uv cotton! Boss, this ol nigguh sho must be heavy wit you! Whutcha do, boss, let 'em ketch you fuckin a mule?"

The cons waiting to weigh up behind me started laughing. Boss Deadeye's face crimsoned and he had a wild-eyed look when he said, "Cap'n, I'm willin to forfit a whole month's wages if you jes look the other way fer five seconds so's I kin throw this worthless sonuvabitch away." With trembling hands, he pointed his double-barrel shotgun at me and laid the hammers back. Those waiting to weigh up scampered out of the way in case he fired.

"Naw, boss," Cap'n Smooth said jokingly, "I don't bleeve this bastard's even worth the price uv a good load uv buckshot. 'Sides, you might splatter nigguh shit all over my boots an mess up my shine." Boss Deadeye lowered his shotgun.

"Whar you frum, nigguh! I spose you one'a them city nigguhs that ruther steal than wek. Whar'd you say you come frum?" Each time I attempted to answer, "Dry up that fuckin ol mouth when I'm a-talkin to you!" With his finger pointed close to my face, Cap'n Smooth shouted, "Do you hear me talkin to you, *nig-guh*?" bouncing his voice off my nose.

"Tell you whut, boss, don'tcha let this sorry bastard even slow down at that water wagon. He ain't picked enuff to pay fer a drank uv water." Back at me, "As fer you, nigguh, you betta gitcha goddamn goat-smellin ass back out yonder an go to pickin that goddamn cotton! I'm gon do sump'n to you if you come draggin yore yaller ass back up to them scales wit another measly forty pounds. You hear me, *nig-guh*?"

He hollered down the turnrow to the officer watching the dump sheets for dirty cotton. "Lieutenant, you betta sho watch this nigguh, an don't let 'em dump *all* 'at cotton he's got on yore foot. Jes might break it!" Walking toward the sheets to empty my sack, I heard him say, "Reason that sonuvabitch can't pick no cotton's cuz he wuz too busy hustlin up decent white men fer his ol mammy to screw 'stead uv learnin sump'n worthwhile."

I emptied my sack and stood to the side waiting for the others to weigh up and empty. Lieutenant Sundown asked in a semiaudible tone, "You didn't have much that time, didja?"

"No sir."

"Well, they's plenny uv it out thar. You betta gitcha self some uv it."

After Chinaman emptied his sack and got a drink, we took off running back down the turnrow to where we'd left off. It seemed like we had been picking for an hour when Boss Deadeye hollered, "Ol Road Runner, y'all raise 'em up an go on over yonder whar they dun set up 'at johnny ground."

We headed down the middles of the rows toward the turnrow. "You dick-eatin bastards betta not be a-knockin 'at man's cotton all over the fuckin ground! Ever sonuvabitch stay walkin in his own middle. First nigguh I ketch a-crossin over 'em rows a-knockin cotton on the ground's gon git a load uv buckshot in his black ass. You nigguhs tighten up an git on up yonder wit that lead-row nigguh 'fore I bust a ball down through this canyon! Ol Road Runner, go 'head! Take 'em on 'way frum heah!"

Road Runner shifted gears, and we struggled furiously for our other gears. We shot down the turnrow like a bunch of gazelles. Within minutes we pulled up at the johnny ground. On one side of the turnrow the flunkies had set up folding tables and chairs for the bosses. By now, all the squads had arrived and we were lined up to go through the chow line. The Number 1 squad first.

As we started through, Boss Deadeye shouted, "Ol Yaller Nigguh, don'tcha git no pan. You jes stand yore rotten ass over yonder back outta the way so's 'em nigguhs thas been a-wekin kin git sump'n to eat."

The other bosses joshed Deadeye. "Hey, boss, is this heah that nigguh whut broke 'em scales wit all 'at cotton this mornin?"

Another chimed in, "How's he gonna keep pickin them bales fer ya if ya don't feed 'em? Come to thank uv it, that nigguh looks lak one'a them import nigguhs. Frum whut I hear, they don't need a heap to eat. They spose to run all day on a liddle bit uv nothin. Ain't that right, nigguh?"

"Hell, boss," another added, "that nigguh don't wont no talk. You kin tell he's swole up. That nigguh's got his mind on sippin lemonade in that free world."

Boss "Eat-Em-Up," the undisputed master at harassing cons and bosses, added his bullshit. "Since you ain't gon feed that ol nigguh, why don'tcha lend 'em yore hat an let 'em fan some'a these fuckin flies. As a gen'le rule, nigguhs whut claim they can't pick cotton gen'ly make damn good fly fanners," he said, cramming food into his mouth. "Boss, know whut?" he asked while chewing. "If I had that ol nigguh in my squad, shit, I wouldn't even *ask* 'em to wek. All he'd hafta do is jes fan the flies an gatter nippers offa me an my fuckin hoss."

I stood off to the side waiting for them to finish eating. Some con said, "Gotdam! Looka heah, heah's a big o' grasshopper in my pan!"

The con next to him reached over, pretending to grab it. "Lemme have dat piece uv meat, man," he joked.

With the meal over, Boss Deadeye hollered, "Awright, alla you Number One nigguhs, git out heah on 'is turnrow an line up in twos." We quickly paired off in two columns so he could take the head count. He rode his horse from end to end. "Go 'head!"

I was back on my row again and nothing had changed. I kept falling behind, Cap Rock came over at Boss Deadeye's request to pick off my row, and Boss Deadeye stayed on my ass. My shirt stuck to my back and the sweat sloshed inside my brogans. My parched throat got drier and drier and the sharp pains in my back were excruciating.

Shortly, Boss Deadeye yelled, "Ol Road Runner, that man's beckin fer us again. Y'all raise 'em up an head on to them scales."

The sun's hot rays had dried most of the early dew from the cotton. It was much lighter now, which was evident as Cap'n Smooth called out the weights. "He's got one seventy-five!" That was Road

Runner. Cap Rock weighed up next. "He's got one eighty-five!" He
outweighed Road Runner because of all the cotton he had picked off
my row. The weights ranged from 130 pounds to Cap Rock's 185. So
far, Cap'n Smooth hadn't said a word to anybody who had weighed
up ahead of me.

I hung my sack on the scales. Cap'n Smooth jumped back in a
comical gesture and hollered out, "He's got fifty-five pounds! Boss,
you must'a whispered sump'n in this nigguh's ear. Nigguh, you betta
go to gittin some more uv 'at cotton! That ain't near bouts enuff.
You hear me?"

"Yes sir," I said, dragging my sack away.

Before I reached the sheets, he shouted, "Nigguh, don'tcha be
a-wearin 'at fuckin sack out draggin it up an down this goddamn
turnrow! Pick it up an tote it! You ain't got a double handful uv cotton, an you gonna jes drag it roun lak it's too heavy fer you to tote!"

I emptied up. Since nothing had been said to the contrary, I
headed to the water wagon. Water Boy Brown poured up some more
water from the two canvas-covered wooden barrels, refilling the four
tin buckets. He could barely pour for squabbling with some cons
who had already gotten their drinks. They were at the front of the
wagon aggravating the two old mules, Ol Coal Oil and Ol Fannie.
Ol Fannie had been screwed so many times by convicts that when
one of them patted her on the rump, she automatically raised her
tail up. When a con touched either of the mules, it caused them to
move the wagon a few feet.

Water Boy Brown finally said, "You ignant muthafuckas, let dem
mules 'lone befo I take one'a dese ax hannels an ram it up one'a y'all's
asses. Gotdam stupid muthafuckas! Dere's some mo nigguhs back
heah still tryin to gitta drank!"

Still, they would not stop, no matter what he said. Like a bunch
of mischievous little boys, they enjoyed teasing the mules and antag-
onizing Water Boy Brown.

The water was hot as piss and so salty it was almost slimy, but it
was my first drink since we'd left the building and tasted as good as

Coca-Cola. I noticed instead of wasting water by spitting it on the ground, it was spat into the empty cotton sacks. Whatever water was left in the cups went into the sacks too. Wetting it "makes the cotton weigh mo."

When the tail row emptied his sack and gulped down his last swallow of water, Boss Deadeye yelled, "Y'all git on 'way frum heah. Go 'head!"

Like bats out of hell, we sped back to our rows and started picking again. The scorching sun beat down on the fields, casting a mirage in the distance. To shield themselves, bosses wore handkerchiefs beneath their cowboy hats and had capes draped around their shoulders. Rays of blistering sunlight beamed on Boss Deadeye's wet back as he stood in his stirrups, exposing the soaked seat of his pants that no doubt added to his bad-tempered disposition. Shotgun barrels held in sweaty hands forced the bosses to hang them downward by the stock, hitting against their horses' shoulders, causing them to buck. Sweat pouring, we worked our way closer to the sun. "Go 'head! Git that row!"

It was late in the afternoon. A few courageous clouds dared to shield us from Ol Sol, momentarily causing shade-giving shadows to dance across the fields. Barring an occasional abusive remark by a boss or the "go 'head" command, and except for the rattling of the cotton stalks being stripped of their precious white gold, it was quiet. All across the field cotton sacks inched along like giant caterpillars as black bodies dressed in white bobbed up and down like prairie dogs, bending, stooping, sweating, crawling, picking, and popping those sacks with an uncanny rhythm each time a handful was thrust inside.

I wasn't quite as far behind as I had been earlier in the day, and Boss Deadeye was behind somebody else for a change. I hollered, "Pourin it down over here, boss!"

Finally, "Go 'head an pour it down."

Turning my back to him, I directed every single drop into my sack.

We picked and picked. Cap'n Smooth had already gone to the building, leaving Lieutenant Sundown in charge of the field force. I understood why the cons called him that. The sun was sinking low and there was no indication that we would be knocking off anytime soon. On the turnrow ahead, he leaned so precariously off the side of his horse the stirrup almost touched the ground. It looked like any minute his saddle was going to slip down under the horse's belly.

Sundown looked right sitting atop a horse—a real Gary Cooper-looking cowboy. He was tall and slim, neat as a pin, and his tailored shirts fit like a glove. He sat unconcerned, smoking a cigarette and staring off into the sunset. He and his horse were motionless, except when the big dark bay periodically swished her tail or he took a drag off his cigarette.

For once I was even with the squad because the work pace had slowed considerably. Most of the squad were watching for Sundown to raise his hat. I passed several of them as I hustled for every boll of cotton I could get. I had more in my sack now than I'd had all day. The strap was cutting into my shoulder each time I pulled against it. The sun was gone, even the reddish-orange glow had disappeared over the horizon. We picked on. Sundown raised his hat at twilight.

Boss Deadeye yelled, "Awright, you Number One nigguhs, brang 'em sacks on back heah an put 'em on the end uv yore row." After the head count, he called, "Go 'head! Ol Road Runner, take these ol thangs on to that house." Hollering up ahead, he ordered, "Boss, git them goddamn drag asses outta the way up thar an let this Number One squad come by."

Some of the other squads had gotten to the turnrow before we did, but it was a law of the bottoms that no squad walked or worked in front of Number 1. They pulled over. "Ol Road Runner, go 'head, nigguh!"

While standing at the back gate waiting for Boss Deadeye to get his shotgun and pistol checked in, I noticed that neither the warden nor the captain was there with the hog law book. I didn't know what was going on and didn't care so long as I could make it back to the tank and get on my bunk. That evening I found out it was a traditional policy of Big Devil's (a gift of sorts) not to punish on the first day of picking season. "He gives us dat day to warm up an git broke back in."

When Boss Deadeye had finished checking his weapons, he said, "You nigguhs, go 'head!"

Inside the yard midway between the back gate and the back door, we stripped so the line of waiting guards could shake us down. The ten of us who lived on Number 3 tank made a mad dash for the showers to get in and out before the rest of the squads got into the tank. As usual, Big George sat on the ledge above the commodes so he could eye-grind our naked, wet bodies. Thanks to Sundown, by the time we finished showering it was totally dark outside.

After supper I got on my bunk. To hell with the domino table and card games. I scratched my head and winced. My fingers were sore and puffy, and the cuticles and under my nails were full of cotton burr tips. I picked them out with my teeth the best I could, but some would have to fester before coming out. I massaged my swollen, aching knees, hoping that would ease the stiffness. Lying on his bunk, Beer Belly looked over at me. "This shit's gon take some gittin use to, man," I told him.

"I tell you, I been pickin side by side wit a nigguh all day long an never got no furtha behind 'em dan the end uv his sack. An I be damn if dat nigguh wudn't beatin me fifteen or twenny pounds ever weigh-in. I couldn't figger where in the hell he got all dat cotton frum or whut he wuz doin I wudn't doin. But I sho learnt in a hurry. Dey's a trick to it. You hafta learn it. You gon see."

Before I could ask what the trick was, the call came: "Count time!"

Count time over, all was quiet. With no fans and very little fresh air, the hot, sticky, stinking air from stinking feet made sleep difficult. But I was dead tired and dozed off. Voices and the tank door opening and closing woke me. Toe Sucker had been put out of the tank again, for the umpteenth time. He had gotten a double lip-lock on somebody's toe during the night and must have nibbled a little too hard and woke his prey. Half-asleep, I raised up on my elbows.

Beer Belly said, "Ain't nobody but Toe Sucker hustlin some mo toe jam."

Unable to go back to sleep, I heard whispering from the next row of bunks. Half opening my eyes, I saw a couple of cons pouring lighter fluid all over Iron Head's sheet-covered body. The cons called him Iron Head because he could hit his head with his fist and it sounded as if he were hitting an empty bucket. He was so good at his ventriloquist trick few realized he actually made the sound with his mouth.

While he loudly snored and snorted, they finished dousing his bunk and returned to their own. One of them lit a cigarette and thumped it on Iron Head's sheet. A second or two later, *whoosh!*

In flames he jumped up yelling and cussing, ran toward the front of the tank, then realized all the water was in the back. After a quick U-turn, he ran down the alley hollering and slapping at the flames, trying to put his sheet out. He made it to the showers, jumped in, and turned on the wrong faucet, the hot water. He was dancing a jig and had the shower area looking like a steam bath.

The tank was in an uproar. The boisterous laughter caused Boss Wise-Em-Up to holler down, "They's some wild-assed nigguhs in heah tonight. Some'a you ol wild-assed nigguhs gonna hafta talk ta that warden in the mornin. You betta git down on it." Then he asked Iron Head, "Didja make sho you got all that far [fire] put out? Don't wanna set this whole fuckin buildin a-far."

"Yassuh, boss, it's all put out," he said as he went back to what was left of his mattress. "Wisht I knowed whut muthafucka it wuz dat dun dat. I betcha dat warden hafta burn me offa his ass."

Of course everybody was pretending to be asleep now, but snickering under their covers. Iron Head mumbled on until Slope Diddy said, "Say, muthafucka, dry up dat fuckin mouf an go ta sleep befo you git dat ol iron head melted sho nuff!" Iron Head lay down on his bunk and quickly went back to snoring.

Tomorrow came and with it the inevitable. Hades couldn't possibly be any hotter. We had been entombed, packed inside a four-by-eight steel and concrete chamber and sealed up like a can of beans. As we stood naked in our urine and sweat, the heavy stench was overpowering. The small supply of oxygen depleted with every panting breath the nine of us took.

No face basin, no water, no light, and a fifty-cent-piece-size hole in the center of the rough, unfinished concrete floor served as the lavatory. The nine of us writhed and twisted for space like maggots in a cesspool. All the darkness and sweltering heat vacuum-sealed inside when the solid-steel door slammed shut. This was the pisser.

I was the second man to enter and hurried to one of the back corners. Each time someone squirmed for position everybody in the dark furnace was disturbed. A fight nearly broke out when a con tried to lie down. If one punch was thrown in the blackness, fists would fly like a bunch of blind men fighting.

I had been well schooled in how to suffer, to withstand punishment as if it were a challenge, suffering nonetheless. I knew how to cope, been there before; but after so many hours, my legs were cramping. I had to get out of that corner. "Say," I said, "I know a way we kin make it easy on ourselfs."

A voice shot back, "Ain't nothin gon make dis shit easy, man. Dey got us crammed in dis hot muthafucka lak sardines."

Then another, "Whut kinda plan you got, man?"

"Look," I said, "if five uv us line up frum this corner I'm in to the door, with our faces to the wall, then four uv us kin take turns sittin an squattin on the floor next to the other wall."

"Sounds awright to me," somebody said, "but how come we gotta face the fuckin wall while them four nigguhs is squattin down 'hind us?"

"Yeah, man, how come?"

"Well, facin the wall would keep us frum blowin our hot breaths on each other an we wouldn't be danglin our dicks in the faces uv the ones on the floor."

"Yeah, but den yo ass would be."

"I know," I said, "but it won't stick out as far."

We agreed to try it, and rearranged ourselves in the cell. The nine of us stood, squatted, and sat in that hellish coffin until the next morning, when it was time to go back to the cotton patch and try to satisfy the hog law book.

The following day in the fields, Deadeye stopped his horse on the end of my sack. I tried to move forward but couldn't. "Boss, yo hoss is on my sack."

"Shet yore mouth an go ta wek!"

I pulled the strap off my shoulder, wheeled around, grabbed the horse's muzzle, and punched him in the nose. He let out a loud whinny and reared, throwing Boss Deadeye to the ground and causing him to drop his shotgun. "Cap'n! Cap'n! Thar's a crazy nigguh over heah!" That little fracas got me another stay in the pisser and "assault on a dumb brute" on my record. During our next altercation he blew away the end of my cotton sack with his shotgun. I cussed him out, landing me back in the pisser for "refusin ta wek."

My next weigh-in netted another stint in the pisser. Three or four days of that, they let me out and I was back in the fields. When I finally made it to a hundred pounds, I was cuffed to the bars in the hallway. My wrists were fucked up from hanging on the cuffs, my hands were full of festers from cotton burr tips, I hadn't had much to eat, and I was steady trying to keep up with the squad.

One day when Boss Deadeye called me back to fuck with me and had his shotgun aimed at my head, I hollered, "If you don't shoot, yo mama's a punk! If I had that shotgun, I would'a killed you yesterday, muthafucka!"

"Naw, I ain't gon kill ya. I'd be doin you a favor an I ain't never dun no nigguh no favor in my life. Now git on back ta pickin that man's cotton!"

I was getting skinnier and skinnier. I thought I was going to starve to death that first cotton-picking season. But as the season wore on and after at least a dozen more trips to the pisser and several more bouts with the cuffs, my picking skills improved considerably. Just like Beer Belly said, those "miss-meal cramps" have a phenomenal effect on the development of cotton-picking speed.

When the next cotton-picking season rolled around, I managed to average with the squad more often than not. By the end of the season, in October, I was doing a lot better than Road Runner even.

He'd gotten in bad health; his endurance and speed had waned. He lost that other gear and was struggling just to bring up the rear out on the turnrow. We knew it was only a matter of time. He was like an old lion being cast out of the pride.

If the hog law book didn't get him cut out at the back gate, Boss Deadeye got him for "laziness." Finally, his laborious wheezing and coughing up blood got so bad, the medical team diagnosed TB and had him transferred to the Walls hospital. After he got shipped, Boss Deadeye put Cap Rock on as the lead row. The turnrow had taken its toll on Road Runner, but there were plenty more to take his place. One thing we never seemed to run short of was manpower.

I knew it was almost a cardinal sin if a convict talked back to a boss or refused to obey *any* order. He got an ass whipping, the handcuffs, solitary, or a combination of all three. However, if someone got caught jacking off or fucking, Big Devil and the bosses made a joke of it, like with Fistfucker.

Fistfucker was heralded as the tank jack-off champion and played pants-pocket pool even while holding a conversation. Big Devil decided the best solution to the problem was to make him sleep with his wrists tied to his bunk. Whenever he hollered "Alley, boss," Forty had to rush and untie him.

So when Flea Brain and Pork Chops got caught fucking, they had to stand side by side on the soda water boxes under the picket, the usual punishment when Big Devil deemed the offense an insignificant part of prison life. While standing on the boxes this time, they argued so much it led to a shoving match and both fell off. The picket boss hollered down orders for them to stop, but they kept right on quarreling.

Flea Brain had been aptly nicknamed because he acted like his brain was no bigger than a flea's. He spent every waking hour thinking and talking about the love of his life, Pork Chops. Flea Brain was the more aggressive and vocal of the pair. Pork Chops, on the other hand, was extremely humble, no spirit, like a brokenhearted dog in a pound. When he was a young man, the tear sac under his left eye was damaged by a blow from the barrel of a policeman's revolver, causing his eye to drip most of the time and making him look even sadder.

Pork Chops helped keep himself and Flea Brain in smokes by washing the socks of cons in return for their cigarette butts. Nevertheless, Flea Brain would not allow the washing services to last very long. When Pork Chops went back to the same con twice to wash his socks, Flea Brain would cuss to the top of his tongue-tied voice, "Poke Chops, I gittin tied yo shit! You tink you smar muddafucka. I be wachin yo ass, hoe! Don'tcha tink I ain't!"

Pork Chops's left eye started dripping heavier when Flea Brain chastised him. He'd say, "Go on, man. Go on, man. Lemme 'lone, man," and try to get away from Flea Brain, who followed him all over the tank fussing. They "fought" in the tank all the time about any and every thing.

After their lovers' spat in the hallway, the picket boss made them sit in separate corners. Flea Brain began his amorous pitch as Pork Chops sat quietly in his assigned corner. "Baby, you knows I luvs you." He babbled on and on. Finally, the picket boss yelled down for him to shut up, but he never quit professing his love. He harassed the picket boss and Pork Chops all night long with his lovesick jabbering.

The next day, Sunday, Big Devil was in the guards' barbershop in the front of the building getting his weekly hair trim and shoe shine. Afterward, he came through the short corridor that led past the commissary to underneath the inside picket. In his blue gabardine suit, black shoes shining like glass, and light gray, short-brimmed Stetson hat, he looked like a Philadelphia lawyer and could easily have passed for one—that is, until he opened his mouth.

Flea Brain and Pork Chops jumped up from the floor and greeted him, "Mornin to you, Warden, suh." Big Devil looked through his gold-rimmed glasses at them as if they were two big piles of horseshit. Flea Brain immediately told the warden how he had caught Pork Chops traipsing around "washin the same nigguh's socks twice."

By the time Flea Brain finished running it down, Big Devil agreed, "Somethin must be dun." To prevent future problems, he decided, "Sometimes marryin has a way uv settlin crazy-assed nigguhs down."

He phoned the back-gate picket boss and told him to send in Big Mama James, who was a trusty working in the welding shop. Since trusties work seven days a week, Sunday was just another workday for them. When Big Mama James came in the building, Big Devil told him to go back to the shop and make two wedding bands out of some nuts.

While Big Mama James was gone, Big Devil hollered upstairs to the Number 5 tank building tender, "Send that ol preacher down heah!"

Rev came downstairs. "Good mornin, Warden. How are you?"

Ignoring his greeting, Big Devil said, "Ol Rev, I want you to perform me a weddin ceremony. You thank you got sense enuff to do that?"

"Oh yassuh, Warden," said Rev and ran back upstairs to get his Bible.

In twenty minutes it was chow time. After the meal all of us, excluding the white cons, were ordered to remain to witness the "weddin." Rev stood in the aisle way waiting with his Bible neatly tucked under his arm. Big Devil ordered Flea Brain and Pork Chops to strip and get up on one of our mess hall tables. Then he told Rev to begin the ceremony. Big Mama James acted as best man and handed them the rings when Rev got to that part. They put the rings on each other's fingers and Rev pronounced them "man an wife." After which, Big Devil ordered them to embrace.

Most of the audience exploded in laughter. Since the wedding was at chow time and our pans were still on the tables, we showered the newlyweds with food scraps. The cons and bosses were really enjoying the warden's show. Especially us, because it afforded the opportunity, however short-lived, to go acceptably berserk without fear of punishment.

Finally, Big Devil halfheartedly ordered, "Awright, you nigguhs knock that shit off!" Even after his command, somebody slung gravy, which splattered his suit. He demanded quiet again and we settled down. He gestured for Flea Brain and Pork Chops to get off the table. Up to that point in the festivities, Flea Brain had been grinning and enjoying himself while Pork Chops stood dejected with his hands folded over his privates, his left eye leaking like a tiny waterfall. Gravy and molasses dripped from his lowered head. Not once did he attempt to wipe it from his face or body.

"I'm gonna give you two nigguhs an early Christmas present," Big Devil said.

Then he issued the order for Cap'n Foots to transfer Flea Brain to Number 1 tank, placing him on the other side of the building from Pork Chops. After they dressed, Flea Brain reached out to touch Pork Chops's hand for a last farewell as they filed out of the mess hall, one going east, the other going west.

12

It was early December. The rain was freezing as fast as it hit the ground. Icicles hung on the outside window ledges. The radiator pipes that hung along the inner ceiling popped sporadically. Already we had been laying in the building for two days and were getting on one another's nerves. This was my second Christmas and almost my third year at Retrieve. I'd begun to feel like an old-timer.

The saddest part about the Yuletide season was the way each of us tried to hide our loneliness. If we had the holiday blues, however, it was by choice. Big Devil took great pains to make our Christmas in hell merry. Cons were standing on bunks hanging decorations that Big Devil made the bosses chip in and buy after Hollywood had this festive brainstorm and sold him on the idea.

The outstanding punks on each tank were selected by Hollywood and the building tenders to do the decorating. Afterward, Big Devil would inspect the five tanks to determine which was the prettiest. The chosen tank's members were allowed into the Friday night picture show first. After the white cons, of course.

Very quickly, the tank activities slowed after the decorating spree. The sound of hard walking and jingling spurs broke the calm. We knew it was Cap'n Smooth even before he spoke. "Boss, open up all 'em tank doors so's them buildin tenders kin git out heah."

Boss Humpy hollered down, "You wont one frum each tank or all uv 'em, Cap'n?"

Aggravated that he had asked, Cap'n Smooth yelled, "Ever damned one uv 'em!"

Levers were thrown and the noisy steel doors slowly opened. "That cap'n wonts all uv you buildin tenders ta come on out heah under this picket!"

Three building tenders lived on each lower tank and one on the trusty tank. In a matter of minutes all thirteen had gathered underneath the inside picket for a meeting with Cap'n Smooth. As they stood awaiting his spoken word, each had on his most eager-to-please suck-ass expression.

"Tell you whut I want y'all ta do," Cap'n Smooth began. "First, how many uv you nigguhs kin read an write?" Several shuffled their feet and looked down at the scrub-polished redbrick floor, indicating they were the ones who could not. "Well, you nigguhs whut kin, I want y'all to go back in them tanks an git the names an numbers uv ever one uv 'em nigguhs who needs a set uv teeth."

Big George asked, "Cap'n, does you want da names an numbers uv jes dem nigguhs whut ain't got no teefs atall, or does you want dem nigguhs' names whut's got some teefs lef?"

"Naw, nigguh! I don't want y'all gittin no nigguh's name whut's got some teeth in his mouth. That warden wants to take care uv them nigguhs first whut ain't got no teeth atall. Nigguh, whut made you ask a goddamn crazy-assed question lak 'at in the first place? If a nigguh's got two or three teeth uv his own, whut the hell does he want some more fer?"

The question Big George asked must have had some validity, or why did Cap'n Smooth climb up in the inside picket and phone the front office to get further clarification? Afterward, he descended. "Now, les go over this shit again, so's I kin see if you nigguhs understand whut you spose to do. I want y'all whut kin read an write to go back in them tanks an git the names an numbers uv ever nigguh whut ain't got *no* teeth atall. An git the names an numbers uv ever one uv them nigguhs in thar whut's got one eye missin. Don't none uv you crazy bastards ask me if I mean 'em nigguhs that ain't got no eyes atall, cuz we ain't got no no-eyed nigguhs in heah," he said sarcastically.

When they turned and started to leave, he called out, "Jes you nigguhs hold up! I ain't finished wit y'all yet."

One mumbled, "Naw suh, Cap'n. We wuzn't leavin, suh. We jes thought you wuz through wid us, Cap'n."

"I'll tell you when I'm through, nigguh. Now, where wuz I? Oh yeah, afta you dun got them nigguhs' names an numbers an dun give 'em to the picket boss, I want y'all to git a big-mouthed nigguh, a medium-mouthed nigguh, an one uv 'em little-mouthed nigguhs whut's got teeth frum the east side, west side, an Number 5 tanks. Git 'em up to the front uv them tanks so's they kin bite them false teeth molds when Ol Nolan brangs 'em down heah. Now, I'm through wit you nigguhs. Take y'all's rotten asses on back in 'em tanks an do whut I told y'all."

"Yassuh, Cap'n."

The cry went out on all five tanks to those who needed false teeth and artificial eyes. Big George presided over the east-side tanks' registration. Yelling loudly so residents of both tanks could hear, he said, "Awright, you nigguhs git down on dat bullshit an lissen up! Dat cap'n wants alla y'all's names an numbers whut needs a set uv dem false teefs an dem dat ain't got but one eye. Dat warden gon give y'all some. So alla y'all dat ain't got no eyes an teefs, come on up heah an give yo name an number ta Ol Slocum." Big George had delegated the signing-up responsibility since his own writing skills were lacking.

Cons from Number 4 tank who needed an artificial eye or false teeth started marching through the now opened door, which separated the two tanks, to enter Number 3 tank, where the domino table had been cleared for sign-up use. Across the hall, the door separating the west-side tanks had also been opened by Boss Humpy so their building tenders could sign up their less fortunates. I never realized there were so many with missing parts. A good third of the cons in the east-side tanks were crowded around the domino table trying to get their names and numbers listed first by Slocum.

Big George shouted, "Say, some'a you nigguhs git back an give dat nigguh some elbow room."

When the last con left the sign-up table, Nolan came down the stairs and stood at the 3 tank door, very neatly attired in his wraparound smock, white tennis shoes, and emergency room cap. B.C., out of Number 2 hoe squad and Bull's replacement on our tank, yelled out, "You nigguhs whut needs teefs, come on up heah to da front so y'all kin hear whut Doc Nolan gon say."

Marble Eye, who was in my squad, didn't hush quick enough for B.C. "Ol Marble Eye, you gon need more'n another gotdam eye if you don't stop runnin yo ol head! You gon need a tractor ta pull my foot outta yo ass. You one'a dem nigguhs whut don't lak ta be tole nothin. You gits swole up when somebody tells you a liddle sump'n," B.C. said while weaving his way through the crowded front of the tank toward the back, where Marble Eye stood.

With one foot propped on his lower bunk, Marble Eye was holding a conversation with a con and completely ignored B.C. When he saw B.C. coming, he took his foot down and one-eyed his way to the center of the alley. "Dis gon be twixt you an me, B.C. An pull-do muthafucka, you ain't gon whup my ass!"

Marble Eye's bold response froze the other goons for a moment. Before they could establish position in alliance with B.C., we, the Number 1 hoe squad members from the two tanks, got between them and Marble Eye to ensure a fair fight. Boss Humpy had a bird's-eye view as he looked down into the tank from his perch. Since it involved a building tender, he wasn't going to interfere.

Both were two-hundred-plus pounders, with muscles like tree stumps from many years in the fields. Both were serving life sentences, mean as hell, and well matched—except for Marble Eye, having just one eye. This was going to be a battle. If either or both were killed, nobody would weep.

B.C. got within a few feet of Marble Eye and lunged. They met head-on in the alleyway and their bodies crashed together like two rhinos. Both hit the floor. Fists were flying as they fought side by side between the rows of bunks. They kicked and hit, each scuffling to get up first. The bunks reeled and rocked as if they were being uprooted from their bolted-down positions in the brick floor.

The cons and picket boss looked on. No one said a word as the fighters continued to pummel and kick each other. Blood was flowing freely from both. They fought on, blow for blow. Their knuckles were bloody, and thick red slobber hung from their noses and mouths. I'd never seen a better fistfight in my life. They fought a good thirty minutes, tussling, wrestling, butting. Everything was fair game in the pen—"ain't no fair" in fighting. Neither gave an inch, but the power of their swings dwindled.

"Awright, thas enuff uv that shit!" Boss Humpy hollered. "You nigguhs break 'em up now!"

The building tenders moved through the crowd toward them. Big George said, "Say, B.C., y'all break it up. Da man's lookin at y'all. Break it up!"

Neither said much when the building tenders parted and shoved them away from each other. However, Marble Eye did mumble as he walked back up the alley, "You ain't gon whup my muthafuckin ass an no other nigguh." And he meant it. If B.C. wanted to show off, he sure should've grabbed somebody from another squad and not Number 1. Everybody in Number 1 hoe would fight.

With this brief interruption over, it was back to the business at hand. Nolan was talking through the bars with Polly, a Number 4 tank building tender, to allow a few minutes for things to get back to normal. Turning his attention to the picket boss, Nolan said, "Boss, will you open Number Three? I need to git those imprints made."

Boss Humpy hated doing anything the cons asked and shot back, "Can't them nigguhs do it through the bars? Ever one uv 'em got them long ol mouths." But because he knew Nolan was working under strict orders from the warden via the captain, the door's lever was belligerently thrown.

"Y'all lissen up heah!" Polly hollered. "You nigguhs lissen up now!"

Nolan made the announcement. "The warden wants me to take

imprints frum three uv y'all wit all y'all's teeth. He wants a big-moufted nigguh, a medium-moufted nigguh, an a bird-moufted nigguh to make yo imprints in this mold. You nigguhs qualified, come on up heah."

Nobody moved forward, there was only feet shuffling and snickering. Nolan looked at Polly, and Polly looked at Nolan. They didn't have a plan for the arisen selection-process crisis. Nolan spoke out, "An the warden said you buildin tenders is gon hep do the pickin."

Polly hollered, "Awright, I ain't gon do dis shit by mysef. The resta you muthafuckas git offa yo asses an git ta pickin."

Building tenders from both tanks began rounding up their choices. Ape was urging Candy along—"Come on now, baby. G'on up dere an bite dat shit so evuh nigguh dat gits a pair uv teef made frum yo mouf will hafta pay me for life. Cuz das lak evuh nigguh whut gits dem teef will be kissin my o' lady. An, baby, you don't want no nigguh kissin you an not payin us, now, do you?"—nudging him forward again.

Ape was cutting back two life sentences. He had gotten one added since he'd been down for choking a con to death with his bare hands. The victim had a knife in his hand, but Ape literally squeezed the air out of him before he ever got to raise it. Candy was doing twenty for midnight burglary. Both were multiple offenders who had grown up at Gatesville State School for Boys and graduated to hell. Ape and Candy seemed content with the life to which they had both grown so accustomed.

By now, several of the star punks had been shuffled to the front and were gathered around the middle domino table, where Nolan and Polly sat. Except for Forty, all the building tenders were there in the interest of their specific punks, each one trying to get his punk to calm down and "stop actin lak a damn fool."

"Say, Nolan," one hollered, "let our woman g'on an bite dat shit an git it over wid. You dun kissed her. You knows how sweet her lips is."

Trying to ignore the comment, Nolan gave out more directives. "Y'all look heah, les git this over wit so I kin git on outta heah. I got a lot uv shit to do to git these molds ready by tomorrow." The once-a-month real dentist would be down to pick them up. "Look, I know alla y'all wants yo, ahem"—clearing his throat—"friend, to give the imprint. But I hafta have three sizes—small, medium, an large. Jes by lookin, y'all know that some'a these nigguhs is 'liminated. You nigguhs whut know y'all's 'liminated, move on back outta the fuckin way an let some'a these other nigguhs git up heah."

A few of those standing around the perimeter of the crowd moved toward the back. Then a few more and a few more. How in the hell did they know they were eliminated?

"Now, les git to pickin somebody," Nolan urged. "Whut bout this nigguh?" he asked, pointing directly at Candy. This brought a howl and a chest beat from Ape. Nolan had played it on the safe side. Nobody offered any opposition to his first suggestion. A few cons whistled and hollered when Nolan said, "Okay, we got one. Candy'll bite the medium-size mold." All the toothless cons bared their gums, grinning acceptance of Candy as the medium imprint biter.

Ape, in his thunderous voice, hollered, "Evuh one'a you mutha-fuckas whut gits a pair uv my baby's teefs is gon gimme a sack'a dust evuh week, or I'm gon do sump'n to his ass!"

Now, to choose the small and large. This was going to be diffi-cult. Things were boiling down to B.C. and his punk, Mama Good Drawers, and Air Hammer (former Number 1 squad member) and his punk, Mama Better Drawers. B.C.'s life sentence was for murder and Mama Good Drawers was doing twelve for burglary. Air Hammer was doing fifty for robbery and Mama Better Drawers got thirty-five for poisoning somebody. All of them, except Mama Good Drawers, could hold their own in the muscle department.

Air Hammer looked at Nolan. "Doc, jes by lookin, you knows my ol lady's mouf ain't big as Mama Good Drawers's." Nolan wasn't about to dispute Air Hammer's word.

B.C. made his pitch for Mama Good Drawers. "You right, Air Hammer, yo nigguh's mouf might be liddler, but it sho ain't as priddy."

"Look, B.C., you knows muthafuckin well I ain't scared uv yo ass, nigguh," Air Hammer blasted back. "An me an you kin settle dis shit in the back or rat now! Cuz it don't make a fuck ta me. I been kinda wantin some'a yo ass anyway."

B.C. pondered his predicament. "Fuck it! Let Mama Better Drawers bite dat shit. I don't want my woman puttin his mouf on nothin but my you-knows-whut. C'mon, baby, les me an you go in the back. I want you ta pick my face."

One more to go—a big-mouthed mold biter. Everybody was moving away from the domino table and slowly drifted toward the back of the tank. For whatever reasons, nobody liked the idea of being selected to provide the large imprint. Except for a few cons sitting on the bench at the front of the tank, Polly and Nolan were without an audience.

"Come on, Polly. Pick somebody so I kin git outta heah. It don't make a fuck who it is," Nolan said.

Polly wheeled away from Nolan and walked over to the five or six cons sitting on the front bench. If a big-mouthed con was what he was looking for, he certainly had found one. Among those on the bench was Gatermouf. Polly pointed straight at him, interrupting Gatermouf's conversation. "Hey you, you wid da big mouf!"

Gatermouf looked confused, even though Polly's finger was aimed right at him. "You talkin ta me, Polly?" he asked in bewilderment.

"Yeah, you nigguh. You got da biggest muthafuckin mouf on da bench. Yeah, I'm talkin ta you. Git up offa yo ass an come bite dis shit for da doc."

Gatermouf didn't move. "Say, man, how come you fuckin wit me?"

"Nigguh," Polly yelled, "if you don't git yo ass off dat bench, you gon need some teefs yosef!"

Gatermouf slowly made his way toward Nolan, grumbling, "I don't know whut y'all fuckin wit me for. Dey's a whole lotsa nigguhs in heah wit moufs bigger'n mine."

Polly overheard. "Who, nigguh? Name somebody! You don't know nobody heah an nowheres else wid a mouf bigger'n yo's."

"Well, if my mouf's so fuckin big, who in da hell gon wear a pair uv teefs made frum my bite? Yeah, smart-assed muthafucka, tell me dat!"

Polly was tired of arguing. "Man, fuck you! Bite dis shit befo I put my foot in yo ass!" Gatermouf reluctantly sank his teeth into the modeling material.

Christmas Day arrived. The purple and red crepe paper hanging from the ceiling sagged from the heat of the radiator pipes. After today, it would be taken down, boxed up, and put away until next year.

The night before, each of us was issued a new shirt, britches, and pair of brogans—the year's ration. The clothes were made by the women prisoners at the Goree Unit. Getting our new clothes was like looking into fortune cookies. Inside the flies of our pants were written "I wish" or "I love it" and other little messages. They also wrote their names, numbers, where they were from, how much time they were doing, and even poems under shirt collars and around the cuffs and tails—any place they felt would escape the eye of the clothes garment inspector. Although the Christmas messages would come out after the first washing, they did add to the merriment of the Yuletide season as convict after convict discovered and showed what was written in his fly "specially" for him.

It was still early morning, and not many cons were up and stirring about just yet. In another few minutes, the tank would be pulsating. Card and domino games would be starting soon, and Big Devil even allowed dice games today. This was the only day of the year that he pulled out all the stops. We could gamble openly in the games and not worry about getting busted. Wasn't much fear of a con being punished today, unless he smarted off at a boss.

Big Devil gave orders to the picket boss to leave the door separating 3 and 4 tanks and the one separating 1 and 2 tanks open so we could "visit" in the adjacent tank. Cons marched through the opened doors like ants. Some just walked through, turned around quickly, and reentered their own tanks. Being able to get out of the tank had more to do with it than visiting.

After our Christmas dinner of turkey and all the trimmings was over, everybody was handed a small paper sack as we walked out the mess hall door. In it were about ten pecans, a super small apple, an orange, and a small walking-cane peppermint stick. Also as we walked out of the mess hall, a cupful of salted peanuts was poured into our hats, which we had been told beforehand to bring to the mess hall with us.

Most of the cons rushed back to the tanks and headed straight for the gambling tables. The small sack and hatful of Yuletide goodies were like five hundred dollars' worth of chips at the Las Vegas casinos. It was hilarious to listen to and watch the betting in those games. "Shoot twenny goobers. Twenny goobers I shoot." At the rate they were counting out their peanuts, some of those games would last all night long. The peanuts were handled so much all the salt and skins had been rubbed off. The gamblers bet a few, ate a few, and squabbled all in between.

The Number 4 tank residents were the lookouts since they could see from their windows whenever somebody came from the front office. One of them sounded the alarm: "Heah comes Cap'n Smooth. He got two nigguhs wit him totin some boxes."

Beer Belly commented, "Maybe he be brangin my prole papers."

Bad Eye answered, "Shit, you ain't gon make no prole 'way frum dis hellhole. You kin forgit dat shit. Nobody knows where dis mutha-fucka is, specially dat prole board. Hell, I been down heah goin on 'leven calendars an ain't never seen nairn down heah yet. 'Sides, dey needs a hellacopta an a pair uv spyglasses jes ta find the road dat comes in heah. An dat's way too much trouble."

"Yeah," Chinaman chimed in, "thas da only reason I ain't dun run off. I don't know where in the hell I am."

Cap'n Smooth came in the back door and up the hall. Two house-boys tagged behind him carrying a cardboard box apiece. "Y'all jes set 'em down heah under the picket," he ordered.

After they sat the boxes down, one asked, "Anythang else, Cap'n, suh?"

"Naw, thas all. Let these two nigguhs back out, boss," he hollered to Boss Humpy as the two trusties turned to leave.

"Merry Christmas to you, Cap'n," they said in parting.

"Yeah."

The full name the cons had dubbed him was Cap'n Smooth Mouth, but they spoke of him as Cap'n Smooth. He was transferred here from one of the northern units when Big Devil took over the camp. He had the notorious reputation for being the "hardest cap'n" in the system, even though he was in his sixties. He was best known for leaping off his horse onto the backs of field workers like Hoot Gibson of the old Wild West movies. He'd fight them man to man and wouldn't allow the bosses to intervene—win, lose, or draw. When he staged these cantankerous melees, he managed to draw a few but never won "nairn."

His idea of weekend fun was to come in the tanks and chase cons down with a pair of pliers to pull out their whiskers or the hair on their heads if he felt it was too long. Sometimes, he put on convict whites he got from the laundry and eased his way into the tanks to catch unalerted crapshooters. He'd sit on a con's bunk unnoticed by the gamblers until he made his presence known: "It's my fuckin shot now." He took all the loot and threw it up in the air. Whoever caught it got to keep it.

The main thing Cap'n Smooth disliked was the "suck ass" tactics the cons used on the officers. By now, the prime suck asses had gathered at their tank doors. With the curiosity of baboons, they were dying to find out what was happening but didn't know how to approach him.

Finally it got the best of one. "Mornin, suh, Cap'n." Smooth didn't answer. Undaunted, "Cap'n, dem sho is some priddy boots." Scratching his head. "Sho would lak ta shine 'em up for you sometime," he said in his best Stepin Fetchit voice.

"Nigguh," Cap'n Smooth said, looking at him as if he were a twice-used condom, "git yore goddamn ass on 'way frum 'em bars 'fore I come in thar and stick these purty boots in yore stankin black ass!" His temper was riled. "You goddamn, rotten-assed bastard! Come up heah fuckin wit me on Christmas. I oughta throw yore maw-dickin ass in that pisser. By God, if it weren't Christmas, thas whar you'd spend the next thirty or forty days!"

The harangued con dropped his head, stuffed his hands into his pants pockets, and began to shuffle away. Looking back over his shoulder like a whipped dog, he muttered, "Merry Christmas to you, Cap'n, suh."

"You jes kiss my Merry Christmas ass," Cap'n Smooth snarled, "you low-down sonuvabitch!" Looking up at the picket, he said, "Boss, now that that sonuvabitch dun quit a-fuckin wit me, I wantcha to call all them ol nigguhs up heah to the front whut needs them false teeth, an git all 'em one-eyed fuckers up heah too."

"Y'all hold it down in thar so I kin hear that cap'n," Boss Humpy hollered into the tanks. "That cap'n wonts alla you nigguhs whut needs them false teeth an ol eyes to come on up heah to the front. Rat now!" He added, "If y'all wont this shit, you betta quit draggin them ol asses roun an git on up heah!"

Cap'n Smooth propped his boot on top of one of the boxes as he talked to those gathered at the tank doors on both sides of the hall. "I'm gonna git that boss to open 'em doors an let you nigguhs come out heah under this picket to git you a set uv these fuckin teeth thas in this box," he said, indicating the one he had his foot atop. "An you ol nigguhs whut needs eyes, they in that box right thar. Y'all understand that?" Then he shouted to Boss Humpy, "Open them doors an let these nigguhs out."

The tank doors opened and the disadvantaged filed out in semiorderly fashion. Bad Eye, One Gone, and Gotch Eye cautiously began opening the eye box while Rat and Gila Monster gingerly opened the teeth box.

They were going at it too gingerly for the captain's impatience, and he barked, "You nigguhs quit a-pickin over them fuckin eyes an teeth! Jes gitcha sump'n an git on 'way frum heah! You rotten bastards kin switch 'em roun when y'all git back in them tanks." Rushing them, he shouted, "Goddamn sonsabitches, gon fuck aroun all day pickin over 'em damn thangs! Jes git 'em an git the hell on back in them tanks!"

Pairs of hands ripped into each box, grabbing what they could.

Cons were putting their eyes and teeth in as they came through the doors. Most of the plates got mixed during the scavenging, and the teeth recipients were busily swapping them to come up with a matching pair. After they did, some were holding theirs over cigarette lighters, heating them in order to bend them into "proper shape."

Our famous baseball pitcher Rat and some of the others made a beeline straight to the gambling tables with their presents and pawned them as collateral to get into the games. I chose to get in one of the other games that played for cigarettes and tobacco. I didn't have any use for an extra eye or set of teeth—yet.

In a nearby game, an argument broke out between Blood Eye and Squat Low. When Squat Low won Blood Eye's eye, he put it in his pocket. Blood Eye didn't like that. "Say, man, take my eye outta yo pocket!"

"Fuck you, man! It ain't none'a yo eye no mo. Dis eye is mine till you pay me my stuff."

"I don't give a fuck, take my eye outta yo pocket, Squat Low. You ain't gon be totin my fuckin eye roun in yo pocket."

"Whutcha want me ta do wit it den?"

"Why don'tcha put it in yo locker."

"Put it in my locker? Nigguh, I don't want that thang lookin at me evah time I go in dere ta git sump'n."

Blood Eye left, soon to return with an empty, all-purpose Bull Durham sack. He pitched it on the table. "Squat Low, put my eye in dis 'bacco sack so you won't see it lookin. Ain't nothin in yo locker my eye wants to see no how. 'Less it's one'a dem homemade fuck books you got."

"Say, Blood Eye, you blockin da cards," Squat Low said as he scooped up the sack and put it in his pocket.

With his mind on the game, he really hadn't paid any attention to Blood Eye, and the fight was on. It didn't last too long because some of the other players quickly broke them apart. But when it was over, Squat Low put Blood Eye's eye in the sack and back in his pocket. "I'll put yo eye in my locker when I git through gamblin."

I asked Good Eye, who was in the game with me, "Say, how come you pick that blue eye?"

"Shit on you, man!" he said, offended. "Dat's da onliest color dey had. It don't make a fuck ta me whut color it is, I can't see outta it no how. Jes long as it keeps da air outta my head an fills up dis gotdam hole, dat's all I wants it to do. So don't be fuckin wit me bout it, man."

After Cap'n "Santa" had come and gone, walking down the alley-way half asleep got real spooky. The dim light of the twenty-watt bulbs cast eerie shadows on the proud eye and teeth recipients' faces. Even as they slept, those with the oversize teeth "grinned" and those with a big blue eye "watched" because their eyelids couldn't close shut over them. All the eyes were one size, extra large. Sending the jumbo, blue artificial eyes down here must have been a good laugh for somebody at the Walls. Passing through the monster colony was worse than walking through a graveyard at midnight. I barely made it to the urinal in time.

The problems those eyes and teeth caused at the face basin every morning turned the area into a battleground. Two or three brawls broke out before we could make it to the chow hall. Some con's big eye fell into the sink as he washed his face just as another was spitting out toothpaste.

"Say, man, don't be spittin dat shit on my fuckin eye, 'less you wants ta die!"

There'd be scrapping back and forth. "Man, fuck you! You oughta keep dat big ol humbolli marble where it b'longs, stuck up in yo ass! Dat's da only hole you got it'll come close ta fittin!"

The fists flew when someone's choppers fell out and got spat on. It was the bell for round one all over again.

13

The Number 1 hoe squad got a late Christmas present. The week after Christmas our guard and nemesis, Boss Deadeye, had a stroke and died. "Yay!" It was mid-January, and Number 1 had been laying in since New Year's. We heard through the grapevine the warden was waiting on somebody "special" to replace Deadeye.

It really didn't matter who they imported. He couldn't possibly be any worse to work under than Boss Deadeye. That one-eyed bastard drove us like sugar-mill jackasses, agitated us from dawn till dusk, and had us punished to no end. As far as most of us were concerned, it was a silent victory—we had outlasted him.

Korea, a trusty who worked as the warden's office porter, had come in for lunch and was at the 3 tank door talking with B.C. while waiting on the call for "short line." The trusties ate thirty minutes ahead of the field force. "That One Hoe won't be layin up on dey asses much longer."

B.C. commented, "I'm sho glad. I'm tired uv lookin at 'em."

"Whoever Big Devil been waitin on jes showed up, an he called him Boss Band." The trusty chow bell sounded and Korea left.

I asked Black Rider, "Didja hear whut Korea jes said?"

"Yeah," he answered drily, "I heard. I sho hope it ain't who he say it is. I worked under him on dat Number Three Ramsey camp back in 'forty-five. Dey transferred him dere cuz he kilt a whole squad over on another camp. I sho hope it ain't him! Boss Deadeye wudn't shit 'pared ta him."

All ten of us began talking about the new boss. Finally, Tennessee spoke with authority. "It happen, it sho happen! Kilt evuh last one uv 'em." He went on, clarifying, "Now I wuzn't in his squad when he dun it. Guess y'all kin see dat. But I wuz on the camp at the time."

Chinaman said, "Say, man, quit hem-hawin roun an tell us whut happen or shut the fuck up."

Tennessee was taking his time with the story. Always out of smokes, he was enjoying the free cigarettes being passed around. He had been on every camp in the system and worked under some of the toughest bosses, had the bullet holes in his legs to prove it, and was lashed so many times in his prison career that his back was striped like a zebra. After bumming a light to fire up the cigarette he had just bummed, he said, "The way I heard it frum some'a the trusties who wek'd roun dem bosses' houses when dat happen wuz dis." He left us hanging as he again stopped to expound. "Now y'all know how the grapevine is. Some you kin bleeve an some you has ta wonder about."

Anxiety got the best of Whitefolks and he could take no more. "Say, alla y'all lissen a minute." He took the floor. "Tell y'all whut, les don't give dis nigguh no mo lights, no mo cigaritts, no mo nothin till he tells us whut he knows!"

Several gave a nod of the head to his suggestion.

"Awright, awright, I'm gon tell y'all. Don't y'all be in such a got-dam hurry. Hell, we ain't got nowhere ta go." With a thick blanket of cigarette smoke filling the air, Tennessee began again. "See, Boss Band had a houseboy, least his wife did"—he chuckled—"whut cleant an cooked for 'em. The way the trusties tole it wuz the houseboy wuz bout ta root Boss Band outta house an home. Dat houseboy wuz really layin it to her.

"Anyhow, him an Boss Band's wife got in a squabble bout cleanin up the house. He spose to talk back to the woman, sassed her out real good when she tole 'em to do sump'n. Nigguh must'a been crazy to thank he could git 'way wit dat. Well, when Boss Band come home dat evenin, she tole 'em the houseboy had sassed her out. She tole Boss Band jes enuff to git 'em punished a lil bit. Jes to show 'em she wuz still his boss, even if dey wuz gittin it on.

"Afta she tole Boss Band, he lef runnin for the buildin. He fount dat houseboy in the tank an tole 'em if he come back to wek he'd kill 'em. Den he went to the warden's house to demand sump'n be dun to his ass. It didn't matta ta Boss Band the warden had jes sot down to eat his suppa. The warden say it could wait till mornin, an he'd look into it.

"But the warden knowed how mean Boss Band wuz an had dat house nigguh hauled off in his car to another camp dat same night. Next mornin, Boss Band come to the buildin an fount out the nigguh wuz gone. The warden wouldn't tell 'em where he sunt 'em.

"When the turnout bell rung, Boss Band took his squad out an tole 'em to wek on 'way frum the others cuz he wanted dem in a cut by dey sef. Whilst dey had dey backs turnt to 'em choppin, he opened up wit dat pump scatter barrel. He mowed 'em down, two an three atta time. Dem whut he didn't git wit dat scatter gun, he finished off wid his .45. Dey say he blowed some'a dem nigguhs half in two. Holes in 'em big nuff to put yo two fists in, all fourteen uv 'em!

"Das why dey calls 'em Kill-a-Band. Cuz when we useta set roun talkin bout it afta it dun happen, we useta say, 'Man, dat boss kilt a whole band uv nigguhs!' His reason wuz dem nigguhs tried to 'git in the saddle' wit 'em. Even afta he dun kilt dat many mens, he nevah missed a day's wek or nothin. All dey dun wuz transfer 'em over to the Ramsey camp.

"We heard through the grapevine he sho straightened out dat One Hoe over dere in a hurry. Hell, he wudn't at Ramsey a month an kilt two mo." Laughing a little, he said, "Dat's when his wife lef him. Dat muthafucka got a graveyard alla his own. I sho hope it ain't him. If it is, yo's truly sho gon put on his travelin shoes!"

Our afternoon leisure was interrupted by the inside picket boss. "Alla you Number One nigguhs, come on outta them tanks an git out on that yard!"

We filed out of our tanks and down the hallway, walking for a change. January's wintry breath strip-searched us at the back door. The sun, just by appearing, showed its bravery. Walking through his shadow to line up against the wall, I glanced at the face half-hidden beneath the wide-brimmed hat. With the sun at his back, he stood motionless. It took a minute or so for the twenty-six of us to stagger ourselves against the wall so each of our faces could be seen by him.

After we were in formation, in a gravelly voice he asked malevolently, "Do y'all know who I am?" His words sounded like the heavy hiss from a deadly serpent. Nobody said a word. He broke the momentary silence. "Well, I know who y'all is, an y'all gonna find out who I am damn quick!"

Standing about six feet tall and maybe weighing one sixty, he looked to be on the older side of sixty. Thumbs tucked in the pockets of his jeans with his weight shifted to one side, he looked intently at each of us. We didn't dare make eye contact with him. Kidskin gloves were neatly stuffed in the empty holster hanging from the extra belt he was wearing. Each bullet compartment contained a round of .45 ammunition. With that many bullets around his waist, he certainly didn't plan on running out. He wore a gabardine khaki shirt, black keen-toed boots, and spurs minus the rowels. There was no crimp in the crown of his black hat; the brim was flat all the way around, exposing the silvery, long sideburns.

When he raised his head enough so the brim no longer hid his sinister-looking face, I stole a peek at his eyes. Their icy blue color contrasted with his heavily tanned, weather-beaten skin, which resembled tarnished leather. He seldom blinked, roving his eyes over us.

"I'm gonna tell y'all one time, an one time alone how I'm gonna deal. First off, if ary one uv you tries to run off, I'm gon kill ya. If ary one uv you 'sputes my word, I'm gon kill ya. If ary one uv you don't do lak I tell ya, I'm gon kill ya. If you lay the hammer down under me, I'm gon kill ya. And if I jes take a notion to, I'm gon kill ya."

Never blinking an eye, he continued his commandments in the same monotone. I was holding my breath after each blunt statement. Was there nothing he wouldn't kill us for?

"I don't wont no conversation wit none'a y'all. Jes y'all do lak I tell ya. I don't know whut y'all dun heard bout me, an I don't give a damn. But I heard you nigguhs jes been drag-assin." Louder, "I'm a-tellin you now, if y'all drag 'em ol asses roun under me, I'm gon kill ya. That last boss y'all had didn't git a goddamn thang outta y'all 'pared to whut I'm gon git. I bet not see ary nigguh comin through 'at back gate wit his shirt not a-stickin to his ass. Ain't gon be no dry nigguhs in my squad." Then he shouted, "*Do you hear me, nigguhs?*"

A few said, "Yassuh," or "We hears you, boss."

"When I'm a-talkin to alla y'all at the same time an I axe y'all do you hear me, ever nigguh betta stop whut he's a-doin an answer me back, 'Oh Lord'! If I'm a-talkin to one'a y'all, 'fore you say *anythang* to me, you betta say aforehand 'Oh Lord.' Is that clear? I'm gonna say it again, an you nigguhs betta answer me right! *Do you hear me, nigguhs?*"

In unison, "*Oh Lawd!*"

"If you nigguhs don't answer me back lak that when I'm a-talkin to ya, then I'm gon bleeve y'all tryin to big-ass me. An if I *ever* ketch any uv that ol punkin goin on in this squad, I'm gon kill ya!"

We had been out on the yard about twenty minutes listening to his death sermon. He reached in his shirt pocket and pulled out a spiral notepad and pencil, slowly sizing us up with his cold eyes. Back and forth he went, looking up and down the line, then settled them on me. "Ol Red!"

Brain locked, I fumbled out a partial "Yes . . . ," then remembered the magic words, "Oh Lawd!"

"Come heah!" I walked over to him. "Kin you read an write?"

"Oh Lawd! Yessuh."

Handing me the pencil and pad, he said, "Go to the fur end an start writin 'em nigguhs' names down, jes lak they's lined up ginst 'at wall."

I turned to leave. "An put yore name down first!"

"Oh Lawd! Speakin to you, boss. Do you want me to write these nigguhs' real names down or their other names?"

"Jes the real uns. I'll learn the others as we go."

It was a near-impossible task. Several of the cons couldn't spell their names, and neither could I. So we just guessed at it and I hoped Boss Band wouldn't notice. After writing all the names, I handed his pencil and pad back, then returned to my place at the end of the front line.

He looked over the names for a moment and closed the pad. "Awright, thas the way I wont y'all to ketch 'em rows, jes lak yore name is writ in this book. You nigguhs gon wek zackly lak y'all lined up ginst 'at wall. If I ketch ary nigguh wekin on a row outta his place in 'is book, I'm gon kill 'em. Now, carry y'all's asses on back in the buildin an be ready to meet that bell come mornin. *Do you hear me, nigguhs?*"

"*Oh Lawd!*"

Walking away, he said over his shoulder, "Boss Band! Thas who I am."

Back inside the tank, I went straight to my bunk and flopped on it, still in shock. I couldn't believe he'd picked me to carry the first row. *Me?* The littlest man in the squad? Whew, *shit!* Gazing at the bottom of the bunk overhead, I thought of running away and even suicide. Fuck! I don't want to be no lead-row man, but his haunting words "if ary one uv you don't do lak I tell ya, I'm gon kill ya" burned in my ears.

My gloom was interrupted when I noticed Black Rider standing next to my bunk, giving me the "last look," as if I were already dead. He took a seat on the vacant bunk across from mine. "Man, he ain't gon have but one gear for you ta put it in, an dat's fas forward. You sho gon hafta bear down on it an step on out, cuz us an him's gon be right 'hind yo lil ass all day long. An you bet not take no long chances, dat muthafucka's a crack shot. Only nigguh he useta shoot at all the time wuz the lead row."

That evening I caught the chow line. Once I sat down at the table, I couldn't eat; my appetite was gone. My belly had more knots in it than a Navy rope and was growling like an old Philco radio dialed between stations. I tossed and turned all night and bolted upright, awakening myself near daybreak, wringing wet with sweat. I knew it was useless to try to go back to sleep. "Alley, boss!"

"Lemme have 'em, boss!"

My knees were shaking as I waited for the next call.

"Number One!"

Like a lightning bolt, I charged down the hall with the Number 1 hoe squad right behind me. When the last man cleared the back steps, "You got twenty-six uv 'em, boss," Cap'n Smooth hollered.

"Thas right."

Clearing the back gate, we got our first work command from him: "Ever nigguh gitta hoe!"

Leading the pack, I veered for the hoe rack. In nothing flat, we had our aggies and took off like rats fleeing from a burning barn. My walking gait was good. Leaning into the wind, I balanced the hoe handle against the crook of my arm with the blade hoisted high in the air.

"Ol Red!"

"Oh Lawd!"

"Head 'em on over to that high-line turnrow an ketch in."

"Oh Lawd!"

Glancing over my shoulder, I saw the other squads coming behind in the distance. We were a good forty yards ahead of the closest one, Number 2. He galloped his horse to stay up with us as we burned rubber going down the turnrow. Three or four miles later we were there.

"Tail-row nigguh! Count off twenty-six rows. Y'all ketch 'em an git on 'way frum heah!"

After Bad Eye stepped off the first row, I caught it—just like it was "writ in the book." I couldn't remember the exact order I'd listed all the names, but I knew Cap Rock's was the first after me. He got his push-row position back. Because Bad Eye's name was the last one on the list, he fell heir to Chinaman's job.

Thousands and thousands of empty rows stared us in the face. The workforce had to "air" the rows out by hacking and pulverizing the soil. It was close to planting time again, and this helped dry the land out faster. We hacked down one side of a row to the end and came back hacking down the other side. The weather had been clear the last several days, and the winter sun dried the top layer of soil.

I was middle ways into the field on my row before I looked back and saw the last squad, Number 8, catching their rows. I sank my hoe blade deep as I could each time I dug it into the soft black gumbo. We had to do more than just break the crust, the rows had to be flattened. On the way back down our rows, we passed Number 2 hoe. They were still about twenty yards from reaching the end for the first time.

Even though a cool, crisp breeze blew across the fields, my shirt was sticking to my back. Just like the lawgiver said, "Ain't gon be no dry nigguhs in my squad." I gutted the inside of my row each time I sank my aggie blade into the earth. It was still hard to believe I was the lead-row man, the pacesetter.

Lunch was short on the johnny ground. We were rushed through our meal by Cap'n Smooth. "Y'all betta hurry up an eat that ol hog an bread, an git on back out yonder an finish up them rows."

We made a pit stop at the water wagon and headed back to work. *It ain't as bad as I thought*, I said to myself with each savage hack. Number 1 hoe had been sailing all day. None of the other squads even got near us. I was holding my own and keeping my row out front. We hacked up and down row after row after row. The sun was going down. Cap'n Smooth had already left the field; Sundown was in charge. He would keep us out until the sun's last glimmer. He didn't hassle the cons, but he sure hated to knock off.

The other squads had slowed down just a hair as quitting time neared, but Number 1 hoe was still driving hard when somebody hollered, "Dere it is, it's in the air!"

We made a dash for the turnrow. After he counted, Boss Band said, "Ol Red!"

"Oh Lawd!"

"Take 'em on to that house. Go 'head! Hey, boss! Pull them goddamn heifers over out the way an let these Number One bulls come on by," Boss Band shouted up ahead. With the right-of-way cleared, he told me, "Ol Red! Bear down!"

"Oh Lawd!" I said, speeding up the walking cadence four more notches, causing the rest of the squad to strike up a trot.

At the back gate we waited for Boss Band to check in his weapons and give the "go 'head" signal. "Ol Red!"

"Oh Lawd!"

"Git over yonder! Resta y'all nigguhs, go 'head!"

For what? I dared not ask.

I stood at the back gate until the last man in Number 8 hoe went through. Out of all the two-hundred-plus field workers, I was the only man cut out. After shakedown, Cap'n Smooth marched me through the gate. As we walked toward the building, I said, "Speakin to you, Cap'n."

"Whut?"

"Cap'n, whut'd I git cut out for?"

He spat tobacco juice. "Dry up that ol mouth. I don't want no talk, nigguh." Once inside, he said, "Boss, hand me down a pair fer this nigguh." After cuffing me tightly to the bars, he told me, "These cuffs'll git a nigguh's heart right."

After I'd been hanging about four hours, the pain made me forget my anger. The cuffs were one thing all the cons agreed on: "They kin make the blind see, the lame walk, an the deaf hear."

I twisted into a hundred different positions seeking relief, hoping to find one that even resembled comfort, but it was no use. The hours snailed by until finally the bright lights were on and the turnkey unlocked me. I made it to the latrine quick as I could, splashed water on my face, and got ready for breakfast. Even though the last time I ate was at the johnny ground, I wasn't all that hungry. Just tired as hell and aching. My rib cage felt like somebody had taken a crowbar and pried those ribs six inches apart.

"Number One!"

At the end of the day when we got out on the turnrow and headed for the building, I didn't let up. The squad was strung out behind me like a string of beads, running to keep up. Occasionally, I heard complaints behind me to "slow dis muthafucka down, man." We were panting when we arrived at the back gate. I was so exhausted I was about to drop, but I wasn't about to show it. I had run them raggedy all day.

"Go 'head!"

I could hardly wait to get on my bunk after supper. I was half-asleep when several Number 1 hoe workers came over to my bunk. "Say, man," Cap Rock said. I opened my eyes. "Whut the fuck wuz dat shit all bout? Rippin an runnin up an down dem fuckin rows lak you wuz crazy or sump'n, an dat man wuz on our asses lak stank on shit. We wuz lucky he didn't cut us all out at the back gate."

Jack Hammer added, "Yeah, man, you wuz messin wit our hog an bread doin dat!"

"Well," I said, "seems thas the way y'all wanna do it. None uv y'all don't thank I kin carry the lead row no how. Hell, I didn't ask for it! Whut wuz I spose ta do? Not take it?"

Their blank stares told me that no matter what I said, I was still unwanted.

Cap Rock spoke up again. "If dat's the way you feel bout it, you know you gon hafta burn ever one'a us out. Cuz afta dis shit you pulled, we gon *carry* yo lil ass a while! An I don't thank you kin hold 'em."

"We'll see," I replied as they walked away. I closed my eyes again, trying to drift off to sleep. My body was bone tired and wanted to sleep, but my mind was afraid to let go completely. I couldn't afford to miss anything; my survival depended on it. Somebody was always waiting for somebody else to fall asleep. In the wee hours the lecherous building tenders went on the prowl. And the creatures of the night (Ol Toe Sucker and Company) came out.

Like Toe Sucker, these vampires lived in the tank's ghetto, the back bunks closest to the commodes. When the tank lights are dimmed, that end is the darkest. Along with Toe Sucker, these phantoms waited until the others went to sleep to attack.

A couple of them were just bold pests and fairly harmless. If they saw a con's leg hanging off his bunk, they'd tiptoe up to him, feel and rub on it, and jack off. The sneakier ones really didn't go for blood and were content just to pass by an exposed leg or thigh, touch it quickly, go on to the back, and jack off while sitting on the commode gazing back up the alley at it. The few who actually climbed in the bunks with sleeping cons and started hunching them got their asses beat so much they finally kicked the habit.

The endless cycle of seasons brought us back to corn harvesting. When we first started pulling it, four huge John Deere were sent to the camp to help us out. The cons operating the equipment, along with their supervisor, were transferred from unit to unit to help with the corn and maize harvests. Every row the combines harvested was a row we wouldn't have to pull by hand. Those fourteen-foot sacks full of corn got mighty heavy to drag down the long, city-block rows.

Number 1 hoe was moving through the wind-tangled stalks like a swarm of hungry locusts. When we got to the ends of our rows, we emptied the heavy, gut-busting sackfuls into the trailers parked on the turnrow. We were high rolling and close enough to take a better look at those rumbling green giants. The machines were doing the whole operation at one time; pulling, shucking, and spitting the kernels into a tractor-drawn cart running alongside.

I looked up from my row to see Big Devil's Chevrolet speeding down the turnrow, leaving a swirl of dust behind. His presence in the field automatically caused everybody to speed up. He stopped directly in front of our squad and got out.

While sitting on the hood talking with Cap'n Smooth and Sundown, Big Devil pointed toward the combines. I was dumping my sackful into the trailer ten or fifteen feet from them when Big Devil beckoned for Boss Band. He walked his horse over to the car. "When yore nigguhs finish emptyin up, take 'em over yonder an y'all ketch in next to them combines. Brang them rows back thisa way," he ordered, motioning across the field.

"Whut if we ketch up wit 'em?"

"Go roun 'em," Big Devil quipped devilishly.

"Awright, you Number One nigguhs, git them goddamn sacks emptied up an git on 'way frum 'at trailer. Some'a you nigguhs gon git a load'a buckshot in yore ass if you don't tighten up! Ol Red!" Whenever he called out my "name," it sounded like he was calling a horse.

"Oh Lawd!"

"Head 'em over yonder an ketch in next ta them combines! Take 'em on!"

As we flew to the rows to catch in, Big Devil sent the other squads in the opposite direction. This left only the Number 1 hoe squad pulling corn on the same side of the turnrow as the combines. We covered the couple hundred yards, fanned out, and caught in headed the same way as the four combines. Cap Rock and I were out front, speeding down our rows. The rest of the Number 1 workers were angled off in handshaking distance of one another. We pulled within twenty yards and were catching up.

Big Devil borrowed Cap'n Smooth's horse. He looked like he was riding a pogo stick, bouncing up and down in the saddle as the horse galloped toward the combine supervisor's pickup. When he reached it, the supervisor jumped out and pulled off his hat. After their brief conversation, the supervisor walked across the field and waved his hands until he got the operators' attention. He gave them a hand signal to rev up their engines, pull out the throttles, and run the machines wide open. They began pulling away from us until . . .

Boss Band shouted, "Ol Red!"

"Oh Lawd!"

He fired a shot in the ground behind me. It was close enough to kick the dirt up on my back. "You bet not let them fuckin combines gitta way frum you! The resta you thangs betta lay wit 'em!"

He rode his horse back and forth behind the squad, using his reins as a whip to drive and prod. "Git them goddamn rows on up yonder wit that lead-row nigguh!"

He shot again—somewhere. I pulled corn so fast it was as if I put it on automatic. All the squad could see was the tail end of my sack. The scent of gunpowder was all the additional motivation I needed. My sack was getting heavier and heavier, slowing me down.

Boss Band spotted my cumbersome handicap. "Ol Red!"

"Oh Lawd!" I said, thinking he was going to shoot again.

"Whenever you git a sackful, jes git out uv it an leave it lay. Resta you nigguhs pull up even wit that lead-row nigguh's sack an git out uv 'em."

He hollered across the turnrow for Water Boy Brown to bring some empties. He dropped the large bundle in the middle of the squad. We grabbed two empties apiece and tore out again. The combines finished their rows and were heading back on others with a fifty-yard lead on us. Boss Band galloped to catch up, yelling final instructions to the water boy: "Have some more sacks waitin at the other end when we git thar."

We spread out across our twenty-six rows and caught in behind the combines. Big Devil watched through his binoculars. I glanced over at Cap Rock. "I'm goin after 'em. Pass the word an tell 'em to come on. Let's show them muthafuckas we kin do it!"

When the word reached Bad Eye, we double-clutched it after those combines like a pack of whippets after a jackrabbit. My sack was full middle ways down the row. I dropped it, unfolded the empty hanging from my free shoulder, and lit out again. When the others evened with my full sack, they did the same. The machines had the edge, they never stopped.

I was gaining. I filled up another sack and got an empty. All my concentration was on those ears of corn. Just like a magician, I made them disappear into my sack. This time when I bent down and straightened up again, I reached the end of my row the same time the combines did. They were catching more rows and going the other way.

The squad finished their rows and got fresh sacks. We took off down the turnrow to catch in, this time right beside them. Boss Band fired again. That last shot evened *everybody* with the machines. The combines were running wide open—but so were we.

The noisy engines drowned out Boss Band. He must have said something, but we didn't hear it. He rode his horse to the front of the squad and I saw his mouth shout out, "Go 'head!" as he leveled his scatter barrel at us.

We passed the combines and beat them to the end by at least thirty feet. The operators shook their heads in disbelief when we went by. There would be no catching us now. We were reaching the ends of our rows a good twenty yards ahead of them every time. We kept it up all day. Big Devil was so pleased with our performance he radioed the agricultural director at the Central Unit to send the heavy equipment trucks to come pick up the combines and "take 'em summers else where they need 'em."

After supper Cap Rock walked up beside me at the face basin. "Lil ol nigguh, we gon run yo ass so damn fas you ain't gon know if you comin or goin!"

"Say, man, fuck alla y'all right dead in the ass! Whut the hell am I spose to do when he shoots an tells me to tighten it up? I don't plan on gittin shot for goin too slow! If you can't keep up, tough shit! Didn't none uv y'all wait for me when I useta be way behind. We been over this shit befo, Cap Rock. If you don't lak the way I'm carryin the lead row, why don'tcha tell it to the man!"

"Look, man, you know you can't hold me if I really wanna pass yo ass. An you sho can't beat me pickin cotton! Only reason I been lettin you stay ahead'a me is I don't wanna job you to the man."

"Bullshit! You ain't been *lettin* me do shit! Cap Rock, I kin outwork you any day uv the week!"

"Lak hell you kin! I'm damn sho gon see when cotton-pickin time comes roun again! I'm gon have dat man on yo lil ass so much you gon wish you wuz dead. Lil nigguh, you don't know who you talkin to! Thas how I got my name," he said, referring to an area in West Texas known as the Cap Rock, noted for growing cotton. "I wuz born an raised in a cotton patch," he boasted.

"An thas where they gon bury yo ass if you keep on fuckin with me! Cap Rock, we don't hafta wait till cotton-pickin time. Me an you kin git it on anytime!"

Later that evening Slocum, who had just returned from the Walls hospital from a hernia operation, told us Road Runner had died about three months ago. Black Rider commented, "Greyhound, Cheetah, now Road Runner. Dem wuz the three baddest lead-row nigguhs I ever run behind, but dat ass-kickin turnrow don't take no shit."

I decided I wasn't going to let "dat ass-kickin turnrow" kill me the way it had them, but it sure was breathing down my neck. It was so bad now that the months ahead would outweigh a motherfucker by ninety pounds. The workers in the squad tried to run me down one by one. On a daily basis, somebody challenged me to a "burnout" by working ahead or walking in front of me on the turnrow. And *nobody* is supposed to be in front of the lead-row man.

Most of the cons were just mouth, and if they could hog you, they would. From experience I knew the first blow generally won the fight, so the very moment anyone threatened, I struck. Boss Band never cut me out for fighting. So rather than race with them one by one, I began hitting them with my hoe, fist, or whatever to make them stay in line behind me. I chopped Kool Aid in the head with my hoe and damn near took off one of his ears for walking ahead of me on the turnrow. When he fell, Boss Band made me and some of the squad drag him off to one side for the water wagon to pick up when it came by.

It was cotton-chopping time again, and we must have been working fast enough to please Boss Band. At least he hadn't shot yet. I looked out of the corner of my eye and saw that Railhead Shorty had pulled up beside me, bucking for my job. "Say, man, gitcha ass back in line where you b'long!" I growled. He kept chopping his row even with mine, grinning and gunning his motor by chopping a little ahead of me, which was telling the boss that I wasn't going fast enough for him. I hollered, "Oh Lawd! Gittin 'em over here, boss!"

"Go 'head!"

We took off. Nearing the ends of our rows for the first time, we chopped side by side. Hurrying to beat Railroad Shorty out on the turnrow to the next set of rows, I tripped over the raggedy legs of my pants, got up quickly, and tore after him. I saw no signs of his letting up as he swooshed his aggie blade between the young cotton stalks, plucking out the weeds, leaving the standard four stalks to the hill.

I shifted into "double nuther" gear and went by him so fast it threw his timing off. In an effort to catch up, he stopped chopping and walked up even with me, leaving a long skip of grass behind him.

Boss Band rode over to check our rows, saw the grass Railhead Shorty had left, and made him go back to rechop it.

He stayed right at his heels, cursing him with every breath, driving him to catch up. Railhead Shorty made it to the turnrow and dropped down on all fours. Boss Band tried to trample him with his big black horse, Ol Satan, who had a cold-blooded disposition and would attack when we got too close.

Railhead Shorty barely rolled out of Satan's path. Boss Band tried again. Railroad Shorty got to his feet, staggered, and stumbled toward the squad, but he fell again. Boss Band hit him with the barrel of his shotgun as he tried to get up. Blood splattered, Railhead Shorty was sprawled out in the middles.

"Ol Chinaman, Ol Mae Widder! Come back heah an drag this rotten bastard out yonder on 'at turnrow. Tell 'at water nigguh to pour some water on 'em when y'all git up thar."

They grabbed an arm apiece and began dragging him. "One'a you nigguhs come back heah an git that sorry sonuvabitch's hoe an take it wit 'em."

Both dropped Railhead Shorty's arms at the same time and started back for the hoe. "I jes need one'a you nigguhs!" They put on the brakes. Boss Band shouted angrily, "Ol Chinaman! Git this goddamn aggie 'fore I shoot both uv you ignorant bastards! Tell that water nigguh when he gits this nigguh revived, tell 'em he betta ketch up wit us, cuz if I havta go to that house 'thout 'em, I'm gon kill 'em. Resta you nigguhs git on 'way frum heah! Go 'head!"

We finished chopping a couple more sets of rows. Railhead Shorty was on his way back, and soon as he got to us, he caught in and started chopping.

Boss Band slowly walked Satan over and stopped him about ten feet from me. I felt his eyes burning in my back. "Ol Red!"

"Oh Lawd!"

"Whar you frum, nigguh?"

Here we go with that "whut color is yore ol mammy" shit again. "Longview, boss." *I don't want no conversation with this muthafucka. Why is he over here fuckin with me?*

"Well, they ain't got no cotton to mount ta nothin in Longview," he commented.

"Nawsuh, they sho don't."

"Whar you learn how to chop cotton lak 'at?"

"Right heah, boss."

"How long you been heah?"

"Goin on five years, boss."

"I wuz watchin yore row when y'all wuz goin up through thar to see if you wuz gon be leavin a buncha them weeds. Goddamn me, I never seed a nigguh racehossin up an down a row lak 'at, an clean it thatta way. Why hell, I knowed that nigguh weren't gon keep up wit you. I'da bet money on it."

He paused a moment. "Thank thas whut I'm gon name you. *Ol Racehoss!* Thas whut I'm a-namin you. You hear me, nigguh!"

"*Oh Lawd!*"

"When I calls you that, you betta answer!" Then he shouted to the squad, "Did the resta y'all nigguhs hear that?"

"*Oh Lawd!*"

"Ol Racehoss, y'all take 'em rows on away frum heah! Go 'head!"

From then on, Ol Racehoss was my name. The bosses called me that, and the cons called me just plain Race, for short.

That night in the tank I got the ten Number 1 hoe workers together and told them, "Some'a y'all think you kin outwork me. Maybe you kin. I ain't gon keep racin y'all one atta time no mo. I'm gon race one mo uv y'all an thas it. I don't give a damn who it is, but I tell you one muthafuckin thing. If I burn out whoever y'all pick, the next time one uv you bastards git in fronta me, I'm gon try to kill him. Who's it gonna be?" I already knew who they were going to choose.

Thirty-Five spoke up. "We pick Cap Rock."

Cap Rock said, "It's okay by me."

"Do we agree that if I win, y'all will quit fuckin with me?" I asked.

They spoke among themselves. "Okay, man, if you burn Cap Rock out, we'll letcha up," one of them said.

"Y'all got a deal, an watch me wear his ass to a frazzle."

They went their way in the tank; I went mine. Tomorrow's race was set; this burnathon was for all the glory marbles.

When we got to the field the next morning and caught our rows, Cap Rock took off down his and got ahead of everybody in the squad. I kept a steady cotton-chopping beat, allowing him to get no more than a few feet ahead of me. He had a good drag and held the lead all the way to the end. Even on the turnrow when we headed to catch some more rows, he walked slightly out in front, jobbing me. The squad knew what was going on, and, by now, so did Boss Band. Cap Rock was "askin" for my job.

Back on the turnrow after lunch, he walked out ahead again. Boss Band had seen enough and hollered, "Ol Racehoss!"

"Oh Lawd!"

"You betta quit yore drag assin, an git to carryin 'at lead row!"

I stepped on out and regained the lead position. "Gitcha jive ass back in line, Cap Rock!" He slacked back just a hair. Looking over my shoulder as we sped down the turnrow, I hollered, "Oh Lawd! Speakin to you, boss!"

"Whut?"

"Takin Ol Cap Rock a round or two when we ketch in!"

"Go 'head!" We'd been cleared to duel. He pitched the fourteen-inch file he kept hanging from the horn of his saddle to Bad Eye. "Put a good edge on both uv them nigguhs' hoes."

This took a few minutes. When Bad Eye finished, he returned the file and retook his place on the tail row. Cap Rock and I waited for Boss Band to give the signal.

"Go 'head!"

Neck and neck we left the blocks. We quickly pulled away from the squad. Boss Band hollered at us, "Y'all carry them rows on away frum heah!" which was cutting us loose from the herd.

It was go for what you know. The pace was brutal—a leg cramper, a shoulder acher, a back breaker until somebody dropped or quit. My race with Railhead Shorty the day before had my body sore. We covered at least four feet each time we dragged our hoes down either side of our rows. This was a duel in the sun, requiring stamina and skill.

I fell back a lick so I could take a better look at his drag and spotted the flaw. He was sinking his hoe too deep. I barely skimmed the ground's crust with mine. Smelling blood in the water, I tightened my gait a notch. On the next set of rows I took a slight lead, pulled away, and kept lengthening the distance. About two hours into the race, I lost count of the rows we'd chopped; but I was so far ahead, it was as if I had sprouted wings like Pegasus and flown away from him.

Boss Band called me back, "Ol Racehoss! Come on back over heah in the squad. This goat-smellin sonuvabitch dun laid the hammer down!" He herded Cap Rock back into the squad, trying his best to ride him down with Satan. "If I ketch another one'a you bastards in fronta Ol Racehoss on 'em rows, I'm gon kill you!" he hollered, adding, "An you nigguhs stop a-crowdin him when y'all out on 'at turnrow. Next nigguh I see a-crowdin him, I'm gon blow the top uv his goddamn head off! *Do you hear me, nigguhs?*" he bellowed.

"*Oh Lawd!*"

Cap Rock and the others wouldn't dare push me anymore. They would work and walk where they were supposed to and let me set the pace. Boss Band would see to that.

14

I was just any other "wild-assed nigguh" under Boss Deadeye. Under Boss Band, I grew into manhood. He got butter from a duck. The hungry years under the Band forged me a body "'thout a ounce uv fat on it." My legs were lean and muscular like a distance runner's, like a racehorse's. My chest looked like I'd been pumping iron, with muscles sinewy as the village blacksmith's. I'd been slow-baked in the sun's oven like the men of the desert, and blended in with the rest. Camouflaged by my desert bronze, I could have been mistaken for a Mexican. But up close, my eyes gave me away. I'd become as one of them, and my color wasn't an issue.

I saw my transformation taking place, reminding me of when I was a kid and watched Lon Chaney Jr. change into the Wolf Man at the picture show. My hands, rough as sandpaper with layers of hard calluses lining the palms, scarcely resembled the ones that used to cast dice. No more blisters from the brogans without socks, my feet had toughened by the miles and miles of turnrow they tread. My sculptured body was tight with nothing inside but guts. That's all I was running on. I'd become the lone gray wolf that had fought his way up through the pack, and was now leading it.

Number 1 hoe became a motorized squad, and we proved it to any nonbelievers by outworking the corn combines. There wasn't much difference between us and the other squads, except we had to do it four times faster with the same quality. Before Boss Band, I was a shadow among shadows, a robot among robots. He brought me from obscurity and placed me at the helm of the ship.

Two years after becoming lead row, I had that "drag," that lick, that rhythm in my shoulders when chopping cotton. I could pluck the small grass shoots growing against the tender cotton stalks and never bruise the stalks. The relentless pressure struck a chord—what mattered became confusing. A different set of priorities, values, thoughts emerged.

Boss Band pushed me beyond any limits I dreamed I had. He forced the word *can't* out of my vocabulary. He gave no alternatives, it was do or die. At times I felt like throwing up both my hands and screaming "Kill me! Kill meeee!" Something within forbade it, and I kept on going.

Working under the Band brought out the best and the worst in me. He was the catalyst, forcing me to think, compelling me to recognize, to look, to become aware of where I was and what was going on all about me. Every smallest thing I learned to appreciate. He drove me into the arms of a friend who later became a lover. As my friend she cooled me off. As my lover she gave me rest. In the free world she'd always been an adversary, a dreaded nuisance. But he opened my eyes to her, and I'll never forget the day I fell in love with the *rain*.

That day, it had been so hot I saw little heat devils jumping on the glistening turnrow. The only dry spot on my body was my throat. That day, the heat made me dizzy and I began to imagine things. I thought I saw a hawk light upon a cloud in the endless blue sky, which held the glaring sun diamond in its navel. Two or three cons had already collapsed in the heat.

We started hollering for rain like a bunch of croaking frogs. In less than two hours, a light shower came from the Gulf and cooled us off. With mouths gapped open like hungry baby birds, we held our faces skyward and stuck out our tongues to catch the drops as they went flickering by. The rain cloud wept her tears and left. We moved to a drier cut across the turnrow and worked on. Ol Hannah must have laughed while drying and sucking the sap from my bones. At least a dozen men had fallen and were dazed and lying under the water wagon. I was near collapse, I just hadn't dropped. The rain blew her cool, soothing breath across my face just before she came again.

I glad-watered but nobody noticed; I was wet all over, thanks to her. Her persistence forced Cap'n Smooth to wave his hat.

Another day Hannah hung high and bore down, asking for it every step we took. All day we'd kept up a hellish pace. As if possessed, the Band drove us with unrelenting fury, and we'd made three revolutions around the other squads. Drag-stepping in our heelless brogans, we glided down the turnrow, enveloped in our own cloud of dust, a shivering mirage.

Suddenly, Satan snorted violently, let out a loud, eerie neigh, and fell over dead, pinning Boss Band underneath. We finally drove the big black bastard down and jobbed him to the man. He wouldn't be biting us in the ass anymore when we got too far behind.

Jack Hammer, Thirty-Five, and Mule rushed back and grabbed Satan by the legs, hoisting him off Boss Band. Like the Pony Express, the livestock supervisor delivered a fresh steed. Looking more evil than ever, he unsaddled the carcass and quickly saddled his replacement. And the Band played on. "Go 'head!"

That evening at the back gate Boss Band cut the three rescuers out to be punished. The next day in the squad he called them back. "I'm tellin y'all heah an now, ain't nary one uv you nigguhs heavy wit me. I oughta kilt y'all fer doin sump'n I didn't tell ya to do. Git yore goddamn asses back to wek!" He fired in the ground behind them as they ran back to catch their rows.

At night in the tank we sat around and joked about who jumped the highest and how long he stayed in midair after Boss Band shot behind us. Tonight, it was Jack Hammer, Mule, and Thirty-Five on the butt end. When Boss Band shot behind them, Mule remained running in flight a good eighteen seconds, according to our "stopwatches." He was declared the top "air walker" in the Number 1 hoe squad.

It was July; the cotton was growing its ass off. Soon, we would start picking. After we chopped it for the last time, we headed to the woods. Acres of bottomland could be cleared before the cotton blossomed. The only good part about working in the woods around the snakes, scorpions, and leeches was that it provided us with a source of meat. Since meat was seldom served in the mess hall, we were allowed to take any critter we could catch to the building to get it cooked. All we had to do was holler "gittin it over heah, boss!" and take out after it.

Boss Band loaned out his pocketknife to clean the catch. One of the feet was left unskinned so the cooks could tell what it was and how it should be cooked. Possums, coons, rabbits, squirrels, armadillos, and any other edibles were run down and caught. Nothing was safe near Number 1 hoe. When somebody in the squad hollered "dere it go," "it" was dead meat.

Some cons were so fast they could catch a running rabbit in a matter of seconds. Each man in the chase got a share of the kill. It was taken in that evening after work and served at supper the next night. Terrible fights broke out when the cook got the meat mixed up and gave it to the wrong cons.

I wasn't allowed to run critters; I had to keep the lick going. Because of this, I got cut in on whatever was caught. Runnin Time caught an owl once and had it prepared in the kitchen. I was going through the chow line right behind him to ensure my piece of the fowl.

The cook came from behind the steam table and handed him a tin pan containing the cooked bird, with the shortest drumsticks I'd ever seen. Runnin Time had a pan in each hand, but he wasn't passing up a thing on the steam table. Owl or no owl. When we got to the chocolate pudding, he held the pan of owl forward.

The flunky looked confused as he waved the ladle over the pan for a place to pour it. They were holding up the line. "Say, man, where you want me ta po dis shit?"

"Dumb-ass nigguh, if dis wuzza turkey an dem wuz cranberries, you'd know where to put it. Po it over dis fuckin owl!"

That night I ate my first and last piece of chocolate-covered owl.

Due to the density of vast underbrush, the woods afforded the best possibilities for escape. With such limited visibility, there was no way the bosses could see all of us all the time. In the woods we were the closest to the "Big Brazie" River, which was the main escape route. Boss Band counted constantly.

Tarzan was in his finest element in the woods. He loved it, and, if anything, the woods weren't wild enough for him. He was a husky, barrel-chested, gorilla-looking con with long hair growing on his muscly arms. He didn't have any top or bottom front teeth, which made him look like he had fangs. When he opened his mouth, it looked like a huge python's.

Whenever Tarzan caught a critter, he didn't waste time waiting for the cooks. He used his fangs to snap its neck. Then he'd bite the head off and spit it on the ground. He didn't want to eat "no brains," but he ate everything else—blood, guts, hair, and all! Usually, whatever he ate was still kicking as he chewed.

Always, after he caught something, Tarzan let out a loud, jungle-like holler that caused Boss Band's horse to rear in fright. All the birds in the trees would fly away, and the small animals scurried to safety. I would have loved for Tarzan to walk up on Bloody Bones out in the woods. That oozy bastard wouldn't have lasted five minutes around him and would have been gobbled up, without the salt.

With all that blood on his face and around his mouth, Tarzan reminded me of a little playmate I grew up with, Marie. But us kids called her Meat Reetie. She was Floyd's sister, even uglier than him, with two-inch Buckwheat plaits all over her head.

Miss Bertha took Floyd, Marie, and me to the creek to catch crawdads. For some reason Miss Bertha always handed the raw liver she bought for bait to Meat Reetie to tote. We'd be walking in front of her, toting the poles and buckets, and look back to see Marie's mouth and face covered with blood. She'd look at us so innocently, with the most blank expression, while smearing it all over her face, trying to hide the evidence. Miss Bertha ended up spitting snuff juice on small pinecones, and we'd catch plenty of crawdads anyway. Meat Reetie looked funny; Tarzan did not.

Nobody liked to sit next to him in the mess hall. We always tried to leave an empty seat between him and us. He slobbered and spat food all over the table as he chewed ravenously. When he said, "Pass de salt," we all leaned back to let his foul breath pass on by. We certainly didn't want to get breath-poisoned by the "funky-breathed muthafucka," as he was referred to under our breaths.

Going to the woods was like going to the big top, a circus without the tent. It wasn't unusual to see cons pulling brush or axing trees with live baby snakes dangling from their earlobes. They applied pressure on the snakes just below the head, forcing them to open their mouths, then clamped them on. Looking at those Medusa-eared jokers, I knew the classification committee had really blown it . . . again. Tarzan wasn't the only crazy one out there, and the woods seemed to bring out our wilder sides.

Because the thick brush and foliage obscured Boss Band's view, it provided cover for Cowfucker. He was always on the prowl for any loose cow unlucky enough to stray into our work area. That sentence he got for "cattle theft" hadn't curbed his lust one bit. I don't know how he could catch one of those half-wild cows without a horse and a real rope, but he kept right on trying. He seemed intelligent enough and had even attended college, but his thinking was definitely screwed up. It's hard to imagine preferring cows over a campus full of coeds, but he boasted many times that "if a cow could cook I'd marry one."

It had been raining recently, and the forest was steaming. Thick swarms of mosquitoes were having a field day, and the spiders, bugs, worms, and other creeping, crawling brigades were stirring about on the forest floor, totally unhampered by our presence. Boss Band split us into three work groups: the cutters, the trimmers, and the brush pullers. We all loaded the heavy logs, except Whitefolks. Boss Band didn't know he had a bad back, but we did. Nobody wanted to lift logs with him as a partner, so when we split up into our regular three-man loading teams, Whitefolks kept pulling brush. Boss Band had a policy about loading logs, "Thar ain't no four-nigguh-size logs out heah. Three's high as they go."

The cutting teams felled quite a few of the tall timbers. It was time for us to pull back to help the trimmers catch up. Then we'd load. Enormous piles of trimmings and underbrush hissed and crackled in the flames no more than fifty feet from our backs. What little wind there was blew all the fiery heat in our direction.

The brush pullers were catching the most hell. They had to get close enough to heave the limbs into the flames, and the more they piled on, the hotter it got. After we helped the trimmers and loaded, my four-man cutting team went back to axing. We worked at a furious speed to get farther into the woods away from the fires. Two men cut at the same time on opposite sides of the tree. Each pair struck their blows in sync with their grunts to avoid hitting the other pair's swinging axes.

When I heard Boss Band holler "Ol Glodine!" I glanced back at the brush pullers. I saw that Glodine's ass was really dragging. Boss Band seemed to take offense at any cons in the squad with girl monikers, and had been driving him all day. "Don'tcha be a-draggin no more uv them damn lil ol twigs up heah to this far [fire]. Go back yonder an grab some more uv them limbs. You goddamn rotten-assed ol whore! I oughta blow a goddamn hole through you! Go to wek!"

Glodine had a strange look on his face when he hurried over to my tree to gather limbs. He walked up so close that Bad Eye had to stop cutting. "Whut's the matter with you, man?" I asked.

"Will one'a y'all chop off my hand if I lay it on dis tree?"

"Man, you crazy? Hell naw! I ain't gon chop off yo fuckin hand," I said.

Bad Eye, a mean bastard doing life, told him, "Put it up dere. I'll chop the muthafucka off."

I stood stunned as Glodine laid his right hand against the tree, mumbling, "I can't take it no mo. I got ta git 'way frum Boss Band an dis place."

Big Louzanna and Cryin Shame, the other pair, stopped when Bad Eye asked, "You sho you wants yo hand chopped off? Ain't gon be no uh-oh. When I hits, it's gone."

Gritting his teeth, Glodine muttered, "Do it, man," and turned his face away.

Bad Eye *whacked* it off, right across the knuckles, leaving Glodine's fingers still dangling and stuck to the tree. Glodine never made a sound, cradled what was left of his hand, and dropped to his knees.

I hollered, "Oh Lawd! Got one with his hand hurt over here, boss!"

Boss Band rode over. "Whut happen ta that nigguh's hand?"

Bad Eye blurted out, "Oh Lawd! Boss, it wuzza axident. I couldn't hep it. The nigguh walked up heah rat in the way."

Boss Band stared at each of us a moment, then rode off. He radioed back to the building with his walkie-talkie for a pickup truck to "come take one in."

We were still standing around after the excitement until Boss Band shouted, "You nigguhs git y'all's asses back to wek! That ain't the first time y'all seed nigguh blood. Git back to wek! Go 'head!"

As our foursome started our lick back up, Big Louzanna kicked off a song. I was sure glad they took Glodine's fingers with him—I wouldn't have wanted to "axidentally" step on them. As the truck hauled him down the turnrow, Big Lou sang "Black Betty's in the Bottoms" whilst our axes spoke our grief and misery.

The next day we were three men short. Replacements for Number 1 hoe were slow to come by. Elefin Head and Cryin Shame got a rare lay-in. They'd got into some poison ivy and "swole" up so bad they couldn't go to work. I saw them before we left the building, and they were hardly recognizable. The last thing Elefin Head needed was for anything to swell up his head; it was already two sizes too big.

Cryin Shame actually looked better. With his face swollen out of proportion, he wasn't his regular old Neanderthal-looking self. He was so named because it was said, "He so ugly it's a cryin shame." Somebody in the tank was always jazzing him about his looks and said things to him that were awfully hard to take.

"Ugly muthafucka, ain't no tellin whut yo daddy must'a accused yo mama uv doin when he seen yo ugly ass."

"Nigguh, if yo daddy's ugly is you, he got ta be somewhere in a zoo. Who you take afta?" Before he could answer, "Naw, don't tell me! I don't wanna know dere's another muthafucka on earth ugly is you."

The cons cracked up at their facetious remarks, and Cryin Shame laughed right along with them. He was one of the nonviolent types, pulling time for arson. Either he didn't understand what they were saying to him, or he didn't care. Maybe he was just glad to get some attention, even this kind.

Their affliction gave me an idea. When we got back to the woods, I was going to get into some poison ivy so I could lay in and rest up too. Soon as we reached our destination and started axing, I caught Boss Band not looking and made a beeline for the first patch of poison ivy I saw. I opened my shirt, scratched my chest and arms with some briars until I bled, then rubbed the poison ivy all over my scratched skin. I sneaked back to the crew and took up my position and resumed cutting.

I was in misery the rest of the day. The salt in my sweat was burning the scratches and I was itching like crazy. *That must be a sign it's workin*, I thought as I showered that evening. I could hardly wait till morning to wake up and be all swollen and get to lie back down. Next morning I immediately began inspecting myself. Nothing had happened. When Big Tom rang, it was back to the big top for me.

Whether Boss Band knew it or not, we had grown accustomed to his style. He had a way of tipping his hand when he started fidgeting with his shotgun. This was one of those days. The activity in the woods was going full blast as we hacked our way deeper and deeper into the bottoms. The falling trees and noisy axes failed to quell the sound of gunshot. We paid little attention to it because a boss was always target practicing or shooting at "somethin" in the woods. Our foursome continued cutting.

Whitefolks kept his voice low as he picked up the brush near my crew. "Boss Band jes shot Rapehead! I thank he dead."

"For whut?" I asked.

"Sshhh! Not so loud, man. I don't want 'em thankin I'm meddlin in his bizness by tellin y'all."

We tapped the tree lightly with our axes, trying not to drown out his half whispers. "I wuz throwin some brush on the pile back dere an jes turnt to leave when I heard the shot. I looked aroun an seen Rapehead fallin to the ground wit a hole in his bosom big as a Black Diamond watermelon! Boss Band wuz talkin to hissef lak he always do, an I heard him say sump'n bout Rapehead wuz tryin ta hide frum him 'hind the pile."

Whitefolks left our area and went back to pulling brush. We passed the word along to the others. Sergeant Buzzard (the dog sergeant) and two or three of the bosses working close by walked their horses over to "see." Buzzard asked, "Whut happen, boss?"

"Rotten bastard tried to 'scape. I had ta throw him away."

Sergeant Buzzard leaned over his saddle, looked down at Rapehead's body, and spat on it. "You beat me to it."

Shortly, a pickup came and we loaded Rapehead's body. Boss Band slow-walked his horse over near my crew and stopped about fifteen feet away. We were working and watching him at the same time as he sat gazing off into the woods, talking to himself. "Rotten bastard didn't b'long in this squad, didn't b'long on earth neither. Sonuvabitch needed killin."

That evening when we got to the building Rapehead's body was lying on the back steps, his eyes open and staring. All the squads had to step over him to get inside, a grisly reminder of what would happen if we "tried to 'scape." I knew now what Tennessee told us had some truth to it—Boss Band was a traveling executioner.

That night the mood in the building was somber and unusually still. When the prison got quiet, the officials got worried. "Them nigguhs is plottin." As long as the cons were grab-assing, fighting, snitching, and lying on one another, the warden didn't have any problems.

I leaned off my bunk and whispered up to Black Rider, "Say, man, wonder whut really made Boss Band so cold?"

"Dat's the way the muthafucka come outta his mama's belly."

I lay back down feeling he was right. It flashed across my mind like a neon sign, *If we don't hurry up an git outta them woods, ain't gonna be many uv us left.*

On Sunday morning, as usual, the inmate preachers were circulating in the tank, encouraging different ones to attend the afternoon service held in the auditorium. We were one of the last units to get a chaplain. The job was given to a feeble old fart who looked like he already had one foot in the hereafter. He pastored over a small church on the outskirts of Brazoria. When he drove up in the parking lot, it took him five minutes just to get out of his car. With the use of his cane, he slow-stepped his way straight to the warden's office. Big Devil made a point to be in his office on the Sundays "Ol Preacher" was scheduled to preach. Their little chats typically lasted until chow time.

The inmate preachers would be watching and waiting for the moment he emerged from the warden's office. When he did, they got the "heah Ol Preacher comes" signal from the 4 tank lookouts. Excitedly, they started yelling to the picket boss, "Comin out, boss! We gotta go hep da chaplain."

With standing orders from the warden, the picket boss unlocked the tank doors. "Alla you ol preachers thas gonna help that ol parson, come on outta thar!"

They met him at the front gate, almost mobbing him as the eight or ten of them jockeyed for positions. One snatched his walking cane, almost making him fall down, and two grabbed him under each arm and were practically carrying him. Another toted his huge Bible, and somebody else had his hat. The rest danced and frolicked in front of him all the way to the building.

Once inside, they let him walk. He headed straight for the mess hall with his followers dogging his heels. He wasn't allowed to eat in the guards' dining room, so he ate in the mess hall with us. He was Uncle Tom, Uncle Mose, and Uncle Everybody Else all wrapped into one. And they treated him that way from the warden on down. To keep him from feeling too bad, the inmate preachers were allowed to sit at the table with him and keep him company. To further illustrate it was "nothin personal," they had the flunkies put a tablecloth on his table. After his belly was full of food and suck-ass adulation, the inmate preachers assisted him up the stairs to the auditorium.

Upon his arrival, another assisting crew took over. These less privileged "preacher aides" weren't allowed to eat lunch with him, but they helped him suit up in his pastoral attire. Robed, with a huge cross hanging around his neck, Preacher took his seat behind the portable pulpit among the six main deacons. They waited for the choir leader, Molly, and the Retrieve a cappella choir to complete their rendition of "Near-o My God to Thee."

The choir finished and the deacons helped prop the old man up against the pulpit. All eyes glued on him, we quieted down, readying ourselves for the sermon. Preacher raised his outstretched arms skyward and called out, "Y'all know y'all got the best *warden* in the system?" Looking back at the deacons, he asked, "Do I hear a amen on *that?*"

"A-men! Aaaa-men! A-men!"

"I'm gon talk ta y'all today bout truf, amen. Truf, amen, thas whut we gon talk bout. Facts is one thang, but unfacts is somethin else. We ain't talkin bout unfacts, naw! We gon talk bout the *truf!* If you know whut the *truf* is, then you know whut I'm talkin bout, amen? Some'a y'all dun forgot whut the *truf* is, an you been livin in a daydream!"

Several "amen"s came from the audience. Preacher was getting revved up. "How long will it be? *How long?*" he shouted at the ceiling. "How long is it gon take befo you come into the light an know the *truf,* the *facts?*" He had the main deacons stomping on the floor, shouting "amen" after "amen," and nodding their heads in agreement with every statement.

"The *truf!* Thas whut we heah to talk bout today." Leaning forward over the pulpit, looking us straight in the eyes, he went on. "Y'all already know that most uv you b'long in heah. An y'all jes hafta 'cept dat. I don't hafta stand up heah an tell y'all dat. Y'all already knows it! *Amen?*"

This "truf" was "amened" the loudest of all.

"Talkin bout *facts!* If you didn't b'long in heah, you wouldn't be in heah. Some'a y'all be dead if you wudn't in heah. Dis place give y'all a new lease on life. The Lawd's been good ta y'all."

He was bombarded with *amen*s.

"Talkin bout *facts!* I don't hafta tell y'all there's only two ways outta heah. Y'all already know the mo trouble you make, the mo trouble you gits. Y'all oughta strive to please yo keepers, amen? Cuz if you *striveeee*"—he covered his ears to keep from deafening himself—"to please yo keeper, the *warden* will sholy set you free. *Amen? Amen!* Thas the *right* way out. Or, you kin git buried heah an hope yo spirit will leave. Amen? Somebody gotta speak for you! Somebody thas got a word that mean somethin. The *warden* kin *speak* them words, amen?"

"Amen, amen."

"It's up to you whut you want him to say. Do *yo part!* An you kin rest assured the *warden's* gon do his'n. It say rat heah in my Bible, talkin bout *truf,* amen? It say rat heah"—he was shouting louder while pointing to a page—"if you make one step towards me, I will make ten towards you. *Do yo part!* Lean on the *Lawd* an *do yo part! Gawd!* an the *warden* will do the rest! An so, les pray."

Some had to be awakened to rise for prayer. We had all heard the "Warden sermon" before. It was the only one he ever preached besides "The Eagle Stirred His Nest." But I thought he would have at least mentioned something about Rapehead.

Preacher's other pastoral duty was to be our counselor. But somehow, every problem any con went to him with was quickly solved by Big Devil. Preacher may have been a free man, but he was the biggest snitch around. It didn't take long for us to figure out it was best not to confide in him. And for God's sake, don't ask him to do something like mail a letter. Instead of just saying "I can't" and not doing it, he went straight to the warden and snitched.

The counseled ones kept getting their asses whupped by the bosses and building tenders after talking with Preacher and got wise to him. So, after church was dismissed the congregation fled. Only the deacons, inmate preachers, and preacher's aides remained behind to help him take off the holy harness and hold a special prayer service. After ministering unto the flock, it was time for Preacher to leave; and they escorted him back to the front gate until next time.

It was no secret that Number 1 hoe was working under a whimsical maniac who drove us mercilessly from sunup to sundown. After Boss Band killed Rapehead, we developed a million and one new ways to watch him while we worked. When he scratched his head, we flinched. When he changed positions in the saddle, we held our breaths and readied ourselves to duck. Knowing he would kill any of us any time without hesitation or reservation, we watched him much closer than he watched us. In his heyday, Road Runner's fastest gait would have been too slow for the torturous pace we maintained for this man. Even though we worked the hardest and the fastest, we knew death sat on a horse just a few feet behind us.

One day while we were chopping cotton, we heard, "Ol Baby Raper!"

"Oh Lawd!"

"Come back heah, nigguh!" Baby Raper trotted back to Boss Band and pulled off his flop-down hat. Pointing with his shotgun, Boss Band ordered, "Git that weed you left thar!" Baby Raper nudged the cotton stalk with his hoe, searching for it. Boss Band glared at him, raised his shotgun, and cut loose with both barrels. He didn't even change expressions as Baby Raper collapsed to the ground.

Cap'n Smooth rode over. "Why'd you hafta waste that nigguh, boss?"

"Well, a nigguh wit a name lak that ain't got no bizness livin, an he damn sho don't b'long in my squad." Then, "Ol Chinaman! Ol Bad Eye!"

"Oh Lawd!"

"Drag that rotten bastard out on the turnrow." When they returned to the squad, he hollered, "Some more uv you nigguhs gon git a load uv buckshot in yore ass if you don't tighten up! Ol Racehoss!"

"Oh Lawd!" *Am I next?*

"Go 'head!"

Ears laid back, I accelerated my chopping cadence and pulled away from the squad. "Y'all betta lay wit 'em!" he commanded and shot in the ground behind them.

One day he called me back in the squad. "Ol Racehoss, is you ever wondered why I ain't dun kilt yore yaller ass?"

"Oh Lawd! Nawsuh, boss!"

"Well, I'll tell you why. I don't let nobody pick the nigguhs I kill. I'll do that myself."

We had cleaned the cotton out of the fields and the tractor squad had plowed the stalks under. We were pulling the last ears of corn off the stalks right across the turnrow from the building when the afternoon sky suddenly turned to night. The lightning in the distance looked as if it were slashing a great big blackberry pie. Cap'n Smooth shouted, "Awright, raise 'em up! That goddamn hurricane's comin! Let's git in that house!"

Rain and hail pounded at our heels as we sped through the back door. It was so dark they had turned on all the lights inside. Heavy thunder jarred the building with every rumble. We barely made it to our tanks before the building tenders were calling, "Chow time!" Chow time? What in the hell was going on? We already ate lunch and didn't know why we were marching to the mess hall in early afternoon to eat again.

No sooner had we gotten back in our tanks than a deafening clap of thunder boomed, instantly followed by a bolt of lightning that struck something nearby, causing the whole unit to go black. Cap'n Foots called for some of the "maintenance squad" (the fifteen white cons) to go check the power plant, which was three hundred yards from the building and close to the front entrance. They were gone a long time but never did get the electricity on. Backup generators, producing about as much light as a birthday cake candle, had to be used.

"Damn, thas a bad muthafucka out dere," Braggs said in a troubled tone.

"I been in twelve calendars. Shit, dis the worst un I seen yet," Cap Rock added in an equally troubled tone.

September 1961, Hurricane Carla struck the Texas Gulf Coast with a vengeance. We huddled in the dark tanks as she kicked ass outside. The employees who lived on the premises within shadow distance of the prison brought their families to the building for refuge and went in the mess hall to wait out the storm. So that's why we ate early.

I watched the water scale the tank walls inch by inch. The bosses said to pull our mattresses off our bunks and take them with us, then moved the 3 and 4 tank inhabitants upstairs into 5 tank, and the 1 and 2 tank cons into the auditorium with the white boys. Hence, all four-hundred-plus hard-core convicts were stacked on top of one another.

Because the water had swelled almost knee-high on the lower level, the families had to move to higher ground. Now, they were lined up like crows on the stairwell, in the hallway that led to the hospital, and in the narrow corridor outside the bars from us. They tried not to look at us, but did every chance they got.

Everyone connected with the prison (convicts, bosses and their families, the warden, his wife, son, and four daughters) was jammed together, either on the stairwell or on the second floor, with only bars between us. The water was rising, as was the fear of being drowned like a bunch of rats in a sewer, unsettling to one and all. We hoped it wouldn't climb any higher, but it did steadily.

The families were forced to scoot higher on the stairwell, making those in the narrow corridor crowd closer to 5 tank . . . and to us. So close, we could have reached through the bars and touched them. When night fell we were in pitch darkness, except for flashlights and cigarette lighters flickering here and there. Near fights and plenty of pushing and shoving went on inside the packed tank that night.

Daylight brought receding waters. Before the next night fell, the families were gone. We reassembled into our humble abode downstairs, which was still ankle-deep in water. Cons with push brooms shoved the remnants of Carla's havoc down the hall so another bunch could thrust it out the back door. The heavy rain had stopped and was now just a drizzle.

Once Carla moved farther inland, the locals in Angleton requested Big Devil's help with some townspeople trapped by floodwaters in a nearby church on High Island. He was more than happy to accommodate and unhesitant to offer our services, knowing it was good for the prison's image in the community.

"Number One!"

Number 1 hoe squad ran down the hallway and out the back door.

"Number Two!"

We got our hoes at the hoe rack and loaded onto the cattle truck fitted with a metal cage specifically designed for hauling cons off the prison farm. About an hour later, the transport truck arrived at High Island. Other trucks pulling horse trailers carrying the horses and dogs followed. Lieutenant Sundown, who was in charge of the operation and rode in the first truck, signaled the convoy to stop before getting bogged down in the mud.

After the bosses unloaded their horses and mounted, Sergeant Buzzard and the dog boys took the dogs a ways off into the woods. With the bosses saddled and ready, we unloaded. Number 1 hoe formed a line of twos while Boss Wilhite ("Cochise" the cons had labeled him) was still trying to get his squad to line up.

With hoes in hand, we stood on the embankment looking down at the flooded road. Boss Band hollered, "Ol Racehoss, take them nigguhs into that water an unblock that road."

"Oh Lawd!"

In mud up to the tops of our brogans, we plodded down the slippery embankment. Even Boss Band's horse was having trouble with his footing. A few steps away from the truck, we were in water up to our bellies. We made it to the road and into the chest-deep water.

Holding our hoes above our heads, we waded side by side toward the church. Until we saw snakes swimming everywhere! *Holy shit!* Mayhem and confusion broke out as cons panicked and hit at them

with their hoes. This place should have been called Serpent Island!
I yelled, "Don't hit at 'em! You'll jes make the muthafuckas mad!
They'll wrap aroun yo hoes an you be swingin 'em above yo damn
heads! Do lak this."

Using my hoe like a canoe oar, I gently stroked the water, trying
not to disturb it any more than necessary. With our hoes stroking
in front of us, we pushed the snakes along on top of the water and
nudged them away. We formed a slow-moving fifty-hoe barricade
with the blades barely skimming the top of the water, synchronizing
our motion to keep the barricade intact and tight. I was steady telling
them, "Y'all keep them gotdam hoes together! Don't be splashin that
fuckin water!"

We veered to the left to break open the levee of debris clogging
the road. Boss Band hollered, "If you nigguhs let one'a them snakes
bite my hoss, I'm gon kill ya!"

I yelled at the squads, "Hold that line! Keep them hoes together!
Move easy!" Somebody pulled a hoe back with a snake wrapped
around his blade. When he jumped, I shouted, "Hold that line!"

Up to their chests in water, the horses were splattering it on our
backs while Boss Band and Cochise kicked it to keep the snakes away.
The horses and bosses were splashing worse than us. I called, "Oh
Lawd! Speakin to you, boss!"

"Whut?"

"Boss, I thank it'd be a lot betta if y'all wuz walkin yo hosses up
on the bank."

From his expression he looked relieved by my suggestion, even if
it didn't come from Sundown, who sat watching atop his horse on
the bank. Without delay Boss Band said, "Hey, boss, let's git outta
this goddamn water. We kin still see these nigguhs jes as good up
thar on the bank." Cochise appeared equally grateful to get out of
the snake-infested waters, seeing as their boots were waterlogged and
they were having hell with their unruly horses.

We used our hoes to direct the snakes the way gauchos use their
horses to herd cattle. When we got closer to the huge wall of tree limbs

and trash, we turned our blades upward and pushed against it, trying to make an opening. I urged, "Put some ass into it! Let's tear this shit down!" Snakes were crawling all over the refuse. "Look out, Cap!" I yelled, then hacked the snake's head off only a foot away from him.

We kept pushing until we poked a hole in the wall, and it gave way. At first only a heavy trickling flowed through, then the murky waters gushed forth, taking huge piles of trash from each side of the hole with them.

Along the banks the trees were filled with hundreds of snakes that had taken sanctuary. Looking like long bananas hanging from the limbs, they must have "heard" the rushing water and began dropping into it like autumn leaves. As the flow carried them toward the opening, we made a V-like trail with our blades turned downward to help guide them through it and out into the Gulf of Mexico.

The water receded rapidly. Before long, most of it had drained off the road. We headed for the church. The people started coming out. Boss Band hollered, "You nigguhs, jes hold it right thar!" Now that the water was no more than a foot high, he and Cochise rode their horses to greet the crowd, which was making its way toward a Red Cross truck parked on the embankment. The workers were handing out blankets, coffee, donuts, and drinking water; and the church folks were grabbing with both hands, especially the water.

Soaked to the bone, we stood on the other side of the embankment and watched. It was late afternoon, and we hadn't had any food or water since we left the building. I pursed my lips. One of the Red Cross ladies turned away from the truck, facing our direction. Coffee thermos in one hand, donuts wrapped in tissue in the other, she asked Boss Band, "Would you like some hot coffee and donuts?"

"You thank you got enuff uv that coffee to give my nigguhs a swallow?"

"They've done such a tremendous job. I think I've got enough to give them some donuts too."

"Ol Racehoss, you an them nigguhs go on over to that wagon an git some coffee an donuts."

Back on 3 tank that evening, Cap Rock said, "Say, Race, lemme axe ya sump'n. Where in the hell didja learn how to herd snakes lak dat?"

"Aw, I useta work on a snake ranch."

He looked puzzled for a moment, and then it dawned on him that I was just pulling his leg. He grinned and capped back, "Man, you fulla shit," and walked away chuckling.

After four years under the Band, the Number 1 hoe members had become the big brothers on their tanks. Hardly a week passed without one of us getting into trouble. We didn't take any of the building tenders' bulldogging shit and stopped them from ganging up on anybody in our tanks. They knew we had nothing to lose. For us, going to solitary was merely a few days' rest from dodging bullets.

Big Tom sounded. When we cleared the back steps, Cap'n Smooth motioned for us to stand to the side. After the other squads cleared the yard, Big Devil came out of the building. When he wanted special work done, he pulled us out of the field to do it.

"Boss Band, take these Number One nigguhs up there by the entrance and clean up that ol graveyard. I'm 'spectin some big shots down heah frum the Walls, an I want that thang cleaned up real good." In an irritated tone, he went on, "I don't know why'n hell they put a goddamn graveyard right next to the entrance to begin wit. It ain't nothin but a eyesore!"

With the warden's instructions over, Boss Band called, "Ol Racehoss!"

"Oh Lawd!"

"Head on over to that hoe rack. Ever nigguh gitta hoe! Go 'head!"

The graveyard was a half mile from the yard. In a few minutes we were opening the fence gate. Boss Band rode through behind us and walked his horse over to one of the fence corners. Facing us, he backed up until the horse's tail was touching the barbed wire. He knew not to get too close when we worked away from the main workforce. Some of us were just as eager to sink our hoes into his skull as he was to put a bullet in ours.

The johnsongrass was so tall it completely hid the graves. We started chopping, but he stopped us. "Ol Racehoss!"

"Oh Lawd!"

"Y'all lay them aggies down. Pull all that grass up by the roots an throw it outta thar. I don't aim fer us to hafta come back up heah day afta tomorrow."

It didn't matter if we had to do it with our hands. They were tough as mule hide anyway. Despite the earth's unwillingness to yield her roots, we quickly uncovered the mounds. The markers bore no names, just dates. Some went back to the 1930s. I heard conflicting stories about who was buried in this old graveyard. Some said they were black, but others called it "peckerwood hill." At first I wondered how could they be white, but then I remembered this was an all-white camp once upon a time.

After we pulled out all the grass, the sixteen mounds had to be reshaped and smoothed over. We picked up our hoes, but Boss Band stopped us again. "Y'all jes leave them hoes alone an start pattin that dirt back on them mounds by hand. I wont this thang to be real purty fer that warden," he said with sarcasm. "Plus, it'll give y'all a chance ta whisperrr . . ."

Suddenly he leaned to one side, fell off his horse, and lay on the ground clawing at his chest and gasping for air. We looked at one another for a second in disbelief.

Elefin Head whispered, "I bleeve Boss Band's dyin."

We walked closer, circled him like a bunch of buzzards, and stood watching. Cowfucker started calling his name, "Boss Band! Boss Band! Kin you hear me?"

"Shit! You jes wastin yo breff. Dis bad muthafucka's dead!" Bad Eye said while poking him with his hoe. "Les take his shotgun an pistol an split! Hell, ain't nobody up heah but us. We kin git a good head start if we leave now. C'mon, y'all, whut the fuck we standin roun for? Dis muthafucka can't stop us."

Thirty-Five said, "If we leave heah wit this muthafucka dead, they gon swear up an down we had sump'n ta do wit it."

"Well, whut we spose ta do?" Bad Eye shot back. "Jes stand heah an watch the flies blow his dead ass?"

I said, "Naw, we ain't gotta stand here an watch 'em, but I agree with Thirty-Five. We sho oughta stay. I'm goin over there in the corner an sit down on my ass till somebody shows up."

The others agreed, and we finally convinced Bad Eye to go along. We sat down together in the farthest corner away from Boss Band. Glancing occasionally in his direction, I thought his shotgun and pistol looked very tempting; but Thirty-Five was right. Chinaman pulled out a fresh bag of "dust" (Bull Durham) and passed it around.

Lieutenant Sundown, usually the officer who checked on us when we worked away from the other squads, rode up and saw the riderless horse standing inside the fence. Half joking, he asked, "Whut y'all dun wit Boss Band?"

I answered, "We ain't dun nothin with him, Lieutenant. There he is layin over yonder."

Thirty-Five added, "We wuz wekin, an he jes up an fell off his hoss. We didn't know whut wuz the matta wit 'em."

Sundown trotted his horse around the outside of the fence to get a better look. "Come on outta thar an line up out heah on this road so I kin count y'all. Ol Chinaman, git Boss Band's hoss an walk him out heah."

After he counted, we sat down beside the road. He radioed the warden on his walkie-talkie. Then he asked, "How long has he been layin thar?" He got several different time spans hurled at him all at once.

Big Devil drove up quickly, got out of his car, and walked around the fence to look. "An ambulance is on the way, but that ain't gonna help him none. Didja talk to these nigguhs bout whut happen to 'em?"

"They all say that he wuz talkin to 'em an right in the middle uv it, he jes fell off his hoss. Sounds ta me lak he had a heart attack, Warden."

"Yeah, guess so. Ol Racehoss, come heah." When he asked me what happened, I told him the same thing we told Sundown.

The ambulance arrived. While the attendants were loading him, Mae Widder mumbled, "That muthafucka sho died hard. He ain't gon have no hoss in the hell he goin to. Dey gon hand dat muthafucka a hoe an put 'em on the lead row wit all dem nigguhs he dun kilt 'hind 'em, drivin his ass. Thas where I wanna go when I die, so I kin hep 'em."

After the ambulance drove away, Big Devil got in his car. As he was turning it around to head back to the building, he hollered out the window, "You stay heah wit these nigguhs. When I git to the buildin, I'll send Boss Robles out heah to take over the squad."

Sundown waved an acknowledgment as the warden sped away. After firing up a Marlboro and exhaling a long stream of smoke, he said in his slow Texas twang, "Well, at least he died wit his boots on. I know y'all sho gon miss Boss Band. Ain'tcha?"

His question drew only silence. And more silence. Nobody faded him on that shot.

15

When we treat man as he is, we make him worse than he is.
When we treat him as if he already were what he potentially
*   could be,*
We make him what he should be.

—Johann Wolfgang von Goethe

The next day in the fields he called the squad together. "My name's Robles. Y'all kin call me Mr. Robles or Boss Robles. I'm gonna call y'all by your names afta I learn 'em all. So don't git your dander up if I say 'hey you' till I git a handle on 'em. Okay? Another thang, I ain't gonna be cussin y'all out. I don't feel like thas gonna be necessary. Do y'all?"

A few heads shook in agreement.

"If any uv you would ruther I call you by somethin other than your prison name, thas fine by me." I knew I didn't have to tell him mine. Every boss that takes over a squad is told the lead row's name before he ever leaves the warden's office. "When we work off by ourselves, we kin let 'em down."

He continued to speak in a manner we were very unaccustomed to hearing—no cursing, no threats. He was talking to us like men who were capable of understanding what he said. "Y'all do what you're supposed to do and act like men. I'll deal with the warden or anybody else I have to. Ain't nobody gonna be tellin me who to cut out at the back gate. Somethin else too. Y'all don't have to git permission befo you talk to me. But since Racehoss is our lead-row man, I'd 'preciate him doin most uv the talkin when it concerns this work. He knows more about it than I do."

Boss Robles sounded too good to be true, a complete contrast to Boss Band and Deadeye. He looked to be in his mid-thirties, wasn't a big man, standing about five foot seven, kinda chubby, and had a pleasant, friendly voice. There was no scowl of disdain on his face—yet. He carried no shotgun, just a six-shooter. He didn't call us "nigguh" and encouraged us not to call one another that. He spoke a foreign language, one we never heard before. He was a different breed from the others, and I wondered how long it would last.

I heard he was a recent hire and had been working with the fencing squad as a utility boss before Big Devil called on him to work our squad. We were just as surprising to him as he was to us, and we stupefied him with the way we worked. He soon learned that he had inherited a squad of "stone-down gorillas," the highest compliment one con gives another. All he had to do was sit on his horse and keep up with us.

It didn't take long to find out if he was for real or not. We were picking cotton with the Number 4 hoe squad picking next to us. Their boss, Eat-Em-Up, walked his horse over to shoot the breeze with Boss Robles. "Howdy do, boss."

Boss Robles said "howdy," very uninterested.

But Boss Eat-Em-Up wasn't the type one could ignore when he wanted to talk. As they were walking their horses side by side, Eat-Em-Up kicked off again. "Goddamn, it's hot! Ain't it?" he asked as he took his hat off to wipe his forehead.

"Yep."

"Say, how'd you manage to git that Number One hoe squad? Damn, you must know somebody. I been carryin this Number Four fer six years. I asked that man to give me them nigguhs afta Boss Band died. I bleeve they worried that poor boss to death. I'd lak to carry them bastards fer jes one month.

"Tell you one thang, you sho hafta watch them ol nigguhs, boss.

If you don't watch yore bizness, some'a them nigguhs'll drap yore britches 'n fuck you rat out heah in this field!"

That got an angry glance from Boss Robles, but he held his peace.

After cramming his jaw full of Red Man chewing tobacco, Eat-Em-Up went on. "Alla them ol nigguhs kin pick hell outta that cotton, but if you don't prod an drive the shit out uv 'em, they'll jes tell you ta kiss they black asses an lay down on them sacks."

Boss Robles continued looking straight ahead.

"You gon hafta fuck wit 'em an have eight or ten uv 'em put in that pisser or hung up on them fuckin bars. Jes ta hep keep the lead outta them ol asses 'n let 'em know you mean bizness. You gotta let 'em know who's runnin it. Don't, an they'll jes take over. Nigguhs is jes lak mules. You hafta make 'em do whut you wont 'em to. A little shower uv leather"—he patted the eight-plait bullwhip he used on his squad—"across the fat part uv they ol stankin asses ever now an then is the best thang you kin do fer 'em. Hell, they love it. You ain't gonna bleeve this, but I had a nigguh come up an thank me fer puttin this whup ta his ass."

Chinaman interrupted his conversation when he hollered out, "Gittin on the job over heah, boss!"

"See, boss, thas whut I mean. I betcha two bits ginst a hoss turd that nigguh don't bit mo need ta shit than I do. Thas they way uv fuckin roun. Ever time one'a mine do's it, I make 'em brang some back on a stick." Then he shouted at his squad, "You nigguhs betta git down on that ol head runnin an git some goddamn cotton in them sacks!"

Able to elicit only an occasional "yep" out of Boss Robles, Eat-Em-Up talked about everything from their low salaries to the weather, but he hadn't come up with a topic yet that interested him. "Whar you frum, boss?"

"West Texas."

"Well, I'm frum Conroe mysef. Got me a big, ol fat half-Injun woman ta cook biscuits an hep keep me warm in the wintertime," he said, spitting tobacco juice on the ground. "I go home on the weekends I ain't on duty. Wit a job lak this, a man's sho gotta regulate his fuckin, ain't he?"

Boss Robles never cracked a smile.

"Say, didja ever hear the one bout the nigguh an white man that wuz on death row? Well, I'll tell it to you jes in case you ain't. See, they had this nigguh an this white man on death row. They wuz in cells side by side. An they wuz gon hang 'em the next mornin. Well, that night that fuckin ol white thang wuz up most uv the night pacin back an forth jus a-bawlin. It got on that nigguh's nerves an he hollered an tole 'em, 'Shet up all 'at cryin an go to sleep.' That ol white thang hollered back, 'How kin I sleep? Don'tcha realize they gon hang me in the mornin?' That nigguh tole 'em, 'Well, I ain't cryin an they gon hang me too.' That ol white thang said, 'Yeah, I know, but y'all's use to it!'"

Boss Eat-Em-Up doubled over with laughter. Seeing no response from Boss Robles, he said, "Say, boss, you sho don't talk much, do ya? You know I been a-tryin ta git somebody to lissen to me fer pert near six years." He looked real serious. "I got a invention that'd cut the cost uv pickin this damn cotton ta nothin. Won't nobody lissen. Best part is, it won't hardly cost nothin to git it goin. It'd save on manpower an everthang."

Finally, he got a response. "How're you gonna do that?"

"Aha, gotcha 'tention, did it? I betcha wanna git in on some uv the profits, don'tcha?"

"What kind uv invention is it?"

"Well, it ain't zackly whut you might call a invention cuz it's been roun ferever. It's plain as the nose on yore face, but people jes ain't smart nuff to use it. I garn-dam-teeya, it weks ever time. I'll tell you whut it is, but you gotta promise to keep it to yoresef."

He had Boss Robles's attention.

"Tell ya whut we kin do," Eat-Em-Up said, looking all around as if he were about to divulge some deep, dark secret. "We kin git us a boat an go out in the ocean an git us some'a them octopussies, brang 'em back, an crossbreed 'em wit these nigguhs. We'll have us some eight-row-at-a-time cotton pickers that'll run on plain ol watermelon juice!" He cracked up at the way he had pulled the new boss's leg.

Boss Robles waited until Eat-Em-Up had stopped laughing. "I want you to git away from me and my squad. And I don't want you comin around no more with that kind uv talk. You stay away from us. Do I make myself clear?"

The seriousness in his voice was enough to convince Eat-Em-Up to leave. He turned his horse and headed back to his own squad. Before he left, he threw back, "If thas the way you feel bout it. Hell, I wuz jesta funnin you."

Boss Robles passed his first test.

About a month later we were going through the cotton like a cyclone for the third time, picking the "tags" (scrap cotton left in the bolls). This would be used to make clothes and bedding for the prison population. I was into my seventh cotton-picking season, and all doubts were settled about who was the fucking best.

At the beginning of the season, Cap Rock and I squared off in a cotton-picking shoot-out with six decks of squares bet. I beat that chump by ninety pounds. It was sweet revenge for the days he picked off my row under Boss Deadeye. He finally knew his place in the squad—behind me. Now my cotton weights topped the field, and I didn't need to piss in my sack anymore.

It was early September. We were more than three-quarters finished with our cotton crop. We finished first every year. Big Devil was nominated each year for the Warden of the Year award. He was the only one in the system to win it four years in succession. Naturally, he was going for five.

His strategy was to pull us out of the field along with the other top three squads and send us over to one of the other farms to "help 'em out." This left the remaining four squads to keep on picking what was left of our crop until we returned, which was his way of letting it be known his farm was so far ahead it could finish first with half the squads. We had been assembled in the auditorium for his preparatory speech.

"I'm gonna send y'all over to the Clemens farm to give 'em a hand. We're fur nuff 'long wit ours to be outta danger befo bad weather hits. Clemens dun fell way behind this year. Ain't no way they gon git dun by rodeo time, 'less we go help 'em. Some'a you nigguhs been over there befo. I'm gonna warn you now. If y'all fuck up over there, you gon git punished over there. Y'all will be under that warden's jurisdiction. I'm out uv it.

"How many uv you nigguhs been over there befo? Raise yore hands." I raised mine along with the majority. "I'm gonna send the lieutenant 'long wit y'all's bosses, an he'll be in charge. I want y'all to go over there an behave y'all's selves an don't be a-fuckin wit them nigguhs. Y'all will be leavin first thang in the mornin."

Clemens, another all-black unit, housed mostly first offenders. Many of us had "graduated" from there. It had nearly twice as many cons as "hell" with its 750-plus count. They could field an army of workers compared to us. True, we had grown to 447, but half were dog boys, cooks, mess hall flunkies, houseboys, garden squad, tractor squad, lot squad, shop squad, dairy squad, turnkeys, building tenders, commissary clerks, and so on. This left eight hoe squads in the fields, with twenty to thirty men each, to maintain over sixteen thousand acres under cultivation.

The next morning we were loaded onto two metal-caged cattle trucks. With about fifty cons to a truck, the Number 1 and 2 hoe squads were inside the cage on the first truck. Numbers 3 and 4 were in the other one. The trucks had seats welded to the floor outside the cages for two bosses to sit on. Boss Robles and Cochise sat at the rear while Sundown rode in the cab with the driver. Pickups pulling trailers with the horses and dogs brought up the rear.

We ate thirty minutes early, and the sun was barely rising when we got on the highway. The fifteen-mile trip took about half an hour, and the driver drove us straight to the field. Heading down the turnrow to unload, we passed the Clemens squads in the field working. Some stopped picking long enough to wave and cheer as we sped by. They knew help was on the way.

I saw two packs of dogs as we passed their dog boy. I thought about how their dogs compared to ours. Theirs were healthy and full bodied; ours were so skinny their ribs could be counted and their hip bones stuck out noticeably. Our old dogs looked as though there wasn't an ounce of life left in them, but those bastards would run a convict until doomsday. They were just like us—lean and mean.

When the trucks stopped, we were about a mile from the Clemens workers. After our four squads unloaded we had to wait, no cotton sacks. Sundown was mad as hell. Clemens was supposed to furnish everything. While waiting for the sacks to be delivered, I couldn't help but notice the condition of the cotton. It was tall and full of morning glory vines and johnsongrass, as if it had never been hoed.

About five minutes later, the water wagon arrived with some sacks. All regulation eleven footers. I couldn't remember the last time we used eleven-foot sacks. We gobbled up the pile, grabbing two apiece. As the water boy turned his wagon around to leave, Sundown asked, "Is this all the sacks y'all got? I kin tell you now, it ain't enuff to hold 'is bunch. You betta git us some more. By the time you git back, some'a these ol bullies'll be waitin."

"Yassuh, I be rat back."

"Boss Robles, go right down yonder whar that turnrow makes a L, an y'all ketch in an brang 'em rows on back thisa way."

When he finished, Boss Robles said, "Racehoss, let's git 'em started."

I caught my usual two rows and took off. The stalks were loaded, and by the time I picked to the end, I had a full sack. I tied a knot in the end of it, got a green boll, marked "Racehoss" on it, and left it lying on the turnrow. Several others had filled their first sacks too and were changing harnesses.

My second sack was over half-full before the water boy came back. When I reached the end this time, I dropped another, marked it, and grabbed two more. The others who needed them did the same. We finished picking about three sets of rows, and then Sundown decided it was time for us to weigh up.

"Boss Robles, brang yores on outta thar an les go to them scales."

When we reached the area where they had set up the scales, we saw Big Devil and the Clemens warden, who the cons had dubbed "Silly Willy," sitting on the hoods of their cars, waiting to hear our weights. I slung my two and three-quarters sacks of damp cotton across the scales, and their weight checker did a double take before hollering, "He's got two sixty-five!" Silly Willy didn't believe it and made me hang them on the scales again. It was right the first time. Cap Rock's wasn't much different, 240.

To empty up I had to pass them, and Silly Willy asked, "Whut do y'all call that nigguh?"

"Ol Racehoss."

"I kin damn sho see why," he said, and he offered to swap Big Devil three trusties for me.

Big Devil just looked at him and grinned, then hollered at me, "Ol Racehoss, you betta quit layin back on that sack an go ta gittin me some more cotton!"

"Yessuh!"

Not a weight in Number 1 hoe was less than two hundred pounds. We got a quick drink and headed back. Word traveled about how much cotton we weighed up compared to the Clemens squads. On that first weigh-up, our four squads picked "almost forty bales," Sundown said. He told us we wouldn't weigh up again until after lunch.

At lunchtime we loaded onto their tractor-drawn trailers and *rode* to the building. "Yay!" We got there and were quickly ushered up to the auditorium, which would be our living quarters for the next few days. It had been prearranged that we, the visitors, would go to the mess hall last.

The inside picket boss told us, "When I call y'all, I wont y'all to go in the mess hall in yore own squad so's I kin git another count. An that warden wonts y'all to stay together an not be a-mixin up wit our nigguhs."

We lined up by squads at the top of the stairs and waited. The mess steward beckoned when he was ready. "Okay, y'all kin go on in," the picket boss said.

The Clemens cons were already eating. A special section had been reserved with a row of empty tables purposely left to keep us separated. A complete hush fell over the mess hall when the infamous Number 1 hoe squad walked in. They stopped eating and gazed as we passed their tables. Boss Band had made my "name" and Number 1 hoe a legend in the bottoms.

Their stares told how we must have looked, and made me realize how different we were. Because of Boss Band, we'd been nicknamed the "death squad." We did look like the walking dead compared to the Clemens cons. They had a fresh-from-the-crate appearance, still wrapped in baby fat. We looked tough and driven. Our heads were noticeably balder and our eyes were hidden hollows that used our faces for backgrounds. Sunken cheeks revealed jowls protruding against hard, weathered faces.

We were raggedy as a nickel mop, and our sleeveless shirts exposed arms like coils of steel. Our britches were full of patches and held up with shoelaces and pieces of rope; they wore belts. They watched and whispered as we ate in sullen silence. Seeing us probably did more to rehabilitate them than anything they had seen thus far. They saw how they could end up if they kept using the prison as a revolving door.

After lunch we picked our way closer to the Clemens workforce. Suddenly, Tarzan let go with his famous jungle scream. Boss Robles's horse reared and bucked. It must have scared the new boss half to death. This was his first Tarzan yell since he'd been working us. After he got his horse quieted down, he managed a weak smile. "What on earth wuz that all about?"

"Ain't nothin, boss. Ol Tarzan jes made a ketch," Thirty-Five rendered.

Boss Robles was still confused until he saw Tarzan bite the head off that lizard and start chomping. He almost fell over backward off his horse. He rode off a ways and started puking. His face was beet red when he came back and he was still wiping his mouth with a bandanna. After regaining some composure, he said, "Damn! Does he do that all the time?"

Bad Eye answered, "Naw, boss, jes when he ketch sump'n."

Boss Robles had been officially welcomed into the Number 1 hoe squad.

It was after two o'clock and we hadn't weighed up since we got back from lunch. With all the cotton in our sacks that we didn't weigh up before, our next weights would really be heavy. I had filled up my third sack when Sundown signaled for us. No one in the squad had less than two. When we got out of the cotton patch onto the turnrow, Sundown immediately noticed that we were just "totin a lil dab" to the scales.

He stopped us. "Whar's the resta y'all's cotton? I know damn well this ain't all y'all dun picked."

I spoke up. "It's on the other turnrow. We had more'n we could tote."

Boss Robles quickly added, "Lieutenant, they filled up so many sacks I told 'em to leave 'em. Ain't no way they could tote all that cotton to the scales."

"Awright, boss, y'all take whut you got onto the scales an wait." He radioed Big Devil. "This is walkie-talkie three to walkie-talkie one."

"Yeah, go 'head, Lieutenant."

"Whut's yore twenny, Warden?"

"I'm over heah by Dow Chemical. Whut's the trouble?"

"We got a problem, Warden. These nigguhs dun picked more cotton than they kin tote. 'Less we pissant it, we ain't got no way to git it to the scales."

"Y'all jes stay where you at. I'll be there in ten minutes. Ten four?"

"Ten four."

Over Sundown's walkie-talkie, we heard Big Devil transmitting with Silly Willy. "Walkie-talkie one Retrieve to walkie-talkie one Clemens."

"Yeah, I heard," Silly Willy responded. "Whutta you wont me to do?"

"Well, fur starters, you kin git them trailers out to the field an haul our cotton to the scales. Thas whut them trailers is fur anyhow."

"Jes hold yore hosses, Alton. I'll git you some trailers headed thatta way. Ten four?"

"Ten four."

By the time the tractor drivers brought our sacks and we sorted them out, Silly Willy and the entire Clemens field hierarchy had gathered. Even "Beartracks," the Ramsey warden, was there. He must have been in the vicinity and heard the message too.

"He's got three fifteen." I quickly unhitched my sacks and emptied.

While I waited for the others to weigh up, Big Devil called me. "Ol Racehoss, come over heah."

I approached his car and removed the bandanna I wore in lieu of a flop-down hat. "Yessuh."

"How much you have?"

"Three fifteen, Warden."

"How much you have this mornin?"

"Two sixty-five."

He was having a field day showing off before the other two wardens. "Thank you gon git me a thousand today?"

"I will if we stay late enuff."

Beartracks asked, "This lil ol nigguh ever picked a thousand befo?"

"I don't know. Have ya, Ol Racehoss?"

"Nawsuh, not yet."

Beartracks continued, "I got a nigguh over on my farm we call Thousand Pound Blue I'd lak to see tie down wit yore nigguh."

"Thank you kin beat 'em, Ol Racehoss?"

"Yessuh, I kin beat 'em."

While the wardens detained me, Boss Robles took the squad back to the field. When I got back, I told them about the contest being set up.

At the day's end our four squads beat the Clemens workforce so bad, Silly Willy punished all fourteen squads. That evening when we got to the building, the Clemens pickers almost overflowed the yard standing on barrels and soda water boxes. They were hanging in the halls and the pissers were full. We had really jobbed them, but it wasn't done maliciously, just naturally.

Early the next morning the three wardens converged on the turnrow for the "cottonathon." After leaving the conference site, Sundown came and got me. It had been decided the contestants would pick in a separate cut, and Sundown would oversee the race.

Out on the turnrow, with Sundown walking his horse close behind me, he said, "Ol Racehoss, I heard that ol nigguh frum Ramsey kin pick purty good. I tell you one thang, that man sho been a-braggin on you. Thar's a lot ridin on this contest, if you know whut I mean," he said, indicating side bets were made.

"Yessuh."

The other two contestants had been assembled by the time we got there. Soon as I walked up, Big Devil told me, "Ol Racehoss, lay yore sack over yonder 'side the turnrow. We gonna give y'all some fresh uns. First, let me go over the rules wit you. I dun told these two. We don't want no buncha leaves, stalks, and stems put in them sacks. If y'all git caught wit any mud balls in them sacks, I can't speak fur these other wardens, but I'm gon do somethin to yore ass. Is 'at clear?"

"Yessuh."

"We agreed to give the winner two cartons uv cigarettes. Second place'll git one carton, an third gits five packs." While he talked to me, the two cons stood off to one side. When he finished he motioned for them. "Ol Racehoss, do you know these other two nigguhs?"

"Nawsuh."

"Well, the next thang we oughta do is innerduce y'all," he said, smiling at the wardens. "This nigguh heah is Ol Totem Pole, an this'n's Ol Thousand Pound Blue."

Silly Willy had entered Totem Pole, the lead row in Clemens's Number 1 hoe squad. They threw him in for good measure, I guess. He didn't look a day over twenty-one and was a tall, gangling con whose profile did resemble a totem pole. Just by looking at him, I knew he didn't have a chance. He didn't look hard enough yet.

Thousand Pound Blue, on the other hand, looked more like us. He was stocky built, about thirty or so. His clothes were the same dingy gray and just as raggedy as ours. His alleged cotton-picking prowess, coupled with his blue-black complexion, had earned him the moniker. He was the lead row in the Number 1 hoe squad at Ramsey, which was a repeat offender unit housing white and black cons—segregated of course.

All the while Big Devil talked to me, Thousand Pound Blue was giving me the once-over. Now, face-to-face, we stared at each other like two well-seasoned warriors about to do battle. Both of us completely ignored the youngster from Clemens.

We got fourteen footers this time. Big Devil must have brought them. He told Sundown to get us started. As we walked away, Thousand Pound Blue turned to Beartracks. "Warden, suh, kin we have any kind uv cigaritts we wants?"

"Any kind you wont, Ol Blue," the warden told him, as if it were already in the bag.

Heading to where we were going to pick, Sundown gave final instructions. "When y'all gitta sack fulla 'at stuff, git out uv it an leave it lay. Somebody'll be by to pick 'em up. Y'all betta be sho an mark y'all's sacks good so's you kin tell 'em apart. Another thang, how many rows y'all ketch is up ta y'all. You kin pick one at a time or a dozen at a time. Don't make a shit ta me."

The cut selected for us was some of Clemens's best. It was low, about three feet tall, and loaded. The soil was semisoft from the morning dew, just right for fast crawling.

Totem Pole asked, "Lieutenant, suh, how you want us to ketch in? I mean, who you want to carry the first row?"

"Don't make a shit ta me."

It wasn't hard working that out among ourselves after Thousand Pound Blue caught the first two rows and lit out. Totem Pole was next and I ended up in third position. We caught two rows apiece. Totem Pole had good hand speed, but he was fighting it. Middle ways into the field, he fell back into the low part of the V. Blue and I were picking side by side.

I began to pull away from him, slightly. I knew that once I got ahead, that was it. I reached the turnrow first and caught the first set of rows coming back, "my" rows. Sundown told us when we got to the end, "Jes wheel aroun an head back the other way." I beat Blue to the end by about four cotton stalks.

I straightened up to rest my back a second and saw the wardens watching us with binoculars. Now, Blue was picking in the middle and Totem Pole was third on the outside. Since I had no idea how long we were going to pick before we weighed up, I let it all hang out while the cotton was still damp.

When I got to the end of my second set of rows, I had another full sack. Empties were at the end of each set in case we needed them. Up in the cloudless sky, the sun said it was around ten o'clock. Sundown had us pick on. It was close to lunchtime when he finally gave the signal. The water boy picked up our full sacks and had them lying on the side of the turnrow when we got to the scales.

Totem Pole weighed up first. "He's got two twenty," the weight caller hollered. Blue hung his two and a quarter sacks on the scales. "He's got two forty." I hung mine. "He's got two seventy-five."

Beartracks looked at Sundown and asked, "Whar in the hell did that nigguh git all that cotton frum?"

In his customary nonchalant manner, Sundown took a puff from his cigarette and looked off in the horizon. "You ain't seen nothin. Hell, I ain't even hollered at 'em yet."

We barely got back to picking before Sundown knocked us off for lunch. This was the first time I had been with my squad since the contest began. As soon as I got on the trailer, they started firing questions. "How much you have?"

"Two seventy-five."

"How much they have?"

"That Clemens nigguh had two twenty. The nigguh frum Ramsey had two forty."

The Clemens mess hall was buzzing when we entered. "That nigguh frum Retrieve beat both uv them nigguhs the first weigh-in."

"Fuck, I don't know why dey even put Totem Pole in it. Shit, I kin beat dat nigguh."

"I heard that nigguh Racehoss is a walkin gin."

When we got back to picking after lunch, I could tell that a lot of the wind had gone out of my two opponents' sails. I picked on away from them, stopping only to mark the full sacks I left strewn up and down my middles. The hot, broiling sun dried all the early September dew from the cotton. I knew my weight would be lighter the next weigh-up, but so would theirs.

Sundown gave the signal to knock off. This time when we headed for the scales, I walked the lead point of our arrowhead formation. Blue and Totem Pole were already conceding.

I hung my three on the scales first and had 260, Blue weighed up 225, and Totem Pole had 215. We got a drink and headed back. One more to go.

I was picking with an easy gait, and we all were picking one row at a time now. They were struggling and knew the race was over for them. In my mind it was over before it started. I had picked cotton under the Band and Deadeye. These chumps didn't stand a chance. Sundown interrupted my thoughts when he rode up beside me. "Ol Racehoss, how long you been out in the fields?"

"Bout seven years, Lieutenant."

He was a man of few words. After the question, he walked his horse back to his original position behind us and lit a Marlboro.

All the squads had been knocked off for the last weigh-up. The Clemens cons were amassed on one side of the turnrow and the Retrieve bunch on the other. Silly Willy ordered quiet so *our* last weights could be heard. I hung my two sacks on the scales and the Clemens captain hollered, "Ol Racehoss got one eighty-five."

The convict weight keeper quickly tallied my total and handed the figures to the captain. "Thas a total uv seven hundred and twenty pounds fer Ol Racehoss." Blue hung his up next. "He's got one ninety-five, fer a total uv six sixty." Then Totem Pole. "He's got one seventy, fer a total uv six oh five. Ol Racehoss is the winner!"

Beartracks, a six-foot-seven Goliath, jumped off the hood of his car, rushed over to Thousand Pound Blue, and hit him in the face, knocking him to the ground. A sore loser, he stomped him repeatedly. I was glad this was our last day here. I was ready to go back "home." I know the Clemens bunch was glad to see us leave.

Big Devil must have radioed ahead because we had fried pork steaks and mashed potatoes with gravy waiting. It reminded me of the time the grand jury convened in Brazoria County and came out to the unit for lunch. It was in July, but turkey and dressing with all the trimmings was served on the line.

Big Devil came to the mess hall. "I'm gonna let y'all lay in this weekend. Y'all git them crops finished up this comin week, and we'll have ice cream next Sadday."

A weekend lay-in during cotton-picking season was as scarce as the hair on our heads. Working seven days a week with a short half on Sunday was a grinding three-month pace. About ten the next morning, the commissary clerk called me to the commissary and told me I had three cartons of cigarettes to "spend." "Boss Robles come by an paid for one uv 'em," he told me.

When I finished swap-shopping, I had a carton left. I bought a new razor and blades, three cans of tooth powder, several bars of sweet soap, lighter fluid for my old Zippo, two bags of oatmeal cookies, and a couple cans of sardines. Enough supplies to last me for a while. *Not a bad day's work*, I thought as I reentered the tank carrying my goodies. I loaned out five packs for the two packs' interest they would bring, and saved the rest to gamble with and smoke.

With two days to rest, what was left of our cotton crop didn't last as long as a snowball in hell, and we got our ice cream.

I had never been to a prison rodeo. We were a little over a hundred miles from the Walls (Huntsville Unit), and I didn't like the idea of freezing my balls off in those open-air trucks. It starts the first Sunday in October, and is held every Sunday during the month. Retrieve was scheduled to go the fourth Sunday this year along with the other two Brazos Bottoms units, Ramsey and Clemens.

The rodeo list had been posted with all those eligible to go. Going to the rodeo was a "privilege, not a right." All the trusties' names headed the list, then the tractor drivers and others who had "jobs," then the field workforce. Big Devil used the hog law book to determine who could go from the field workers.

After I reviewed the list and saw my name, I had to write the warden a note like I'd done in the past, asking (he didn't like the word *request* because he said it was too much like demanding) that my name be taken off. To some, going to the rodeo was the big event of the year.

Chinaman, my regular domino partner, came to the table where I was playing. "Say, Race, is you goin to the rodeo?"

It was my play. "I don't know if I'm goin or not."

He waited until I made my play. "Well, when you gon know, man?"

"Why?"

"Cuz we wanna know, thas why."

"Whut we?"

"Alla us in the squad."

There was no use trying to ignore him, he wasn't about to go away. I had known him long enough to know that sometimes he was a pain in the ass. "Whut the fuck is my goin got to do with y'all goin?"

"Well, if you ain't goin, den dey say dey ain't goin, which means I ain't goin, which means I miss my chance ta see some'a dem big-leg brown sugars. So I wish you'd make up yo mind so I know whut ta tell 'em."

Trying to concentrate on the game and listen to Chinaman at the same time, I said, "Look, man, I'll letcha know!"

He left, only to take a seat on one of the nearby benches. Slamming down five-trey, killing Beer Belly's double-trey, I hollered, "Domino! Count 'em up, muthafucka."

When the game ended, Chinaman asked, "Race, is you made up yo mind yet?" Then he poured it on. "Look, man, you don't know whut you missin. Some'a dem ol gals goin by in cars sho be settin high. Shit, dey know who we is 'n do's it jes so we kin see. An dem broads at the rodeo has on britches so tight, man, if you stuck a pin in 'em dey'd bust."

He went on enthusiastically. "Shit, man! I don't go up dere to watch dem nigguhs git bucked off no hosses 'n tryin to ride some big o' musty-assed bulls. I go to hussle me some jack stuff. Race, I 'member last year when we went up dere. I seen a broad wit a ass so big an fine it give me night fits. When we got back, I nelly jacked mysef to death."

I pondered all he'd been telling me and thought, *Whut the hell? I could sure use some jack material.* I'd just about used up all my memories. "Okay, man, I'm goin," I said, "an you quit followin me fuckin with me!"

Saturday night before the fourth Sunday in October, Big Devil walked underneath the picket. "Boss, open up all uv them tank doors an send them nigguhs in the mess hall thas goin to that rodeo!"

"Alla you nigguhs thas goin to that ol rodeo, the warden wonts y'all in the mess hall!" the picket boss yelled as steel doors opened in a frenzy. Everybody seemed to simply go crazy when the warden spoke, bosses and cons alike.

Big Devil walked through the mess hall barking commands. "Cap'n, I want you to have them laundry nigguhs brang a set uv clothes in heah fur alla these nigguhs. I want ever nigguh to have a new pair'a brogans an a belt. Brang 'em a pair'a drawers. Let them nigguhs try on them clothes to make sho they git a good fit." He never stopped walking. "Give 'em some socks too," I heard him say while passing through another door being held ajar by the turnkey. "I don't want these nigguhs goin to them Walls lookin lak a bunch uv hoboes. An git 'em all a shave an fresh haircut."

"Yessir, Warden. I'll take care uv it."

"Take care my ass! I want it dun now!"

Cap'n Foots left the mess hall running. Later, we went back to our tanks with an armload of Christmas-in-October garments.

At four A.M. the call went out from the picket post, "Alla you nigguhs whut's a-goin to that ol rodeo, les go eat!"

We were rushed through our meal and remained seated. A few minutes later Big Devil came in, all decked out and strutting like a palace guard. He was going too.

The cage-fitted cattle trucks backed inside the yard close to the back door. "Awright, y'all lissen up heah," Cap'n Foots ordered. "When I call y'all's name, give me yore number an go on down the hall an git on the truck!"

Big Devil waited near the back door to inspect us and see that we loaded sixty to a truck. Within the hour, our three trucks cleared the farm with Big Devil leading the way in his freshly waxed and polished Chevrolet.

As soon as we got to the highway, sheriff and highway patrol cars were waiting to escort us to their line of jurisdiction. Another group was waiting when we entered the next county. It was daybreak before we reached the Ramsey and Clemens trucks waiting to join the convoy at a highway intersection.

Unfortunately, we had Boss Eat-Em-Up riding at the back of our cage. "I ain't gon have y'all a-hollerin out the sides uv this truck at them ol nappy-headed gals. First nigguh I ketch a-wavin an a-gawkin gon git sump'n dun to his goat-smellin ass. I wont you nigguhs to be quiet! Another thang, y'all ain't gon be a-runnin all over this truck!"

I wondered how in the hell we were going to be "a-runnin all over" when we were almost sitting on top of one another. Before we got fifty miles down the highway, several cons had already pissed on themselves. Somebody forgot the piss cans. But, with so much wind blowing through the cage, they'd be dry by the time we got to the Walls. Somehow, I got on the wrong side of the truck when boarding and couldn't see off into the cars that went by. Nobody was about to switch for less than two decks.

It was almost noon when we got there. We quickly unloaded and were herded into the latrine area. Afterward, we sat on those hard seats for almost an hour before showtime. Meanwhile, the Goree girls kept us entertained by showing us their "stuff" when the guards weren't looking. We looked and wished.

The whole show lasted about three hours, and then we were heading back to the hell.

I sat in wind-chilled silence thinking about the day's events, recollecting some of the hundreds of pretty girls I'd seen. My head was so damn cold I couldn't help but remember we were the only cons there with bald heads. It started raining before we got halfway back. It was after eight that evening when we stepped off the truck. Cap'n Foots was at the back door. "Y'all go on in the mess hall an take them clothes off an tie them shoes together."

We stripped and filed back to our tanks, where our clothes were ready and waiting. I finally thawed out and went looking for Chinaman. "Look, man, a million years frum now, don't never ask me to go to another one'a them muthafuckas! It ain't worth it." He just stood there, grinning at me like the Cheshire cat.

16

A herd of wild elephants foraging in the African jungle wouldn't make as much noise as we did stripping sorghum cane. The task was threefold, and Boss Robles left it to me to get us organized. I chose the fastest workers to do the cutting and the slower ones to handle the loading. Everybody in the squad helped strip the razor-sharp leaves off the cane going down the rows. Coming back, we split up into sections. The cutters hewed the stalks while the loaders came behind gathering and loading it onto the trailers. When the loaders fell behind, we cutters helped load to keep them caught up.

When we stripped in the afternoon it wasn't too bad, but not so in the early morning, when the cane was still wet with dew and the leaves let go reluctantly. My hands were semisoft from the moisture and almost every time I reached up to the top of a stalk to strip it down, I cut them. My bloody palms looked like they had been sliced repeatedly with a razor blade. I ripped off a piece of my pants leg and wrapped it around my palms. When we knocked off for lunch and got out on the turnrow headed for the building, I noticed I wasn't the only one.

Once we reached the building and got to the tank, I went straight to the face basin. After washing my hands, I saw what a real mess they were. Cadlack, the lead row in Number 3 hoe, came over. "Say, Race, is dat cane messin up y'all's hands lak it is ours?" Instead of answering, I just showed my sliced palms to him. "Whut we gon do, man?"

"I don't know whut *we* gon do. I jes know whut *I'm* gon do."

"Well, whut ya gon do, man?"

"I ain't decided yet."

"When ya do, lemme know. Fuck dis shit!" and he walked away. The turnout bell rang. Back to the cane field. After lunch we quickly finished up where we had left off and caught another set. My hands were bleeding again from more fresh cuts. About midway I stopped. "Boss Robles, my hands is in bad shape," I said, turning my palms up for him to see, "an some uv the others' is too."

After looking at my hands, he shook his head. "I see 'em, Race-hoss, but I flat don't know whut to tell you, except y'all take your time and try to be careful strippin them leaves."

The last part was okay, but there was no way we could take our time. Not us. I worked on a little farther, thought about the pisser, and dropped my cane knife. Fuck it! I quit! And sat down on my row.

The rest of the squad quit. It was a shame this had to happen under Boss Robles, but we wouldn't have done it under the Band. This wasn't the first time our hands had been bloody. We always stripped cane bare-handed, but under Boss Band nothing was supposed to hurt. If it did, we kept it to ourselves.

Soon, squad after squad sat down in the middle of their rows and placed their hands over their heads like we had done. For once, we banded together. The call went out, "Them nigguhs dun bucked!"

Cap'n Smooth told the bosses, "Round 'em all up in one bret an gather up them cane knives."

Then he ordered security phase two. "Y'all drive 'em tractors an trailers up heah alongside these nigguhs an park 'em." He was talking to the convict tractor drivers who were hauling the cane to the syrup mill. They quickly obeyed his orders, and, as soon as they completed the operation, he ordered them to sit with us.

"Some'a you bosses wit them shotguns, tie yore hosses an git up on 'em trailers." Like commandos, they responded and took their posts. Boss Robles was excluded; he only carried a revolver. The "commandos" took it a step further and laid the hammers back.

With all secured, Cap'n Smooth directed his attention to us. "If you nigguhs don't git up offa y'all's asses an git back to wek, you gonna wish you hadda."

He walked Ol Cherry, his big strawberry roan, right into the crowd. We shifted and slid left and right to keep from being stepped on. He stopped in the center of the circle. "You goddamn impudent bastards betta git up offa y'all's asses an git back to wek! Y'all hear me?" he shouted.

We didn't budge. He walked Cherry throughout the crowd. We squirmed, twisted, and reshuffled to stay out of her path. He shot a glance at some of the other bosses who were still on horseback. They got the message and began walking their horses in and out of the crowd, hitting us with the reins, shouting, "Git up offa y'all's asses an git to wek!" They quickly got back in their positions by the trailers when they saw Big Devil's car coming.

Dust was still flying when the Chevy and three pickups loaded with officers and bosses halted on the turnrow in front of us. Some were carrying baseball bats and ax handles. Big Devil sure didn't have on the right kind of shoes for the terrain because he kept tripping over the cane stubs. When he got to us, he yelled, "Who started this shit?" After no reply, he asked, "Cap'n, you know who started it?"

"Well, Warden, that Number One hoe wuz the one to quit first, if thas whutcha mean."

Big Devil tried to get Boss Robles to single one of us out, but he wouldn't. He told the warden we all quit at the same time. Determined to find out "who," Big Devil used another tactic. "Alla you Number One nigguhs that wanna go back to wek, stand up."

Nobody moved.

"Any the resta you nigguhs that wanna go back to wek, stand up," he said, surveying us.

We remained still. He motioned to the waiting bosses to move in closer with their bats and ax handles. Every available man had been brought along, even Cap'n Foots. Big Devil called to him, "Cap'n Franklin, brang 'em cattle prods outta the backseat uv my car."

Hearing that, we nervously shifted positions a little. Cap'n Foots delivered the half dozen or so "stingers," and Big Devil handed one each to whatever bosses happened to be standing nearest him and ordered, "Use 'em." Armed with a bat in one hand and a battery-operated cattle prod in the other, this bunch started kicking and jabbing those on the outer perimeter.

Then they moved into the inner circle and poked us indiscriminately, trying to elicit a response of some kind they could really attack. After this failed, Big Devil ordered them to stop. He pulled back most of his key officers for a conference and decided it was best for us to stay in the field until things were resolved. "Don't want them nigguhs a-tearin up 'at buildin." A good two hours had passed since the sit-down began, and nobody had asked us *why* yet.

I suppose it was prison policy to report a mass rebellion such as this to the bigwigs at the Walls, because before long we heard a plane buzzing overhead. It was the Texas prison system's own. The horses stirred uneasily as the small aircraft circled the field at low altitude and landed on one of the turnrows about a mile away.

Big Devil was there waiting. A middle-aged man got out, hurriedly entered the awaiting vehicle, and they drove away from us. The unit's entire security force had assembled in the field, forming a huge ring around us. The bosses pulled some trailers together on the turnrow and formed a platform. Car doors opened. The visitor and Big Devil slowly walked to the platform and mounted.

"My name is Jack Heard, I'm the assistant director. I'm here to find out why y'all refuse to work. I talked to the warden, now I want to hear what you men have to say. I want somebody to tell me why you quit."

Silence. He must have been crazy asking someone to stand up and talk in front of all these guards, and Big Devil to boot. What was going to happen to the one that did it? He sure as hell wouldn't fly back to the Walls with the assistant director.

He repeatedly asked that somebody stand up and speak, but nobody would. Finally, "If somebody wants to speak up, I give you my word nothing's gonna happen to you for it. Is anybody gonna come forward and speak up, or am I gonna have to issue orders to put y'all back to work?"

Most of the cons in my squad cast their glances at me. I took a moment to weigh the promise he had made, and then stood up. When I did, he beckoned me to come forward. "What's your name?"

"They call me Racehoss, sir."

Big Devil added, "This is the lead row in the Number One hoe squad."

"You want to tell me why you men refuse to work?"

"Yessir."

"Well, tell me then."

"Sir, I ain't sittin down cuz I don't wanna work. It's cuz my hands is all cut up," I said, showing them to him. To my surprise, Cap Rock walked up and showed his. Then all the rest raised theirs to show him.

"How'd this happen? Why don't y'all use gloves?"

"Whut caused it is the sharp edges on the cane leaves, sir. When they wet, it's hard to strip 'em off without cuttin our hands an fingers nearly to the bone. We don't have gloves, sir. They don't sell 'em in our commissary, an even if they did, most'a us couldn't buy a pair."

He looked at Big Devil. "Why don't you have gloves for this type of work?"

Big Devil squirmed. "We got 'em on order, Mr. Heard. We ain't received 'em yet."

His decision was quick. "Take these men to the building. I don't want them back out here till you get gloves. Is that clear?"

"Yessir, Mr. Heard," Big Devil answered quickly.

After the head count, we started walking down the turnrow. Mr. Heard stopped us. "Hey! Y'all come on back here and get on these trailers."

For supper that evening we got two pork chops apiece, mashed potatoes, gravy, biscuits, and all the apple pie we could eat!

This strike ended quite unlike the "buck" that time when it was freezing outside and we refused to go to the spinach patch to pick the frozen shit. After they rang the turnout bell, the inside picket boss hollered, "Number One!"

Since I was supposed to be the first man out, I said, "I ain't goin."

"One!"

"I ain't goin."

"I'm gonna call that number again, and you nigguhs betta git to goin! *One!*"

I didn't move and no one else did, except Hollywood. He was the only man standing in the hallway. Cap'n Smooth told him to go back in his tank and took me to the pisser for "agitatin." When Big Devil found out about it, he gave Hollywood a job and punished all the hoe squads.

No doubt Jack Heard's presence had an influence on the outcome, but the 100 percent seemed to make a difference. We stopped fighting among ourselves long enough to enter into an unknown territory—unity—and became a force with which to be reckoned.

The next morning about nine thirty a truck arrived from the Walls. The commissary clerk (Hollywood) and turnkey unloaded a dozen cardboard boxes full of cloth gloves made by the Goree girls. We were each issued a pair, and we waited for the turnout bell while reading our love notes written inside the fingers.

Once we were out the back gate, Boss Robles had me head for the trailers. We were going to ride to the field! Big Devil purposely had them parked a good three or four city blocks from the back gate, just to show he was still on the throne. As we rode to the field, I thought about Boss Band. He had probably turned over in his grave!

The work situation in the fields changed dramatically. Boss Robles always had treated us like men, but now he acted proud to be our boss. The other squads looked up to and admired us. Just like in the tanks, we became the big brothers in the field. I was able to slow the work pace down so all the squads could keep up. Something totally unacceptable in the past.

Boss Robles lifted the silent system we had worked under for so long. There was no longer the threat of death if one of us stopped working long enough to roll a cigarette. He streamlined the row-hacking operations too. He stopped us from hacking down one side of our row all the way to the end and hacking down the other side coming back. Since we walked right down the top of the row anyway, he convinced Cap'n Smooth we could cover more ground if allowed to slow down a little and hack both sides of our rows while going down them. He was more concerned with the quality of our work than how fast we did it. Of course, picking cotton was still every man for himself, and we still had to face the hog law.

Boss Robles struck up a mild friendship with the old boss over the Number 5 hoe squad. Boss Skeals was too funny to pass up, and I liked to listen to him when we worked beside his squad. They weren't anything to compare to us, but they were good workers.

He never stayed close to them like the other bosses did. He'd be at least twenty-five yards behind. His dialogue was filled with threats. By two o'clock he'd cut all his cons out for the day. But rarely did he ever do it at the back gate.

Totally unconcerned, he'd say, "You nigguhs betta blacken dem rows, blacken 'em, I tell you. You nigguhs go ta sinkin dem hoes up to the eye. Go to movin dat dirt roun lak you aim ta do sump'n. Now I know y'all is all bad an I'm makin some'a y'all mad. But I don't give a damn. Y'all ain't the baddest nigguhs I dun evah seed. I seed a whole lotsa nigguhs badder'n y'all is.

"I'll bet evah one'a you ol thangs is down heah fer murder ta let y'all tell it. Shit, the only thang y'all evah dun kilt is biscuits in dat man's mess hall. Git ta wek an git dem rows on 'way frum heah! I bet y'all thank I'm gon follow y'all's black asses all over dis man's plantation an not do sump'n to you. I kin tell you rat now, thas a damn lie! Jes wait till we git ta dat back gate."

Boss Skeals had been carrying the Number 5 hoe squad for many years, but he couldn't name four cons who worked under him. Well beyond the sixty-year mark, he had a grubby old prospector look about him. He always needed a shave and his clothes were always dirty, stained with missed tobacco spits. He had a terrible odor and a running sore on the right cheek of his ass. A big wet spot showed through the seat of his pants whenever he wasn't in the saddle.

He'd worked around black cons for so long, he developed the mannerisms and even talked like them. He had more experience guarding convicts than any of the field bosses. Prior to coming to Retrieve, he served twenty years as a guard at the Angola Prison in Louisiana, had retired from there, and drew a pension. He loved to talk about Louisiana. The cons in his squad who had served time in Angola or happened to be from Louisiana had it made. All they had to do was let him talk and throw in an occasional "Thas right, boss," and go through the motions of working.

That is, until he saw Big Devil's car in the fields. When that happened, he immediately shifted his conversation to chewing the con out for "laggin back," threatening to cut him out at the back gate if he didn't tighten up.

I overheard him doing that one day with Braggs, one of the few he knew by name. He was carrying on a two- to five-year Louisiana conversation with him. Somehow, Big Devil's car got by him and he didn't see it in time to straighten his act. Big Devil pulled his car right behind our two squads and parked.

"Boss Skeals!" the warden shouted. He didn't hear and kept right on talking. "Boss Skeals!" a little louder this time.

Somebody in his squad finally said, "Boss Skeals! Boss Skeals!"

"Whut the hell you wont, nigguh? Can't you see I'm talkin? Thas whut's wrong wit you nigguhs now, always buttin in somebody's bizness!"

The con finally got a word in. "Boss, I wuz jes tryin ta tell you the warden is back dere callin you."

"Ol Braggs, you bout the sorriest nigguh I evah seed," Boss Skeals said, leaning forward in his saddle to really let him have it. "Don't you thank I gits tired uv watchin you drag yo ass aroun? *Whut'd you say?* Nigguh, you bet not open yo mouf! How come you won't go ta wek? How come you make me beg you ta wek, nigguh? Why you so bitterly ginst it? Is wek evah kilt anybody in yo family? Is you evah heard tell uv anybody dyin frum it?"

"Nawsuh, boss," Braggs answered and kept on working. He, like the rest of the squad, knew it was all just a charade.

"I tell you whut, nigguh, I'm damn sho gon see if I can't *beg* dat man into doin sump'n ta yore rotten ass when we gits back ta dat house!" Big Devil sat on the hood of his car trying to keep a straight face. After thoroughly chewing out Braggs, he asked, "Did I hear some'a y'all say sump'n bout dat warden 'while ago?"

"Yessuh, boss, we been tryin ta tell you the warden's been callin you."

"Well, why in the hell didn't y'all say so?" Shifting all blame onto the squad, he said, "You damned ol thangs be runnin dem ol moufs so goddamn much, a man can't hear hissef fart. Git ta wek!"

Removing his hat quickly was the fastest move he'd made all day. He slowly turned his horse around and began walking it toward the car. Hat in hand, he greeted Big Devil. "How you feelin, Warden, suh? You doin awright today, suh? Sorry I tuk so long in a-comin, I didn't know you wuz back heah. But as you knows, these nigguhs be runnin them ol moufs worse'n a bell clappin in a goose's ass. I jes got through tellin one uv 'em he betta quit runnin his ol head. I'm sho glad you showed up. He'll take his ass ta wek now."

"Whut nigguh is it thas givin you trouble?"

"Warden, suh, you know whut I come ta learn?"

"Whut's that, Cliff?"

"Alla dem ol wide-mouf apes look so much alak I can't hardly tell 'em apart." Scratching his stubby chin, he went on, "I can't thank uv dat nigguh's name to save my life. But I know whut I'm gon do, I'm gon cut the whole damn batch out. Dat way, I'll git dat rotten bastard. Whut wuz it you wonted ta see me bout, Warden?"

Big Devil had as much fun as anybody listening to Skeals's thigh-slapping humor, but he wasn't about to let the boss off the hook for not adequately guarding his squad. "Skeals, you betta go to watchin 'em nigguhs an make 'em go to cleanin them rows. Yore nigguhs is goin down through there leavin half a that wek."

"I'm sho glad you seed that, Warden! I been callin dem rotten bastards back all day. I'm so tired uv it I jes don't know whut ta do.

Dey won't lissen ta me, Warden. Warden, now dat you's heah, kin I axe you a favor, suh?"

"Yeah, whut is it, Cliff?"

"Warden, would you take my hoss an ride out in dat field an tell dem rotten bastards uv mine how *bad* you wont sump'n dun to dey black asses?"

Nobody was about to sit in the saddle after him, above all, the warden. "Cliff, whut I called you fur is to tell you I kin see y'all's rows a mile away. Them nigguhs uv yourn is jes flat out big-assin you."

"You right, Warden, you sho right! Only thang keepin me frum killin some uv dem rotten bastards is I don't wanna give yore farm no bad name."

"Whutta you mean?"

"Whut I means is the way you runs the damn thang. You the bes warden I evah been under. Ain't no mounts uv money dat could git me ta take on yo worries. Thas why I do's evah thang I kin ta try not ta worry you no more'n I hafta. Is sump'n worryin you, Warden?"

"Yeah! Sump'n's worryin me. It's worryin hell outta me the way you let them ol nigguhs uv yourn jes drag 'long, lak they waitin fur the damn flies to blow 'em."

"Warden, I'm soooooo glad you said dat I don't know whut to do! Jes soon as you leave, I'm goin over yonder an put dem rotten sonsabitches ta wek, one way or another. I dun had enuff."

"How come you can't do it while I'm heah, Cliff?"

"Well, Warden," Skeals replied, looking at him point-blank, "I respects you too much. I don't wont you nowhere round when I gits back ta dat squad. I couldn't stand fer you ta see whut all I'm gon do. 'Sides, I couldn't sleep tonight knowin I dun messed up yore suppa."

Big Devil didn't have a comeback for that much tarnished humility. Shaking his head, he got in the car and drove away.

All the squads got to the end in good succession, and we quickly lined up and headed back. I slowed it down a notch to allow Number 8 to work their way up even with the rest of us. We were still snickering at Boss Skeals's conversation with Big Devil.

When all the squads got lined up and were working side by side again, I looked over at Cap Rock and said, "Let's rock 'em." Cap Rock picked up the lick, and the con next to him, and the next, and so on down the line until our two hundred hoes were hitting together thunderously, causing the earth to tremble beneath our feet. I cut loose with one of our work songs, and the two-hundred-con choir sang the response.

"We got forty-four hammers rangin in one line," I sang.

"Forty-four hammers rangin in one line," they echoed.

"Ain't no hammer heah that rangs lak mine."

"Rangs lak mine."

"It rangs lak silver, an it shines lak golddddd."

"Rangs lak silver, an it shines lak gold."

"The price for my hammer rangin ain't never been told."

"Ain't never been told."

"So les raise 'em up higher, an then drop 'em on down."

"Drop 'em on down."

"They can't tell the difference, when the sun goes down."

"When the sun goes down."

We must have sung Boss Skeals and his horse to sleep. While we were singing, his old horse had wandered behind another squad. Both had their heads hanging down. Boss Cochise detected Boss Skeals had fallen asleep and alerted the others not to awaken him. The horse and Boss Skeals came right out on the turnrow still following the wrong squad. We watched him go down the turnrow, dead asleep.

Once all the squads were out on the turnrow, the bosses felt they'd let the joke go on long enough. Cochise hollered, "Hey, Boss Skeals! Hey, boss!"

Boss Skeals flinched and sat up erectly. Eyes blurry, he looked around and didn't see the three or four cons he knew. "Yeah, whut is it, boss?"

"Boss Skeals, I hate ta 'sturb you, but you been followin the wrong squad." The other bosses cracked up.

Boss Skeals waited until they finished laughing. "Dey all nigguhs, ain't dey?" he asked matter-of-factly.

Besides Boss Skeals's antics, the tractor squad was a main attraction. They put on a show for us when they plowed nearby. They plowed the rows straight as arrows with the front wheels of their tractors reared up like motorcycle daredevils.

Thirty-Five plowed while steering with his feet and rolling a smoke. Crazy Folks filed on a "piece'a sump'n" he hustled at the shop, making rings, tie clasps, and other sellable "jewelry" as he tilled the soil.

The "toast ridin" feat was the grand finale. They all lined up and leaped off their moving tractors, ran along beside them, undid their water jugs strapped to the hoods, took a drink, "salud," crossed over in front, and remounted on the other side. It was no secret that those jugs were usually filled with "chock" (a home brew made from potatoes, sugar, yeast, dried fruit, and water). At any given time any of them could have been busted for PWI (plowing while intoxicated). It was no secret either that the tractor squad was the "warden's nigguhs" and could get away with it.

Their bosses didn't hassle them since they were all good workers, or the warden wouldn't have assigned them to the squad. They were the first ones called out to the fields in the morning and the last ones to come in at night. Seven days a week, rain or shine, the tractor squad went out.

To keep the farm looking clean and the roads smooth, on Sundays the warden would have Pug and Brady drop the cultivators on Brady's hot rod tractor and hook on the cable-drawn two-by-twelve planks to drag-sweep the main turnrow, which was the road leading into the unit. When we were up in the auditorium, we could see them through the windows as they performed their no-holding-on-to-nothing-allowed "plank-skiing" stunt. We bet on each ride.

They took turns riding the planks, while the other zigzagged the tractor across the road, trying to throw the plank rider off. Going full speed, the driver would lock one of the wheels and turn sharply to create a wide, sweeping "pop the whip" effect. When this didn't get it, the driver was the loser and they'd switch places. According to our score, the match was three to one in Pug's favor.

Something was really going on; I thought maybe the feds had taken over. Never had so many big shots from the Walls administration visited our unit back to back. The week before it had been a group from the Education Department down to teach us a word-association memory technique, and then it was the prison system's clinical psychologist, Dr. Gates.

"Any man can change for the better, but he gotta want to. He's got to have that itchin, achin, burnin desire for self-betterment." When I first saw Dr. Gates I thought he might have been the governor. He spoke eloquently while at the same time using layman's terms we could understand. He told us, "I'm going to start a pilot program of group counseling sessions where we can talk out our problems through discussions and interacting with one another.

"The program will begin next Thursday afternoon and will be held each Thursday thereafter for sixteen weeks. Those who are selected to attend will only work a half day on Thursdays. Selection of the twelve participants will be left to the warden's discretion."

"He sho didn't hafta say dat," somebody mumbled.

The only logical reasons I could come up with as to why Big Devil selected the twelve of us was either he'd gone crazy or he didn't give a damn if it worked or not and was just appeasing the administration. We were all field hands, except Hollywood and Rev.

After Big Devil finished laying down "the law" about classroom behavior, he asked, "Y'all got any questions?"

Nobody had any. That is, except for Flea Brain. "Yassuh, Warden. How come y'all don't put Poke Chops in heah wit us?"

Big Devil didn't dignify Flea Brain's question with an answer. Instead, he shot him a scornful look and dismissed us.

Thursday rolled around. "Funny-school day," the cons had labeled it. The count was clear and Boss Humpy let us out.

When we entered the auditorium, Hollywood and Rev were already seated, chatting with Dr. Gates. They got a head start because their trusty tank door was kept unlocked and they could wander about at will. We sat anxiously waiting to be included.

"Good afternoon," Dr. Gates greeted. "I already met these two fellas. Why don't we get acquainted? I'm Dr. Gates. Let's start with this fella right here. What's your name?"

Flea Brain didn't give Cowfucker a chance to speak and blurted out, "How come y'all ain't got Poke Chops in dis class?"

"I didn't know y'all were allowed to eat up here," Dr. Gates joked. "Next time I'll try to remember to bring something."

The class erupted, and so did Dr. Gates, which I'm sure made Boss Humpy wonder what in the hell was going on. Proud Walker explained between laughs, "Dr. Gates, he ain't talkin bout pork chops you eat."

"Well, if we're not talking about the kind you eat, somebody wanna tell me what we *are* talking about here?"

Proud Walker, in his finest hour, was quick to decipher the Pork Chops intrigue. "Dr. Gates, he talkin bout another nigguh *named* Pork Chops."

"Nowww I got it. Thanks for helping me out." The class had gotten back to semicalm, and Dr. Gates directed his attention to Flea Brain. "What's your name, fella?"

"Flea Brain."

"Why do they call you that? Do you know?"

"Yassuh, it's cuz my brains ain't no bigger'n a flea."

"How do you know that?"

With foolish pride, he answered, "Das whut da warden say an da warden don't lie."

"And you believe that your brain 'ain't no bigger'n a flea' just because the warden said it?"

I thought, *You better watch out, Doc, you're treadin on thin ice. If you don't, Wise-Em-Up's nightly heralds uv "you gonna hafta talk ta that warden in the mornin" will ring true for you.*

"Well, now that I know Pork Chops is a who, why do you want him in the class?"

Flea Brain was not the bashful type when the subject was Pork Chops. "Jes cuz I luvs him an he need to be where I is, an I need to be where he is."

"In other words, you feel that your friend Pork Chops should be in the class because you're in it."

"Dr. Gate, he be mo'n a 'frien.' Poke Chops be my woman," Flea Brain sheepishly added, "an sometimes I his'n."

Silence.

"Oh, I see."

Overwhelmed by his frankness, Dr. Gates jumped at the opportunity to do a full Flea Brain analysis. "Do you feel it's wrong to have sex with a man?"

"Dat's all dat's in heah. I gits punished when I gits caught jackin off. Most uv us can't git to dem cows, mules, an hosses lak dem lot nigguhs. Whut we spose ta do?"

Flea Brain had stymied the good doctor. "If you don't want to be in the class because Pork Chops isn't in it, the best thing for us to do is get you out of it. You go on downstairs and have a seat under the picket. I'll talk to the warden on my way out."

After Flea Brain left, we spent the rest of the afternoon listening to the good doc describe his escapades as an "RAF pilot in WW Two." Even with Flea Brain gone, he had his work cut out for him. There was the silent bunch: Earthworm, Crazy Folks, Bad Eye, Cowfucker, and me. Nelly Nothin, Proud Walker, Bow Wow, and Fistfucker were the vocal dunces, who tied up the class with their illogical questions and arguments.

Rev and Hollywood were the ad-libbing duo. They tied up the class expounding on Dr. Gates's statements. Their suck-assism was the most boring part of the class, but Proud Walker would come to the rescue with his cockeyed questions that caught the good doctor off guard.

Dr. Gates would be going hot and heavy. "A man is judged by his behavior. A man is no better or worse than his behavior makes him. You are no more or no less than what you've become up to this very moment. We're the sum total of our behavior."

He should have finished before he stopped to ask if we were "with him." Proud Walker apparently wasn't. "Dr. Gates, sump'n bout dis I don't unnastan."

"What is it you don't understand?"

"Whut is behavior in the first place an how does I know I gots one?"

"Everybody has a behavior, Proud Walker. Sometimes it's good and sometimes it's bad, just like anything else."

"Well, if it's bad an it's jes lak anythang else, how come ya can't git it took out lak yo 'pendix when dey gits bad? Is it some kinda disease or sump'n?"

"No, it's not a disease."

"Well, if it ain't no disease, how come it takes a doctor ta fix it?"

As the weeks wore on, the good doctor repeatedly talked about pride, fair play, humbleness, and respect for others whenever Proud Walker hushed long enough to let him finish a thought. He was doing his level best to convince us we could "change," but he didn't "unnastan" this was no place for fainthearted gentlemen.

At the end of the sixteen weeks, we held our graduation exercise in the auditorium and received our certificates of completion. My first . . . for anything.

The next morning, Friday, it was business as usual. After Big Tom sounded, Cap'n Smooth hollered up the hall, "When you Number One an Two nigguhs come out, pull over to one side an wait. Awright, lemme have 'em, boss!"

"Number One!"

Soon as I cleared the steps, I veered the squad over by the laundry. Number 2 did the same. It took about fifteen minutes to get the count clear. Then Big Devil came out onto the yard. "Boss Robles, Boss Wilhite [Cochise], y'all go git some picks an shovels. Take y'all's squads roun in front uv my office an I'll meet y'all."

"Yessir. Okay, Racehoss, let's go git us some tools."

We got them and met the warden on the shell road in front of his office. "Boss Robles, Boss Wilhite, I want y'all to go right out there"—Big Devil pointed to the open field of johnsongrass—"on the other side uv 'at parkin rail an commence diggin."

We stood poised and ready to dig up the world. "Tell y'all whut, I best walk over there wit y'all an show you zackly whut I want." Walking across the road, he instructed, "Brang y'all's squads on an follow me." He walked to the center of the field and pointed down. "This is where I want y'all to start."

"Whut're we diggin, Warden?" Cochise asked.

"A fishin pond."

"How big's it gonna be?" Cochise asked.

"Well, itta be plenny big enuff when I git dun wit it."

Looking at the area, I thought, *He ain't bullshittin.* And with two squads digging it with picks and shovels, I'd discharge the rest of my sentence on it. Big Devil "walked it off." According to his calculations, the pond would end up being one hundred feet by one hundred feet. "An we're goin down a fur piece, bout six to eight feet."

"Warden, you ain't plannin on goin fishin in it no time soon, is you?" Cochise asked.

Big Devil smiled mischievously. "Jes soons y'all git it dug."

The two squads kept their motors on low idle, hoping Cochise would hush and let Big Devil go on about his business. Just his presence made everybody nervous as whores in church.

"Warden, you gonna stock it?" Cochise asked.

"Goddamn, Wilhite! It wouldn't be no damn fishin pond if it weren't no fuckin fish in it!"

Boss Robles, waiting for an opening, asked, "Warden, you got any more orders before we git started?"

"Yeah, take yore Number One nigguhs an spread 'em out in a circle heah in the middle. You nigguhs spread out in a circle roun me. Spread out wide nuff apart so y'all got room to wek."

Then he had Number 2 encircle us. "Now thas the way I want y'all to start. You Number One nigguhs start diggin in the center heah, an pitch 'at dirt back to these Number Two nigguhs. They'll throw it back outta the way. We'll build up the levee as we go. Awright, y'all git at it."

The area was near the officers' housing, namely Cap'n Smooth's house. Most of the cons and bosses hated working close to the houses, and especially that close to the warden's office. Whenever we walked past the warden's house, we had to pull off our flop-down hats whether anybody was home or not, which was the main reason I started wearing a bandanna. Failure to pull off your hat was the pisser (for being disrespectful). The same thing went for his car.

After the second week of digging, we had the "pond" all to ourselves. We didn't do it on purpose, but we jobbed the shit out of Number 2 hoe. We'd been digging out so much dirt and pitching it back, they couldn't shovel it back fast enough and we had a hole that looked like a double-ring donut. This pissed Cochise off and he started cursing them for not keeping up. Cap'n Smooth's wife overheard his "foul language" and ran him in to the warden. Big Devil came out to the pond and sent them back to the fields. Fuck!

Big Devil compensated for the loss of manpower. We worked in the hole as our "regular" job five days a week, and all the screwups in the building, as well as in the field, carried on the project nights and weekends as punishment. After about ten weeks the hole was taking on the shape of a huge pond. The more we dug, the more I despised the sight of a shovel and a pick.

Tuesday evening when we came in, Boss Humpy hollered down in the tank, "Ol Racehoss, lay in in the mornin to ketch 'at chain!"

"Yahoooo!" I couldn't help it. It had been so long since I talked to the parole man I'd just about given up. After almost eight years, I made it.

17

. . . and violated parole for aggravated assault with a deadly weapon.

Déjà fuckin vu! After only a year, I was stepping back into hell again. I felt like kicking my own ass as I walked through the back door of Retrieve. With a pair of nuts hotter than a comet's tail, I had been out just long enough to get my belly full of pussy and my nose cut off. With no credit for the time I was out, I picked right up where I left off, going yonder way on the rest of that funky thirty-year sentence, which amounted to about ten more years. With commutation time, eighteen calendar years discharge a thirty-year sentence.

Soon as I got my things put away in the same old Number 3 tank, the picket boss sent me to the front office. "Welllllll, Ol Racehoss! Couldn't stay out, couldja? Jes can't make it in that free world, kin you? Nigguh, you wudn't gone long nuff fur 'em to give away yore bunk, wuz you?"

Not so, I got another bunk *and* locker, but I didn't interrupt just to dispute that. I'd rather have been shot down and shit on at sunrise than have to face him, let alone listen to his shit.

Then he noticed the scar running from my left jawbone up across the bridge of my nose to my right cheek that hadn't completely healed. "Whut happen to yore face? Whut'd you do, git to fuckin wit somebody's gal?"

"No sir, Warden. I wuz in a car wreck an went through the windshield. It cut my nose off."

"Thas too bad, Ol Racehoss, but it still looks lak yore nose."

"Yes sir, it is. I had it wrapped in my handkerchief. When I got to the hospital, they wuz able to sew it back on."

He thought for a minute. "Bein a field hand didn't do you much good in the free world. Go upstairs to the E an R [Education and Recreation] Department in the mornin an tell Meabs I said to put you on Ol Sonny Wells's job. I'm sendin him to the Walls to cook fur the director. Thank you kin handle 'at?"

"Yes sir."

"You do whut he tells you, an you bet not let them nigguhs be a-usin that place fur no whorehouse neither."

"Yes sir."

As I was about to leave, he added, "I'll call in there an tell the inside picket boss to let you out wit the rest uv them buildin nigguhs in the mornin."

The next morning I ate breakfast on the short line, then went upstairs to my new workstation. I walked into the little office, sat down, and began looking at all the paperwork piled on each of the two desks. Hanging on the wall behind the larger desk was Mr. Meabs's master's degree in physical education from Southern Mississippi.

The floors were already shining from last night's cleanup, so I got the feather duster and started dusting off the library books. It was getting pretty close to eight o'clock.

When Mr. Meabs topped the stairs and entered the auditorium, I stopped dusting and spoke. He kept right on strutting like a blind rooster, as if he didn't hear me. I followed him, stood in the doorway, and waited for him to get settled at his desk before giving him the warden's message.

Without looking up at me, he said, "Who're you?"

"Racehoss, Mr. Meabs. Yesterday the warden told me to tell you to put me on Ol Sonny's job."

"You got a GED or high school education?"

"No sir."

"Can you type?" he asked, still avoiding eye contact.

"No sir."

"Can you run a picture show projector?"

"No sir, but I kin learn."

Finally he looked up. Clearly startled by the long, unsightly scar on my face, he stared at it, then looked down at his desk and began grumbling about all the paperwork and typing that had to be done. With a noticeable lisp, he said, "What in the heck I gon do wit shumbody who don't have a education, can't type, an can't run a projector? I sure wis the warden would lemme be in on choosin people to work in here."

I spent practically the entire day in the auditorium, and he hadn't said another word to me. Since I didn't know what routine he expected, I went to him and asked.

"Well, Racehoss, the main tang is keep the auditorie spic-an-span, cause we can't nebber tell when the warden migh' come up here an look aroun."

"You don't hafta worry bout the auditorium bein clean. I'm gon see to that. Do you mind if I use the typewriter to practice on after we close up the auditorium?"

"It's awrigh' wit me, but you nee' to git permission from the warden to stay up here atta count time."

That evening after he left, I unlocked the projector room and examined the equipment. By the time our Friday night showtime rolled around, I ran the projector with ease.

Each night after all the activities were over, I cleaned up the place and lugged the old Royal typewriter downstairs to sit under the picket to practice so I wouldn't disturb the white cons. It was coming slow. I'd hunt and peck on it until two or three in the morning. I dropped all attempts at holding my hands like typists do and used just the index and middle fingers on each hand. In a few weeks I could type faster than Mr. Meabs, and he used all of his fingers.

Occasionally, Mr. Meabs let me help in the office by stapling papers, removing paper clips, and sometimes filing. Bit by bit I became familiar with the office routine, started studying, and eventually got my GED. My typing was good enough now for me to type all the reports as well as manage the office in his absence. He began showing up at nine o'clock instead of eight, then ten, eleven, two, et cetera.

Meanwhile, Hollywood had suck-assed Big Devil into believing he could help make us better. And got permission to formulate the Brotherhood, a self-improvement program held every Saturday night. We "changed" so much it became Big Devil's favorite rehab program.

First hour—Fellowship.

The star punks served unsweetened Poly Pop in paper cups Hollywood had panhandled from Foots. While the band played ("*Uugh!*"), Okinawa sang "Come Back, Baby" and "Blind Man Standin on the Corner" ("*Uuuugh! Arrrg! Booooo!*").

Second hour—role-playing situations between the cons and the bosses. Tonight, I played the role of Mr. Meabs. I had worked around him long enough to mimic his fast-paced lisp to perfection. The audience was rolling in the aisles with laughter. After my performance the night lieutenant, who sometimes sat in on the meetings, came up to me and said he never laughed so hard in his life and was still laughing as he walked downstairs to his station in the mess hall.

Monday morning before the night lieutenant left, he ran into Mr. Meabs and told him in jest he didn't know he had a convict twin. "Ol Racehoss kin sound jes lak you. Saturday night at Brotherhood I laughed so hard I cried when he imitated you."

Mr. Meabs came straight to the office. "What's this I hear bout you mockin me Sadday nigh'?"

"I wudn't mockin you, Mr. Meabs. We role-play at the meetins all the time. That's the main part uv the program. I jes showed how you won't speak to none'a the convicts, an how I—"

He cut me off and told me "nebber" use him as a subject again and stormed out. Working in the office with him after that was hard. He sulked and pouted like a little boy, and hardly spoke to me. He started monitoring my work to the point of harassment, searched for dust along the windowsills and examined every piece of paperwork.

When he found a mistake, he wouldn't let me correct it. Instead, I had to do the whole thing over.

The PIP (Point Incentive Program) quarterly report time had rolled around again. We were graded quarterly for work, conduct, attitude, and "other" program participation. The points we earned had a definite bearing on our being considered for release on parole. If we didn't have eighty points during the previous quarter and came up for parole, the case wouldn't be considered. The PIP was tied in to just about everything, and side-hustle points could be obtained for attending Alcoholics Anonymous, church, singing in the choir or playing in the band, and being a trusty. Those who failed to maintain the eighty points were kicked out of GED classes. In addition, there would be no job promotions, and making trusty was out of the question.

I stayed late several nights in the auditorium typing the 470 individual forms, getting them ready for mailing. It took almost a week, but I had them ready by the first day of the month ending the quarter.

During that week, Mr. Meabs spent little time in the office. All the cons on the camp had been PIP rated, except me. All the forms were ready for his signature. The third day after our reports were due, the warden got a call from the Walls Education Department inquiring about them. He called me to his office and chewed my ass out.

"Warden, they ready, except for my sheet. They won't accept partial reports. All I'm waitin on is Mr. Meabs to grade me."

"I don't give a damn whut the holdup is, y'all betta git them damn reports off to them Walls!"

"Yes sir, Warden."

Mr. Meabs didn't come to work until late that afternoon. As soon as I saw him, I reminded him about my rate sheet. He hardly slowed down long enough for me to talk to him. "I be back in the mornin an gray [grade] you."

The next morning I placed my form on his desk, on top of the stack. He couldn't possibly miss it. He didn't show. Later that morning Big Devil sent for me.

Fuck it! I went back to the office, looked in the files, and pulled the last quarter's report. I had 110 points out of a possible 300. I circled the same ratings he gave me before, signed his name, and got the package off in the truck mail.

The next morning he came to work on time for a change. Soon as he walked into the office, he asked, "Where you PIP forms?"

"Mr. Meabs . . . the reports are gone. I mailed them off yesterday."

"Who grayed you?"

"Mr. Meabs, the warden wuz on my ass. He called me out to his office again about them reports."

"Who grayed you?" What I said seemed to shoot right over his head. He had one thing in mind—getting even and getting rid of me.

"I did. I copied my last quarter grades."

"Who shined 'em?" he asked, putting the lid on my coffin.

I swallowed down some air. "I signed 'em."

"You mean you forge my name?"

"Yes sir, if that's whut you wanna call it."

He had me, and we both knew it. Everybody knew Big Devil's policy: "If you git run in, you git punished." It didn't matter if the con was in the right or not. In less than fifteen minutes, I was standing in front of the warden's desk. Mr. Meabs had told him that I was impudent, forged his name, used my own judgment, and didn't consult him.

"Ol Racehoss, I thought you wuz doin a pretty good job up there. But, guess I wuz wrong," the warden said and took a chew of tobacco.

Big Devil and I had done this tango before. As many times as I'd had to face him over the years, I learned the hard way how much he hated it when a convict locked eyeballs with him; but as mad as I was about being "run in" for what amounted to nothing, I did it anyway. Knowing he was holding all the cards and the longer I speared him with my eyes the longer my punishment would be, I cast them to the clock on the wall, not wanting to overload my ass. After he spat tobacco juice into a bucket next to his desk, he said, "You know my rule, Ol Racehoss."

"Yes sir," I said and looked over at Mr. Meabs, who lowered his eyes.

Big Devil phoned the inside picket boss and told him to send the duty officer out to his office. "Boss Tetus, take Ol Racehoss roun there an put his ass in 'at pisser."

I'd lasted eighteen months on the job.

On the way, Boss Tetus asked, "Whut the hell ja do, Ol Racehoss?"

"Nothin."

As we approached the compact building just outside the back gate, Boss Tetus said to the boss who met us, "How you doin, boss? Got any empties back thar?"

"Sho, boss. Hell, ain't been nobody back thar in a week." Interrupting himself for a second, he said to me, "Take off yore clothes an git up on them scales."

I stepped on the scales, and he ran the weight balance back and forth a few times before saying "A hunnert an forty-two pounds" and recording it on a door card.

"Well, boss, I best be gittin on back, he's all yourn."

"Yeah, well, come back an see me when you got some more bizness. Okay, les go, Ol Racehoss." After passing a couple of cells, "It's been a while, ain't it?"

Silence.

"Contrary bastard, ain'tcha? You stayed out a whole lot longer'n I figgered you would. You got the whole hotel all to yoresef. Which room you wont?" He opened and closed a few of the doors, took a brief look inside, said "Whew!" while holding his nose. "They all the same, which'un you wont?"

Silence.

"Okay, if thas the way you feel bout it, I'll jes put you way back heah in the last un. That way, if we git some more customers, you be outta everbody's way," he wisecracked.

When we reached the last cell he unlocked the solid steel door, stepped inside, and unlocked the inner door. I stepped up inside and my eyeballs jumped to grab the last flicker of light before he sealed the four-by-eight tomb. A concrete slab jutted out from the wall for a bed; a four-bit-size hole in the center of the floor served as a commode. No electrical outlets for lighting, total darkness. A cup of water and a biscuit a day, and every sixth day a full meal. I knew the routine. Solitary and I were no strangers.

But I had grown soft from being out a year and then working inside for the last year and a half. I didn't expect to be put back in here, especially on some bullshit. When I worked in the fields, it was a refuge, a place to get away for a few days to rest. To go to the pisser from the fields was honorable, to go from a job was a disgrace.

If the boss could have seen through my back, he would have seen the tears streaming down my face. The slamming of the two steel doors still rang in my ears. Sitting naked on the slab in pitch-black silence, I hung my head as the tears bounced off the floor onto my feet. Other times, I took a seat and sang all the songs I knew over in my mind. But this time I felt like I was smothering, buried alive.

Sweat poured. Gritting my teeth, I hugged and rocked myself, trying to squeeze back the consuming fear, trying to keep from going off the deep end. What if something happened? A fire, flood, war—would they remember to come let me out so I could run too? Tears flowed. I panted for the thin air. My hot breath made the hellish hotbox feel like a steamy swamp. My nostrils burned from the suffocating stench of piss, and the sweat running down my body made a puddle under my butt. I squeezed myself tighter and tighter. Mouth dry, thirsty, tired, hungry, angry. The pressure from the walls was closing in, and I leaped off the slab.

I pounded my knuckles against the unyielding concrete wall until they were wet with blood. Then the sudden sound of rushing water demanded my immediate attention. Frantically I felt along every crevice and seam, hoping not to find water seeping in. Louder and louder. I got on my knees and held my ear over the floor's hole. I started scratching the hole. Nothing. Covering my ears with my hands, I discovered the source and listened to the blood rumbling up and down my fingers. My heart was beating like an African drum, pounding so hard my chest vibrated to the beat.

With the agility of a panther, I sprang up and ran around the cell. Then rolled on the floor like a ball. With outstretched arms, I clung to the low ceiling by my nails. I mauled myself, scratching and tearing my body. All the miles and miles of rails I rode, this was how far I'd come. I knew I had reached my row's end, and was nothing more than an empty-hearted outcast. Weeping bitterly, I wished there was something I could do to release some of the pressure. Like a dying dog, I had already peed myself.

Slumped exhausted on the slab in utter despair, I covered my face with both hands and cried out from the depth of my soul, "Help me, God! Help meeee!"

A. Ray. Of. Light. Between. My. Fingers. Slowly uncovering my face, I saw that the whole cell was illuminated as if a twenty-watt bulb were turned on. The soft light soothed and I no longer was afraid. Engulfed by a Presence, I felt it reassuring me. With the quickness of a shadow, it comforted me and made my tears flow back into my eyes. No pressure anymore, I breathed freely. I had never felt such well-being, so good, in all my life. Safe. Loved. I lay back on the slab with outstretched arms, absorbing it all. There was nothing to see, but I knew something was in there with me and it had to be God. I hardly got the words out of my mouth and He was there.

And the voice within talked through the pit of my belly, "Don't you worry about a thing. But you must tell them about me." Unlike a command, it was a sweet, gentle asking. I said yes with all my heart, yet I wondered with uncertainty, *Who am I to do that? I'm nothin but a lowly convict. Who do you want me to tell?* No answer.

There was no more darkness in the cell or in me. A change had taken place. I slept peacefully and hungered not. I paced blissfully in the soothing light. Never before had I felt so totally loved, and that's really all I'd ever wanted. The biggest need in my life was fulfilled in an instant. And I loved God back. My capacity to love was restored, and He proved I wasn't without feelings, I wasn't dead. Blackened by the soot of evil, yet reclaimed.

He unlocked the shadowed prisms of my mind. Through feelings, every thought was crystal clear. My life winded down before my eyes like the film in a projector set on reverse. He made me happy to feel love again in my heart for Emma. This was the first time I ever looked at the situation and took into consideration that she had her problems too. I just happened to have been there, and glad I was. I realized I was just as guilty for blaming her as she was for blaming me. He took that yoke off and sent all my regrets into exile; they became painless memories.

He never left me, He sat beside me, He held me in his arms. The caring was so magnified, such a loving touch; there aren't enough words I could ever say that would even come close to describing the feeling. I didn't care if they ever let me out. When the boss opened the door, I hesitated. I didn't want to leave my cell.

"Betta brang yore ass on frum thar befo I keep you in heah another twenny-eight days!" he shouted at me.

I stepped into the hallway and glanced back. *I sure hope He comes out with me.*

"Go git on them scales." When we reached the front, I stepped up on the scales to be weighed. He was stunned. "One forty-seven!" He rechecked the door card. According the the scales, I had gained five pounds. He said somebody had been slipping me food but didn't pursue it and let me go on to my tank.

After that, God was real. There will be no mistake; it is I. He found me in the abyss of the burnin hell, uplifted and fed my hungry soul, and filled me with His love. I didn't walk out of that cell glowing like Moses, but I knew that something had changed in me, that I wasn't the same man anymore. And I knew He would be with me for the rest of my days.

As soon as I walked back through my tank door, I felt guilty for not blurting out what had happened in solitary. But I knew if I told it, they would think I was crazy. I felt better when I thought, *Maybe He meant when I could.*

I took a shower and wasn't quite finished lacing up my brogans, getting ready, when Boss Humpy hollered down, "Ol Racehoss, that warden wonts you in his office."

In a few seconds, I called back, "Comin out, boss."

On the way to the front gate, my mind was running a hundred miles a minute. *Whut the fuck could he want this time?* I thought as I stepped through the gate.

"Yes sir, Warden," I said as I entered his office doorway.

He finished signing some papers on his desk, looked up, and handed them to me. "Take ease in there an give 'em to Boss Jack."

I quickly did an about-face back into the outer office, handed them to Boss Jack, and returned. Big Devil reared back in his chair and looked me over. "Ol Racehoss, do you thank you got sense nuff to iron my shirts 'thout burnin a hole in 'em? Thank you kin fry eggs 'thout the lace on 'em?"

"Warden, I don't know much bout cookin an I never ironed nobody's shirts befo, not even my own." If he was offering me a houseboy job, no way. I'd rather go back to the fields than work around the houses. Even back to the pisser. Working around the women meant nothing but trouble, and I had enough trouble without any help from them.

"Well, I kin see you don't wanna wek at my house."

"No sir, Warden. It ain't that I don't wanna work at yo house, it's jes I never dun that kinda work befo. I'm mo uv a field hand."

As he cleaned under his nails with a small pocketknife, he asked, "How much typin didja do fur Meabs up in the auditorium?"

"Most uv it. I did all the monthly an quarterly reports."

"Didja type letters?"

"Yes sir."

"You thank you kin keep yore mouth shet an not be a-tellin 'em nigguhs in the buildin my bizness if I put you to wek out heah in my office?"

"Yes sir."

"Boss Jack! Come in heah. This is Ol Racehoss," he said after Boss Jack entered. "He's gonna be wekin heah in the office wit you an kin help out wit some uv the typin, or whutever you need 'em fur." Looking at me, he said, "You'll be wekin under Boss Jack, but I still run the farm."

Boss Jack's expression changed; he didn't like the bragging remark. He went back to his desk in the outer office. The devilish look on Big Devil's face as he picked up the phone told me he enjoyed needling him. He dialed the inside picket. "Boss, I'm sendin Ol Racehoss back in an I want you to move 'em up to the trusty tank. Yeah, an leave word fur 'em to let 'em out in the mornin wit the trusties. Right, he'll be wekin out heah in my office. Yeah, thas right, jes add 'em to yore trusty count." After he hung up, he told me, "Ol Racehoss, when you go back inside the gate, stop by the laundry an tell 'em I said give you some new whites to wek out heah in."

Everything happened so fast. I changed in the laundry room from my old dingy gray clothes into the new starched and pressed whites (that fit). Just like that! I had been given "the job," the warden's bookkeeper! I'd expected the worst, to be back on a row with a hoe by now. As a rule when we got busted off a job and put in the pisser, it was back to the fields. And I remembered, "Don't you worry about a thing."

As soon as I was inside the building, Boss Humpy hollered down, "Ol Racehoss, git alla yore stuff, I'm movin you up in Number Five tank."

I quickly emptied my locker, put everything in my pillowcase, and went upstairs. I walked over to the barber area and started chatting with Hip Cat, the barber. He said there was no special night for shaves and haircuts, and he gave them whenever the cons asked. He was a pleasant contrast to Crip, wore fireman-type suspenders, and looked like he was past fifty.

I already knew the trusty tank door was kept unlocked, "jes let the picket boss know where you goin." We had a pretty long talk before the trusties started coming in for lunch. I knew everybody who lived on the tank. Some had been in the squad with me, others used to live in 3 tank. I'd handled each of their PIP cards at least a hundred times, and knew most of their prison numbers by heart I had typed them so often.

On my first night in the trusty tank I found out that when it came to gambling and watching *Gunsmoke*, they were no different from the bunch in Number 3 tank. The TV benches were full of loyal fans. In the opening scene when Marshal Matt Dillon walked out in the streets to draw his gun with the crook, stopped, and relaxed his left leg, the cons went wild. The moment the marshal moved into his drawing stance was the part that got it! They all were on Matt's side. After watching their enthusiastic reaction to *Gunsmoke*, I knew it was just another tank full of cons, only called something else.

After we'd eaten breakfast on the short line, the call for "trusties" went out. We cleared the back gate. Each trusty went to the Peg-Board outside of the pisser building and punched out. When I got to the board, my name wasn't on it.

"Stand to one side an let the rest uv these nigguhs come on by," I was told. After they checked out, the boss asked me, "Whar in the hell do you thank you goin, Ol Racehoss?" half joking. "Ain't no peg up thar fer you."

"I'm goin round to the warden's office, boss."

"Whut're you gon be doin in the warden's office?"

"Workin, boss."

"Well, you jes stand heah till I call the inside picket. Ain't nobody told me nothin bout it."

After he slammed down the phone, I had to listen to the rules governing trusties coming in and out of the back gate. "I ain't gon letcha back in the yard unless you been shook down. Jes cuz you trusty don't mean nothin ta me. You don't hafta strip, but you'll be searched. Is that clear?" I started walking away, and he said, "I'll hafta make you a peg."

"Yessir."

Approaching the front office, I wondered how I was going to get in. I figured it was too early for anybody to be there yet. Surely Big

Devil kept the office locked. Walking past the drawn venetian blinds, I saw the lights were on. I stepped inside the door. Sundown was sitting at one of the side desks, drinking a cup of coffee and smoking a cigarette. "Good mornin, Lieutenant."

"Mornin, Ol Racehoss," he said in his usual low-key voice. "I already dun made coffee. I didn't know whut time you wuz gon git heah." I told him about the delay at the back gate. "Well, I'm gen'ly heah by six. If I beat you, I'll go 'head an make the coffee. When you git heah first, you make it. You kin make coffee, right?"

"Yessir," I said, thinking this was more than I had ever heard him talk.

"The warden told me an the cap'n yestiddy he wuz gon put you out heah." Blowing smoke and looking away from me, he went on, "You dun got you a damn good job heah, Ol Racehoss. You sho betta play yore cards close to yore chest." The conversation ended when Smooth and Buzzard arrived.

I didn't want to sit and listen to their bullshit, so I stepped out and went into the visiting room next door. The trio was long gone before the warden arrived about seven thirty. He called me into his office and handed me a set of keys.

"This is a extra set of keys to the front door, desks, an file cabinets. I don't know which is which, you have to figure that out. Boss Jack usually gits heah round eight, an he'll tell you whut he wants you to do. One uv them keys fits my desk too. You might need to git somethin out uv my drawers sometimes."

"Yessir," I said, returning to the outer office area.

Talking from his office, he told me, "I tell you somethin you oughta do quick as you kin. Learn whut's in 'em fuckin file cabinets. Boss Jack's the only one who kin find a damn thang in 'em an most uv the time he's gone when I need 'em. I come up heah the other eenin afta quittin time an spent damn near two hours huntin fur last month's livestock report. Never did find the damn thang. I had to call his house. So learn that quick as you kin."

"Yessir."

"Another thang. If I wuz you, I'd stay 'way frum 'at auditorium 'less you on office bizness. That way, you won't git in no more trouble."

"Yessir."

He was gone when Boss Jack came, and I was going through one of the four-tier file cabinets. "How'd you get in the file cabinet?"

"The warden gave me the keys."

"That's okay then, I just wanted to know how you got in them. Sit down and let me talk to you a minute. How far did you go in school?"

"I got a GED."

"From what I gathered in the warden's office yesterday, you can type."

"Yessir. About forty words a minute. I'm not all that fast, but I'm accurate."

"Well, that's plenty fast enough. Do you know anything about debits and credits?"

"Not much, only whut I learned when I wuz takin an ICS [International Correspondence Schools] course in accounting."

He went to the closet and got a copy of every form used in the office. "Here, take these and learn them by name and what each looks like. Afterwards, I'll show you how to fill them out. By the way, you better go put the flags up. You'll find them folded up in the back of the visiting room." As I was leaving, he added, "I'll sure be glad when the warden decides to get another porter out here."

I found Old Glory and Texas, ran them up the flagpole, and returned. "I don't know if the warden told you anything or not," he continued, "so I'll just start at the beginning. You work seven days a week. Until we get a porter, you have to keep the office clean, floors waxed and all. On Sundays, you work in the visiting room." He looked out the window. "Say, did you know you got the flags upside down? The American flag should always be hung on the top. Do you know what it means when flags are flown upside down?"

"No sir."

"It's a distress signal. If an airplane was to fly over and see those flags flying that way, the pilot would think we were in distress."

"Well, Boss Jack," I told him, "I don't know about you, but I'm sho in distress. I ain't never seen this many forms in my life." We had our first good laugh together.

"Well, don't worry, you'll get the hang of it."

Boss Jack's persistence prevailed and the warden assigned Jewel to do the porter work, freeing me to concentrate on the bookkeeping. With Boss Jack's patience and instructions, in a couple of months I could handle all the paperwork and knew the filing system.

He literally turned the work over to me, all the monthly reports, posting the inmate records, and even the employee payroll. This provided him with more coffee-drinking time over in the guards' dining room. He wouldn't drink the coffee I made in the office for the others. "That belongs to them and I don't want any part of it," he would say. After I got the procedures down pat, I had some free time too and signed up for more correspondence courses.

Big Devil liked to spend as much time driving in the fields as possible and was in and out of the office, mostly out. He didn't like the administrative "crap," and would much prefer seeing how things were running on the farm for himself. He'd walk through the building and kitchen or drive in the fields surveying the work that needed to be done. Sometimes he came to the office on the weekends, but he usually didn't stay long.

When working on the weekends, I had the office to myself. Jewel had no interest whatsoever in the office other than keeping it clean. He spent his leisure time sleeping in the visiting room. One Saturday after the warden had come and gone and Jewel was fast asleep in the visiting room, I decided to satisfy my curiosity and see what Big Devil had in his desk. While rummaging through it, I ran across the Warden's Handbook in his middle drawer. I kept sneaking back until I read the whole book.

Rules regarding the employee payroll had been explained to me by Big Devil and Boss Jack. "Nobody" opened the big brown envelope containing the checks before the warden got it. The envelope was to be placed on his desk "intact." I had orders not to tell the bosses the checks were there until the warden left the office. He took his check, Cap'n Smooth's, Sundown's, Cap'n Foots's, and Boss Jack's. Because of their educational gap and varied social backgrounds, the warden made sure that he handed Boss Jack his check personally, just to keep it straight who was paying whom. Boss Jack didn't like being in the office with all the bosses either, so as soon as he got his check, he left too.

Buzzard stayed out of the way at the back of the crowd and waited for everyone to get their checks and leave. After the time in the warden's office when he had to "sign" some papers regarding his retirement, I knew the secret. When the warden handed him the pen, Sergeant Buzzard held it with a death grip and his hand trembled. It took him a good fifteen seconds to draw the two uncrossed streaks of lightning.

Boss Eat-Em-Up couldn't read or write either, but he could at least make an X. I signed his name on the payroll for him too. Cap'n Foots, with his seventh-grade education, could do only a little better. The warden didn't have a single ranking officer on his immediate staff who had a high school education, and none could put together a report on their operations without help from Boss Jack or me.

Boss Jack and I were caught up with our work in the office. As usual, to keep from being in the office while the warden was there, he was over in the officers' mess hall drinking coffee. After Big Devil and I were left alone in the office, the warden called, "Ol Racehoss, come in heah fur a minute."

"Yessir," I said, stepping into his office.

"I wanna ask you somethin. Who do you thank is the ugliest, Ol Cryin Shame or Ol Pug?"

I didn't answer and started laughing. Pug's face looked like a Pekingese, especially around the nose and mouth; and Cryin Shame was just plain ugly.

"I'm serious, which one uv 'em do you thank is the ugliest?"

"Warden, neither one wouldn't win no beauty contest."

Realizing I still hadn't caught his drift, he said jokingly, "Hell, nigguh, I thought you wuz keepin up wit thangs heah in the office. I'm talkin bout that letter that come in heah the other week or so bout plastic surgery. Well, we got another one today."

As he talked on, I recalled the letter. It had stated that one of the universities had gotten a grant to do research on the use of plastic surgery as a corrective measure for criminal behavior. According to the letter, the researchers believed the way a person looks has a definite bearing on his or her personality and criminal behavior. They were asking for a volunteer to undergo the operation.

"I gotta pick somebody to send up to them Walls. Hell, all the doctors in the world couldn't make Ol Cryin Shame look no betta. Changin his face ain't about to stop 'at nigguh frum stealin. He needs a whole new head." Pondering for a moment, he said, "Ol Pug's my choice cuz ain't nothin gon help Ol Cryin Shame. He's jes crazy is hell; the penitentiary's the best place fur 'em. So I tell you whut, go 'head an make out some transfer papers on Ol Pug an les git 'em on 'way frum heah on Black Betty."

18

From all indications, we were going to have a big Juneteenth celebration. Giving us a good meal and the day off was the warden's
precotton-picking-time "rally" and a way to celebrate emancipation
all in one fell swoop. This got our engines heated up. When the
cotton blossomed, it wouldn't last long. That's when we repaid him.

Big Devil issued orders to Cap'n Foots to feed us fried chicken
and watermelon, plus we had a big baseball game scheduled Saturday.
Our team, the Yellow Jackets, was playing the Ramsey Hardhitters
for the southern division championship.

Even though Mr. Meabs was the manager of the team, Big Devil
did the managing. He made the final decision as to who played on
the team, using the hog law book to make most of his selections.
"If a nigguh don't pick nuff cotton, he can't be on my ball team,"
he declared.

When the Yellow Jackets beat another team, it was ice cream and
cake; but when they lost, it was the soda water boxes for the rest of the
night. Big Devil punished the whole team when they got beat, and
those who errored the game off were punished more severely. Being
number one was an obsession of his, whether it was producing the
first bale or winning a baseball game. Baseball was the only convict
activity in which he showed an interest.

A few intermittent showers started on the Thursday before the big
game. Big Devil immediately called in the building for Mr. Meabs

and told him to get some tarpaulins from the tractor shop and cover the diamond.

Friday afternoon the showers were gone. Big Devil began his usual roaming about the farm, checking things out. He knew every inch of it, just like Road Runner and I did, only he drove it. While surveying his sixteen-thousand-plus acres, he went down Hog Pen Alley and passed by the baseball field. He saw standing water on the diamond and no tarps.

When he returned, he slammed the screen door behind him, went directly into his office, and called for Mr. Meabs. He crashed down the receiver and sat at his desk cursing. "Goddamn diamond's jes full uv puddles. That sonuvabitch didn't do whut I told him!"

Mr. Meabs stepped into the office with a big grin on his face. With both barrels, the warden let him have it. "You spose to be soooo goddamn smart! Got a big ol piece'a paper hangin on yore wall, but you ain't got sense nuff ta cover up a fuckin diamond!"

Mr. Meabs's small, pudgy frame shrank six inches as he stood in the warden's doorway. "You know whut, Meabs? I don't know nothin you *kin* do, cuz you ain't dun a damn thang since you been heah. Them nigguhs been a-runnin 'at goddamn schoolhouse. All you been doin is settin up there on the hard part uv yore rotten ass takin all the credit."

Mr. Meabs mumbled something but was interrupted. "Shet yore mouth when I'm talkin to you! Next time you disobey my orders, I'm gon see that somethin gits dun to yore ass!"

I stopped typing and looked into his office. I saw the backs of Mr. Meabs's pant legs shaking from his trembling knees. During a pause in the blistering ass chewing, Mr. Meabs said in a soft whimper, "I'm sorry, Warden. I git busy and flat forgit."

"Busy, my ass! You ain't never been busy a day in yore life," Big Devil retorted. He went on sarcastically, "You spent alla yore time a-goin to school gittin educated. Well, it sho as hell didn't help you none. Meabs, I been a-puttin up wit way more uv yore shit than I oughta. Take yore goddamn ass outta heah, an see if you got sense nuff to go roun to that mess hall an git a mop an bucket, an git yore ass down to that ball field an dry up 'at diamond. I bet not see a speck uv water on it when you git through!"

Meabs left the office running. Soon after he left, I left. I made it my business to be standing by the back gate when he came out with his mop and pail hung over his shoulder. He was whistling like a jolly little elf on his way to cookieland with the mop balanced over his shoulder and the pail hanging from the mop head.

Having been reduced to a molecule of shit just a few minutes ago didn't seem to have fazed him one bit. Regardless, I hadn't felt this good about anybody getting eaten up and spat out since Emma sliced Arthur Johnson across the cheeks of his ass with that butcher knife. The score had been evened, and I didn't lift a finger.

The Juneteenth celebration got under way as planned. A few trusties were still out working, but they would take off early for the ball game. After the fried chicken lunch, we went out on the yard and ate our piss chunk. Each con was allowed half a watermelon, so we were full as ticks and waiting for the main event.

Everybody was there, the building was left empty. Whenever the Yellow Jackets played at home, the warden demanded 100 percent attendance, with the only exceptions being the picket bosses, and even they watched with binoculars. The whole ball field was encircled by bosses on horseback.

Plenty of candy wrappers were rattling while our team was on the field warming up. Rat was on the mound for us today! "*Rat! Rat! Rat!*" the chanting began.

He was the Satchel Paige of the prison system and could throw a ball hard as a mule can kick. When Rat was pitching, the warden wouldn't let anybody do the catching but Pee Wee, who stood a fraction over four feet. The warden liked the way Pee Wee "talked it up" with Rat between pitches. Extra padding was sewn into Pee Wee's mitt, but with Rat on the hill, it would be all busted out by the end of the game.

The warden sat on the hood of his car going over the game plan with Mr. Meabs. "Heah dey come," somebody in the bleachers shouted as the big-caged truck bringing the Hardhitters turned onto Hog Pen Alley. The free-world umpires arrived and held their conference with Big Devil, Beartracks, Mr. Meabs, and the Ramsey team manager. After they'd set the ground rules, the game got under way.

The first three batters up for the Hardhitters, Rat mowed down. He threw nine pitches that sounded like nine cannon shots hitting the mitt, and he knocked Pee Wee back from home plate nine times. But Pee Wee jumped right up, dusted off the seat of his britches, and resumed his catcher's stance, never missing a beat.

Pounding his mitt, he'd yell, "Thas the way, baby kid! Turn over in yo hide! C'mon, baby kid! Turn me over. Make me see upside down!" *Boom!* "Thas the way! Why don'tcha knock me down some time?" *Boom!* "Thas the one, baby kid! Thas whut I'm talkin bout! Put it rat heah! Lemme have that same one again!" *Boom!* Down and back he'd go.

The bleachers bunch whooped and hollered, "Rodent's right today! Dey can't see it cuz dat nigguh's throwin dirt up dere!"

"Man, dat nigguh's kickin high!" someone hollered, referring to Rat's knuckles dragging the ground each time he cocked his leg and reared back.

The Hardhitters' best pitcher, Coach Whip, who was a sidearmer, was no less effective with our first three batters. The pitchers' duel went on inning after inning, with only one scratch hit given up by Coach Whip. Through six innings, Rat struck out eighteen batters and was well on his way to breaking his own strikeout record.

Top of the seventh, their best hitter, Swahili, was up. Rat reared back and fired. The pitch was ripped into right-center field. The outfielder bobbled the ball, and it was a stand-up double. We let out an excited sigh in the grandstand.

The next hitter sacrifice-bunted and the runner was safe at third. One out. Big Devil called "time out" and summoned Rat over to the car. "If you lose 'is game, nigguh, I'm gon do somethin to yore goddamn ass!" After the pep talk Rat bore down, and the next batter went down swinging. Two away.

He went into his full windup. A bleacher fan yelled, "Look out! Heah he comes!" The third-base runner was stealing home, and Rat uncorked one to cut him down. The force knocked Pee Wee at least six feet back. The runner slid across home and was standing up dusting off his britches by the time Pee Wee got back to the plate. Rat struck out the next hitter for number twenty.

In our half of the inning, we got two hits but couldn't push anything across. On through the top of the ninth, Rat had a total of twenty-four strikeouts, but we were still behind one to nothing. Rat was also the best hitter on the team and would be the second batter coming up in the last of the ninth.

Rock Island, our first baseman, was the first man up. He hit a long fly ball the center fielder ran down and caught. Rat was at the plate. First pitch, he smacked a double down the left-field line. Big Devil jumped off the hood of his car, shouting. Popeye, our next-to-last hope, swung at and missed the first two pitches from Coach Whip. Then he hit a little blooper to the shortstop. Two down.

Big Devil headed for Mr. Meabs, who was standing next to our players' bench. If a rabbit was in the hat, Big Devil was going to pull it out. Since the game had been so crucial throughout, both teams had exhausted their player rosters.

The Yellow Jackets had used every player, except West Texas. The warden held a strategy conference with Mr. Meabs. Pee Wee was scheduled to hit with the tying run still at second. West Texas couldn't help but overhear Mr. Meabs tell the warden that he had used all of his pinch hitters. West Texas butted in, "Warden, suh, lemme take a bat."

"Git away frum me, nigguh!"

Mr. Meabs took his shot below the belt with a chance to lisp his displeasure at having West Texas on the team. "Wes Texis, you can't hit the ball. You don't eben pra'tice when you out here."

Undaunted, West Texas pleaded, "Warden, suh, I picks a lotsa cotton for you. I ain't got to play in no game yet."

True, the warden knew he was no ballplayer to begin with, and let him sit on the bench and watch two practice days a week. At forty-five, West Texas was still one of the best cotton pickers on the farm. The warden kept him on the team because of that and to give him the two days to rest up. He had a way of looking out for the older convicts who were good cotton pickers.

Big Devil conceded, "I don't give a damn if he ain't been practicin. Let 'em hit. Least he got sense nuff to do whut I tell him." *Touché!* "He can't do no worse'n 'em other rotten bastards who couldn't hit a goddamn bull in the ass wit a bass fiddle. Gitcha a bat an go on up air an lay into one!"

Since he'd never played a game, West Texas had never been issued spiked shoes. So he dug in at the plate with his heelless field brogans. He fouled off the first two pitches. Coach Whip got wild and threw three balls in a row. Things were so tense you could hear a boll weevil piss on cotton.

The three-two pitch was on its way, and it was just what the warden ordered. *Smack!* West Texas hit it deep. The outfielders watched as the ball flew over their heads. Because there was no fence, there were no automatic home runs. The center fielder was running at full speed trying to catch up with the ball, and the bosses were galloping their horses behind him.

It rolled damn near to the turkey pens, a good six hundred feet from home plate. The center fielder finally caught up with it as West Texas was falling down rounding second. He'd already fallen going to first. The bleachers rocked with excitement as he stumbled to get up. Rat scored.

Three players lined up in the outfield for the relay back in. When West Texas rounded third, he was almost out of breath and looked like he was running in slow motion. The warden rushed out between third base and home, urging him on. "Come on, nigguh! C'mon, git ready to *slide!*" The throw was finally coming in. West Texas fell again and started crawling. Big Devil ran up to him, screaming, "Git up! Git up! Git up, nigguh! *Git uuuuup!*"

West Texas stumbled on toward home, collapsing headfirst at the plate and putting his hand on the bag. "*Safe!*" by a hair.

We won two to one, ice cream for all. That is, except for the player who bobbled the ball and allowed their runner to reach second. He spent the rest of his Juneteenth on a soda water box.

Big Devil was on the bright side of sixty. He enjoyed sitting around talking with his old law enforcement and hunting cronies who stopped by the unit on a regular basis for a free cup of coffee and meal. Reared back in his executive chair, he told them tale after tale about things that had happened during his illustrious career, which he had begun as a field boss on Ramsey. Then he was mess steward on Clemens, where he got promoted to warden. After the white cons were transferred away, he was sent to Retrieve to take over.

"They shipped off all 'em ol white thangs befo I got heah. An when I took over 'is camp, they handpicked the worst nigguhs frum the other units an shipped 'em to me. So, I started out wit nothin to begin wit," he told his full-bellied audience.

He pointed to the gruesome eleven-by-twenty-five framed photograph hanging on the wall behind his desk. It showed a headless convict sitting at the end of one of our mess hall tables. In the photo Redwine sat perfectly erect with his hands still resting on the mess hall table, a lighted Lucky Strike clamped tightly between his fingers. Except for his missing head, everything in the picture was normal.

Big Devil joked, "Some flunky got tired of bein Ol Redwine's gal-boy an chopped his goddamn head off!"

I had heard the story from the cons on their tank. They say Redwine, one of the building tenders on Number 1 tank, had been kicking the flunky's ass and raping him at will.

The decapitation took place at lunch after we'd passed through the chow line and were seated and eating. As usual, the flunkies were bringing the steam pans up and down the aisles offering second helpings. When the victimized flunky walked down the row of tables where Redwine was seated, he stopped behind him long enough to pull a meat cleaver from underneath his apron. He made one swooshing swing, and *blop!* Redwine's head hit the floor like a cabbage. Even though the blood was gushing out from the stump where his head had once been, the photo showed Tarzan seated across from him, still eating.

With a pompous air Big Devil chuckled and said, "It took a while, but I dun tamed most uv these nigguhs." Then he hollered to me in the outer office, "Ain't that right, Ol Racehoss?"

"Yessir, Warden."

"Take Ol Racehoss. When he first come heah, he useta git punished all the time. Turned out ta be my top hand. Would y'all bleeve 'at nigguh won the cotton-pickin championship ginst the top pickers frum Ramsey an Clemens? But he's dun got some education now, so I put him out heah to be my bookkeeper. Ol Racehoss," he called out.

"Yessir."

"Holler up air an tell 'at picket boss ta call in the buildin an have 'em send Ol Steeple Head out heah."

"Yessir."

After Big Devil's bragging about the gore and cotton picking, it was time to send for the unit jester to further prove how "tame" we all were.

That dubious distinction fell upon Ol Steeple Head, who was black as a crow and slightly built. His records said he was forty-nine and a six-time loser. His most striking feature was the shape of his pyramidal head, with little room at the top for any brains to be stashed away. He practically grew up in the Gatesville State School for Boys. With six convictions for nonviolent crimes, he'd spent most of his adult life in prison.

Regular as clockwork every Saturday night, he dressed up in his "hustlin rig" and took a seat on the bench at the front of Number 5 tank. With Jockey drawers, a rolled-up T-shirt around his chest, a pair of raggedy hose smuggled in by the trash wagon trusty, and some homemade garters, he was ready. Sometimes his work brogans were still covered with dried mud and horseshit from his job at the horse lot. And to top it off, he smeared Noxzema on his face and tied a red bandanna around his bald, cone-shaped head.

Since he wasn't "classified" as one of Retrieve's star punks, he didn't rate room service in Doc Nolan's dentist office. So Steeple Head took care of business in the shower area, obscured from the inside picket boss by a partial brick wall. He charged three packs of Bugler, two for him and one for the building tender Ol Bugs for the use of the motel and posting a lookout.

When business was slow, the cons on the tank teased him just for the fun of it. "Say, priddy mama, you know my credit's good an I'll straighten you on draw day" (payday, the day cons receive their scrip books).

Steeple Head was an old pro and knew when they meant business. Jokingly, he'd shoot back, "Naw, baby," very submissively, "yo credit may be good, but I can't light it up an smoke it." Imitating a woman, he'd go on, "'Sides, it's the wrong time uv the month.'"

As soon as I finished second-handing Big Devil's command, the outer picket boss was third-handing it to the inside picket boss. In no time at all, from the office window I saw Steeple Head running at full speed down the sidewalk for the front gate. The lever was thrown; the gate flew open.

I heard the crashing noise of his fumbling and falling into the office screen door. It sounded like he was breaking in. He finally jerked the screen door open and entered. After slipping and sliding on the freshly waxed floor past my desk, he almost skidded right by the warden's door. He grabbed hold of the door-frame; if not, he would have slid on by and hit the wall.

Panting, he said, "Yassuh, heah I is, Warden, suh."

"Whut took you so goddamn long?" the warden shouted. That was a cold shot because Steeple Head had been scuffling his ass off to get there. "I sunt in there half a hour ago fur yore rotten ass, an you jes now draggin in heah!"

"I come fas as dey lemme out, Warden, suh."

"Jes shet yore goddamn lyin mouth! You been a-lyin ta me ever since I knowed you, nigguh. Whut makes you thank I bleeve *any* goddamn thang you say?"

Steeple Head started weeping. As Big Devil paced around him, his menacing six-foot-two frame towered over Steeple Head, adding to his nervousness. "Y'all know whut I dun fur this nigguh? I helped git 'em out uv the penitentiary. Didn't I, nigguh?"

"Yassuh."

"I got a friend uv mine over in Brazoria to take him in an give 'em a job. The man paid 'em a salary an let 'em live right there on the place. He even let this nigguh drive his ol pickup truck. An all the while he wuz bein good to 'em, you know whut he wuz a-doin? The rotten bastard wuz a-sneakin back out heah gittin in my hog barn. The sonuvabitch wuz brangin that ol cheap wine out heah an him an the night-hog nigguh would pile up in my barn, git lickered up, an screw all night. The lot boss wuz pullin down some sacks uv feed an found this sorry nigguh a-layin up there 'sleep, buck nekked. I had him 'rested; they 'voked his prole an sunt his rotten ass right back heah to me." Big Devil failed to mention that Steeple Head's arrest cleared the livestock report of "unaccountables" from day one.

Steeple Head had been shamed to his knees and pleaded for forgiveness. Between sobs he begged some of the half dozen men in the office, "Y'all pleeze hep me!"

One of them said, "You know, Alton, I'm willin ta take a chance on this nigguh's word an say I bleeve he's a-tellin the truth when he says he wuz tryin ta git heah fast as he could."

Big Devil joked, "Why goddamn, Haley. You gittin weaker'n a bottle uv piss in yore old days. If I wuz ta let you, hell, you'd be askin me if you could take this nigguh home wit you."

They all laughed as Steeple Head sobbed on, puddling up the floor. Big Devil continued to conversationize with his buddies, ignoring him completely. "This nigguh's still crazy, but not as bad as he wuz. The rotten bastard never could keep up wit the squads in the field, so even afta he fucked up an come back, I give 'em an easy job in the lot squad. All he has to do is saddle 'em bosses' hosses ever mornin an have 'em ready by turnout time. Does the bastard 'preciate it? Why hell no! The sonuvabitch gits the bosses' saddles mixed up an puts 'em on the wrong hosses all the time.

"Ol Steeple Head," Big Devil called to him in a milder tone.

"Yassuh?"

"That'll be enuff uv 'at now. You hear me talkin to you?"

Steeple Head sprang up, stood at rigid attention, the crying ceased.

In second gear, Big Devil went on, "Tell ease people jes how long I been a-puttin up wit yore black ass."

"All my life, Warden, suh. You been had me all my life. You raised me to whut I is today," he said with pride.

"Nigguh, don't stand there an blame 'at shit on me!"

"Warden, suh, I do everthang you tells me to. You been my daddy."

Big Devil's buddies laughed, and one of them joked, "Aha, so thas why you lookin out fer 'em." They laughed harder, all except Big Devil.

With no forewarning, he burst out, "Tell 'em how many times you been fucked. You bet not lie. *You hear me, nigguh?*"

"Warden, suh, I ain't gon lie to you. Warden, is you talkin bout since I been heah altogether, or since I been heah wit you?"

"See whut I been tellin y'all. Did y'all hear that? Whenever I try bein nice to this nigguh, he turns aroun an gits smart-alecky wit me. Naw, nigguh, I ain't talkin bout the number uv times you been fucked in yore whole damned prison career. Hell, this addin machine can't add up numbers 'at big. Jes stick wit who dun it since Sadday night."

Steeple Head began calling off the names one by one with Lassie-like obedience until Big Devil stopped him. "Ol Racehoss, go over yonder ta them guards' quarters an tell the officer on duty ta git over heah."

Any time the warden sent for somebody, whether convict or guard, he came posthaste. In two shakes of a deer's tail, the on-duty officer was in the warden's office getting instructions. "Git out yore pencil an pad an write these nigguhs' names down when Ol Steeple Head tells 'em to you. When you finish writin 'em, go in that buildin an put them nigguhs on some soda water boxes. I'll let 'em down."

According to Steeple Head's tally, four cons had had sex with him since Saturday night. After writing their names, the duty officer wheeled around, headed to arrest the fingered ones.

Big Devil asked one of the law enforcement officers, "Didja brang that apparatus wit you this time?"

"Yeah, I did."

"Okay, hook 'er up an plug 'er in. Les see how much she'll burn."

The polygraph machine buzzed and clicked with each adjustment. Steeple Head stood mesmerized, his watery eyes glued to the machine's dials flickering back and forth.

"Damn! She kicked all the way up ta fourteen-forty!" the officer adjusting the dials said dramatically.

"Thas enuff ta fry the hairs off a gnat's ass three hunnerd feet away! These portable ones is damn near good as Ol Sparky. He won't feel a thang," another officer commented.

Steeple Head's eyes got bigger and his ear-to-ear grin shrank to a mere pucker. Beads of sweat popped out on his forehead. Big Devil fixed an intent stare on him while waiting for the officers to finish their "adjustments." He got the "she's all ready to go" nod and lit into him again.

"Nigguh, how much more uv yore shit do you thank I kin stand? How long do you thank I oughta wait 'fore I do somethin bad to yore ol rotten black ass?" Steeple Head tried to speak. "Jest shet yore lyin mouth an set yore stankin ass down over there in that chair!" he ordered, pointing to a chair by the machine left vacant for him.

This was the first time Steeple Head ever balked at the warden's command. Big Devil spat out the order again. "Ol Steeple Head, set yore ass down in 'at goddamn chair lak I told you! An cut out so goddamn much'a that sweatin too, befo you trigger this damn thang off."

Scared and confused looking, Steeple Head backed slowly toward the chair and sank down in the seat. Pleading more desperately, he said, "Pleeze, suh, Warden! Don't let 'em do it! Pleeze, suh. Warden, I ain't lied to you bout nothin. Pleeze, suh!" Tears streamed. His body shuddered and trembled uncontrollably.

With a deep sigh of faked remorse, Big Devil ordered, "Go 'head an hook 'em up. I've gone fur as I'm goin to wit this nigguh."

The officer began wrapping the long black cords around Steeple Head's body. "Raise yore arms straight up, lak this," he said, showing Steeple Head what he meant. "Lak this, nigguh! Raise up yore goddamn arms!" he repeated impatiently.

Steeple Head sat rigid as stone.

"This is the dumbest nigguh I ever seen in my whole life!" the officer said.

"Well, I dun already told y'all that. Tell you whut, if you can't git 'em wrapped roun his chest an under his arms, jes wrap 'em roun his fuckin legs. They'll git the job dun wherever ya put 'em."

The officer began again, but Steeple Head jumped straight out of the chair as if being ejected by a giant coil. "Warden! Oh Lawd! Have mercy, Warden! Oh Lawd! Warden! Nawsuh, Warden! Pleeze don't let 'em wrap me up in dis stuff! Pleeze spare me, Warden! Don't turn yo back on me! I'm a good nigguh!"

"Set yore goddamn ass back down in 'at chair! You bet not make me havta put you in it!"

Steeple Head sank back down in the chair. To intensify and prolong their game, the officer slowly wrapped the cords around him. First, his legs, then underneath the bottom of the chair, looping them around his lap and on up around his chest.

Finally, all systems were go. The warden issued the order. "Okay, go 'head an crank 'er up again."

Just as the officer reached for the switch, Steeple Head unzombiezized. Thinking they were going to electrocute him, in a terror-stricken voice he screamed "*Oh no!*" and bolted up with the chair still strapped to him. He fell down and kicked and hollered hysterically while rolling and twisting on the floor trying to free himself.

He managed to get the chair off his back but was still entangled in some of the cords. Struggling to his feet, he almost knocked the officer down as he broke for the door. Off the table crashed the polygraph machine, scaring him even more. Out the front door and down the sidewalk he ran, dragging the cords behind.

The game backfired. Big Devil's cronies were cracking up at the unexpected finale as the warden ran a short ways down the sidewalk chasing Steeple Head and yelling, "Come back heah, you crazy sonuvabitch! Come back heah!"

Big Devil stopped after hollering one more "You betta come back heah, you ignorant bastard!" But it was useless. Steeple Head was long gone, heading down Hog Pen Alley. On his way back to the office, the warden told the outside picket boss, "Radio the lot boss an tell 'em I said go down to the lot an brang Steeple Head back up heah."

When Big Devil returned to the office, the officers assured him the equipment hadn't been damaged. A few minutes later, the lot boss escorted Steeple Head into the office, saying, "I found 'em hidin in the loft in the hay barn, Warden."

"Whutta you got ta say fur yoreself, nigguh?" Big Devil roared.

Head lowered, looking at his feet, Steeple Head mumbled, "Nothin, Warden."

"You dun tore up a thousand dollars' worth uv 'quipment! Whutta you thank I oughta do to yore crazy ass?"

"I dunno, Warden, suh," he trembled out.

"Naw, you don't know! Thas cuz you don't wanna know!" While the warden raked him over the coals, Steeple Head was shaking like a dog trying to shit a peach seed. "Tell you whut I'm gon do fur you, nigguh. Hell, I ought not ta do nothin fur yore rotten ass," he declared with a faked change of heart.

Steeple Head begged, "Pleeze, Warden, suh. I be merciful for anythang you do for me."

"Well," Big Devil continued, "I ain't gon take it out on you fur a-scarrin up my floor wit that chair while you wuz a-floppin roun lak a damn chicken wit its head cut off. An I ain't gon do nothin to you fur tearin up guvment property, but I am gon havta do somethin to yore rotten ass fur runnin outta heah 'thout permission."

"Yassuh, Warden. Thank you, suh."

"See if you got sense nuff to go roun to that back gate an tell 'at boss I said put yore rotten ass in that pisser."

With a look of relief, Steeple Head left trotting off to the back gate. A small price to pay for proving we were all "tame."

Working so closely with Big Devil, I was afforded a bird's-eye view of his chameleonic personality. His callous dealings with Steeple Head were just e pluribus unum in his repertoire of management styles. He moved in and out of situations with the bosses and cons with ease, never showing the same face twice. He kept us off balance with his unpredictability. He was the devil one minute and a near saint the next, with a degree of humanity and understanding of which I would never have thought him capable. It was like working for Dr. Jekyll and Mr. Hyde. He knew all the cons personally and had the uncanny ability to deal with each one on an individual basis. Those who acted like men, bosses included, he treated with a measure of respect; those who didn't came face-to-face with Mr. Hyde. He was the best Dr. Jekyll I'd ever seen with Hip Cat.

After living on the tank with Hip Cat for a couple of years, I knew of his deep love for his mother. He was an only child. Unlike most of the cons on the tank, he never talked about old girlfriends and sex. Instead, he talked about his mother and how close they were. His locker was full of neatly tied bundles of letters from her dating back twenty years.

One day while I was in the barber chair, he went to his locker and returned with a badly worn photo of his mother that he'd painstakingly wrapped in cellophane from cigarette packs. Though it was faded in places, I could easily see the resemblance and felt privileged to look at it, especially after he said, "I don't let everbody see this."

During one of our talks he told me, "I ain't seen her in twenty-four years."

"It's been a long time since I seen mine too," I commented.

"I know how she feels, Race. I know she wants to see me. I wanna see her too, but not lak this. I tell her in ever letter I write to git that out uv her head. I don't want her comin way down heah. It's too far for one thang, an she's too old to make a trip lak that all the way frum Paris" (Paris, Texas, near the Oklahoma border).

It was Wednesday. I was taking a break in the visiting room when I saw the taxicab pull up out front. An elderly black woman got out. Assisting herself with a cane as she walked toward me, I knew she was Hip Cat's mother because they sure did favor.

"Young man, can you tell me where the warden's office is?"

"Yes, ma'am," I said, holding the screen door open, "it's right here." After we entered, I told her, "Wait here, ma'am."

"Thank you."

I stuck my head in the warden's office. "Pardon me, Warden. There's a lady out here to see you."

"Tell her to come on in." She stepped inside his office. "Whut kin I do fur you?"

"Are you the warden?"

"I'm the warden."

"Well, sir, I come down here to see my son, Alonzo Curlee."

Offering her a seat, the warden asked, "How long's it been since you seen him?"

"Twenty-four years," she said without a doubt.

Big Devil began telling her the visiting rules. "Sundays is visitin day, an visitin hours is frum nine to eleven in the mornin an frum one to three in the eenin."

He hardly ever broke that rule unless prior written permission was granted through the Walls. I had seen him turn away lawyers who came down to the unit to see their clients.

"I didn't know y'all had certain times," she said, adding sorrowfully, "an I came on the bus all the way frum Paris. Warden, please, sir, can't I see him even for jus a minute?"

"Ol Racehoss!"

"Yessir."

"Tell the picket boss to call inside an tell 'em to send Ol Alonzo Curlee out heah." While waiting he said to her, "I'm gon let y'all visit *this* time. Me an Ol Hip Cat, thas whut we call him, go back a long ways" (he was referring to their having been at Ramsey together). "He's been a pretty good hand. I thank he's got one uv the best attitudes on the farm."

The outside picket boss let him through the front gate. Hip Cat entered the outer office and stopped at the warden's doorway. "Yes sir, Warden."

"Come on in. There's somebody heah to see you."

When he stepped inside the door and saw his mother sitting to the side, Hip Cat was totally speechless. She stood up. Then he cried out "Lawddd!" and wrapped his arms around her. They embraced. Weakened by the shock of seeing him, her legs gave way and they both almost fell when she went limp. He gently helped her back into the chair.

He dropped to his knees weeping and she cradled his head against her bosom, rocking back and forth and stroking his face. She cooed, "Hush, Alonzo, hush. Les don't cry. The Good Lawd brought us together again. I been prayin so hard for this day to come."

This was the only time I had ever seen a show of compassion in Big Devil. He was sniffling as he stepped out of his office, pulling the door shut behind him. "Don't let nobody in my office till I git back," he told me.

He got in his car and drove off. He'd broken another rule; a boss is supposed to be present during all visits with free-world people. About thirty minutes later, he returned and took a seat in the outer office with me.

Hip Cat opened the door after a while and Big Devil went back in and sat down behind his desk. I couldn't hear all of what they said, but I did overhear him telling Hip Cat's mother, "The next time Ol Hip Cat comes up fur prole, he's got a good chance uv makin it."

Breaking another rule, offering hope.

While waiting for the taxi from town, she thanked him for his kindness. As Hip Cat assisted her out the front door, she looked over her shoulder and said, "I'm gon pray for you, Warden."

When she got to the sidewalk she stopped. "You keep on bein a good boy so you can hurry up an come home to Mama." Hip Cat did get out, and we learned a short time after that he had died from natural causes. At least he died at home with his mother and not in the pen.

And the warden was the worst Mr. Hyde I'd ever seen two weeks later, on the Sabbath. The visiting room was packed. It was my responsibility to issue freshly starched and pressed whites to each con that the boss brought out for a visit. Before entering the visiting room, the con changed into the pristine whites, giving the impression he dressed that way all the time. Once the visit was over, he put his dingy grays back on.

The cons had dressed out in the back room and were seated on one side of the long glass-partitioned counter. As a fringe benefit, Big Devil allowed me to be the runner to the Coke machine for the cons and their visitors so they wouldn't lose any time visiting. Plus, it was a security measure since visitors weren't permitted to hand anything to the cons. I was into my third or fourth trip and busily passing out the drinks when, unexpectedly, the warden stepped in.

He stood in the doorway for a minute or two, looking things over. A well-dressed, middle-aged, light-complexioned lady turned around in her seat and asked, "Pardon me, are you the warden?"

"Yeah."

With a friendly smile, she said, "Do you mind me askin you how my son is doing down here? Has he been behavin himself?"

Still leaning against the doorway, Big Devil cast his eyes across the counter on her son, contemplated for a moment, then looked back at the mother. "How many children you got?"

"I have just the two. My daughter here"—she pointed to the teenage girl sitting beside her—"and my son."

With the same empty face, he shook his head. "You ain't got no son. You got two gals," he said, turned, and left. Exit Mr. Hyde, leaving the con's mother in a state of shock.

*   *   *

For the past year it had been rumored that a warden rotation plan was in the making. The grapevine was right again. The administration assembly line rolled out the plan in a memo that sent Big Devil through the roof. It stated that he would be one of the first wardens rotated because he had been at one unit for so long, and, henceforth, wardens would be rotated every five years.

Besides dismantling the longtime dynasties, Dr. George Beto, the new director of the Texas Department of Corrections, would be assigning an assistant warden and farm manager to each unit to help free the wardens so they could focus more on their administrative duties. Dr. Beto became known as "Walking George" because he'd show up on foot in front of a given Texas prison, at all hours of the day or night, ready for an inspection and tour.

Big Devil ranted and raved to Boss Jack and me, "I been runnin 'is farm over twenny years, an now they gon ship me off summers else. Up till now I been goin 'long wit all their educated puke, but I'll be goddamned if they gon start runnin me roun frum pillar to post!"

He fought the new policies tooth and nail, but he would be transferred to the multiracial Eastham Unit, and the Eastham warden would be transferred to Retrieve. The assistant warden and farm manager would be down within the month.

A mood of uncertainty swept through "hell" as it slowly but surely sank into the quicksand of progress. In addition to the warden rotation, the administration was raising the educational requirements of the prison employees and would be doing all future hiring rather than leaving it up to the individual wardens. No more walk-ons like Boss Humpy. Current personnel would be frozen in their positions until they met certain educational standards and could pass written examinations for promotion. Longtime employees who were below the new standards would have job performance evaluations done to verify their proficiency in maintaining their positions.

When Retrieve's personnel learned of the new orders, there was near pandemonium. Most of the officers and bosses were justifiably worried about their futures. Education was never one of Big Devil's main criteria for employee selection. He used to boast that he had only completed the eighth grade himself. A large portion of his staff didn't graduate from high school. Many didn't get out of grade school. I knew Buzzard and Eat-Em-Up were scared to death since they couldn't even write their own names.

With only a month left until the warden's transfer, things at Retrieve were sadder than the horses that pulled President McKinley's casket down Pennsylvania Avenue . . . until Black Betty came. She left a lone passenger. On my way back to the office to deliver his record to the warden, I leafed through it and thought there must have been a mistake. After the warden looked at it, he phoned into the building. "Send Ol Pug out heah."

I was looking through the file cabinet, and Pug walked by without my seeing him. He went directly into the warden's office. "Ol Pug, is that you, nigguh?"

"Yessuh, it's me, Warden!"

"Ol Racehoss, come in heah an look at this nigguh."

I definitely wanted to see him because I sure as hell didn't recognize him at the back gate. I went in, and after seeing Pug up close, I still had a hard time believing it was him. Instead of looking like a pug-nosed Pekingese, now he looked like Pinocchio, with a long pointed nose, big ears, and thinned lips.

"Goddamn, nigguh! If you wudn't black as the ace uv spades, you'd look jes lak a white man."

Pug grinned from big ear to big ear.

"Do you lak 'is new face better'n you did that other'n?"

"Yessuh, Warden. I laks it jes fine."

"Lemme ask you somethin. Where'd they git all 'at meat frum to make you that nose an them ears?"

"Mostly off my behind, Warden."

Seldom did the warden ever laugh out loud, but now he laughed so hard he was in tears. Pug and I got tickled and started laughing with him. "You mean to tell me, out uv all the places on you, they had to take some uv yore ass an put it on yore face an ears? You know whut that means, don'tcha, nigguh?"

"Nawsuh."

"Well, it means that you'll be walkin round a-smellin yore ol goat-smellin ass fur the rest uv yore life!" Big Devil was still laughing when he said, "Go on roun to the shop an tell 'at boss I said give you a tractor an send you on out to the field. Be sho an tell 'em who you are, an if he don't bleeve it, tell 'em I said call me."

That night on the tank Pug stood before the mirror until count time, primping. Proud Walker and a few others went to the back purposely to tease him. Proud Walker asked, "Pug, lemme axe ya sump'n, man. Did you pick dis face or did dey do it? I lak'd you the other way when you look lak a bulldog. Now you look mo lak a anteater wit dat long snout dey made you."

At last Proud Walker said something with which I agreed. Pug was ugly as sin before his surgery, but now, with his "new" Anglo features, he looked like an uglier somebody else.

The same week Pug came back, Trigger Bill met his doom. He had finally convinced the warden to take him off as building tender and let him work in the shop squad. While he was a building tender, Trigger Bill had made plenty of enemies. Once he left the protection of the building, retaliation would just be a matter of time. Big Devil still relied on Doc Cateye to run the hospital, so when he wanted to know, he called him. Cateye diagnosed Trigger Bill's death as having been due to poisoning. He explained, "Somehow he must'a got into some'a that cotton 'secticide, cuz, Warden, I smelt it on his breath. Smelt lak he'd been drankin sump'n else too, lak that ol chock."

The trial of the decade was under way. The warden interrogated the entire tractor and shop bunch. "Warden, dat nigguh had a bad habit uv slippin roun drankin other folks' stuff, if y'know whut I mean. Das prob'ly whut happen to 'em. Somebody must'a fixed up a special batch for 'em," one explained.

Wash stated, "Warden, suh, I ain't sayin I'm one uv 'em, but I know dat dem other nigguhs chips in an buys sugar outta the mess hall an makes 'em up a batch uv chock. An dey say Ol Trigger Bill didn't never chip in. He snuck aroun watchin where dem other nigguhs hid dey jugs at an he drunk it all up, an be blowin his breff in dem other nigguhs' faces."

Trying to trip up the testifier, Big Devil asked, "How do you know he wuz sneakin round drankin up y'all's home brew?"

"Nawsuh, Warden, I wudn't watchin 'em. I be doin my wek lak I spose to. I jes heard dem other nigguhs talkin dat *wuz* watchin 'em. See whut I'm sayin, suh?"

"An I don't spose you kin remember none uv their names either?"

"Nawsuh, I sho don't, Warden. You knows me, I try ta tend to my own bizness when I'm out dere."

Even though in a roundabout way every one of them confessed that Trigger Bill had been poisoned and gave their renditions of why, nobody knew who. Big Devil didn't buy that his chock stealing was the sole motive he was murdered, and told them so. But because the tractor and shop squads were so vital to the farm operations, Big Devil wasn't about to put them all in the pisser and leave them there until somebody confessed. So he ruled there was inconclusive evidence and the case was closed: "Death by suicide."

Big Devil didn't get to laugh long about Pug's makeover. Security got its first slap in the face when Sergeant Buzzard and Rattler let one get away. This was the first successful escape from the burnin hell in many years. Retrieve's once notorious reputation for not "lettin 'em git outta the bottoms" had been stained.

The warden's impending transfer caused an exodus of old-timer personnel, especially those he failed to get transferred to Eastham with him. The director stuck by his guns that each warden would be allowed to take only his convict cook. Boss Jack was finally getting to have the last laugh.

Cap'n Smooth had in thirty-seven years and suddenly decided to hang up his spurs. Lieutenant Sundown, who had come to Retrieve with Big Devil over twenty years ago, resigned and went to work with the local sheriff's department. The laundry supervisor requested and was granted a transfer to another unit. The shop, lot, and garden supervisors all retired. Buzzard, after thirty years, was quitting the dog trail and put in for his retirement to begin the day that Big Devil departed.

Even the two old water wagon mules, Coal Oil and Fannie, got out a month before the warden was to leave. They rode off into the sunset for the soap factory and, we hoped, were *not* pulling the water wagon in mules' heaven.

The wheel of fortune had stopped spinning and teetered toward reverse. The burnin hell (Big Devil's domain) was going up in flames, and he could do nothing to stop it. While others wailed and gnashed their teeth, Big Devil stayed out of the office and kept mostly to himself. He went fishing a lot in "his" pond, the one I had helped dig. His move to Eastham was a bitter pill that he was forced to swallow. Starting over again at a multiracial unit with more than two thousand untamed cons was going to be a real challenge to his wardening philosophy. He sure better not leave his handbook behind!

19

1968

On the morn scheduled, the curtain fell on Big Devil's long reign over hell.

That evening the replacement warden from the "Ham" arrived. I recognized him from his photo in the prison administration's annual directory. But I had no idea the face in the book would be attached to a giant's body, and I readily accepted the stories I'd heard about his prowess as a defensive lineman at Texas A&M.

He walked into the warden's office and sat down behind the mahogany desk. "I am sitting in the right seat, ain't I?"

"Yes sir," I answered, but he sure didn't look right sitting in it.

"How much time you doin?"

"Thirty years. I'll pull my record if you want me to, Warden."

"That won't be necessary. I'll take a look at it later."

"Warden, do you need me to get anything out of your car?"

"No. I've got a lot of junk in there, but I'll take it on down to the house. The van will be here later tonight with the rest of my things. I'll git somebody to unload it tomorrow. That's a pretty long drive down here," he said, adding, "That'll be all."

Within a few months after the new one's arrival, he was baptized with a sit-down strike in the fields, an escape attempt, and a near riot in the mess hall. Work slowed down in the fields for the first time in many moons. The squads no longer worked on Saturdays, and it didn't look like we would finish our harvest first. The unit rapidly lost its manicured appearance as the weeds took over.

We were shown a laissez-faire style of "wardening." Each evening after he had supper, the warden routinely returned to the office to catch up with his paperwork. Afterward, he headed for the building and went in one of the lower tanks to play dominoes with the cons. With the door locked behind him, he stood at the domino table and waited his turn.

When he went in one of the east-side tanks, we could look down from the trusty tank and see him at the domino table. He seemed right at home, and made as much noise as they did slamming the dominoes and squabbling. At first, the cons were leery of him; but after he passed around his ready rolls freely, they were glad to have him in the game.

Boss Wise-Em-Up didn't dare holler, "Y'all betta git down on it. Some'a you ol wild-assed nigguhs gonna hafta talk ta that warden in the mornin!" We had gotten used to his evening tank visits, and on Saturdays he spent practically the entire day inside the tanks. Even though there was always a domino game going over at the guards' quarters, he preferred playing with the cons.

Sometimes while waiting his turn at the table and rocking on his heels, he'd lose his balance and reel backward. The cons standing around would catch him before he fell. He'd thank them, and they laughed and kidded him about it, going so far as to say, "Warden, I sho wish I felt good as you feels."

In the office the assistant warden and Boss Jack were discussing him. Boss Jack commented, "His breath smells like a distillery."

"Yeah, I know. How in the hell can I maintain building security while he keeps volunteering himself as a potential hostage?" A few days after their talk, the assistant warden made out a request for a transfer, which was granted. He was sent to the Darrington Unit, and promoted to full warden.

The Walls administration got wind of the warden's tank escapades. A few weeks after the assistant warden went to Darrington, a big sedan from the Walls kicked up gravel wheeling into the parking space. The three officials (one I recognized from the cane patch) walked briskly past the warden's office and on through the front gate.

Once inside, they struck up a trot, hurrying down the sidewalk and on into the building. It was Saturday. About ten minutes later, four were coming back. They had busted the warden red-handed in Number 3 tank playing dominoes. He led the way into his office. They closed his door. I got the message and left.

After their sedan sped away, the warden walked down the sidewalk headed to his house, shoulders sagging. The outside picket boss got a radio message a few hours later and hollered it down to me, "The movin van'll be here Wednesday."

Monday in the truck mail a letter came from the Walls Education Department. I had been selected to attend heavy equipment school at A&M and was to be transferred to the Walls on Thursday for processing. I had no idea how they came up with my name; I hadn't applied for anything.

Later that day it came in on the teletype that the warden from Central would be the next replacement and was scheduled to arrive on Thursday. We'd probably pass each other along the highway.

Wednesday afternoon I helped the warden put his trophies and other personals from the office into his car. That night I packed my little shit and was ready to vacate hell too.

After the heavy equipment school ended, I was assigned to a bulldozer sitting idle at the Darrington Unit. When the work was completed at Darrington, I was sent to work at Prerelease, Ramsey, Ellis, Ferguson, and then on to Eastham.

Whatever cost was involved for the training I received, they were certainly getting their money's worth out of me. When my mail finally caught up with me, I wasn't surprised that I had gotten another year's parole set off. The board read their hog law book on me and determined that being back five more years wasn't "near bouts enuff," as Cap'n Smooth would say.

The truck-driver guard slowed the diesel transport to a stop in front of the Eastham Unit tractor shed. I unchained and quickly unloaded the machine. When I was finished, he took me to the back gate and had me put on the count, then checked me in to the building.

The building officer told me to sit down against the wall, and he walked away down the long hall. About half an hour later, another officer walked over and ordered, "Come with me."

I walked slightly behind him for at least two city blocks down the main artery before we made a sharp left into a smaller hallway. When we reached the closed door with "Warden" written above it, he knocked lightly.

"Yeah, come on in." I recognized his voice immediately.

When we entered, the officer quickly removed his cap, placing it under his arm. "Is this him, Warden?" he asked.

"Yeah, thas him. That'll be all."

The officer politely closed the door on his way out.

"Ol Racehoss, goddamn, been a long time since I seen you," Big Devil said in a tone that sounded like he was glad to see me.

"Yes sir, it sure has, Warden. How you doin, sir?"

The spark in his once fiery eyes had dwindled to a flickering ember. The lines of time threaded his face, and his hair was white as snow. He looked tired and old, well past his prime.

"Aw, fair to middlin, I guess. Lotta diffrunce in this farm an that other one though," he added.

"Yes sir, I imagine it would be."

"Almost four times as many heah an most uv 'em young ones that ain't learnt how to do time yet," he commented. Taking a look at my record there on his desk, he said, "Looks lak you been movin roun quite a bit."

"Yes sir, I sure have."

"You had a chance to go back down there yet?"

Jokingly I responded, "Warden, I doubt if I'll be sent back to Retrieve. We did all the heavy equipment work with our hoes and shovels befo you left."

He smiled and said, "Set down," motioning toward one of the office chairs, offering me all the courtesy he would a free-world man, except the handshake. "Y'all run that other warden 'way frum there in a hurry. Didn't ya? Got 'em busted to 'sistant warden. Whut wuz the matta? Wuz he too hard on y'all?" he asked sarcastically.

"No sir, I don't think that was it."

"How come they sunt you over heah?"

I already knew I wouldn't be here if he hadn't requested me from the master list of heavy equipment operators. "They said you needed some work done with the dozer."

"Yeah, well, I got a little drainage wek an some clearin I want you ta do."

He leaned back and began naming off the Retrieveites who had gotten out, come back in, and were here with him. "Ol Proud Walker, Ol Bay City, Ol Steeple Head, an Ol Cryin Shame." Then, bragging, "Them ol bastards got word to me soon as their asses landed in them Walls, wantin to come where I wuz. So I told 'em to send 'em on. Ol Forty's over heah too. Have you heard whut happen to Ol Pug?"

"No sir."

"Well, that new face didn't help him much. That ignorant bastard didn't last a hot minute afta he got out. He went to Houston an got to big-assin wit some ol woman an she stabbed him in the heart wit a ice pick an kilt him. An you'll never guess whut Ol Bay City dun. He's gotta be one uv the craziest nigguhs I ever seen. As good a damn mechanic as he is, he got busted in a cafe. The owner caught him drunk, settin down in front uv the jukebox takin the screws out uv it to steal the nickels an dimes. The owner held a gun on him till the police got there. I can understand it when some'a these nigguhs that ain't got no talents come back, but there ain't no excuse fur a nigguh lak Ol Bay City to keep runnin in an out uv heah.

"An Ol Steeple Head shouldn't'a been sunt back at all fur whut he dun. That crazy sonuvabitch wuz runnin frum a nigguh who'd whupped his ass. 'Thout even lookin back, Ol Steeple Head shot over his shoulder an hit that nigguh right betwix the eyes, kilt 'em dead as a hammer." Laughing, he told me, "That nigguh cried an begged the judge out uv a measly three years.

"Ol Cryin Shame robbed a man's place, then set down on the steps an waited fur the police to come take 'em to jail. I always knowed that nigguh couldn't make it in the free world." Big Devil added, "He don't havta worry bout it no more. They filed the bitch [habitual criminal] on 'em an give 'em life 'is time."

After bringing me up to date on the "old stomping ground cons," he put on his Stetson. "Come on, I'll show you roun the farm."

He drove up and down turnrow after turnrow, pointing out all the agricultural improvements he'd made. "When I first come heah, trees an underbrush wuz growin all up to there," he said, pointing over to some freshly plowed land. "I dun added more'n two thousand new acres uv farmland to this place. Tell you somethin else, I put these sonsabitches to wek too. It wuz some bastards in heah who'd been layin up on their asses in that buildin so long, they'd dun flat furgot how to wek!"

He boasted, "I put a stop to 'at shit in a hurry. Ol Racehoss, when I come up heah, they had about three hunnert nigguhs an Mexicans wekin in the fields. None uv them ol white thangs wuz wekin atall. Now, I got over forty squads."

"Warden, do they work together in the same squads?"

"Well, not zackly. They wek in the same cut sometimes, but I ain't got roun to mixin 'em up yet. Course when one uv them ol white thangs fucks up in his squad, I take him out an put his ass in a squad wit them nigguhs fur a couple uv weeks. Weks ever time. Don't take much uv that to git his heart right an make him put his ass in high gear."

When he reached the place where he wanted me to start working the dozer, he stopped the car and told me what he wanted done to prevent water from standing in the area after it rained. He said I'd be working under the farm manager, and would be coming out in the mornings with the tractor squad.

As we were driving away, he continued, "Tell you somethin else too, most uv these bosses wuz doin jes lak they damn well pleased, which wuz nothin. It took some doin, but we got it straight that I weren't gon put up wit their trifflin shit. They got the message afta I run off a batch uv 'em."

When he ended the tour, I was let out at the back gate. "Boss, put this nigguh on yore trusty count an let 'em go on in the buildin," Big Devil instructed.

The trusty tank was empty except for the building tender, Ol Forty. The warden had given him the same job he'd had in the hell. As soon as I put my belongings away, we sat down and had a long chat. He told me he had filed a writ because he had served his forty-year sentence, explaining, "Hell, Race, it don't take but twenny-four calendars to do forty. I dun nine years befo I made prole an I been back over seventeen. Somebody fucked up, man. I been heah two years too damn long! Dumb as I is, I kin figger dat out."

He reaffirmed what the warden had told me earlier. "Big Devil put dese muthafuckas to wek, an I mean everbody. Ain't no mo uv dat layin-roun shit."

The next morning when the call came for the tractor squad, I caught out with them and headed for the tractor-shop area. I was checking the fuel and oil in the dozer when an officer dressed in snappy western wear, who looked to be in his mid-forties, walked up. "I'm the farm manager. You gon be runnin 'is thang?" he asked.

"Yes sir. The warden told me what y'all want done."

His expression flashed anger. "Ain't you the nigguh I seen ridin round wit the warden yestiddy?"

"Yes sir, he had me in the car with him."

"Oh, I git it," he said disdainfully, "you another one uv the warden's nigguhs."

"No sir, I'm just a nigguh sent here to do some heavy equipment work for y'all."

"Whut's yore name?"

"They call me Racehoss."

"Well, Mr. Racehoss, when you git through dilly-dallyin round wit 'at machine, do you thank the warden would mind if I told you to go on an git started?"

I got on the machine, fired it up, and walked it down the turnrow. After twenty days, I had the big drainage ditch cut and was ready to start clearing stumps.

Then, when the equipment service truck from the Walls arrived on its regular run, they brought along my trainee helper, a young white con. In the training program I had been instructed how to train new operators and knew this would be part of my duties. While two of my former A&M classmates who were assigned to the service truck were checking the machine, the service-truck boss went over the trainee details with me.

"They want you to let him ride on the machine with you while you're operatin it so you can tell and show him what you're doin. Then let 'em run it with you ridin. When he gits to where he can handle it pretty good, let him do it by himself as much as possible so he can git the feel of it. With you watchin, of course. I think he knows the front end from the back. He told me when we was comin out here that he had run a front-end loader once. You don't need filters or nothin, do you?"

"No sir," I said.

He and his two helpers left.

My new trainee told me he was twenty-four, that this was his first time in the pen, and that he was from some little town in northeast Texas, serving three years for burglary. None of this meant a hill of beans to me. What mattered was that I had somebody to help me, so I could take a break from the dozer sometimes and give my back a rest.

The on-the-job training was paying off. Gene was getting better and better as the days went by and could run the machine alone, but wasn't quite good enough yet to work it in close quarters. I was leaning against a tree no more than fifteen feet away, watching him spread some backfill, when the farm manager drove up.

He stopped and shouted to me, "Ol Racehoss, git over heah! Gitcha goddamn ass on the back uv this pickup! I'm takin you to that buildin."

Climbing onto the back, I asked, "What for?"

"Jes shut yore damn mouth an git on!"

He drove off, spinning the wheels. On the way in he radioed ahead that he was bringing in one of the heavy equipment operators. Big Devil must have intercepted the message, because he drove up at the same time the pickup stopped at the back gate. The farm manager got out of his truck and walked the few feet around to the driver's side and leaned on the door.

"Whut's the matta?" the warden asked.

"Warden, I wuz brangin this nigguh in to have 'em put in the pisser."

"Fur whut?"

"Fer one thang, when I drove up out there in the field a while ago, Ol Racehoss wuz standin off up under a shade tree makin 'at white boy do all the work."

The warden beckoned for me. I jumped off the truck bed and walked over to his window. "You hear whut the farm manager said?"

"Yes sir."

"Is he tellin the truth?"

"Yes sir," I answered, totally surprised that he'd ask. Never had I heard Big Devil question an officer's word. "Warden, my helper had only been on the machine bout five minutes when the farm manager showed up. I was doin what I was told to do by the service-truck boss who brought 'em. He told me to let 'em run the machine much as possible. I'd dug the stumps up and he was spreadin some backfill when the farm manager drove up."

Leaning on the steering wheel and never looking up, Big Devil said, "Boss, you kin go on back to doin whutever you wuz doin, cuz I know you must'a been mighty busy." The farm manager's face reddened more when Big Devil said, "Git in the car, Ol Racehoss," and took me back to the machine.

The warden kept finding little projects, keeping the machine busy, overextending his allotted time limit. The farm manager started driving out almost daily, taking Gene off in the front seat of his pickup. Sometimes they'd be gone for over an hour. When Gene would get back, he said the farm manager had him doing "somethin." And I left it at that.

Soon after Gene's accusation, Big Devil held court in his office. My two former A&M officer classmates testified that they did indeed find a new oil and air filter buried. The farm manager and my helper took them to the "exact spot." My reason for burying the filters, Gene said, "I don't feel like messin with 'em."

The warden questioned me. "Didja do that, Ol Racehoss?"

I looked him straight in the eyes. "No sir." I turned and looked across the office into the face of my helper. "Warden, why don'tcha ask him how they got there. He's the one that's been ridin aroun in the pickup with the farm manager, and they're the ones who found 'em."

Big Devil smelled a rat. He mulled over the testimony a few seconds, then said, "Since y'all's the ones"—he pointed to the two service-truck bosses "that brung this ol thang over heah, y'all take 'em back wit you when you leave." He yelled out of his office to his clerk to start processing transfer papers.

One of the bosses ventured to ask, "What do you want us to do with him when we git him back to the Walls? Warden, sir, we need to have some reason for bringin 'em back."

"Do the same thang wit him ya did befo you brung him over heah."

The boss went a step further. "But, Warden, no disrespect, sir. What's the reason?"

"Oh, I see. You havta have a reason to give 'em, huh? Well, tell 'em the reason is I don't want the rotten-assed bastard on my farm, an if they have any problem wit that, tell 'em to call me."

After I'd been caught in the middle of a power struggle, the day for me to leave Eastham couldn't come quick enough. Orders finally came from the Walls to transfer me and the dozer to Coffield, the new unit under construction. As we turned onto the iron-ore-covered road, the compound of galvanized buildings loomed ahead. The truck driver followed the road around the buildings and stopped at the shop. At the loading dock, a truck from Wisconsin that had brought down a monstrous Number 9 Caterpillar was waiting to exchange it for my smaller one.

The normal check-in procedure at all the other units I'd been on began at the back gate. This time the driver drove to the office. No one was in the outer office when we entered. He called out, "Is anybody in here?"

From inside the warden's office came "Whutcha got?"

The driver handed him my record, then left. It was Silly Willy, the former Clemens warden. He was rotated in the first round too. He glanced through my papers briefly, then looked over his horn-rimmed glasses and asked, "Ol Racehoss, kin ya still pick 'at cotton?"

"No sir, not like I useta. That was a long time ago, Warden."

"They tell me you're a pretty good 'quipment operator. Well, you sho come to the right place. Plenny uv work heah to keep ya busy. You kin plan on stayin heah awhile."

He asked what I thought of my new dozer, said there was enough work here for a regular heavy equipment squad, and assigned me to it. After our chat, he phoned inside and had an officer sent to his office.

I followed him through the long, barnlike galvanized building with chicken-wire-covered windows, surmising security wasn't the long suit for this unit. With so much construction work, most of the five hundred cons were of trusty caliber, if not already trusties. The large majority were skilled construction workers, giving birth to another prison.

Each hangar-type building was divided into two tanks. A tin wall with an open doorway separated them. Only a barber was in the tank when I arrived. This was my first unit without building tenders. He walked with me down the rows, pointing out the vacant bunks. It looked to be about a hundred bunks in all. He said the white cons lived on the other side of the wall. Throughout our conversation, he talked about how different it was here compared to the Ferguson Unit, from whence he came.

I read the tank's bulletin board and saw that college classes would begin soon. I had been traveling around so much the last three years that I was never at one unit long enough to take some courses. Silly Willy seemed certain I'd be here for a while, so I decided to enroll.

He was right. There was plenty of work to do on the 23,000-acre unit, clearing timber, plowing root stumps, building roads and bridges, getting the land ready for farming. I was putting in a lot of hours and working seven days a week, but the warden worked out a schedule allowing me to come in at four o'clock on the afternoons I had classes. I continued the writings I'd started a few years earlier and had filled up ten composition tablets.

The letter was lying on my bunk when I came in from work. Besides the Christmas card the Salvation Army sent every year, this was the first mail I had ever received. I opened it cautiously, the way they did those eyes and teeth boxes.

> Dear Bubba,
>
> I hope you doing fine. It took a long time for me to find where you was. It's Mama. She just hanging on. She got gan-green in one of her legs from the fleabitis and she got kidney failure to. They got her hooked to a machine. I talked to a lawyer about getting you out to come see her. The doctor say he would personally call the Board to request that you come. I hope and pray they let you. I want to see you so bad. Been a long time, hasn't it. I love you, Bubba.
>
> > Your sis,
> > Pat

I was called out that evening. Letters containing news of illness, death, or other urgencies are viewed as motivations for escape attempts. Silly Willy told me to lay in the building tomorrow, and he phoned inside to inform the building major. Back on the tank, I got the letter from under my pillow and reread it. It had been so long since I'd seen Emma, I was unable to picture her clearly. My mind slowly drifted back over the years.

The next morning I was called out to the laundry and issued some free-world khakis, shirt, and shoes. I'd been granted a five-day emergency reprieve. The deputy sheriff from Gregg County was waiting for me in the warden's office. After I'd been shackled for transport, he led me to his car. The trip from the Coffield Unit near Palestine to Longview took about an hour and a half.

In the Good Shepherd Hospital parking lot, he removed the leg and waist chains but left the wrist cuffs. I got slightly nauseated by the strong hospital odors when we walked through the sliding glass doors. A brief stop at the admissions desk; the deputy got directions to Emma's room. We were on the right floor and walked briskly down the wheelchair-and-gurney-lined hallway. Heads turned, and I was so ashamed to come in this condition.

Pat looked up the hall, saw us, and came running. After the kisses and hugs, she asked the deputy, "Do you have to keep the handcuffs on 'em?"

"Ma'am, these are my orders. If you want to talk to the sheriff bout it, that's all right with me."

Pat told me, "Befo we go in, I'm goin over here and phone the sheriff."

While she was phoning, I waited in the hall exchanging greetings with her boyfriend, T.J., and Emma's three sisters Pat had summoned from Dallas. I hadn't seen any of them in years. Pat's conversation with the sheriff's department necessitated the deputy going to the phone. Afterward he walked over to me, removed the cuffs, and left the hospital. Five days of freedom at such a price.

Pat said, "Bubba, I'm so glad you could come, but she won't know who you are," and she began to cry. "She been in a coma for three days."

"I'd like to go in alone, Pat, if that's okay with you."

"Sure, Bubba. I'll wait out here with T.J. and them."

I was startled by how old and frail Emma looked, more like ninety than sixty-six. I reached over the railing and touched her shoulder. "It's me," I said. Her eyes opened slowly. Barely able to move her fingers, she motioned for me to come nearer. I held her hand and leaned my face close to hers.

As she struggled to speak, her lips trembled. In low, short whispers, she said, "Mama knowed you wuz comin. I wuzn't bout to go nowhere till you got here. Move back a little so Mama kin look atcha." Still holding her hand, I straightened my body. Opening her eyes wider, she looked me over through the flowing tears. "Is me an you still buddies?"

I saw the life-light in her eyes waning. Fighting back my own tears, I answered, "The best kind, Mama."

A faint smile crossed her lips. With her gaze fixed on me, she drifted off into death. Thank God! we got the chance to make our peace. My turning point had been five years earlier in a solitary confinement cell. If I hadn't changed, there's no way I could have responded quickly enough. The feelings were there; I loved her. I only regretted she beat me asking.

I was on a bench warrant in Pat's custody until the funeral was over. She bought me a navy blue suit and the accessories, and put some money in my pocket. It surprised me that the funeral was held in a church and not at the funeral home.

The pastor began the service by saying, "A member she may not have been, but I can say one thang for Emma Sample, she give mo to this church in dollars an cents over the last few years than fifty percent uv the membership. So do she have a right to be in this church for her funeral? I just wanted to clear the air on that point."

He said he had visited with her twice a week over a long period of time and had gotten to know her. "I can tell the bereaved I know in my heart Emma Sample is in heaven. If there was ever anybody I been close to as they neared death that I felt been saved, it was her. In the last few months befo she passed, she got close to her God and was prepared to die. She was not afraid. As she put it, 'I'm a big girl.'"

The small church was filled. I had no idea this many cared enough to attend. Even Mr. Milton, the liquor store man, closed up and came. The faces of the congregation were somber. Emma had told Pat that she didn't want "no whoopin an hollerin," just organ playing. She even picked the music the organist played throughout the service. I could almost hear her singing along.

As I stood at the casket for the last viewing, I pulled out *two* one-dollar bills, folded them neatly, and slid them beneath her hand. I knew she wouldn't want to run into Blue and not have any money to bet she "bar it."

Pat offered to be my parole plan, but because she had been busted a couple of times for gaming operations at her house, I felt living with her would be unacceptable to the board. Besides, I didn't want to put any heat on her by having a parole officer coming in and out. Instead, I submitted a plan to go to a halfway house in Houston.

Nine months after the funeral, it was December, and the snowflakes were softpedaling their way to the ground. The heavy equipment boss came to the tank and called for me. Since it was Sunday, I was on towing standby. When we got out in the pickup, the boss took me to where I had parked the machine the evening before. Once I got to the bogged-down log truck, it took only a few minutes to hook on the cable and pull it out. I towed it far enough up the road so the driver could make it the rest of the way to the sawmill on his own.

The equipment boss said he had to drive to the other side of the unit and close some cattle gates, reminding me, "We're tryin to git everthang closed up. Ain't gon be many uv y'all wekin next week cuz most uv the bosses'll be off fer Christmas. Why don'tcha go over in the woods an make yoreself a far [fire]. I'll be back adder while an gitcha."

It didn't matter; I was in no hurry to get back. The tank was heavy laden with holiday melancholy, and I felt better being outside. The woods had become a refuge. I pulled Big Bertha off the road and walked her through the sparse timberline of spruce and speckled ash. Deeper into the woods, I came upon a little stream and stopped.

I saw movement in front of the small brush pile on the other side, a brown cottontail. I shut the engine down to low idle and quickly got my three-foot rabbit stick from behind the seat. I eased out of the cab onto the dozer track. Just as the rabbit jumped, I threw my stick and turned it a flip. I was on it like a duck on a june bug and, as quickly as possible, ended its struggling.

From the cache of tools in my toolbox, I soon had it skinned, gutted, and washed in the stream. Seasoned with the salt and pepper packets I stockpiled from my sack lunches, it was roasting on a tree-branch rotisserie in no time.

Leaving my fire, I crossed the stream and got on the dozer to walk it over. Pausing for a moment, I looked at the picturesque winter wonderland and felt like I was in the middle of a Christmas card. The crystallized flakes splashed off the naked branches and sparkled like Roman candles before joining their snowflake pals blanketing the forest floor. Not wanting to disrupt the little stream's serenity, I decided to leave Big Bertha where she was and walked back.

Occasionally, one of the icy pellets found its way down my shirt collar, but for the most part the yellow slicker suit kept me dry. I squatted, turning my rabbit slowly over the flames. There was a break in the silence. Squinting, I saw a white man approaching on horseback.

He stopped his horse eight or ten feet from the fire and said amicably, "Hello there, how you doin? I could smell it cookin all over the woods." Smiling, he went on, "All I had to do was follow my nose. Got enough to share?"

"Sure, come on. It's almost ready," I answered, surprised that anyone was nearby but glad to have his company, even though I'd never seen him before. Noticing the long hair under his cowboy hat, I wondered how in the hell he managed to wear it that length when all the other cons at the unit had short GI haircuts like mine.

Finished with tying the reins around a spruce, he came over and squatted beside me, ungloved his hands, and warmed them over the fire. "Merry Christmas to you, pardner," he said.

"Same to ya."

"Is that your dozer parked over yonder?"

"Yep. That's Big Bertha."

We gazed into the flames and took turns picking off bits of the rabbit. "What're you doin out here in the snow?" I asked. "I thought everybody was in watchin the football game."

"Roundin up some strays."

"If you hadn't smelled this rabbit, you might've missed one," I joked.

I liked his easygoing style and got around to telling him about being out nine months earlier for my mother's funeral. Then I said, "I talked to the parole man back in September but ain't heard nothin yet. They get somebody all werewolfed up, then nothin. Nada. Zilch."

He stopped chewing and said with an air of certainty, "Don't worry bout a thang. You'll make it." We finished our rabbit feast. "I thank you for sharin with me. I guess I betta be movin on. So long, pardner."

"Good luck with your roundup."

He mounted and then disappeared into the thicket. Stomping out the fire, I realized I didn't know anything about him and hollered, "What's your name? What buildin you on?"

I guess he didn't hear me, I thought and resumed my fire stomping. It started snowing much harder, so I climbed on Big Bertha and waited until the boss came and took me in.

Monday evening when I got to the building, an inner-unit truck-mail envelope was on my bunk. When I opened it and saw the parole release slip inside, I got weak in the knees. The gift of gifts—I'd be out in less than a month.

Every morning when the trusties went out, I watched for my rabbit-eating "pardner" to tell him the good news, but I never did see him again. I finally gave up trying to find the ghost rider in the snow.

The day before my release I arrived at the Walls and was ready for shakedown. The bunch of us who came in on Black Betty were quickly herded into the security station for the strip search, jammed inside the little room like cattle. Naked, we squirmed closer to the doorway of a larger room, where we would be searched. A guard stationed near the entry door of the smaller room yelled, "You bastards scrouge up in there! I got some more people waitin to git in heah." Black Bettys were bringing them from other units to be released, transferred to a different unit, or assigned to this one. Looking down the line while waiting my turn, I noticed those ahead inspected by the older guards moved through the line much faster. The younger bosses were more thorough.

My turn came. I put my clothes, shoes, and other personals on the counter. I completed the "open your mouth, spread your cheeks" part as the young guard watched. He raked my shoes and clothes to one side, indicating it was okay to start putting them back on. I was almost finished buttoning my shirt and cramming my cigarettes and Zippo back in my pockets when he began to leaf through one of my composition tablets stacked on the counter.

"What're these?" the young guard asked.

"Just some tablets I've been keepin notes in."

"How long you been here?"

"A long time, boss, seventeen years altogether."

He read aloud from the tablet in his hand, "My life was spent in darkness. And then there was Light." With a smart-ass smirk, he asked, "What kinda shit is that?"

He pitched the tablet into the barrel with the rest of the things they'd confiscated, then tossed in the others. Five years of writing thrown in the trash like garbage.

"You ought not have no trouble rememberin. Next!"

20

The prison-made khaki pants and shirt I had been issued, which clearly told I was a newly released, didn't provide much protection against the cold January morning as I walked through freedom's gate. I turned my collar up and tucked my chin in to duck the icy breeze, slid my hands into my pockets, and took off trotting to the Trailways bus station four blocks away, leaving all the lost time behind.

I bought a four-dollar ticket to Houston and waited for the bus. The whores were running in and out of the station like moths, trying to pick up whatever little change the newly released cons had after paying for their bus fares. Parolees received ten dollars mustering-out money, those discharged got fifty. Some cons didn't even make it out of Huntsville. They spent all their money on pussy and booze, got into trouble, ass thrown in jail, and were back inside the Walls before they could get out of town.

Twenty-six days prior to my forty-second birthday, with six bucks in my pocket, I was paroled to New Directions ex-offender halfway house, founded by Sonny Wells, a former Retrieve inmate. The second day, I enrolled in night classes at the University of Houston, financed by the Department of Vocational Rehabilitation. The fifth day, I got a job working for a black newspaper, a hundred bucks a week. Two of my parole criteria had been satisfied; I had a place to stay and a job.

The dice "started hittin." After a month I moved out of the halfway house into my own apartment. I had never been in a newspaper plant before, let alone worked in one. But in about a year and a half, I was promoted to general manager. Meanwhile, I'd put together a very decent wardrobe and bought a new car.

I was sitting in my office, busy as hell, with deadlines to meet. It was county election time and the politicians had been coming and going all day, each hoping to garner the newspaper's support. They knew the *Forward Times* packed plenty of clout in Houston's black community, and they shook hands with everybody they met along their course to the publisher's office.

Looking out from my glass-walled office, I saw him when he came in and watched him take the same handshaking, handing-out-pamphlets route as the rest. He worked his way to my office. With a light rap on the glass door, it was my turn. He opened the door partways and poked his head in, glanced at the nameplate on my desk. "Mr. Sample, can I bother you for a minute or two?"

"Sure, come on in and have a seat."

He extended his hand and we gripped. After he took a seat and looked again at my name on the nameplate, which was followed by the words GENERAL MANAGER, he said, "I know you're a busy man so I'll get straight to the point." He handed me one of his pamphlets, which I put on my desk. "I'm Jack Heard. I'm running for sheriff of Harris County and I'd like your support," he told me, garnishing it with a great big politician smile.

I leaned back in my chair and stared at him for so long he began to get a little uneasy. "I know who you are," I said, "but you don't know who I am, do you?"

Looking me over more closely (a cop look), he replied, "Nope, can't say that I do," with a hint of a smile. "Guess you got me there."

"You were assistant director at the state prison. Your office was in Huntsville at the Walls, right?" He nodded. "You remember that time the convicts had a sit-down strike in the cane field at Retrieve? They flew you down in a state plane. You stood on a trailer bed and asked the cons to tell you why they refused to work. I was the first man who stood up and showed you my bloody palms." I held my palms in the air the same as I had done in the cane field. He looked at them and his eyes lit up, astonished.

"Ol Racehoss, they called you . . . I think."

"That's right. That was a long time ago."

With a genuinely cordial smile he stuck out his hand and we shook again, this time with much more gusto. Still at a loss for words, he said, "Well, I'll just be damned," with an incredulous look on his face, seeing me in a place where I ought not to be.

"You got my vote, Mr. Heard," I told him, although I couldn't vote at the time, "but as for the newspaper endorsing you, you'll have to talk to the publisher about that. But I'll sure put a good word in for you."

"'Preciate it."

"Now that you're here, would you like to know the rest of the story about that cane strike?"

"I sure would."

"After you chewed the warden's ass out and flew off, that night we had pork chops and all the apple pie we could eat," I said, chuckling, and he laughed. "You really got the warden's attention."

"Did you ever get those gloves?"

"The very next morning."

He laughed again. Glancing at the nameplate, he said, "Sure looks like you've been doing all right for yourself. When did you get out?"

"A little over two years ago."

"I'm just flabbergasted at how far you've come since the cane field days." He leaned forward in his chair and said in a serious vein, "Let me ask you something. No offense and I'm just being curious, what do you think it was that turned you around?"

"That cotton sack!" He really cracked up this time. I felt compelled to tell him, "Mr. Heard, it would have turned out different in that cane patch if it wasn't for you. Thank you for what you did for us."

"Well, you're certainly welcome, Raceh—" He looked at my nameplate. "I mean, Albert." Then he continued on his way to the publisher's office.

What were the odds of something like this happening? Jack Heard seeking my help just as I had hoped for his long ago in a cane patch. A billion to one probably! I did everything in my power to gain his endorsement from the newspaper. He won the election by a landslide.

I could hardly wait for the weekends. Soon as five o'clock Friday came, I headed for Longview to be with Pat. We had been apart for too many years. With each visit we grew closer and closer. We were the only family left, and really enjoyed each other.

She had managed to go to cosmetology school and ran a beauty shop in her house. But like Emma, she also ran dice games on the weekends. I usually managed to arrive right in the middle of the crap game, but she'd leave the table and we'd sit in the living room talking and laughing until we both got in the game.

During one of my weekend visits, it was nearing dawn and the crap game had finally ended. All the players were gone, except the few who couldn't make it. Three of them were piled up on the daybed in the back room. After losing all their money, they filled their bellies with Pat's collard greens and ham hocks, fried fish, and hot-water corn bread. They were drunk and sleeping peacefully.

Pat and I sat talking at the crap table. "Bubba, since it done boiled down to jes me and you, what you want me to do bout yo funeral and stuff in case I outlive you?"

"Well, you can make sure I got my shoes on. I don't wanna be tippin around on them hot coals barefooted."

"C'mon, be serious, Bubba." I saw the deep concern in her face.

"Awright, jes see that they don't cut up my clothes and spread 'em out over me. Have 'em put 'em on me. I don't wanna meet my maker with my ass out behind."

"Okay," she said, laughing a little, "you got it. I give you my word that's the way it'll be done." Then, out of the clear she asked, "Bubba, you scared of dyin?"

"No, but it ain't somethin I'm lookin forward to. Why all this talk about death and dyin? I know we got somethin else we can talk about besides that."

"I know, but I wanna talk about it. That's what's wrong with people today. They don't ever talk about things like this. Then when the time come, they don't know what to do. Anyway, we can't quit talkin about it. I ain't had my turn yet."

"You ain't plannin on leavin no time soon, are you?" I kidded.

"But jes in case, Bubba," she said without a smile, "I want you to say everything at my funeral. And I don't want it in no church. The funeral parlor's good enuff. Most of all, I wanna be buried close to Mama."

I was quiet.

"Are you listenin to me?"

"Yeah, I'm listenin."

"Okay, promise me you'll do it."

"I promise."

She explained the relationship she had with her ex-husband, Roy Lee, as well as the one she had with T.J. She interrupted herself. "Boy, am I glad I got a big bubba I can tell all my secrets to, the way they do in them love story magazines I read all the time."

She started crying. I walked over and put my arms around her. With her head buried against me, she whimpered like a little child, "Bubba, I want you to always know one thing, I love you with all my heart." Crying more profusely, she said, "We're all we got." After blowing her nose and wiping away some of the tears with the hankie I'd handed her, she said, "God, I miss Mama. Sometimes I feel so all alone, Bubba."

Holding my sister close and crying too, I told her, "You're not alone, Pat. I'm right here with you. C'mon, cheer up. We're gon make it jes fine. Watch and see. C'mon now," I urged, "let's stop cryin and have a drink together."

After we'd shared a small shot of vodka, she said, "I'm okay now. I guess we been needin to cry together for a long, long time. Bubba, lemme ask you sump'n. Have you seen Mama? You know, like in a spirit or a dream?"

"No . . . have you?"

"Yeah, I have. I've seen her. I see her all the time."

"Aw, c'mon, Pat."

"No foolin. Sometimes I be doin sump'n, turn around, and there she is."

"Don't it scare you?"

"Course not, it's Mama. She wouldn't hurt me."

"Does she talk to you?"

"Naw . . . that is, up till about a week ago. Bubba, please don't think I'm crazy, but jes like you know you lookin at me right now, that's how sure I am it was Mama."

"What'd she say? C'mon, tell me. You got my ears wide open."

"The other night I got in bed and fixed myself in a good readin position. You know I hafta keep up with my *True Confessions*. I wasn't asleep, Bubba. I looked up from my magazine and there she was sittin on the foot of the bed, jes lookin at me. She looked so troubled I asked her why she was so worried. She said, 'I'm worried bout you. Be careful, baby. We should'a poisoned him when we had the chance.' 'Who, Mama?' I asked her. 'You know who I'm talkin bout.' An jes like that, she was gone. What you think, Bubba?"

"I don't know what to tell you, except the same thing Mama said, be careful."

Sunday morning when I was ready to head back to Houston, Pat walked to the car with me. "Bubba, don't stay away long."

I stuck my head out the window. "Don't worry, I'll be back soon. You got me hooked on them collard greens."

I worked hard during the days and was tired at the end of them. One night the ringing of the phone woke me. Half-asleep, I picked up the receiver and said "Hello."

"Bubba, is that you?"

I glanced at the radio clock, 2:15. "Hello," I repeated. "Pat? Speak up, I can hardly hear you. Say that again."

"This is Clara, Pat's friend across the street."

"Okay, I'm with you, what's up?"

"I'm callin bout Pat. She been shot."

"Is she dead?"

"I don't know, but you betta come quick. The police an ammalance is over there now. They brangin her out on the stretcher."

"Where will they take her?"

"Good Shepherd."

"Who shot her? Do you know?"

"Naw. Wait a minute! I see 'em. The police is puttin Roy Lee in the car."

"Thanks for callin, Clara. I'm on my way."

I threw a few things in my bag and hit the road. It had just been a week since I was up there. About four hours later, I was exiting onto Highway 80 on the outskirts of Longview, heading for the hospital. Once through the familiar electronic doors, I walked up to the admissions desk. The corridors were empty and the big clock on the wall showed 6:23.

"Pardon me, ma'am. Do you have Patsy Hicks here?"

"Just a moment," she said, and she fingered through the cards. "Yes, she was brought in a few hours ago. Are you a member of the family?"

"Yes, I'm her brother. Can you tell me anything about her condition?"

Reading from the record, she said, "Multiple gunshot wounds. She's in ICU. Her doctor will be in around nine."

"Can I see her?"

"No sir, the doctor left strict orders not to allow any visitors until after he sees her this mornin."

She directed me to an area where I could get some coffee and wait, assuring me that when the doctor arrived she'd let me know. Waiting for nine o'clock, I drank a gallon of coffee and went to the john a half dozen times.

"Doctor," the nurse said, "this is Miss Hicks's brother."

"Hello, come this way." He placed the folders he was carrying on the desk. "I'm gonna level with you. Pat's been very seriously injured, so seriously, I dare not tell her just yet. She's got fifteen gunshot wounds from a small-caliber weapon scattered over her body. Fortunately, all the bullets went through and didn't hit any vital organs. But she lost a lot of blood. If we can make it through the next week or so without complications, she's got a fair chance. But in situations like this where the patient is totally immobile, there's always a possibility of blood clotting. Her being a diabetic could also cause problems with the clot-preventive medication. How's your stomach?"

"Okay. Why?"

"It gets much worse. Half of a broken Coke bottle was inserted into her vagina. It has caused major problems. I haven't told her that yet."

My first reaction was shock. My next was I wanted to kill Roy Lee so bad I could taste it. He was one lucky motherfucker to be in jail. "Is she conscious?"

"Yes, she's conscious. She's sedated, but I talked with her just a little while ago. She's fairly coherent."

"Can I see her? Just to let her know I'm here. I won't disturb her."

"All right, but only for a few minutes."

The admissions nurse directed me to the intensive care unit. When I entered, the green-clad nurse met me at the door. "I'm here to see my sister, Patsy Hicks."

"Okay, she's in that room," she told me, pointing through the glass window.

"Is it all right if I go inside?"

"Yes, but don't touch anything," she warned and returned to her station.

As I stepped inside, a cold chill ran over me. There were tubes in Pat's nose, both arms, and lower body. I quietly approached the big-wheeled gurney. "Pat, Pat," I said softly, "can you hear me? It's Bubba, I'm here."

She turned her head ever so slightly in my direction and whispered, "Oh, Bubba, I'm so sorry I had to worry you."

"Hey, buddy, you can't worry me. I love you."

"Bubba, that sonuvabitch went crazy," she said weakly. "Mama warned me," she said, and a tear trickled down her cheek.

"Was it Roy Lee?"

"Yeah, I want you to promise me you won't get in no trouble." She was fading out. "It ain't worth it . . . don't go back down . . ." The drugs took over.

After leaving ICU, I saw T.J. "Hi, Race. I got here soon as I heard bout it. Is she gon be awright?"

We stepped to one side of the hall. I told him what the doctor had told me, all but the last part.

Over the next few days either T.J. or I remained at the hospital. On the fifth day, Pat was moved from the ICU to a room that I realized was right next to the one in which Emma had died. I saw her doctor and expressed how good I felt about how she was doing.

"Don't get too optimistic just yet," he cautioned. "The next few days will be the most crucial. It's a miracle she's made it this far."

Regardless of what he said, I was optimistic. She looked so much better as the days wore on, and had even sipped a little soup. She seemed to be gaining strength.

The next three days she was in very good spirits. We talked, and she told me the whole story. "I was in a financial bind, Bubba, and needed six hundred dollars right away to take care of some bills. Roy Lee came by the house and we got to talkin and I mentioned I needed six hundred dollars from somewhere—and quick. He offered to lend me the money and said to pay 'em back whenever I could. He'd been after me to take him back, but we been divorced for nearly six years, and I don't love him. He knew that, but he couldn't stand that I was in love with T.J.

"We had a good game goin, and T.J. was at the house when Roy Lee came over. He got in the game, and befo long, him and T.J. were arguin. And there I sat in the middle. It was gettin mo serious and

I knew T.J. was gettin ready to jump on 'em. I felt like he would really hurt Roy Lee so I asked him to leave. He thought I was takin sides with T.J., which I wasn't. But he couldn't see it that way and stormed outta the house.

"It was past midnight Sunday when I got home. I got a funny feelin, specially when Buster didn't bark. I figured he must be sleepin and didn't hear me. He's gettin old too. I unlocked the door, stepped inside, and locked it behind me befo I turned on the lights.

"There sat Roy Lee on the couch with a rifle layin 'cross his lap. It scared me so bad, all I could think to say was 'Whatcha doin sittin up here in the dark? How'd you get in?' Bubba, he never said a word. I started for my bedroom, where I keep my pistol. That's when I saw Buster on the floor . . . dead.

"Befo I could reach my room, he got up and started shootin. I tried to grab him. I managed to get my hands on the rifle barrel, but he kept on shootin. I remember him knockin me back away from him. I don't know how many times I was shot, but I could feel the burnin inside me. I fell to the floor. He reloaded, stood over me, and shot some mo times. I played dead. I believe if I hadn't, he would've reloaded again. Then I passed out. How many times did he shoot me?"

"The doctor said it was more than a dozen."

"Damn, I sure was lucky."

"Yep, you sure are."

She was more cheerful on the sixth day than she'd been since it happened. But she did mention that if she didn't make it, she wanted me to give her rings to Mae Rose, T.J.'s sister. "She's been a real good friend to me." Joking, she went on, "You get everything else, the house with the mortgage and all the unpaid bills. But at least that ol car's paid for."

I emphasized, "But you gon make it, sis. You're comin along fine."

"Yeah, but jes in case."

She took a turn for the worse on the ninth day and grew much weaker. The blood clotting was out of control. The next day she lapsed into a coma. Standing at her bedside, I watched her chest rise and fall for the last time. Never before had I felt so helpless. We'd had so little time together since I'd been out of prison. My heart ached and I felt near collapse as I helped lift her stretcher into the ambulance and rode along to the funeral home to make arrangements.

The chapel overflowed. There wasn't enough seating room, and people lined the walls. I fulfilled my promise to her and gave the eulogy. She was buried next to Emma. I settled her financial matters, gave her rings to Mae Rose, and left. Pat's death was a shattering, unexpected blow that left a hollow hole in my chest. I could hardly get my breath as I looked down the highway before me. Night had fallen and the road was long. Listening to the tires thump across the highway seams, I couldn't help but wonder, *What happened to "Don't you worry about a thing"?*

I had to somehow put the painful loss in a safe place in my mind. I threw myself into my work. I didn't go back to Longview for the trial. After it was over, T.J. called me at work one day and told me Roy Lee had been sentenced to thirty years. How ironic, the same sentence I got for robbery.

SIPPING LEMONADE

In 1974, three months after Pat died, the director of the halfway house program, Sonny Wells, came to my office at the newspaper and offered me a job. I accepted and became the business manager for the ex-offender program, funded by the Criminal Justice Division. In December of the same year, the miracle of miracles happened. A statewide search had been launched by a very popular "maverick" state representative, Ronnie Earle, to find an ex-convict to direct a newly created prison-release program out of the Office of the Texas Governor. After a lengthy interview he passed the dice to me, and I was appointed project director of Project STAR (Social Transition and Readjustment).

The penalty for possession of four ounces or less of marijuana had been reduced to misdemeanor status, but the legislature failed to make the law retroactive for the hundreds of inmates previously sentenced as felons. Using executive clemency, Governor Dolph Briscoe pardoned the inmates. Project STAR was created to help them find employment. Those affected would bypass the six-week prerelease program designed to plug them back into society. This was my job, to provide counseling and job placement assistance. It also meant that, since I was the program, I had to hurry!

By the first of the year, when it kicked off, I had contacted literally hundreds of potential employers across the state by phone and in person regarding hiring ex-offenders. Much to my amazement, after some straight talk about the matter and answering questions about the "risks," the majority were willing to "take a chance."

By the time the first prisoners were released under the new program, I had job possibilities and somebody for them to contact already lined up. Of course, the individuals still had the responsibility of nailing it down; that's where the "how to" and "sharing personal experiences" counseling came in. Armed with "big papers" bearing the governor's signature, I was authorized to enter the prisons and counsel my clients prior to their release.

At the guard level I was "that nigguh frum the Guvner's Office," but in the wardens' offices I was "Mr. Sample." The convicts viewed me with pride, "a stone-down gorilla," and called me "Mr. Racehoss." As for me, it was an emotional high every time I entered the gates simply because I knew I could leave when I was ready.

Of the 476 prisoners affected under the new law, 305 needed assistance. At the end of 1975, follow-up data on those who had been assisted by Project STAR showed it was a success. Of the 305 I assisted, only 3 had been rearrested.

"I don't remember the numbers," Ronnie Earle said in later years, "but I used to have a certificate from the Department of Labor, because this was the most successful ex-offender rehabilitation program in the United States."

On my final trip to the Walls to visit my last client, I recognized somebody I hadn't seen in years, Big Devil's son. I remembered when he was just a kid and used to come up to the office and hang around hoping I could come out and toss the football with him.

I walked over to the security desk where he sat and spoke. He recognized me. "Hi, Racehoss," he said, extending his hand to shake.

"Hi, Alton Jr. How long have you been workin for the prison system?"

"Aw, bout two years. Ever since I got outta the Navy."

"How's your dad?"

"Aw, jus fine. He retired, you know."

"Naw, I didn't know. I didn't think he'd ever leave the pen."

"Well," he said and shrugged his shoulders, "you know how that goes. Him an Mama got 'em a little place in Lovelady an settled down."

The doors were unlocking. "Say, Alton Jr., I gotta run. Here comes my client. When you see the warden, tell 'em hello for me."

"Okay, sure will."

After seeing that the new releasee was safely on the bus at the station, I got in my car and drove away from Huntsville. Traveling along the highway listening to the music on the radio, mind wandering, I realized I had made a wrong turn somewhere when I saw the sign LOVELADY 17. That sure wasn't the way to Austin. I started looking up ahead for a place to turn around. Then decided, what the hell.

Five hundred yards after I entered Lovelady, I pulled into an Atlantic Richfield service station. The attendant came out and said, "Yes sir."

"Hi, I just need some information. Can you tell me where the Walkers live?"

"Sure kin," he said, pointing. "See 'at little road"—no more than twenty feet away—"jes turn right there an follow it on roun till you come to a big oak tree. Thas where it makes a Y. Stay to the right an you'll dead-end in they front yard."

It was no road, it was a path. I followed it as directed and ended up in the front yard of a white frame house with a big porch with a swing. I parked in the driveway and walked up to the front door. *Knock! Knock!*

His wife came to the door. "Yes?" She didn't recognize me, but I remembered her.

"Is Warden Walker in?"

"Yes."

"Would you tell him somebody's here to see him?"

"Jesta minute. Alton, Alton!"

"Yeah?"

"There's somebody here to see you."

"Okay, be there in a minute."

I stood to one side with my hands clasped in front so he could see them. After stepping onto the porch, he exclaimed, "Ol Racehoss!"

"That's right, Warden."

"Damn! When did you git out?" Motioning toward the porch swing, he said, "Have a seat."

"In 'seventy-two."

"Well," he said, smiling, "you beat me out by little better'n a year."

"I didn't know you retired till I saw Alton Jr. over at the Walls."

"Yeah, I helped git him on over there," he boasted. "Whut wuz you doin over at the Walls?"

"Meetin a convict."

"I see. Whut kind uv wek you doin?"

"I work out of the Governor's Office, the Criminal Justice Division."

"Is that so? Aw, I see," he said, mixing surprise with sarcasm, "you one'a them big shots now."

"No sir, I'm not a big shot." Adding my own dab of sarcasm, I said, "I'm still just Ol Racehoss. I bet you don't even know my real name."

After a silence, "Whut all do you do?" he asked.

"Well, have you heard about the marijuana release program?"

"Yeah."

"I'm the project director."

"Well, I'll be. I didn't know you wuz headin up 'at program."

"Yes sir. I left the Walls after my client got out, made a wrong turn, and ended up on the road to Lovelady."

"Well, Ol Racehoss, I'm glad you did. Where you livin now?"

"I moved from Houston to Austin about a year ago."

"Frum whut I hear, Houston ain't nothin but a trusty shack. Half the people who git out wind up in Houston. I betcha a third uv Houston's population is ex-convicts. When you wuz livin in Houston, didja ever run 'cross any uv the old-timers?"

"I sure did," I said, adding, "I went to a halfway house for ex-cons when I got out. Know who was runnin it?"

"Who?"

"Ol Sonny Wells."

"You don't say? Ol Sonny had a good head on 'em. He'll do awright if he don't start makin 'at chock," he joked, referring to the time Sonny's chock he had stashed in the kitchen exploded. "I heard Ol Cateye went to Houston too. You ever see him?"

"Yes sir, I saw him. Last I heard he was workin for Dr. Gates. Ol Ottie Dottie works for Sonny at the halfway house, and I saw Flea Brain standin on a street corner in Galveston. He's still just as funny as ever. And Ol Forty's workin at the halfway house too, got him a buildin tender job. Ol Thirty-Five's preachin in Fort Worth. And let me see, who else? Oh, you'll never guess who else I saw."

"Who?"

"Pork Chops. I went to a movie one night and after takin my seat, I heard somebody sayin, 'Racehoss, Racehoss!' I looked around and it was Pork Chops. He said he had a job workin at a cafe and doin just fine."

"I'm glad to hear that. I hope they all kin stay out."

We sat in the swing chatting just like two old cons. "Last time we wuz together, Ol Racehoss, that damn farm manager wuz afta yore ass."

"Yes sir, that's right." His memory was uncanny as we talked and talked about yesteryears. "Warden, how come you hung 'em up? I thought you'd probably stay around till they tore all the buildins down."

"Yeah, well, I planned to, but then I thought about it an talked it over wit Ol Miss. I decided it wuz time fur me to git out. I spent the betta part uv my life in prisons. I don't wanna have nothin else to do wit 'em. I'm through. I dun my time," he said, adding humorously, "Hell, Ol Racehoss, I dun more time than you did. But I got my belly full in a hurry afta they let the convicts take over. Befo I left the Eastham farm I had a dozen lawsuits filed ginst me."

"For what?"

"Violatin somebody's civil rights, brutality, all kinds uv stuff. Say!" he said, smiling devilishly. "Since you wek fur the guvner an everthang, I might need you to testify fur me."

"Aw, you don't need my testimony. You'll make it all right." I thought about it for a moment and decided to tell him. "Warden, do you remember that time you put me in solitary when Mr. Meabs ran me in?"

"Yeah."

"Well, I want to thank you for that."

"Why?"

"I've never told this to anyone before. God came to me while I was in there that time, and my life hasn't been the same. I just wanted to tell you that."

Big Devil sat silently, head bowed. Then he looked up and hollered into the house, "Ol Miss, brang us two glasses uv 'at lemonade," rocking the swing gently with his foot. After Ol Miss handed us the frosty glasses and went back inside, he said, "Ol Racehoss, I bleeve you gonna make it this time. An I'm glad I had somethin to do wit helpin git yore heart right."

"That's where you're wrong, Warden. You didn't have shit to do with it," I told him and sipped my lemonade.

Bama, Sally B, and Elzado (in that order) died within ten years after Emma's death in 1971. Rest their souls.

The Retrieveites

———

Ol Cadlack, Florine, High Pocket, Pile Driver, Dog, Mae Perl, Cuero, Bull, Sally, Big Six, Chicken, Judy, Mellaman, Fort Worth, Fistfucker, Marble Eye, Piss Ant, B.C., Jelly, Round Head, Navasota, Misusin Slim, Annie, Look-Em-Down Red, Lil Chicken, Big Low, Skinny, Maude, Tangle Eye, Road Runner, Bernice, Gilflirt, Texicana, Cattle Gap, Fish Head, Brass Mouf, Flea Brain, Calf Eye, Choppin Charlie, Garden Slim, Middlebuster, Crip, Baldy, Lil Alfonso, Flyin Home, Pickhandle, Big Mama James, Track, Beaumont, Mus Havit, Rag, Mufflejaw, Sarge, Cuz, Big Filet Mignon, Spider, Slope Diddy, West Texas, Kotch Tom, Moon, Bighand, Doc Cateye, Lunchmeat, Hound, Motormouf, Skeet, Pork Chops, Chubby, Nolan, Trigger Bill, Snake, Cowboy, Runnin Time, Forty, Lil Hand, Rabbi, Hawk, Ape, Pig Eye, Unca Moze, Dumplin, Round Rock, Good Eye, Rooster, Iron Head, Mattie, Stump, Walkie Talkie, Cornflakes, Bugs, Toe Sucker, Shadow, Dead Man, Skindown, 84, Polly, Buster, Hook-Em Bill, Swapout, Big Louzanna, Wetback, Beer Belly, Mae West, Buckjump, Wild Man, Lay-Em-Down Shorty, Rev, Duck Eye, Bird Eye, Yeller Gal, Fishgil, Water Boy Brown, Ax Man, Cross Cut, Soda Cracker, Dishpan, Turkey Slim, Rock, Whickabill, Kilgo, Rastus, Two Moufs, Cap Rock, Chinaman, Scrap Iron, Mule, Tin Horn, Coon, Rock Island, Moose, Sleepy, Corsicana, Bones, Tree,

Buttermilk, Ox, Dragline, Sardine, Gatermouf, Polecat, High John, Gypsy, Bad Eye, Mama Good Drawers, Ollie, Crazy Folks, Owl Head, Cutbelly, Naomi, Tarzan, Guvner, Black Pete, Firebug, No Ass, Crosshauler, Korea, Speedy, Hafahead, Rat, Mama Better Drawers, Lookinback, Cowfucker, Jaybird, Candy, Babysetter, Air Hammer, One Gone, Calico, Gotch Eye, Mammy, Gravedigger, Sue, Goat, Railhead Shorty, Cablecar, Spriggs, Polkadot, Chili, Dakota, Gila Monster, Pauline, Cresote, Dangalang, Squat Low, Glodine, Pulldo, Lil Hal, Big Time, Short Shorty, Witherspoon, Fartnot, Eel, Talco, Shadrack, Blood Eye, Black Rider, Tennessee, Birdseed, Whitefolks, Sicamo, Jack Hammer, Booty Green, Snot Man, Mae Widder, Scarecrow, Kool Aid, Tiny, Fo Eyes, Slocum, Radio, Feets, Peebaby, Rapehead, Pee Wee, Slats, Lillian, Fishhook, Cryin Shame, Gallopin, Three-Eighty, 44, 35, Hut, Hole in the Head, Ostrich, Pank Eye, Dreamer, Elefin Head, Happy, So-Peter, Carnival, Water Well, Crybaby, Braggs, Nose, Sheep Shit, Brady, Collard Greens, Hammerlock, Pick a Head, Racehoss, Space Man, Baby Raper, Killa, Snout, Mabel, Pug, Hollywood, Backsticker, Peckahead, VD, School Teacher, Sof Head, Midnite, Way Lay, Skintight, Proud Walker, Rearback, Rockinchair, Box, Midget, Soapsuds, Earthworm, Amarilla, Big Ear, Bow Wow, Frenchy, Police, Eaglepaw, Fenderbender, 7 Fangers, Knees, Neck, Nelly Nothin, Old Folks, Backtrouble, Dizzy, Lil Ear, Claw, Kangaroo, Hip Cat, Watermelonman, Tumbleweed, Pitchfork, Alabama, Popeye, Squarehead, Eightball, Duckbutter, Arcola, Snakedoctor, Jewel, Greyhound, Rabbit, Big Ada, Stripes, Possum, Jesse James, Ticktock, Hiwatha, Choker, Waco, Gasoline, Bat Man, Hercules, Bay City, Wolf, Pincushion, Top 'N Bottom, Redwine, Sparkplug, Appleass, Spooky, Waterbaby, Ragmouf, Ottie Dottie, Corinne, Halliburton, Steeple Head, Blacknite, Waxahachie, Goldfront, Shine, Picklehead, Molehands, Underground, Meat Cutter, Ace, Big Cross, Bubble Eye, Wash, Kong, Waskom, Jabbo, Sonny Wells, Razorback, Goosey, Monkey Man, Bulldog, Tomball, Preacher, Rosebud, Twin Chin, Black Scotty, Bill Davis, Penny, Smallchange, Liverlips, Grunt, Big Mexico, Dolly, Molly, Butterbean, Tarbaby,

Peanut, Goree, Doubledeuce, New York, Earlytime, Bug Eye, Grasshoppa, Bicycle, Minnie, Patch over the Eye, Arkadelpha, Packrat, Mank, Picturedrawer, Logcabin, Unca Frown, Smiley, Crazy Mo, Nicklehead, Sack Man, Tadpole, Jap, Bummabee, Flagpole, Gladiola, Willie B, Saddlehead, Teacake, Buttcut, Blackgal, Deepwalkin Dad, Copout, Monkeywrench, Dallis, Shot Man, Hambone, Willie Mae, Cornbread, Ragmop, Squirrelhead, Gertrude, Okinawa, Cave Man, Suzy Q, Prizefighter, Storyteller, Angola, Broth 'N Law, Fly, Flea, Montana, Speck, Hop, Deathrow, Frostbite, Blaine, Minnow, Dummy, YoYo, Lurline, Puppy, Pillowcase.

Afterword

In late 1974 my mother was in a terrible car accident, and I came to Houston with my young daughter, Amber, to care for her. My mother had worked as a counselor at New Directions Halfway House for ex-offenders when Race was the business manager, and they had become good friends. Stepping into my mother's apartment, Race had a huge smile on his face, exuding manliness and confidence. I had never met anyone like him. His magnetic personality, great sense of humor, and depth of sensitivity drew me to him instantly. When serendipity blossomed into true love, it took us both by surprise. My mother recuperated completely, and Race and I were married on Valentine's Day 1976.

Government funding for ex-offender programs was quickly dwindling as the prison population exploded; consequently, Race transitioned out of the correctional field and became superintendent of the Construction Division for the city of Austin. I had a great job in the HR Department at Lockheed. We were happily living the American dream—beautiful new house, two new cars—in spite of the challenges we faced as an interracial couple in the heart of Texas.

But something was amiss. The voice in solitary that said "You must tell them about me" echoed through Race's mind like a drumbeat, getting louder and louder until he couldn't ignore it any longer. Sharing his life-changing epiphany and remarkable story of overcoming the odds soon became an obsession, something he felt compelled and destined to do. "I'll help you," I told him. In 1982 our lives took a dramatic turn when we quit our jobs and then sold our home to buy us time to write his autobiography.

He got an old typewriter at a Hispanic-owned junkyard that he affectionately nicknamed Señor, and I borrowed an IBM Selectric typewriter. Running on faith, we hunkered down in a house we had leased for six months, hoping the book wouldn't take any longer. By then Amber was in the sixth grade, and luckily the school bus stopped right in front of our house. We were all set to go, except for one thing. Race had no idea where to start. He finally decided to skip the beginning and focus on prison life because it was so fresh in his memory. I was his sounding board, editor, and retypist.

Hunting and pecking at a respectable speed on Señor, Race banged out much of the book. I was reading and editing it. Still, no beginning. Writer's block. Weeks went by, time slipping away, money running out. Around three one morning he shook me awake and said, "I got it." By the time the sun came up, he had written "Prelude." This was Emma's beginning, the stories she told him about her shattered childhood, which set the stage for his.

We were humming along once again. And then the bottom fell out. We got a phone call from the young couple who owned the house, giving us notice that they had put it on the market. The next day as we sat working at our typing tables a private bus stopped in front of the house. The real estate agent walked the twenty or so people to the front door and showed them around as we worked. After that, she brought clients almost daily, thank God one at a time.

After two weeks of this, we got another phone call from the owners. "They sold the house," I told Race glumly, "and we got thirty days." We needed more time, so I called the young woman back. She said they had ended up selling the house to her parents and she would call them to see if they would delay their move. She asked me how much time we needed. "Three months," I told her.

Race said waiting for that phone call was like waiting to get out of the pen. Finally, the phone rang. The young woman said her parents agreed and we had our three months. I thanked her immensely, and we went back to work with a fierce determination. Three months later we loaded our belongings into the back of a U-Haul truck and headed to our next rental house. I was carrying the completed manuscript under my arm.

Because Race knew the black vernacular was going to be difficult for a publisher and that he would want to be very involved in the editing process, he submitted the manuscript to a local publisher, Eakin Press. The hardcover of *Racehoss: Big Emma's Boy* came out in the spring of 1984. That December, Race was on *The Studs Terkel Program* in Chicago, and his interview with Studs later won the New York Festival's International Radio Programs Awards Gold Medal. A rep from Ballantine Books heard the show, and they bought the rights to the mass market paperback. It came out in January 1986, and the movie producers began swarming us like sharks. Movie rights were optioned twice and sold to Sean Hepburn Ferrer, who became a dear friend, and over the years we wrote numerous screenplays adapted from the book. In 1999 Sean filmed Race performing a one-man show of the book onstage at the University of Southern California, and this became the powerful documentary *Racehoss*.

In early April 2005, Race was diagnosed with stomach cancer that had spread to his lymph nodes. He was told he had "a few months" to live. Upon hearing this death sentence, he replied, "I ain't scared to die," and proceeded to tell the two doctors in the hospital room about his miracle in solitary confinement. He never stopped telling that story, and he never could tell it without tears.

Race and I would go through this together, like we had everything else. I couldn't imagine not having him in my life, and every moment with him became precious, knowing they were now so few. Race was strong in his faith. He prayed. He was ready, at peace with it. Me—I was a complete mess.

We talked about going to Longview to visit Emma's and Pat's grave sites, something he had wanted to do for many years. The last and *only* time we went to Longview had been thirty years earlier. We'd arrived too early for the person we were visiting to get off from work, so we waited outside his house, which was in a black neighborhood out in the country. Race sat on the hood of our car. I stood in front of him as we talked while Amber played in the front yard. Then we heard a loud cracking sound coming from across the road, and then another. With the second crack came a bullet whizzing right between our heads; I could feel the vibration of it sailing past my face. Race jumped off the hood, and the three of us squatted behind the car. We waited a few minutes, then made our way to the car doors and jumped in. He backed out of the long driveway in the direction of the bullet and burned rubber taking off down the road.

I insisted that we make the four-hour drive while Race was still able. When we arrived at Jordan Valley, a small cemetery nestled under some tall pine trees, he said there were no headstones on their graves, just markers, and that he couldn't remember where they were but knew Pat was buried right next to Emma. We walked the whole graveyard front and back, over and over, hoping to see their names on the markers. After three hours of walking, it had become a hot afternoon and Race was getting tired and woozy. I was dead set on finding the graves, but he said, "When you do your best and it doesn't work, that's all you can do. They know we came and tried. That's what counts." The trip zapped all his energy, and I wished I hadn't pressed him to go. He grew much worse very quickly and passed on May 19.

A natural-born storyteller, Race loved to write and was a master with words, capturing the moments like a Kodak and bringing them to life on the page. After Señor bit the dust, he preferred writing in longhand, using sticky notes, scraps of paper, old envelopes, and tablets. He could get more on one of those little sticky notes than I could on a sheet of paper. He wouldn't use a computer. I guess after he saw what damage I could do with one (once losing a hundred pages), he decided against it. My most treasured possessions are the thirty years of notes and writings that he left me.

Race wanted his book to inspire and give hope to others. I'm deeply grateful to Scribner for introducing this extended version of *Racehoss: Big Emma's Boy* to a whole new generation of readers and, in so doing, celebrating my husband's extraordinary life.

"Miss me. Remember me and miss me," he once said.

Not a day goes by that I don't.

—Carol Sample
(2017)

Reflections of a Book

November 29, 1983

You will tell them about Emma and me. You will go temporarily to stand alone, apart and away from me and the expert, loving, gentle hands of Carol guiding what you say, but don't worry about a thing; when you get through standing tall like we know you do, they will see the love, care, and tenderness that is in every fiber of every page, the carbon in every pencil mark, every blotch of ink. It's not so different from the time Emma got run out of town and I had to stand on my own. You don't need no help from us; many words as you got you sho know what to say. We loved teaching you how to talk, to speak eloquently. You will not be ashamed when introduced to strangers, daring them. Our hearts go with you and soar with you as you fly to take your place among the inhabitants of the word world, where you can tell them about us. We were born anew in you, fulfilled, and no change shall come upon you unnecessarily but merely to polish your shine. The mold is set, the die is cast readying for your baptismal resurrection into everlasting forever, carrying us along on your powerfulness. Your expression and method, your unique style and care and frankness will be viewed by great minds; and great minds will respect and admire you through us.

About the Author

After seventeen years and several stints in prison, Albert Race Sample became the first ex-convict in Texas to work out of the Office of the Governor, to serve as a probation officer for Travis County, to be on the staff of the State Bar of Texas, and to work as a division head for a department in the city of Austin. He also appeared as a keynote speaker at the Texas Corrections Association convention in 1976 along with U.S. Representative Barbara Jordan and soon-to-be governor of Texas Mark White.

In recognition for his work in the field of corrections and rehabilitation of ex-offenders, he received the prestigious Liberty Bell Award and two Services to Mankind Awards. In 1981 he was recognized as the Outstanding Crime Prevention Citizen of Texas by the Texas Crime Prevention Association for implementing a crime watch program utilizing city employees. After the publication of his memoir in 1984, he was interviewed on *The Studs Terkel Program* in Chicago, which won a New York Festival's International Radio Program Awards Gold Medal in 1985. He received the Gabriel Award in 1986 for outstanding achievement in broadcasting, and in 1987 he received the Angel Award from the 700 Club.

Albert Race Sample was granted a full pardon and restoration of all civil rights in 1976. He resided in Austin, Texas, with his wife until his passing in 2005.